STUDIES IN RICHARD HOOKER

The Folger Library Edition

of

The Works of Richard Hooker

General Editor

W. Speed Hill

STUDIES IN RICHARD HOOKER

ESSAYS PRELIMINARY TO AN EDITION OF HIS WORKS

Edited by

W. SPEED HILL

THE PRESS OF
CASE WESTERN RESERVE UNIVERSITY
CLEVELAND & LONDON
1972

to Emita

CONTENTS

EDITOR'S PREFACE

Unlike his distinguished predecessor, John Keble, the contemporary editor of Hooker's *Works* can by no means assume a constant or cohesive scholarly interest in them. Keble's edition may seem unduly narrow in the focus of its commentary and unduly pious in its retention of Walton's *Life* as the gateway to the *Laws of Ecclesiastical Polity*, but it climaxed a publishing tradition of remarkable continuity and homogeneity, and it enjoyed a comparable longevity of its own in its many reprintings—including that in the Everyman's Library—since its appearance in 1836. By contrast, contemporary interest in Hooker is more varied and more specialized than in Keble's day. It has been so parceled out among various scholarly disciplines —each of which has its own reasons for reading him—that we are in danger of losing sight of the wholeness of Hooker's own vision and of the ordered exposition and argumentation he so valued himself. Like the six blind men and the elephant, scholars who share a common interest in the man and his work find themselves cut off from one another by allegiance to their disciplines, each with its own corpus of scholarship to be mastered, each with its own information networks, formal and informal, which they as individuals constitute and to which as scholars they contribute. To be sure, symposia, newsletters, institutes and central research libraries, personal travel and correspondence—all mitigate this process of professional individuation and compartmentalization. But the process itself seems inexorable and irreversible.

In such a context, then, it becomes altogether appropriate that such a central repository of our literary culture as the Folger Shakespeare Library should have undertaken to sponsor a new critical edition of Hooker's *Works*, for an edition is above all a gathering together of the results of widely dispersed scholarly investigations in order to establish and elucidate a single, major text. As a preliminary to that edition, the present volume of essays was commissioned by the Press of Case Western Reserve University. A single example of why it is needed will suffice. Among the contributors whose training and professional activity was not in literary history, not one had heard of David Novarr's magisterial study of Walton's *Lives*, published in 1958. Yet Novarr's analysis of Walton's *Life of Hooker* documents in fascinating and irrefutable detail the process by which the posthumous Books of the *Laws* were denied authenticity for centuries, and he shows how the man and his image for subsequent readers—Keble not excepted—was fixed in a mold whose origin was the legitimization of the Restoration Episcopate. This image was not seriously modified until the well-known work of C. J. Sisson, published in 1940, and the image is still very much with us. That Novarr's equally significant work is less well known precisely to the scholars who would find it most illuminating is no reflection on the scholars in question; rather, it is a consequence of the structure of the profession, for a book on Walton, as "literature" not "history," is reviewed in journals not ordinarily read by historians or theologians. The essays brought together in this volume, then, are meant to bridge just such gaps between the disciplines. They represent cross-talk among specialists who share a common interest in Hooker but who come from different countries of the scholarly world and who in their customary communications address distinct audiences.

Dr W. D. J. Cargill Thompson, Lecturer in Ecclesiastical History at University of London King's College, writes as a student of political thought in the Reformation. In a closely reasoned essay, he argues that Hooker's political philosophy—*pace* the attacks on its coherence by H. F. Kearney and by Peter Munz—is essentially coherent and unified, that the defense of the Royal Supremacy in Book VIII follows logically and inevitably from the principles enunciated in Books I–III. As such, it is a welcome vindication of Hooker's achievement from an historian who is fully cognizant of the polemical character of the *Laws* and no less alive to the fact that much of what Hooker says had been said before in the sixteenth century. Yet the very sweep of his own essay suggests that for many scholars today the most revealing context for Hooker's treatise remains, in general, the history of political theory, and, in particular, the history of the Tudor constitution.

Dr H. C. Porter, Lecturer in History at Cambridge University, is likewise concerned with Hooker as apologist for the Tudor constitution. But whereas Dr Cargill Thompson seeks to demonstrate the logical coherence of Hooker's *Laws*, Dr Porter's essay is concerned to uncover the extensive root system of the work in the two generations that preceded its appearance in the 1590s. The constitutional revolution effected by the Henrician Reformation in the 1530s, the Erasmian tradition in the English church in the persons of Cromwell, Cranmer, and Ridley, the policy of *moderatio* of Elizabeth's first archbishop, Matthew Parker, the traditions of English common law available to Hooker at the Temple where the *Laws* was conceived and first written, as well as the immediate and more familiar arguments of Jewel and Whitgift, Hooker's own patrons— all are shown to contribute importantly to Hooker's epic. The essay makes no pretensions to being definitive—it casts its nets too wide— but it does suggest how very complex the fabric of contemporary allusion in the *Laws* is, how multiple the contexts that need to be recovered if the modern reader is to assess the *Laws* with full accuracy and sympathy.

My own essay takes the years of Hooker's residence at the Temple as its primary focus, and it argues that much of the later ambiguity of the work can be seen as the outgrowth of the book's early history. In its reconstruction of the immediate circumstances of its conception and of the local and topical nature of its sponsorship by Edwin Sandys, the essay is a documentation, *in extenso*, of Christopher Morris' remark that the *Laws* is above all a *livre de circonstance*, and it suggests ways by which it is possible to discriminate between Hooker the man and Hooker the polemicist. Much of its bibliographical and textual evidence, though historical in nature, is of less interest to the historian of ideas than the literary historian. Still, great books have multiple and distinct contexts into which we must place them, and the history of the composition and publication of the *Laws*, however tangled, provides a useful corrective to those who often forget that books, like ideas and institutions, have their own history.

Professor John Booty teaches church history at the Episcopal Theological School, Cambridge, Massachusetts. His wide-ranging investigation of the uses and abuses of Hooker in the years during which Anglican theology was assuming its characteristic shape is illuminating in its very tentativeness, for it suggests how Hooker's views, enunciated as they are for us with such distinctive force, were to his immediate contemporaries less a landmark than a part of the ongoing process by which the Church of England defined the source and nature of its authority in the early seventeenth century. Like Dr Porter, Professor Booty eschews the logic of self-contained argumentation in favor of the untidy evidence of actual citation by a variety of later writers who had occasion to adduce Hooker's authority to buttress their own arguments. At the same time, he shows with admirable fullness the centrality of Hooker to nascent Anglican theology in the years after Elizabeth's death and before the Civil War.

By contrast, Egil Grislis, Professor of Historical Theology at Hartford Seminary Foundation, Hartford, Connecticut, treats Hooker as a theologian, rather than as a part of the history of an institution. But his essay—no less than Professor Booty's—is an exercise in the definition of the *via media*, for it draws together in comprehensive fashion what Hooker himself had to say on the necessity for "consensus" as an authentic witness to truth and on the nature of the authority of Scripture. It thus sets forth Hooker's teaching on those twin poles of the Anglican position—tradition and Scripture—central to Hooker's own theology and to the position his church took in the sixteenth century. As part of a longer study of Hooker's thought, the essay promises to make good John S. Marshall's thesis that Hooker's *Laws* constitutes a kind of *summa* of Anglican thought or, perhaps more accurately, a kind of *institutes* of the English church.

Finally, Georges Edelen, Professor of English at Indiana University and, like myself, a student of English Renaissance literature, offers a scrupulous and sensitive analysis of Hooker's style that is suggestive in inverse proportion to the scale of the investigation. He shows how a writer of such fundamental honesty and skill as Hooker inevitably reveals in the syntactical structures he employs the very structure of his mind. It is a measure of our distance from Hooker that a consideration of his famous style should habitually be relegated to professors of English, for the rhetorical tradition of which he was a part insisted upon the unity of style and substance, whereas it was the tradition he himself deplored—that of Peter Ramus—which introduced into our view of rhetoric the contrary assumption of a style separable from content, a tradition that lies behind our own wholly negative contempt for "mere rhetoric."

But style was not then the backdoor it has since become by which nonhistorians, nonchurchmen, and nontheologians enter the spacious precincts of the *Laws*. And it may well be that the most satisfactory explanation for a number of otherwise troubling ambiguities in Hooker's life and work lies in a fuller appreciation of the significance of his training as Renaissance humanist. It sets aside the problem of Hooker's philosophic originality, for none of the humanists saw their intellectual role in these terms. It explains his aversion to "innovation," his allegiance to the established church, for the humanists consciously looked to the past as a guide to the present, and they were historically associated with the Tudor dynasty from the reign of Henry VII on. It places in context Hooker's evident sense of history, as revealed, for example, by the way he handles the scriptural texts offered as proof texts by the Puritans. Most importantly, it accounts for the singular originality of form of the *Laws*, so consciously unlike the point-by-point debates that his twin patrons, Jewel and Whitgift, had conducted with Harding on the one side and Cartwright on the other. His humanism is the logical outgrowth of the patronage of his uncle, John Hooker, Exeter's resident humanist for half a century; of Jewel, whose library at Salisbury Hooker may have used; and of the traditions of Corpus Christi College, one of the distinctively Renaissance foundations at Oxford, where Jewel had been Professor of Rhetoric before the Marian exodus and where John Rainolds—a notable hellenist, who lectured on Aristotle's *Rhetoric* and was later active in the preparation of the Authorized Version of the Bible—was Hooker's tutor. Finally, it accounts for his willingness to give over the private world and comparative peace of an Oxford college fellowship for the treacherous and frustrating public world of the Temple, if for the civic and dynastic loyalties associated with the earlier humanists we substitute Hooker's evident loyalty to the church in which he had found his home.

If this portrait be accepted—and the sketch needs fleshing out—it would suggest that we need not apologize for the evident fact that Hooker's importance lies less in what he had to say than in how he said it. This has always been implicitly recognized by readers who have not gone to him for specific aid in support of one or another doctrinal or political position within the Church of England. But even among professing Anglicans, such as Bishop McAdoo, one meets that same truth in a different form: it is Hooker's tone, or "method," that is distinctive, rather than any isolatable content matter. (Indeed, the jest that the Church of England was saved by a "good prose style" makes the same point.) It would bring Hooker the stylist back into a position of centrality, whether we choose to view his rhetoric with skepticism, as does Dr Cargill Thompson, or admiration, as does Professor Edelen. One then need no longer regard his acknowledged virtues as a stylist as irrelevant to his role as theologian, political theorist, or apologist for the church.

I suspect that if there is a problem here, it is less an acceptance of the importance to an understanding of Hooker of the ideals set forth in sixteenth-century humanist thought, for this can be had at comparatively little intellectual expense, but the acceptance that this represents a positive, substantial, and honorable position intellectually, that a learned, wise, and systematic concern for the forms of discourse and the style of expression does not render a man an intellectual nullity, socially irrelevant, callous to the *real* concerns of men and society. Within the tradition itself, as it was reiterated with

some frequency, it was precisely the dichotomy of form and content
—or of style and social ends—that was "irrelevant," that a responsible
concern for men and for society implied a mastery of the skills of
discourse and the courage to employ them within the world of
men for humane and socially productive ends. It is this tradition,
fathered by Cicero and set forth most fully in his dialogue *De oratore*,
that was revivified by humanists such as Erasmus in their educational
programs throughout the sixteenth century and that allows us as
justly to link Hooker with the imaginative writers of his day as with
his fellow apologists for the church.

W. SPEED HILL

Oxford
July 14, 1971

ACKNOWLEDGMENT

Expenses for the preparation of this volume have been under-written by grants-in-aid from the Graduate School of Arts and Science of New York University, from the American Council of Learned Societies, and from the Folger Shakespeare Library. To each of these institutions I wish to record my gratitude for their support of this volume and of the Edition of Hooker's *Works* to which it is preliminary.

W.S.H.

STUDIES IN RICHARD HOOKER

THE PHILOSOPHER
OF THE "POLITIC SOCIETY"
Richard Hooker as a Political Thinker

W. D. J. Cargill Thompson

I

Forty years ago Hooker's reputation as a great political philosopher appeared to be beyond dispute. Writing in 1928, J. W. Allen could say, "not merely as a controversialist but as a political thinker, he was incomparably the greatest Englishman of the sixteenth century and on the Continent he had few compeers,"[1] and it is a verdict that most historians until recently would unhesitatingly have endorsed. Today Hooker's standing as a political thinker is much less certain. The past forty years have seen the appearance of a number of studies which, in a variety of ways, have profoundly modified the traditional interpretation of his political thought. While some old problems have been resolved and some long-standing myths have been exploded (one hopes) forever, new issues have arisen—especially in the last twenty years—which have challenged the accepted assumptions of a generation ago, and it is arguable that the nature of Hooker's achievement as a political philosopher is more open to question at the present day than at any time in the past. The announcement of a new critical edition of Hooker's works, therefore, provides an appropriate opportunity to review the developments that have taken place in the study of his political ideas in the present century and to attempt a reappraisal of his significance in the history of political thought.

The treatment of Hooker's political ideas illustrates the difficulties that have hampered the progress of Hooker scholarship in the twentieth century. In spite of the advances that have been achieved in certain fields—notably in bibliography and biography, where the researches of literary historians, such as R. A. Houk, David Novarr, and, above all, C. J. Sisson,[2] have done much to elucidate the problems of the posthumous books and to establish the facts behind Walton's fictions—Hooker has always been in many respects an inadequately studied figure. While he has never been neglected in the popular sense, he has tended to fall into the category of thinkers who are more written about than studied, and both as a theologian and as a political theorist he can hardly be said to have attracted the degree of scholarly investigation which his eminence demands. Although his name figures in all the textbooks, the number of serious historical studies of his thought which have appeared in the twentieth century has been remarkably limited, and little detailed research has been done, even in recent years, either into his political theory or into his theology in general. As a result, there has been a tendency for much modern writing about Hooker to be uncritical in character and lacking in depth and for the same stereotyped judgments to be repeated from writer to writer.

At the same time, the study of Hooker's thought has also been handicapped by the "politic use" that has been made of him in the past. For over two centuries his political philosophy was interpreted very largely through the distorting lens of Locke's *Second Treatise,* and although the manner in which Locke deliberately exploited Hooker's reputation in order to give a semblance of respectability to his own revolutionary arguments is now generally recognized, it is a tribute to Locke's effectiveness as a political propagandist and to the all-powerful influence of Whig historiography in the eighteenth and nineteenth centuries that until as recently as the 1920s and 1930s Hooker was universally regarded as an exponent of the theory of social contract, and few myths have proved more difficult to dislodge than the belief that Hooker's views were, in all essentials, identical with those of Locke. In a similar fashion, the historical understanding of Hooker has also been hampered by the influence of Anglican hagiography. Not only has a large proportion of the general books written about Hooker in the present century been the work of Anglican churchmen—many of them High Churchmen, who have attempted to interpret him from their own ecclesiastical standpoint— but in a more subtle way the traditional Anglican image of Hooker has exercised a profound influence on the way in which he has been treated by secular historians. Thus it is a remarkable commentary on the power of Anglican tradition that until the publication of Sisson's *The Judicious Marriage of Mr. Hooker* in 1940, Walton's picture of the "dove-like," if henpecked, Hooker was accepted unquestioningly by most historians, halo and all. Again, secular historians have tended, in general, to accept the conventional Anglican view of Hooker as a great irenical figure, whose mind was above the ephemeral party conflicts of his own time, ignoring or playing down the essentially polemical character of the *Laws*, just as they have tended, in general, to accept Hooker's claim to be regarded as the first major apologist for the Church of England, overlooking his debt to predecessors such as Whitgift. It is perhaps also because of the unconscious influence of Anglican hagiography that until recently Hooker's intellectual greatness as a philosopher was assumed to be self-evident, and it is only in the past twenty years that historians have begun to question the logical consistency of his thought.

The primary task of Hooker scholarship in the twentieth century has therefore been to break away from the stereotypes of the past. Admittedly, it is a task that has not always been clearly recognized or actively pursued. It is significant, however, that the most important developments in the interpretation of his thought have come about in the main through the realization that there was a large element of myth in the traditional interpretation of Hooker and that it was necessary to start by reexamining the preconceptions of earlier historians. While it does not follow that all the criticisms that have been leveled against the traditional conception of Hooker are necessarily justified, and some of the new views that have been put forward are highly contentious, there can be little doubt that the iconoclasm of a handful of twentieth-century historians has done much to advance the understanding of his thought.

As a broad generalization, one can say that the modern interpretation of Hooker's political theory has evolved through three, or perhaps four, main phases. At the beginning of the twentieth century he was still regarded primarily, as he had been in the eighteenth and nineteenth centuries, as the forerunner of Locke and one of the originators of the doctrine of social contract. Typical of the prevailing attitude among English historians in the early years of the century is Sir Sidney Lee's comment in the third volume of the *Cambridge Modern History*, published in 1904: "Hooker...made a contribution of first-rate importance to the theory of government, both civil and ecclesiastical. He anticipated the great Whig doctrine of the seventeenth century, that government had its origin in a primary contract between the governor and the governed, and he endeavoured to prove that the constitution of the Anglican Church rested on such an implied contract, from which there was no right of withdrawal" —a view which hardly differs from that expressed by Hallam eighty years earlier.[3] On the other hand, although at the beginning of the century Hooker's name was frequently mentioned in works dealing with the history of political thought and his importance was beginning to be recognized by Continental historians, such as Jellinek and Tröltsch,[4] his ideas were rarely discussed in detail, and it was not until the 1920s that his writings began to attract the serious attention of historians of political thought both in England and on the Continent. In Germany, for example, a number of writers began to take an interest in Hooker's religious and political ideas in the years immediately following the First World War, among them Wilhelm Pauck, whose pioneering study of Bucer's social theory, *Das Reich Gottes auf Erden* (1928), included a pertinent section on Hooker's theory of church and state.[5] In England, too, interest in the study of Hooker's political ideas was given a new momentum by the writings of such scholars as Norman Sykes, R. H. Murray, and J. W. Allen,[6] whose chapter on *The Laws of Ecclesiastical Polity* in his *History of Political Thought in the Sixteenth Century* is one of the most perceptive short surveys of Hooker's political theory to have appeared in the past fifty years. However, with the notable exception of Allen, who attempted to set Hooker firmly in the context of his own age, most writers on Hooker in the 1920s continued to see him primarily as a precursor of the seventeenth century, both in his views on the origins of government and in his ideas of natural law.

This traditional way of looking at Hooker was largely undermined in the 1930s by the writings of A. P. d'Entrèves, whose *Riccardo Hooker: Contributo alla teoria e alla storia del diritto naturale* (1932) constitutes a landmark in the development of the modern study of Hooker. In the first place, it was the first full-scale monograph to be devoted to the study of his political philosophy and the first attempt to set his ideas in their historical tradition, and it is still perhaps the best book on the subject, although unfortunately it has never been translated into English.[7] Secondly, it entirely altered the perspective from which Hooker was normally viewed by emphasizing the essentially medieval character of his thought. Not only did d'Entrèves challenge the prevailing orthodoxy that Hooker was to be seen primarily as a social contract thinker, pointing out that it was anachronistic to interpret him in terms of Locke and that it was very doubtful whether Hooker could properly be said to have held a theory of social contract at all,[8] but he also suggested that it was equally anachronistic to interpret Hooker's conception of natural law in terms of Grotius and the seventeenth century. In d'Entrèves' view, Hooker's contribution to the development of the concept of natural law—which he regarded as the most important aspect of Hooker's political theory—could be properly understood only if it was seen not as the precursor of the "rationalist" theories of the seventeenth century but rather as the culmination of the medieval scholastic tradition of natural law "as a part of the eternal order which God has imposed upon Creation."[9] D'Entrèves was by no means the first scholar to emphasize Hooker's debt to Aquinas and medieval scholasticism, but he was the first to analyze it in detail and to make

7

it the key to his interpretation of Hooker. While he did not deny that Hooker's ideas formed an important link between the medieval and the modern world and that he was—to quote from *The Medieval Contribution to Political Thought*—"a Janus-like figure, facing two different if not opposite worlds,"[10] for d'Entrèves, Hooker's essential significance as a thinker lay in the fact that he came at the end of the medieval tradition, that in his aims and his outlook he looked backward to the thirteenth century rather than forward to the seventeenth.

The next two decades saw the publication of several studies of Hooker's political ideas but little fresh development in the interpretation of his thought. Gottfried Michaelis' Göttingen doctoral dissertation, *Richard Hooker als politischer Denker*, published in 1933, was, in fact, written before the appearance of d'Entrèves' book, and it might be said to epitomize the early twentieth-century German view of Hooker. Although like d'Entrèves he stresses Hooker's debt to Aquinas in his treatment of natural law, for Michaelis the real interest and importance of Hooker lies in his role in the development of the theory of social contract. While emphasizing that the ingredients of Hooker's thought were not original and that he was building on the foundations laid by a succession of late medieval and sixteenth-century writers, he argues with Jellinek against Gierke in favor of the view that Hooker rather than Althusius has the best claim to be regarded as "the first representative of the classical social contract doctrine,"[11] while, like Sir Sidney Lee, he makes the concept of social contract the key to the understanding not only of Hooker's theory of government but also of his theory of church and state (pp. 86ff.). However, if Michaelis undoubtedly exaggerates the degree to which Hooker can properly be regarded as a social contract thinker, his book contains a useful analysis of Hooker's ideas, and for the most part it has been unjustly neglected by English-speaking scholars.

In 1935 C. W. Previté-Orton published his important British Academy lecture on Marsilius of Padua, in which he argued on the basis of internal parallels that Hooker's thought owed much to the influence of Marsilius, especially in the later books[12]—an idea since taken up and developed by a number of writers on Hooker. Of even greater significance for the study of Hooker's political ideas in England was the publication in 1939 of d'Entrèves' volume of Oxford lectures, *The Medieval Contribution to Political Thought*, the last two chapters of which were devoted to Hooker. These two lectures consisted largely of a *résumé* of the arguments of his *Riccardo Hooker*, and in themselves they added little to what he had said before. However, they played an influential role in helping to make d'Entrèves' ideas better known among English-speaking scholars, and by treating Hooker in the same context as Aquinas and Marsilius of Padua they served to reinforce his picture of Hooker as an essentially medieval figure who stands at the end of the medieval tradition of political thought.

During the period immediately after the war two further studies of Hooker's political ideas appeared in England, but neither can be said to have advanced the understanding of his thought. E. T. Davies' *The Political Ideas of Richard Hooker* (1946) was essentially a work of popularization, designed to present Hooker's ideas to the intelligent layman—useful but largely derivative, while it suffers, like most works of popularization, from a tendency to oversimplification. More scholarly in its pretensions but equally derivative was F. J. Shirley's *Richard Hooker and Contemporary Political Ideas*. Although not published until 1949, it was mainly written before and during the war and draws heavily on the work of Michaelis, largely without acknowledgment.

By 1950 Hooker's reputation as a political thinker appeared to be firmly established. He was generally recognized as the most important English political theorist of the sixteenth century, while the work of d'Entrèves appeared to have reinforced the traditional English and Anglican conception of Hooker as a great systematic philosopher. In 1952, however, the basic significance of Hooker's achievement was suddenly called in question by the appearance of two studies, both of which independently cast doubt on the validity of Hooker's claim to be regarded as a great logical thinker. The first, a short but provocative essay in *The Cambridge Journal* by H. F. Kearney,[13] went so far as to dismiss Hooker's claims to greatness altogether, arguing not only that he was "too much caught up in the ephemeral problem of his time to be considered great" but that there was a fundamental inconsistency in his argument arising from his failure to reconcile the dichotomy between a "rationalist" and a "voluntarist" conception of law (pp. 303–04). According to Kearney, although Hooker started off by discussing law in terms of reason, like St. Thomas, he ended by virtually identifying it with the will of the crown, like Marsilius and Thomas Hobbes. "It may be argued therefore with justice," Kearney concluded, "that though Hooker begins with Aquino, he ends with Padua" (p. 307). The same words might have been used with equal appropriateness by Peter Munz to describe the principal theme of his book, *The Place of Hooker in the History of Thought*, also published in 1952. Although working along different lines from Kearney, being chiefly concerned with the problem of Hooker's theory of church and state, Munz also arrived at the conclusion that Hooker's argument was flawed and that although he started off as a Thomist he ended as a disciple of Marsilius of Padua. According to Munz, it was Hooker's tragedy that he set out with the aim of expounding a theory of church and state based upon the principles of Aquinas but was unable to reconcile these principles with the realities of the Tudor political situation. As a result, he was forced imperceptibly to shift his ground, and when he came to justify the Royal Supremacy in Book VIII, he found himself increasingly tending to adopt the political arguments of Marsilius of Padua, with their Averroistic implication that the state was a purely secular institution. Munz suggests that it was Hooker's failure to reconcile these two opposing tendencies in his thought that accounts for the incomplete state of the last three books, for as the work progressed he became increasingly aware of the inconsistencies in his position, and in consequence the work slowed down and was still unfinished at the time of his death.[14]

The attacks of Kearney and Munz represent the most important development in the interpretation of Hooker's political theory since the publication of d'Entrèves' *Riccardo Hooker*. The only serious attempt that has been made to defend Hooker's theory against the charge of inconsistency is to be found in an article entitled "The

Coherence of Hooker's Polity: The Books on Power," by Arthur S. McGrade, published in 1963.[15] In this article McGrade rightly insists that the arguments of the later books can only be properly understood if they are interpreted, as Hooker himself intended, in the light of the general principles enunciated in the first four books. However, his argument is primarily directed against Kearney's thesis that Hooker moved from a rationalist to a voluntarist or positivist conception of law, and while he effectively disposes of Kearney's arguments, he does not discuss the more fundamental issues raised by Munz.

This lack of response to the attacks of Kearney and Munz may indicate a waning of interest in Hooker as a political theorist, which may itself be simply a reflection of the fact that the study of the history of political thought has been becoming increasingly unfashionable in English, and perhaps American academic circles as well, over the past two decades. Certainly, it is significant that, apart from McGrade's article, the only noteworthy contribution to the discussion of Hooker's political ideas that has appeared since 1952 is Christopher Morris' admirably balanced chapter in his book *Political Thought in England: Tyndale to Hooker*, published as long ago as 1953.[16] Perhaps equally significant is the fact that neither of the two most recent works on Hooker has been concerned, except marginally, with his political ideas, although each in its own way touches on the problem of his intellectual consistency. J. S. Marshall's *Hooker and the Anglican Tradition* (1963) is, in effect, a forceful reassertion of Hooker's claim to be regarded as a great systematic thinker, since he argues that Hooker's conscious purpose in writing the *Laws* was to produce a theological *summa*, modeled on the *Summæ* of Aquinas.[17] However, Marshall overstates his thesis, and the general credibility of his interpretation is marred by his pronounced Anglo-Catholic bias and his misunderstanding of the realities of Tudor religious history. A much more cogent study is Gunnar Hillerdal's *Reason and Revelation in Richard Hooker*, published in 1962. Although Hillerdal is concerned primarily with Hooker's theological ideas and not with his political philosophy, his work has interesting parallels with that of Munz. For, like Munz, he raises the question whether Hooker was successful in reconciling two opposing traditions of thought—in this case, his Aristotelian-Thomist philosophy of reason and his Protestant theology of grace and predestination. Hillerdal argues that Hooker was unable to do so and that, although he attempted to gloss over the logical contradictions inherent in these two positions, in fact the argument of the *Laws* is constructed around two basically inconsistent conceptions of grace and reason.

The philosophical and theological issues dealt with by Hillerdal are not directly relevant to the interpretation of Hooker's political ideas and, in consequence, lie outside the scope of this essay. Nevertheless, there can be little doubt that the general problem that Hillerdal raises—the problem of the logical coherence of Hooker's thought—is, in the different form in which it is presented by Munz and Kearney, the most important issue that confronts the student of Hooker's political ideas today. Was Hooker the great systematic philosopher and apologist for the Church of England that most modern scholars have assumed? Or was he, in fact, intellectually inconsistent, his argument flawed by fundamental logical contradictions? In other words, is *Of the Laws of Ecclesiastical Polity* to be regarded as a masterpiece or as a failure—a failure, perhaps, on a grand scale, but a failure nonetheless, because in it Hooker was forced to compromise his principles in order to meet the realities of the system which he was trying to defend?

In attempting to answer these questions, it is necessary to make a distinction between Hooker's purposes and his method of argument. As the rest of this essay will try to show, an examination of the logical structure of Hooker's argument suggests that his theory was more consistent than his recent critics have allowed. On the other hand, throughout the *Laws*, Hooker was continually arguing to a brief, and he cannot easily be acquitted of the charge of subordinating his political ideas to the needs of the immediate controversy. In assessing Hooker's significance as a political philosopher, therefore, it is important to take account not only of the question of the logical consistency of his ideas but also of the motives that governed the writing of the *Laws*.

II

Any discussion of Hooker's political ideas must start from the fact that *Of the Laws of Ecclesiastical Polity* is only incidentally a work of political theory. It is not in any formal sense a treatise on the principles of government, like Bodin's *De Republica*, nor is it a discourse on the nature of the English constitution, like Sir Thomas Smith's *De Republica Anglorum*, although much of Hooker's argument is taken up with questions of political philosophy and constitutional practice. Nor is it primarily—as Marshall, for example, has recently argued[18]—a work of theology, an exposition of the principles of Christian doctrine, although again in the course of the book Hooker deals at length with theological issues. Essentially it is a work of apologetic, a defense of the constitution and practices of the Church of England against the attacks of its Puritan critics. It is, as Christopher Morris has rightly said, a *livre de circonstance*, which has its roots in the controversies of the Elizabethan church.[19] As such, it is primarily a work of polemic, designed to serve the same purpose as Whitgift's writings against Cartwright and the Admonitioners in the 1570s and the writings of Bridges, Bancroft, and a succession of Anglican divines in the 1580s and 1590s, whose aim was the refutation of Puritanism and the defense of the Elizabethan Settlement.

Most modern commentators on Hooker have tended to underplay the polemical purpose of the *Laws*, but this is a mistake. It is true that, as a work of propaganda, it is conceived on a grand scale and that both in its style and in the range of its arguments it is greatly superior to most sixteenth-century works of controversy. Hooker's aim was to produce a reasoned justification for the Elizabethan church, and the fact that his book is still regarded as a classic, while other equally significant works of the period are largely forgotten, is a measure of his success. Nevertheless, neither Hooker's aims nor the types of argument which he used differed substantially from those of other Anglican apologists of the day. It is conventional to praise Hooker for his moderation and fair-mindedness in debate, and it is true that, by comparison with Bancroft or the overbearing Whitgift, both his language and the manner in which he conducts his argument are commendably temperate: he never descends to the sort of vituperation which disfigures so much sixteenth-century polemical literature. Nevertheless, although Hooker's moderation is in keeping with what we know of his character, it is also a conscious literary device. When Hooker appeals to the Puritans at the beginning of the Preface to "think not that ye read the words of one who bendeth himself as an adversary against the truth which ye have already embraced; but the words of one who desireth even to embrace together with you the self-same truth, if it be the truth" (Pref.i.3),[20] he is simply adopting the language of literary convention, and it is important not to be misled by such remarks or by the solemn manner in which he delivers them into mistaking the true purpose of the *Laws*. Like Whitgift and Bancroft, Hooker had two principal objectives in writing the *Laws*, the defense of the *status quo* and the refutation of disciplinarian Puritanism; and it is an indication of the essentially partisan character of the work that at no point in his argument, even when dealing with more obvious abuses such as pluralism and nonresidence or the lack of preaching ministers, was Hooker ever seriously prepared to concede that the Puritans might be justified in their criticisms of the Elizabethan church.

Nor, in spite of his apparent moderation, was Hooker any more fair-minded to his Puritan opponents than Whitgift or Bancroft. Hooker's Preface has often been praised by Anglican writers for its masterly insight into the nature of Elizabethan Puritanism.[21] In fact, it is a skillful exercise in denigration which sets the tone for the rest of the work.[22] Hooker's aim throughout the Preface was to discredit the Puritan cause, partly by exposing the novelty of the Calvinist system of discipline and partly by impugning the motives of the Puritans themselves. The manner in which he set about the task is made clear in the famous description of the institution of the Genevan discipline with which the Preface begins (ch. ii). Hooker's account of Calvin is a calculated piece of misrepresentation, a deliberate attempt to undermine Calvin's reputation among his readers. While professing the greatest respect for Calvin as a person and as a theologian, Hooker, in effect, accuses him of perpetrating a pious fraud, for he implies that Calvin's original reasons for instituting his system of discipline were pragmatic and that he only put forward the claim that it was of divine origin in order to induce the inhabitants of Geneva to accept it the more readily.

Hooker adopts similar smear tactics in order to undermine the credit of the Puritans. He accuses them of setting up their own private judgment above the authority of the church (Pref.vi). Following Bancroft—on whose Paul's Cross Sermon he drew heavily in chapter iv—Hooker attempts to drive a wedge between the Puritan clergy and their lay supporters by suggesting that the latter are principally motivated by the desire to lay their hands on the wealth of the church and that "the chiefest thing which lay-reformers yawn for is, that the clergy may through conformity in state and condition be apostolical, poor as the Apostles of Christ were poor."[23] He hints ominously that among the consequences that are likely to follow from the establishment of the Puritan discipline are the destruction of the Queen's Supremacy, "the overthrow of all learning," the decay of the universities, and even, he suggests, without a shred of evidence, the abolition of the common law and its replacement by Scripture as "the only law whereby to determine all our civil controversies" (viii. 2–4). As a final smear, he resurrects the hoary sixteenth-century bogey of Anabaptism as an example of the dangers to which the unfettered exercise of private judgment in matters of religion can lead.[24] If Hooker is at his most tendentious in the Preface, it is important to bear in mind that the motives which he imputes to the Puritans throughout the book are necessarily suspect and that, in particular, for his own polemical purposes he deliberately exaggerates the biblicism of the orthodox disciplinarians, making it out to be more extreme than was, in fact, the case.

The arguments that Hooker uses in order to defend the Church of England against the demands of the Puritans for the establishment of the Presbyterian system of discipline are also very similar to those of earlier Anglican apologists. In general, modern scholars have tended to ignore the question of Hooker's debt to previous Elizabethan writers, partly on the mistaken assumption that Hooker's predecessors, such as Jewel and Whitgift, contributed little that was positive to the defense of the Church of England. In fact, Hooker's debt to them was considerable. Hooker was by nature an eclectic, and although—apparently as a matter of deliberate policy—he never refers to contemporary Anglican writers (with the exception of Jewel) by name, whereas there are frequent references to the works of his Puritan opponents as well as to the writings of older classical, patristic, and medieval authors, there can be little doubt that Hooker drew heavily on the works of his contemporaries. Apart from the echoes of Bancroft that are apparent in the Preface, there are clear traces of the influence of Jewel in his defense of custom and tradition in Book v[25] and of the influence of Saravia in his treatment of episcopacy in Book VII.[26] Further research would probably reveal evidence of extensive borrowings from the works of lesser figures such as John Bridges and Robert Some. Hooker's outstanding debt, however, was undoubtedly to Whitgift, whose writings provided the basis for his attack on the general grounds of the Puritan position in Books II, III, and IV. Indeed, it is hardly an exaggeration to say that the whole argument of the *Laws* is largely an elaboration of the principles enunciated by Whitgift in his *Answer to the Admonition* (1572) and his *Defence of the Answer* (1574). It was Whitgift's writings that provided the main theoretical foundation for the Anglican defense of episcopacy in the 1570s and 1580s, and it was he who first developed, in relation to the question of church government, the two concepts that lie at the heart of Hooker's own defense of the Elizabethan church: first, the concept that there is a fundamental distinction to be drawn between matters of faith, which are essential to salvation and which are clearly laid down in Scripture, and "external" or "outward" matters of religion, which are "not commanded or prohibited in scripture" and are therefore to be regarded as "things indifferent"; and second, its corollary, that each individual church has the right to determine its own external forms of worship and church government "according to the state of times, places, and persons."[27]

What distinguishes Hooker from his contemporaries is, first of all, his attempt to give a broader philosophical foundation to these two concepts by relating the concept of "things indifferent" to the traditional medieval theory of the hierarchy of divine law and by treating the church as a species of "politic society," entitled to the same degree of autonomy in nondivine matters as other forms of civil society, and secondly, his method of argument. In comparison with other sixteenth-century works of controversy, the most striking feature of the *Laws* is the manner in which Hooker presents his case against the Puritans. Instead of adopting the normal sixteenth-century procedure of taking one or more works by his opponents and answering them individually in laborious detail, page by page and sentence by sentence—a method which makes so much sixteenth-century polemical literature so tedious to read and which accounts for the oblivion into which writers such as Whitgift have sunk—Hooker set out to construct a systematic reply to the arguments of the Puritans, starting from first principles, with a general attack on the basic assumptions underlying the Puritan "platform," before proceeding to a detailed refutation of their specific charges against the practices and constitution of the Church of England. Significantly, although Cartwright is the writer whom he cites most frequently, Hooker does not concentrate his attack on any one Puritan author but draws his examples from a wide range of Puritan pamphlets, including the *Admonitions to Parliament*, the writings of Walter Travers and Edward Dering, Dudley Fenner's *Counterpoison* and *Defence of the Godly Ministers*, John Udall's *Demonstration of Discipline*, and the Marprelate Tracts.

The seventeenth-century church historian Thomas Fuller described Hooker's style as "long and pithy, drawing on a whole flock of several clauses before he came to the close of a sentence."[28] The same metaphor might be applied to Hooker's method of argument. The *Laws* was conceived by Hooker as a carefully structured whole. The argument is built up step by step, with each section designed to follow on logically from what had gone before. Although only the first four books were published in 1593, it is evident from the descriptions that Hooker gives of the plan of the whole work in the

Preface that the eight books were designed from the outset as a logical entity and that the first four books were written with the arguments of the later books in mind.[29] Hooker himself gives an illuminating description of his method of argument at the beginning of Book I:

> For as much help whereof as may be in this case, I have endeavoured throughout the body of this whole discourse, that every former part might give strength unto all that follow, and every later bring some light unto all before. So that if the judgments of men do but hold themselves in suspense as touching these first more general meditations, till in order they have perused the rest that ensue; what may seem dark at the first will afterwards be found more plain, even as the later particular decisions will appear I doubt not more strong, when the other have been read before. [I.i.2]

As A. S. McGrade has pointed out, this passage has an important bearing on the problem of Hooker's intellectual consistency, for it indicates that Hooker himself regarded the whole work as a coherent entity and that he placed great emphasis on the need for his arguments to be studied in their entirety. At the same time, it also implies that the arguments of the *Laws* are of two kinds: in the first four books Hooker is concerned with what he terms "general meditations," that is, with the discussion of broad issues of general principle; whereas in the last four he is chiefly, though not exclusively, concerned with "particular decisions," with the refutation of the particular charges leveled by the Puritans against the Elizabethan church.[30] On the other hand, as McGrade rightly insists, it is essential for the understanding of Hooker's overall purpose that the later books should be studied in conjunction with the first four. Hooker intended his two types of argument to be complementary, and his discussion of "particulars" in the last four books presupposes the general conclusions previously established in Books I–IV. Consequently, Kearney's criticisms of Hooker fall to the ground, for he makes the mistake of treating Hooker's pronouncements on law in the later books as if they can be discussed without reference to the general principles enunciated in Book I.

In fact, there is a case for suggesting that Hooker's argument in the

Laws falls into three distinct parts, rather than two, since Book I is in many ways quite different in character from the other three books of "general meditations." Books II, III, and IV are each concerned with refuting certain general propositions put forward by the Puritans in support of their claims, and the arguments that Hooker uses in these three books are not noticeably different from those of Whitgift and other Anglican apologists of the period. Book I, on the other hand, consists of a general philosophical disquisition on the nature of laws and "politic societies" which has no parallel in contemporary Anglican polemic and which is deliberately couched in noncontroversial language, although it prepares the way for the anti-Puritan arguments of the later books. Thus the structure of the work can best be understood if it is seen as being divided into three constituent parts: Book I, consisting of a general philosophical introduction to the whole work; Books II–IV, which are directed against the basic general propositions underlying the Puritan platform; and Books V–VIII, which are concerned with defending the polity and practices of the Church of England against the detailed charges brought by the Puritans. On the other hand, the fact that Hooker was deeply concerned with the logical structure of his argument and that he planned the *Laws* as a coherent whole does not in itself prove that his arguments are consistent. What it does mean is that any discussion of the problem of Hooker's consistency must take account of the fact that he intended his arguments to be treated as a unity and that, in particular, he intended that the later books should be read in close conjunction with the first four.

Both Hooker's aims and his method of argument are extremely important for the understanding of his political ideas. Hooker's primary concern in the *Laws* was the justification of the existing constitution of the Church of England, and to a greater or lesser degree all his arguments are directed to that end. His political arguments are no exception. They are an integral element in the whole work, and they can only be properly understood if they are seen as part of the intellectual weaponry that he employs against the Puritans.

The implications of this for the study of Hooker's political philosophy are most important. In the first place, it means that the nature of the political issues that he discusses in the *Laws* is largely determined by the overall purposes of the work. He was not writing a general treatise on political philosophy, and it is significant that he does not concern himself with some of the most important political problems of the day. In particular, he virtually ignores the most hotly debated issue of the late sixteenth century—the question of the right of resistance. The explanation for this omission, which has sometimes puzzled historians, is almost certainly to be found in the fact that he did not consider the issue germane to his argument. Conversely, those subjects which he does choose to discuss are usually introduced for polemical reasons in order to further his attack on Puritanism. Thus Hooker's discussion of natural law, which is generally regarded as one of the most significant aspects of his political thought, has an important role in the development of his general argument against the Puritans, for it was intended to provide a philosophical basis for the traditional Anglican concept of "things indifferent." Similarly, Hooker's insistence on the principle that laws derive their validity from consent is designed, in part at least, to lend support to his argument that the laws of the Church of England are binding on the Puritans because they have been established by the consent of the church as a whole. Secondly, it is necessary to bear in mind, when studying Hooker's political ideas, that his conclusions were largely determined in advance. As a political theorist he was not engaged in a work of abstract, philosophical speculation; he was seeking to justify the *status quo*. Hooker accepts the existing constitution of church and state in England as given, and even when he appears to be discussing political questions in general terms, as in Book I and at the beginning of Book VIII, in reality the underlying purpose of his argument is to provide a theoretical justification for the English system of monarchy and, in particular, for the Royal Supremacy.

What distinguishes Hooker, then, as a political thinker is not the originality of his conclusions, for in essentials he was as conservative in his political outlook as most Elizabethan Englishmen. Nor is it even the originality of his theoretical arguments, for in point of fact there is little in Hooker that had not been said before. Rather, it is the extraordinary range of his learning and his ability to combine different strands of thought into a coherent whole. Hooker's outstanding characteristic as a thinker is his eclecticism. As a theologian, he was well versed not only in the writings of the Fathers and the sixteenth-century Protestant Reformers, but also in the works of the leading scholastics of the thirteenth and fourteenth centuries. Moreover, for the purposes of the immediate controversy he appears to have read most of the Puritan pamphlets published between 1570 and 1590, as well as some, at least, of the principal tracts written by Anglican apologists in reply. Similarly, as a philosopher he was steeped in the writings of Aristotle and Aquinas, and he drew heavily on both of them for his political ideas. Here again, however, his eclecticism is apparent. For if Aristotle and Aquinas are the two most obvious influences on his political thought, he also had an extensive knowledge of sixteenth-century political literature, and he was familiar with the writings of the Protestant monarchomachs, some of whose ideas on the origins of government he borrowed while rejecting their conclusions. Nor was Hooker's reading confined to works of theology and philosophy, for one of the most notable features of the *Laws* is the extent of his knowledge of contemporary English legal and constitutional theory.

It is hardly surprising that Aristotle should have been a major influence on Hooker's philosophical thought, since Oxford was still a stronghold of Aristotelianism in the second half of the sixteenth century. A more difficult problem, which still requires further investigation, is the source of Hooker's interest in Aquinas. However, although more research is needed into the question of the influence of scholasticism in the late sixteenth century, there is a growing body of evidence which suggests that Hooker's concern with scholasticism was by no means as exceptional as has often been assumed. D'Entrèves has pointed out that the works of most of the leading scholastic theologians were available to him in his own college library at Oxford. There is in existence a catalogue of the library of Corpus Christi, made in 1589 only a few years after Hooker had ceased to be a fellow, which shows that the college possessed copies of works by Alexander of Hales, Bonaventura, Albertus Magnus, Aquinas, Scotus, Ockham, and Gerson, and there is other evidence to show that the writings of Aquinas and Scotus were being read and discussed by some of Hooker's closest associates at Oxford in the early 1580s.[31] At the same time, it is becoming increasingly apparent, as the result of recent research into the history of universities in the sixteenth and seventeenth centuries, that the study of scholasticism survived the Reformation even in Protestant countries and that there was a widespread revival of interest in the writings of the scholastic theologians in England, as well as on the Continent, in the later years of the sixteenth century.[32] In the present state of research, Hooker's position in relation to this movement is obscure, and it would be interesting to know to what extent he was himself a pioneer or was simply following in the footsteps of others. Even in his study of scholasticism, however, his eclecticism is apparent. If he considered Aquinas "the greatest amongst the School-divines" (III.ix.2) and drew more heavily on him than on any other scholastic writer, he also had a high appreciation of Scotus, whom he described as "the wittiest of the school-divines" (I.xi.5). Hooker, in other words, was far from being a doctrinaire Thomist. He used St. Thomas when it suited him, but he viewed the *Summa Theologica* with the same critical detachment with which he viewed the rest of his sources, and it is important not to exaggerate the extent of Aquinas' influence on his thought. Throughout the *Laws*, Hooker borrowed freely from a wide range of writers, and his debt to Aquinas was certainly no greater than his debt to Aristotle or Whitgift.

III

Hooker's treatment of political questions follows the general pattern of the argument of the *Laws*. In Book I he is concerned with "generalities"—with the nature of law in general and the problem of the origins of "politic societies." In Book VIII he is concerned with "particulars"—primarily with the defense of the Royal Supremacy against the implied criticisms of the Puritans, but also, incidentally, with the nature of the king's "power of dominion" in the secular as well as the ecclesiastical sphere. However, since there is considerable overlap between the arguments of Book I and Book VIII, for purposes of discussion it is more convenient to consider Hooker's political ideas under three heads. First, his theory of law, and in particular his concepts of "the Law of Reason" and "Human" or positive law. Second, his theory of the origins of society and government and his conception of constitutional monarchy as the best form of civil government. And third, his theory of church and state, as expressed in his defense of the Royal Supremacy. At the same time, in examining Hooker's political ideas it is necessary to bear in mind Bishop Paget's comments on the importance of the word "presupposes" in Hooker's vocabulary,[33] for Hooker's political ideas are closely interwoven, and just as the arguments of the whole work were built up stage by stage, so the "particular decisions" of Book VIII "presuppose" the "general meditations" of Book I. Equally, it is important to remember that the *Laws* is a work of ecclesiastical controversy and that, even at his most general, Hooker's political arguments have a purpose to fulfill in the overall structure of the book.

This is particularly the case with Hooker's theory of law, which is the basis not only of his political philosophy but also of his whole apologia for the Church of England. Hooker's theory of law plays a key role in the general argument of the *Laws*, since it was designed to provide a philosophical justification for the two basic principles on which the standard Elizabethan defense of the established order in the Church of England rested, the concept of "things indifferent" and the claim that each national church had the right to regulate its own external forms of worship and government. The primary purpose of Hooker's argument was to show that the Puritans were in error in holding "that Scripture is the only rule to frame all our actions by" (Pref.viii.4), and that in consequence the principal reason that they put forward for opposing the existing laws and ceremonies of the Church of England—the fact that they were not in accordance

23

with what was laid down in Scripture—was entirely without foundation. In fact, for polemical purposes Hooker deliberately went out of his way to exaggerate the degree of authority which the Puritans attributed to the Bible, by accusing them of holding "that one only law, the Scripture, must be the rule to direct in all things" (II.i.2) and of making "the bare mandate of sacred Scripture the only rule of all good and evil in the actions of mortal men" (II.viii.5). In practice, the disciplinarian Puritans never adopted such an extreme position. Although there are passages in Cartwright's writings which can be construed in this sense, Cartwright always recognized a clear distinction between the authority of Scripture in the church and its role in the sphere of man's temporal life. While he held that "in all our actions, even civil and private, we ought *to follow the direction of* the word of God," he held that "in matters of the church and which concern all there *may be nothing done but by the word of God*" and, in practice, he did not deny the validity of either human reason or civil laws in the temporal sphere.[34] Moreover, even in the church he was prepared to allow that some things were not prescribed in Scripture but were "left to the order of the church, because they are of that nature which are varied by times, places, persons, and other circumstances, and so could not at once be set down and established for ever," although he was careful to qualify this by adding, "and yet so left to the order of the church, as that it do nothing against the rules aforesaid."[35] Thus the real issue in debate was not, as Hooker tried to suggest in order to prejudice his readers against the Puritans, whether Scripture was the sole law to be followed in all things, but how far the authority of Scripture extended in matters of religion— whether, in other words, precise rules were laid down in the Word for the external government and worship of the church, or whether the authority of Scripture was binding only in matters of faith.

Hooker's argument was basically an extension of Whitgift's. What he set out to demonstrate was that although Scripture was sovereign in its own sphere and, contrary to what the Church of Rome taught, everything necessary for salvation was clearly revealed in the Word, nevertheless Scripture was not the only law that God had provided for mankind. Starting from the Aristotelian premise that everything in nature has "some fore-conceived end for which it worketh" and that in order to achieve this end it is necessary that the operations of every creature should be governed "by some canon, rule or law" which directs it to the attainment of its own end (I.ii.1), Hooker argues that God has laid down different laws for all his creatures, which determine the order of their being. The first law, which Hooker terms "the *first law eternal*" (iii.1) in order to distinguish it from the eternal law that God has laid down for his creatures, is that law by which God himself is governed; for "God . . . is a law both to himself, and to all other things besides" (ii.3). This law differs from all other laws in that it is not imposed by a superior being on an inferior, but is imposed by God on himself by "his own free and voluntary act": it is "that order which God before all ages hath set down with himself, for himself to do all things by" (ii.6). By contrast, the essence of all other laws consists in the fact that they are laws that God has imposed on his creatures, either directly, in the sense that he has laid them down himself, or indirectly, in that he has conferred on his creatures the power to make laws for themselves, as in the case of human laws. It is for this reason that Hooker sees all other forms of law—irrespective of whether their precepts are eternally binding or not—as forming part of what he terms the "*second law eternal*," which is the eternal order of the universe which God has set down "to be kept by all his creatures, according to the several condition wherewith he hath endued them" (iii.1).

This "*second law eternal*" Hooker divides into five main categories "according unto the different kinds of things which are subject unto it." First, "*Nature's* law," by which he means the physical laws of the universe which govern the behavior of "natural agents"; secondly, the "law *Celestial*," by which angels are ruled; thirdly, "the law of *Reason*," "which bindeth creatures reasonable in this world"; fourthly, "*Divine* law," which is that law which God has revealed to men in Scripture; and fifthly, "*Human* law," which comprises the laws that men make for themselves on the basis of the law of reason or divine law (iii.1).

What distinguishes man from all other creatures is the fact that he is subject not to one law only but to several different kinds of law, according to the different aspects of his being. As a natural agent, he is subject to the same physical laws as other natural creatures; as a rational being, he is subject to the moral precepts of the law of reason; while as a member of a civil commonwealth or a church, he is subject to the particular human laws imposed by those societies.[36] At the same time, man is also a spiritual being, with a higher end than mere temporal felicity in this life, and it is for this reason that God had laid down certain supernatural laws in Scripture, which men could never find out by "the light of nature" alone, in order to lead them to salvation (I.xi.4–6). It is this function of revealing to man the truths necessary for salvation that Hooker sees as the primary purpose of Scripture. While he does not deny that Scripture contains many other precepts besides those specifically relating to salvation, he insists that "the principal intent of Scripture is to deliver the laws of duties supernatural" (xiv.1) and that the existence of Scripture does not mean that other laws are to be regarded as superfluous (xvi.5). Thus for Hooker the essence of his argument against the Puritans is embodied in the principle that "wisdom hath diversely imparted her treasures unto the world" and that, accordingly, "we may not so in any one special kind admire her, that we disgrace her in any other; but let all her ways be according unto their place and degree adored" (II.i.4).

From the point of view of Hooker's political theory, the two most important aspects of his theory of law are his concept of the law of reason and his concept of human or positive law. As has frequently been pointed out, Hooker's theory of natural law, like his concept of the hierarchy of laws in general, is closely modeled on that of Aquinas, whom he quotes on a number of occasions.[37] However, one should perhaps not lay too much emphasis on the significance of Hooker's debt to Aquinas, for although Hooker undoubtedly made extensive use of St. Thomas, Aquinas' views on natural law were hardly unique, and his ideas were largely an elaboration of the official teaching of the medieval church. Like Aquinas—and, indeed, like most late medieval theologians and political theorists—Hooker sees the law of reason, "which men commonly use to call the Law of Nature" (i.viii.9), as the universal moral law which God has laid down for all men and which all men are capable of understanding through the faculty of reason. For Hooker there are four main characteristics of the law of reason: first, it is divine, since God is its author (iii.1); secondly, it is universal, for it is binding on all men as they are rational beings and not simply on Christians (iii.1), as is borne out by the fact that the knowledge of its precepts "is general, the world hath always been acquainted with them" (viii.9); thirdly, it is ascertainable by the power of reason, "for the Laws of well-doing are the dictates of right Reason" (vii.4), and it is through the faculty of reason that men arrive at a knowledge of the principles of natural law, although, as Hooker is careful to insist, this does not necessarily mean that every human being has a perfect understanding of the precepts of natural law, since manifestly this is not the case, but simply that "there is nothing in it but any man (having natural perfection of wit and ripeness of judgment) may by labour and travail find out" (viii.9); and fourthly, it is the basis of all human or positive laws, which are deductions or extrapolations from the law of reason (iii.1).

There are differences between Hooker's treatment of the law of reason and the popular medieval and sixteenth-century conception of the law of nature, but these are largely of a technical, philosophical character and are due to the fact that, like Aquinas, Hooker attempts to explain man's understanding of the principles of natural law in terms of Aristotelian epistemology. The popular medieval belief was that the knowledge of the law of nature was innate in mankind, since God had implanted or engraved its precepts in the hearts or minds of men. It is interesting to observe that Hooker himself sometimes appears to conform to this view, as when he adopts the language of popular usage and speaks of men as carrying "written in their hearts the universal law of mankind" (i.xvi.5), or when he describes the law of nature as "an infallible knowledge imprinted in the minds of all the children of men" (ii.viii.6). However, in his main discussion of the law of reason in Book I, he rejects the idea that the knowledge of the principles of the law of nature is innate in mankind, arguing, like Aristotle, that at birth the mind or soul of man is a *tabula rasa*— "as a book, wherein nothing is and yet all things may be imprinted" (I.vi.1)—and that men only grow to knowledge by degrees. Instead, he follows Aquinas in putting forward the view, which again is essentially Aristotelian in origin, that as "in every kind of knowledge some such grounds there are, as that being proposed the mind doth presently embrace them as free from all possibility of error, clear and manifest without proof" (viii.5), so the precepts of natural law comprise a series of self-evident propositions which man is capable of discovering for himself through the light of reason.[38] At the same time Hooker also follows Aquinas in holding that the precepts of the law of nature fall into different categories, for while "the main principles of Reason are in themselves apparent" (viii.5), other, more specific maxims of the law of nature are known by deduction from these first principles.[39]

One difficulty, which is implicit in all theories of natural law but is posed in an acute form by Hooker's rejection of the concept of innate ideas, is how one can know for certain what "the dictates of right Reason" really are. Hooker, in effect, suggests three answers at different stages of his argument. As a theologian he puts forward the conventional medieval and sixteenth-century view that God has provided confirmation for the precepts of the law of nature in Scripture, in order that "the rule of divine law should herein help our imbecility, that we might the more infallibly understand what is good and what evil" (I.xii.2). But he also holds that there are two natural ways by which men can discover what the laws of reason are. The first and safest method is to go back to first principles and endeavor to determine by abstract reasoning what the causes of goodness are. This "is the most sure and infallible way, but so hard that all shun it" (viii.2). Hooker, therefore, suggests that there is a second method. This is to seek to discover empirically what all men have thought the principles of the law of nature to consist of, for "the most certain token of evident goodness is, if the general persuasion of men do so account it." In Hooker's view, the fact that a proposition is universally held to be true is an almost infallible indication that it must be. "Wherefore although we know not the cause, yet thus much we may know; that some necessary cause there is, whensoever the judgments of all men generally or for the most part run one and the same way, especially in matters of natural discourse.... The general and perpetual voice of men is as the sentence of God himself. For that which all men have at all times learned, Nature herself must needs have taught; and God being the author of Nature, her voice is but his instrument. By her from Him we receive whatsoever in such sort we learn" (viii.3). The implication of this is that it would be impossible for all men to agree unless God had caused this to happen and that God himself must, therefore, be the author of all universally held propositions. This argument is also of interest because it suggests that Hooker's approach to natural law was closer to that of Grotius and the seventeenth century than d'Entrèves would allow.[40] Although Hooker would not admit—any more than Grotius himself did—that the law of nature could exist if God had not first laid it down, nevertheless, by suggesting that one possible way of ascertaining the principles of the law of reason was to try to discover what all men believed to be true, Hooker was, in effect, advocating the same empirical method that Grotius was to adopt as the basis of his inquiry into the principles of the law of nature in the *De Iure Belli et Pacis*.[41]

The view has sometimes been put forward that Hooker's theory of the law of reason represents a departure from the teachings of the earlier Protestant Reformers and that in emphasizing the concept of the law of nature he was consciously going back to an older tradition of thought which had largely been lost sight of at the Reformation.[42] However, this is an exaggeration. The sixteenth-century Reformers did not, as one school of modern historians has maintained, either reject or even substantially modify the traditional medieval concept of natural law.[43] On the contrary, as J. W. Allen rightly pointed out in his chapter on the *Laws* (p. 188), the theory of natural law was held just as strongly, if perhaps not always so consistently, by Protestants as by Catholics in the sixteenth century, and it is a mistake to assume that it had no place in Protestant teaching. It is true that the Protestant doctrine of original sin entailed an even lower view of human nature than the modified Augustinianism of the medieval church, with its semi-Pelagian concept of free will, and it is notorious that Luther and the other early Reformers often spoke in extremely disparaging terms of human reason and Aristotelian philosophy. But it is necessary to set these remarks in their proper context. When Luther denounces reason as "the devil's whore" or when he pours scorn on the "pig-philosophers" and "pig-theologians" of the later middle ages, what he is attacking is not the use of reason as such but the application of human reason to questions of faith, which in his view lie beyond the scope of reason.

Basic to Protestant theology was the Ockhamist distinction between faith and reason, and it was this distinction, coupled with the belief that man's spiritual faculties are utterly vitiated by the Fall, which led the early Reformers to insist that human reason was entirely inadequate to deal with matters of faith and that the only authority to be followed was that of Scripture. On the other hand, this did not mean that they denied the validity of reason in the temporal sphere. On the contrary, it is one of the basic assumptions of Luther's political theory that the temporal and spiritual orders are completely distinct and that in the temporal order God has placed man under the rule of reason and natural law, which he sees as the basis of all human laws.[44] Similarly, all the Protestant Reformers took it for granted that the knowledge of natural law was not confined to Christians but was to be found among all men, and in proof of this they appealed—as Hooker himself did—to the evidence of Romans 2:14, where St. Paul declares that "the Gentiles, which have not the law, do by nature the things contained in the law."[45] Against this it has to be admitted that the Reformers, in general, took the view that the knowledge of natural law had been partially obscured in men's hearts as a result of the Fall and that, in consequence, men were rarely capable of grasping the principles of the law of nature in their entirety without divine aid. This was not in itself a new doctrine, however; it was essentially the position of the medieval church, and it was not interpreted as meaning that the precepts of the law of nature were no longer valid. Instead, the Reformers tended to argue, again in medieval fashion, that it was for this reason that God had confirmed the commandments of natural law in Scripture, especially in the Decalogue, in order that men might be reminded of its teaching—a view which, as we have seen, Hooker himself held.[46]

Thus there is no substantial difference between Hooker's conception of natural law and that held by all the leading Reformers. Basically, they all agreed that natural law represented the divine moral law which God had imposed on all men from the beginning of the world and that knowledge of it was common to all peoples. At the same time they also held that natural law was the basis of all secular law and that Christian rulers were under the same obligation to observe the law of nature as they were to observe the revealed law of God. Where Hooker differs most significantly from the orthodox Reformers is in the much greater degree of respect that he shows for the power of human reason. Unlike them, he does not envisage the possibility of any conflict arising between reason and revelation in ordinary circumstances. Rather, he sees them as operating in close harmony, the purpose of Scripture being to "perfect" the light of man's "natural understanding...that the one being relieved by the other, there can want no part of needful instruction unto any good work which God himself requireth"(I.xiv.5). Hooker also went out of his way, apparently deliberately, to flout orthodox Protestant opinion by suggesting that it would not be possible to interpret Scripture at all without the aid of human reason (III.viii.11). On the other hand, Hooker did not have an eighteenth-century belief in the unlimited power of natural reason. In the first place, he insisted that everything that he said "concerning the force of man's natural understanding" must always be understood with the qualification "that there is no kind of faculty or power in man or any other creature, which can rightly perform the functions allotted to it, without perpetual aid and concurrence of that Supreme Cause of all things" (I.viii.11). Secondly, he admitted that man's knowledge of the law of nature was corrupted by the Fall; this is one of the reasons why he considers that human laws are necessary, since, as a consequence of the Fall, men are no longer naturally inclined to obey the law of reason voluntarily (ix.3–4). Thirdly, Hooker did not believe that all men have the same capacity for understanding the precepts of the law of nature. Certain categories of people, he held, have no knowledge of the law of reason whatsoever and need to be guided by other men: children, who are too young to understand it; "innocents," who "are excluded by natural defect"; and madmen, who have temporarily lost the use of their reason (vii.4). But even among the rest of mankind, who have "the light of reason" to guide them, there are different degrees of understanding of the law of nature, for its precepts are not all equally easy to discern. "The first principles of the Law of Nature are easy; hard it were to find men ignorant of them. But concerning the duty which Nature's law doth require at the hands of men in a number of things particular, so far forth hath the natural understanding even of sundry whole nations been darkened, that they have not discerned no not gross iniquity to be sin" (xii.2). Thus it is significant that when he comes to discuss the making of human laws, Hooker specifically recommends that "none but wise men" should be employed in devising such laws, since "men of common capacity and but ordinary judgment are not able (for how should they?) to discern what things are fittest for each kind and state of regiment" (x.7).

Hooker's theory of "Human" or positive law follows logically from his concept of the law of reason.[47] For him, as for most medieval thinkers, human laws are necessary for two main reasons: first, because, as a result of man's fallen nature, men are incapable of observing the precepts of the law of nature in its entirety of their own volition and they therefore need to live under the compulsion of positive law; and second, because the law of reason only lays down general principles and does not provide for all the contingencies of human life and, in particular, for the needs of "politic societies." Human laws, therefore, are of two kinds: first, those which embody the principles of natural law but give them the sanction of positive law, which Hooker terms "mixedly" human "because the matter whereunto it bindeth is the same which reason necessarily doth require at our hands, and from the law of reason it differeth in the manner of binding only"; and second, those which he terms "merely" human, because they "make that a duty now which before was none" and relate to matters which are not laid down precisely in the law of nature but are left to men's discretion to regulate as they think fit. To illustrate the first category, he cites the instance of laws forbidding polygamy and marriage within the prohibited degrees, both of which are condemned by the law of nature; as an illustration of the second, he cites the case of laws relating to inheritance, which may legitimately vary from society to society (I.x.10). Human laws may thus be said to differ from the laws of reason in three major respects: first, they are coercive, for they carry the sanction of positive force, and any breach of them will be punished by the authority that has appointed them; secondly, they are of only local validity, for they are binding only on the society that has made them and not on all men, except in the case of the law of nations, which Hooker treats separately (x.12–13); thirdly, insofar as they are "merely" human, they are mutable, for if circumstances change, they can be altered. Theft, for example, is always punishable, since it is contrary to the law of nature, but the punishments imposed for it may vary, for "the kind of punishment is positive, and such lawful as men shall think with discretion convenient by law to appoint" (x.6).

The two most significant aspects of Hooker's theory of human law are, first of all, his insistence that all human laws derive their ultimate validity from consent, and secondly, his application of the concept of human law to the sphere of ecclesiastical law. Hooker's theory of human law is closely linked to his theory of "politic societies," and, just as it is one of the basic axioms of his theory of government that all government (except in the special case of rulers who derive their authority directly from God) ought to be founded on the "consent of men," since no man has a natural right to exercise political authority over his fellow men, so equally it is one of the fundamental principles of his theory of law that laws can only derive their validity from the consent of the people who are to be governed by them.[48] "Laws they are not therefore which public approbation hath not made so" (I.x.8). Consent, however, may be expressed in a variety of ways, and he is careful to insist that it is not necessary that all individuals should "personally declare their assent by voice sign or act." Laws, he points out, may be said to have the consent of the people if they are passed by their representatives, acting in their name, as in the English Parliament. Similarly, the edicts of absolute monarchs are binding on their subjects—"whether they approve or dislike it"—because absolute monarchs enjoy their authority either by divine appointment or by consent of the people. For the same reason, Hooker holds that men have a duty to observe the laws and customs established by their predecessors:

And to be commanded we do consent, when that society whereof we are part hath at any time before consented, without revoking the same after by the like universal agreement. Wherefore as any man's deed past is good as long as himself continueth; so the act of a public society of men done five hundred years sithence standeth as theirs who presently are of the same societies, because corporations are immortal; we were then alive in our predecessors, and they in their successors do live still. [I.x.8]

Essentially, Hooker's theory represents a sophisticated version of the traditional English constitutional doctrine that the king had no power to make laws without the consent of his people. However, his discussion of the concept of consent also has a direct bearing on the controversy with the Puritans. By stressing the principle that men are bound by the laws made on their behalf by their representatives as well as by those made by their predecessors, Hooker was, in effect, reinforcing his general contention that the Puritans had a duty to conform to the laws of the established church, since such laws had been instituted by the public consent of the whole people.[49]

Of equal significance for Hooker's attack on Puritanism was his application of the concept of human law to the external laws of the church. One of the key arguments he uses against the Puritans is the idea that the visible church, and the "particular" local churches of which it consists, must be viewed from two different aspects. It is not only a spiritual society, it is also a species of "politic society." It is, as he puts it, "both a society and a society supernatural." As such it is governed by two different kinds of laws. As a "society supernatural" it is bound by "a law supernatural, which God himself hath revealed concerning that kind of worship which his people shall do unto him." As a "natural society," however, it requires external laws of government, like other forms of "politic society" (I.xv.2–3). These external laws are not laid down in Scripture but are left to the discretion of each individual church to determine as it shall think fit, an argument that he develops in detail in Book III. "Touching things which belong to discipline and outward polity, the Church hath authority to make canons, laws, and decrees, even as we read that in the Apostles' times it did. Which kind of laws (forasmuch as they are not in themselves necessary to salvation) may after they are made be also changed as the difference of times or places shall require" (III.x.7). The external laws of the church in matters not relating to salvation are, therefore, in essentially the same category as other human laws, for they possess the same characteristics as other forms of human law. They are positive; they are mutable; they are made by the consent of the church as a whole; and they are binding on all the members of the particular church which has established them, unless and until they are abrogated by the consent of that church.

IV

The interlocking character of Hooker's political ideas is illustrated by the close connection between his theories of government and society and his theory of law. In his view, the first point of distinction between the laws of reason and human laws lies in the fact that, whereas the former "do bind men absolutely even as they are men, although they have never any settled fellowship, never any solemn agreement amongst themselves what to do or not to do" (I.x.I), the latter are the products of human society. His investigation of the nature of law, therefore, led him on naturally to consider the nature

of "politic societies" and the problem of how they came into existence. Hooker's principal ideas on the subject of society and government are to be found embedded in his discussion of the nature of
human law in the famous tenth chapter of Book I. However, he
subsequently elaborated these ideas in chapter ii on "the power of
dominion" in Book VIII, and it is necessary to consider the arguments
of the two books in conjunction.[50]

Hooker's theory of society and government may be described in
very general terms—like that of Aquinas, from whom, however, he
differs significantly on many points—as an attempt to reconcile
Aristotle's concept of the state as a natural institution with the traditional Augustinian doctrine of the church that government is a consequence of the Fall. For Hooker, there are two main reasons why
society and government are necessary. The first is to be found in the
fact that men have a natural need to live in society. Although he does
not actually quote Aristotle's dictum that "man is a political animal,"
he does maintain, like Aristotle, that men cannot live on their own
and that "therefore to supply those defects and imperfections which
are in us living single and solely by ourselves, we are naturally
induced to seek communion and fellowship with others" (I.x.I). On
the other hand, he also accepts the traditional medieval and sixteenth-
century Protestant belief that government is a necessary consequence
of man's fallen nature. In Hooker's view, it is the fact that human
nature is corrupt and men no longer capable of living together without strife and envy which makes the existence of government imperative for mankind. For he is prepared to concede—and here he differs
from Aristotle—that there is "no impossibility in nature considered by
itself, but that men might have lived without any public regiment."
"Howbeit," he continues, "the corruption of our nature being presupposed, we may not deny but that the Law of Nature doth now
require of necessity some kind of regiment, so that to bring things
unto the first course they were in, and utterly to take away all kind
of public government in the world, were apparently to overturn the
whole world" (x.4).

However, although the general philosophical assumptions underlying Hooker's theory of government and society are Aristotelian, and although there are frequent echoes of the *Politics* in both Book I and Book VIII, Hooker does not attempt to follow Aristotle at all closely in the details of his argument. On many points he either rejects or substantially modifies the teaching of "the arch-philosopher" in accordance with Christian doctrine or the political thinking of his own age. Where Hooker differs most conspicuously from Aristotle is in his account of the origins of civil society. Hooker holds, like many late medieval and sixteenth-century theorists, that political societies owe their existence not only to man's natural instinct for association but also to some kind of agreement, either formal or tacit, made by men when they first came together to form societies.[51] "Two foundations there are," he writes, "which bear up public societies; the one, a natural inclination, whereby all men desire sociable life and fellowship; the other, an order expressly or secretly agreed upon touching the manner of their union in living together. The latter is that which we call the Law of a Commonweal, the very soul of a politic body, the parts whereof are by law animated, held together, and set on work in such actions, as the common good requireth" (I.x.1). For Hooker, in other words, the state has a dual origin: in one sense, it is a natural institution that has its roots in man's basic human instincts; in another sense, it is a rational construct, since it is the product of human reason, which leads men to unite together to form societies.

The concept of human reason plays an important part in Hooker's theory of the origins of society, as one would expect, since he sees the formation of society as being the direct result of the application of the principles of reason to the needs of man's natural life. Thus he considers that it was through reason that men first learned to perceive the benefits of living together in society. In particular, he holds that it was through reason that men were brought to recognize that the only way whereby the conflicts and strife engendered by the Fall might be avoided was "by growing unto composition and agreement amongst themselves, by ordaining some kind of government public, and yielding themselves subject thereunto; that unto whom they granted authority to rule and govern, by them the peace, tranquillity, and happy estate of the rest might be procured." For men

knew that no man might in reason take upon him to determine his own right, and according to his own determination proceed in maintenance thereof, inasmuch as every man is towards himself and them whom he greatly affecteth partial; and therefore that strifes and troubles would be endless, except they gave their common consent all to be ordered by some whom they should agree upon: without which consent there were no reason that one man should take upon himself to be lord or judge over another. [I.x.4]

Hooker's emphasis on the necessity for some form of "composition" or "agreement" among men before government can be established is the most important principle of his theory of government, for it is the basis on which all his subsequent arguments about the nature of political authority and the validity of human laws rest. In his view, consent is the only rational foundation for human government, since no human being possesses a clear and indisputable right to exercise authority over his fellow men. Thus while he does not explicitly reject Aristotle's view that there is "a kind of natural right in the noble, wise, and virtuous, to govern them which are of servile disposition," he implies that this cannot be proved, and he therefore argues that "for manifestation of this their right, and men's more peaceable contentment on both sides, the assent of them who are to be governed seemeth necessary" (I.x.4). Similarly, while he is prepared to allow that the law of nature gives fathers supreme authority "within their private families," he cannot perceive how this authority can extend beyond the limits of the individual family. Consequently, he holds that "over a whole grand multitude... impossible it is that any should have complete lawful power, but by consent of men, or immediate appointment of God" (x.4). According to Hooker, the only valid exception to the principle that power, if it is to be lawful, must be based on the consent of the governed is in the case of rulers who receive their authority directly from God. However, the exception is more important than might appear at first sight. For in Book VIII he suggests that there are two classes of rulers who fall into this category: first, those who are called directly by God, "which thing he did often in the commonwealth of Israel"; and secondly, those who enjoy their authority by right of conquest, since the latter may be said to owe their position to the direct intervention of divine providence, "for it is God who giveth victory in the day of war" (VIII.ii.5; Houk, pp. 171, 170).

On the other hand, Hooker was capable, as we have seen, of interpreting the concept of consent very broadly, and the same principles that apply in the case of human laws also apply in the case of the compacts or agreements by which political societies are instituted. Thus he does not posit the necessity for any formal contract or agreement before society can come into existence, since he makes it clear that consent may be given tacitly as well as positively. In his first reference to the idea of a compact, he talks of "an order expressly or secretly agreed upon" (I.x.1), while later he speaks of power being "either granted or consented unto by them over whom they exercise the same" (x.4). In a similar fashion, when discussing the nature of royal authority in Book VIII, he suggests that what he terms "the articles of compact" may be modified in the course of time not only "by express consent, whereof positive laws are witnesses," but also "by silent allowance famously notified through custom reaching beyond the memory of man" (VIII.ii.11; Houk, p. 176). Again, just as in Book I he had argued that men are bound by the laws passed by their predecessors even though they have not consented to them themselves, so in Book VIII he argues that subjects are bound by "the articles of compact" which their ancestors have made with their rulers, either at the time of the first institution of government or by subsequent "after-agreement," and he refuses to allow that they have any power to alter them unilaterally. Although he holds that initially the "power of dominion" was vested in the people,[52] he considers that once government has been established and authority conveyed to a ruler, it is to all intents and purposes irrevocable.[53] Hence his insistence that "such things therefore must be thought upon beforehand, that power may be limited ere it be granted" (VIII.ii.10; Houk, p. 176). Equally, Hooker was prepared to extend the concept of consent to include absolute monarchies.

For he held that no single form of government was enjoined in the law of nature,[54] and while in general he appears to take the view that absolute monarchs owe their authority to right of conquest, he does not rule out the possibility that absolute monarchy might be established by consent.[55] Moreover, he suggests that even monarchies that were originally founded by right of conquest may come in the course of time to acquire the sanction of consent, since they may be transformed by "means of after-agreement" into "that most sweet form of kingly government which philosophers define to be 'regency willingly sustained and endured, with chiefty of power in the greatest things'" (VIII.ii.11; Houk, p. 176).

Given these assumptions, it is clear that Hooker's outlook differed radically from that of Locke and the majority of seventeenth-century social contract theorists. In the past, Hooker has frequently been cited as one of the earliest representatives of the theory of social contract, and the view has even been put forward that he was the first thinker to propound the doctrine in its classic form.[56] It is now generally recognized that not only is this conception of Hooker too simple, but it has its origins in an historical myth, since it can be traced back directly to the way in which Locke and other late seventeenth- and early eighteenth-century Whig writers and politicians appealed to the authority of Hooker in order to provide the theory of social contract with a respectable pedigree.[57] Although Hooker undoubtedly anticipated certain aspects of the seventeenth-century doctrine of social contract, there are major differences between his concept of a compact of society or government—he does not clearly distinguish between the two—and the fully fledged theory of the social contract which emerged in the seventeenth century, and it is very doubtful whether he can properly be classified as a social contract thinker.

In the first place, Hooker's interest in the idea of compact was philosophical, not political, and his theory lacks the ideological overtones that characterized most seventeenth-century social contract thinking. Historically, the theory of social contract as it evolved in the late sixteenth and early seventeenth centuries was closely associated with the idea of the right of resistance and the doctrine of popular sovereignty. The majority of seventeenth-century social contract theorists—whether they emphasized the idea of a contract of society or the older concept of a contract of government—were concerned to prove that political authority was ultimately derived from the people and that a ruler who broke the terms of his original contract might lawfully be resisted or deposed by his subjects. By contrast, Hooker was primarily interested in the idea of compact as a means of explaining how society and government came into existence, and it is hardly accidental that at no point in his argument does he draw the inference that, because society originates in some kind of "composition" or "agreement," subjects are entitled to resist their rulers. Secondly, the manner in which he stated his theory of compact was much more tentative than that of most seventeenth-century contract theorists. Not only was he careful to qualify his theory by insisting that consent might be given tacitly as well as positively, with the result that it is impossible to accuse Hooker of falling into the error of supposing that society and government were founded upon an actual historical contract, but he was also prepared to allow that in certain circumstances governments might be established legitimately without any kind of agreement on the part of the people. His theory also differs from Locke's in two other important respects. First, he was prepared to recognize the validity of all forms of government, including absolute monarchy, since, unlike Locke, he did not consider that it contravened the law of nature. Secondly, as d'Entrèves has emphasized, his theory of compact does not involve Locke's individualistic conception of natural rights—a concept that hardly existed in the sixteenth century.[58]

The main point of difference between Hooker's political philosophy and that of the social contract theorists, however, lies in the fact that what Hooker held was a theory of compact or consent rather than a theory of contract. Whereas the keynote of the theory of social contract, in whatever form the doctrine was expressed, was its emphasis on the contractual nature of political authority and the reciprocal rights and obligations of rulers and subjects, the basis of Hooker's theory was not the idea of contract but the idea of consent. What

Hooker was concerned to emphasize in his account of the origins of society and government in Book I was the principle that men could not be subject to any form of government except by their own consent. Although he talks of men "growing unto composition and agreement amongst themselves" (I.x.4), he does not suggest that such agreements constitute contracts in the legal meaning of the term, nor does he claim that the fact that government originates in consent creates any kind of contractual relationship between rulers and ruled. In Hooker's view, consent was a necessary precondition without which, in normal circumstances, society and government could not come into being; however, in marked contrast to Locke, he held that the institution of government was, for all practical purposes, an irreversible act, and that, once the people had consented to be governed in a certain way, they had no power either to withdraw the authority which they had conferred on their sovereign or to alter the terms on which it was held, except with his voluntary agreement.[59] Correspondingly, Hooker's conception of the political obligations of rulers was fundamentally different from that of the majority of social contract theorists. Although he laid great stress on the responsibilities which rulers owed to their subjects—and, in particular, he held that in a limited monarchy the king had a duty to abide by the laws and customs of the realm—it is clear that like most medieval and sixteenth-century political thinkers he believed that these obligations were of a moral rather than of a legally enforceable character and that only God had the power to punish a tyrannical ruler.[60]

It has been argued by d'Entrèves that, although Hooker cannot be said to have held a concept of the "contract of society" (*pactum societatis*) in the sense in which this was understood in the seventeenth century, it is possible to find traces in his thought of the older idea of a "contract of government" (*pactum subjectionis*), especially in Book VIII.[61] But it is doubtful whether this is really the case. It is true that there are passages in Book VIII where Hooker appears to use the language of contract, as, for example, when he talks of "the articles of compact," made when kings were first instituted, which show "how far their power may lawfully extend," or when he speaks of "that first original conveyance, when power was derived by the whole into one" (VIII.ii.11, 9; Houk, pp. 176, 175). However, one should be careful not to read too much into such phrases. Hooker never states that the "original conveyance" of authority from the people to the prince creates any kind of contractual relationship between the two parties, and it is clear from the context of his remarks that what he has in mind when speaking of "the articles of compact" is not a formal contract of government of the kind that figures in the writings of some of his more radical contemporaries, such as Buchanan, but rather the ancient laws and customs of the realm, which it is the duty of monarchs to observe. These laws and customs derive their validity partly from immemorial usage and partly from positive law.[62] Hooker's concept, in other words, is closer in spirit to the traditional medieval conception of fundamental law than it is to the idea of a *pactum subjectionis*, for although he holds that the ancient laws and customs are binding on rulers, he does not recognize the existence of any sanctions that can compel rulers to observe them other than those of conscience and the fear of divine judgment.

Hooker's theory of compact can thus be summed up as a theory of how society and government came into existence rather than a theory of contract in the seventeenth-century sense of the term. For, although his views on the origins of government undoubtedly foreshadow those of the seventeenth-century social contract theorists, the idea of contract—whether in the sense of a contract of society or a contract of government—plays no part in his thought, and it is, in fact, entirely alien to his political philosophy. On the other hand, it is equally important not to exaggerate the novelty of his theory of the origins of "politic societies." The idea that society or government was founded on some kind of agreement or compact was coming to be held by a growing number of political theorists in the second half of the sixteenth century, and most of the arguments which Hooker puts forward in the *Laws* can be paralleled in other works of the period, notably in the writings of some of the Protestant monarchomachs and the late sixteenth- and early seventeenth-century Jesuits.

One writer whose theory of the origins of civil society has particularly close affinities with Hooker's is George Buchanan, the Scots humanist and Reformer, whose *De Jure Regni apud Scotos* was published in Edinburgh in 1579 and in London in 1580. Although Hooker never refers to Buchanan by name, the *De Jure Regni apud Scotos* was one of the most famous political pamphlets of the late sixteenth century, and it is difficult to believe that Hooker was not familiar with its contents or that he did not borrow from it, consciously or unconsciously. Many of the most distinctive features of Hooker's theory are also to be found in Buchanan's dialogue, and the arguments of 1.x.1–5 in particular appear at times to follow Buchanan very closely. Like Hooker, Buchanan attributes the origins of political societies to two factors: first, man's natural instinct for association, which he shares in common with many of the beasts and which leads him instinctively to shun solitude and to seek the fellowship of his own kind;[63] and secondly, "that light infused by God into our minds," which "some call Nature, others the Law of Nature," which teaches men to perceive the utility of joining together to form civil societies (p. 7). Like Hooker, too, Buchanan lays great emphasis on the divine character of the law of nature, so that he can argue simultaneously—very much as Hooker does—that society is created by the voluntary agreement of men, who recognize the practical advantages of mutual cooperation, and that it is God who is the only "Author of humane Society," since it is "that Divine Law rooted in us from the beginning" which is "the cause...of mens incorporating in political Societies" (p. 8). Buchanan also anticipates Hooker in suggesting that at the beginning, when society was first instituted, kings were not bound by any laws but "the lust of Kings stood instead of Laws," and that it was "the insolency of Kings" which compelled men to recognize the need to have fixed laws and to constrain their rulers to observe them (p. 13).[64] On the other hand, Buchanan differed fundamentally from Hooker in the use to which he applied his theory. The primary purpose of the *De Jure Regni apud Scotos* was to justify the right of subjects to resist tyrannical rulers, and, in contrast to Hooker, Buchanan specifically argues not only that the king is under the law but that "there is then a mutual paction betwixt the King and his Subjects" which entitles the latter to take up arms against a ruler who breaks the terms of the covenant or contract under which he holds his authority (pp. 65–66). Such views were entirely contrary to Hooker's traditionalist conception of political authority. It is, therefore, scarcely surprising that Buchanan's name is never mentioned in the *Laws*. If Hooker was influenced by Buchanan, as seems probable, he would hardly have been prepared to acknowledge that some of his leading ideas were derived from such a notorious exponent of the doctrine of the right of resistance.

In theory, Hooker held that not only were all forms of government equally valid but that, in principle, they were all equally divine, since God's sanction could be given in various ways and the ruler who was appointed directly by God, the absolute monarch whose power was founded on right of conquest, and the ordinary ruler who derived his authority from popular consent could each be said to exercise his office by divine right.[65] However, it would be wrong to infer from this that Hooker regarded all forms of government as being equally good or that he was indifferent to the details of political organization. In practice, as he made clear when he turned to the discussion of "particulars" in Book VIII, he had no doubt that the best form of constitution was one where the law, in Aristotle's phrase, was king. "Happier that people whose law is their king in the greatest things, than that whose king is himself their law. Where the king doth guide the state, and the law the king, that commonwealth is like an harp or melodious instrument, the strings whereof are tuned and handled all by one, following as laws the rules and canons of musical science" (VIII.ii.12; Houk, p. 178).

In Hooker's view, the two basic foundations of good government were popular consent and the sovereignty of the law, the latter being in practice the more important. However, he was careful to qualify his remarks on the sovereignty of law by insisting that the powers of government should not be restricted excessively. "I am not of opinion," he writes, "that simply always in kings the most, but the best limited power is best: the most limited is, that which may deal in fewest things; the best, that which in dealing is tied unto the soundest, perfectest, and most indifferent rule; which rule is the law; I mean not only the law of nature and of God, but very national or municipal law consonant thereunto" (VIII.ii.12; Houk, pp. 177–78). For Hooker this ideal was represented by the type of limited monarchy which was to be found in England, "wherein though no manner person or cause be unsubject to the king's power, yet so is the power of the king over all and in all limited, that unto all his proceedings the law itself is a rule" (ii.13; Houk, p. 178), and "where the people are in no subjection, but such as willingly themselves have condescended unto, for their own most behoof and security" (ii.7; Houk, p. 173).

Hooker's theory of the English constitution is of particular interest, because it represents an attempt to combine his own philosophical belief in the consensual origins of society and government with the traditional constitutional doctrines of the English common law. For a sixteenth-century theologian, Hooker displays an unusual knowledge of contemporary legal and constitutional ideas, which has often been attributed to the influence of his years at the Temple, although it is perhaps more likely that it reflects the personal influence of his friend and former pupil, Sir Edwin Sandys.[66] Whatever the sources of his legal knowledge, one of the impressive features of Book VIII is the extent to which Hooker appears to have absorbed the principles of the common law and the expert manner in which he tosses off legal maxims, as if he had been studying the Year Books all his life. The one unorthodox element in Hooker's constitutional thinking lies in his insistence that in monarchies of the English type the king's "power of dominion" is derived originally by "convey-ance" from the people, and that, in consequence, "kings, even inheritors, do hold their right to the power of dominion, with depend-ency upon the whole entire body politic over which they rule as kings" (VIII.ii.9; Houk, p. 175)—a claim that appears at first sight to be more in tune with the theories of Buchanan and the author of the *Vindiciæ contra Tyrannos* than with those of Bracton and Fortes-cue. In practice, however, Hooker had little difficulty in reconciling his belief in the popular origins of political authority with the orthodox conception of the English monarchy embodied in the common law. Although he laid considerable emphasis on the concept of the king's "dependency" upon the people, he took care to make it clear that this "dependency" consisted simply in the fact that the king's powers were originally derived by grant from the people. It did not imply that his authority was subject to popular control or that the people had any right to withdraw the authority which they had conferred on him. Moreover, in the same section of Book VIII, he specifically went out of his way to dissociate himself from the arguments of the *Vindiciæ* by insisting that in hereditary monarchies the natural heir succeeded to the throne automatically on the death of his predecessor by right of birth, without any form of election, and that the ceremony of coronation was not to be construed as an act of investiture by which the new king received power from the people (ii.8–10; Houk, pp. 173–76).

In other respects, Hooker's theory corresponds very closely to the traditional medieval and Tudor view of the English constitution. In the first place, he regards it as axiomatic that the basic principle of the English system of government is that the king is under the law— "*Rex non debet esse sub homine, sed sub Deo et lege*" in Bracton's famous dictum, which he quotes (VIII.ii.3; Houk, p. 169). In Hooker's view the essential difference between absolute monarchy and monarchy of the English type lies in the fact that whereas "kings by conquest make their own charter" and are subject only to divine law and the law of nature (ii.11; Houk, p. 176), in England the powers of the crown are circumscribed by law, and both the extent of the king's authority and the manner in which it may be exercised are determined by the positive laws and customs of the realm. "The axioms of our regal government," he writes, "are these: 'Lex facit regem:' the king's grant of any favour made contrary to the law is void; 'Rex nihil potest nisi quod jure potest'" (ii.13; Houk. p. 178). Secondly, it is clear that underlying Hooker's conception of royal authority is the traditional medieval and sixteenth-century distinction between *gubernaculum* and *jurisdictio*, between the king's "absolute" and his "ordained" power.[67] Although Hooker does not discuss the constitutional powers of the king in detail, except in relation to the church, which is the main concern of Book VIII, he does hold that there is a clear distinction between those things which the king may do in virtue of his supreme power and those which he may not. In civil matters, he writes,

the king, through his supreme power, may do great things and sundry himself, both appertaining unto peace and war, both at home, by commandment and by commerce with states abroad, because so much the law doth permit. Some things on the other side, the king alone hath no power to do without consent of the lords and commons assembled in parliament: the king of himself cannot change the nature of pleas, nor courts, no not so much as restore blood; because the law is a bar unto him; not any law divine or natural...but the positive laws of the realm have abridged therein and restrained the king's power. [ii.17; Houk, pp. 182–83]

Thirdly, as this passage shows, Hooker holds the conventional belief that the power of making laws belongs not to the king alone, but to the king in Parliament, which represents the whole community of the realm, and that, in consequence, the king has no power either to introduce new laws or to alter those that are already in existence without the consent of his subjects.[68] On the other hand, he clearly recognizes—and here again his views are merely a reflection of contemporary constitutional doctrine—that if Parliament alone can pass laws, it is an essential part of the royal prerogative that kings possess the power to veto legislation put forward in Parliament, "which not to give them, were to deny them that without which they were but kings by mere title, and not in exercise of dominion" (vi.11; Houk, p. 244).

From this it is clear that Hooker's conception of sovereignty was essentially medieval and traditional in character. Although he undoubtedly knew the writings of Bodin,[69] his preoccupation with the English constitution appears to have led him to ignore the philosophical issues concerning the nature of sovereignty which Bodin had raised in the *De Republica*. Whereas for Bodin the two essential criteria of sovereignty are, first, that the sovereign is by definition above the law and cannot be legally bound by positive laws, although he is subject to the law of nature and divine law, and, second, that the sovereign is the ultimate source of positive law, since it is his sanction that gives it its effect, Hooker's conception of sovereignty is quite different. For Hooker, sovereignty—"dominion" or "power supreme"—is simply that power which a king exercises over his people. While this entails the idea that the king has no external superior on earth, it is perfectly compatible both with the notion that the king is under the law and with the idea that the king has no power to make new laws without the consent of his subjects.[70] It might be argued that for Hooker, sovereignty in Bodin's sense of the term does not reside in the king but in the whole body of the people, since he holds that the people are the original source of the king's power of dominion and that their consent is necessary for legislation. It is difficult, however, to maintain that this is, in fact, the case. Although Hooker argues that the king holds his dominion "with dependency upon the whole entire body politic," the people in Hooker's theory cannot be said to possess sovereignty in Bodin's meaning of the term, since they have no power to alter or withdraw the authority which they have conferred on the king. Nor can they be regarded as the ultimate source of positive law, since they cannot legislate without the king's assent. In practice, the assumptions underlying Hooker's conception of sovereignty are the exact antithesis of those of Bodin. Whereas Bodin's theory is founded upon the principle that the sovereign must by definition be above the law, Hooker still adheres to the traditional Aristotelian and medieval ideal that the law itself should be sovereign.

Hooker's conception of sovereignty is also traditional in another sense. Although he never discusses the question of resistance directly, implicit in his whole argument is the conventional medieval and sixteenth-century assumption that the king is answerable only to God and that, while he has a moral obligation to observe the law, if he fails to do so, his subjects have no right to take action against him. "For concerning the dealings of men who administer government," he writes in Book II, "and unto whom the execution of that law belongeth; they have their Judge who sitteth in heaven, and before whose tribunal-seat they are accountable for whatever abuse or

49

corruption, which (being worthily misliked in this church) the want either of care or of conscience in them hath bred" (i.1). Unfortunately, Hooker did not develop this theme in Book VIII, except possibly in chapter vi, but it is clear from that passage and from the general tenor of his remarks throughout the book that he shared the orthodox belief of most Tudor Englishmen that rebellion was always wrong and that he was not prepared to countenance it under any circumstances.[71] Hooker, as we have seen, did not hold a contractual theory of government, and in the context of the sixteenth century there was nothing inherently incompatible between the idea that the king was under the law, or even between Hooker's claim that political authority was originally derived from the people and the standard Reformation doctrine that subjects had no right to resist their rulers, however tyrannically they might behave.

V

Hooker's principal purpose in Book VIII was not to explain or defend the English constitution but to justify the Royal Supremacy, and it is this aspect of his political theory which has emerged as the main focus of controversy in recent discussions of his thought. Criticism of Hooker's theory of church and state is not a new phenomenon. In the past he has frequently come under attack from churchmen and historians alike for his alleged Erastianism, and to many modern Anglicans his forthright defense of the Royal Supremacy and his assertion of Parliament's right to legislate for the church have been a source of continuing embarrassment. In the past twenty years, however, the question of Hooker's treatment of the problem of church and state has taken on a new significance as a result of the arguments put forward by Peter Munz in his study *The Place of Hooker in the History of Thought*.

Munz's study raised two issues, in particular, that are of fundamental importance for the overall interpretation of Hooker's political thought. First, it raised the general question of Hooker's intellectual consistency, arguing that, contrary to popular belief, Hooker did not have a single, coherent theory of church and state, but that he shifted his ground in the course of writing the *Laws*. Secondly, it raised in a more extreme form than either d'Entrèves or Previté-Orton had done the question of Hooker's debt to Marsilius of Padua. According to Munz, as a logical edifice the *Laws* is essentially a failure, for although Hooker's original aim was to formulate a theory of church and state which would be in accordance with the philosophical principles of Aquinas, in practice this proved to be an impossible undertaking, since he was unable to reconcile St Thomas' hierarchical conception of the relationship between grace and nature, church and state, with the facts of the Tudor constitution. In consequence, like other Tudor political theorists, he found himself increasingly drawn toward the Averroistic arguments of Marsilius of Padua, with their logical implication that there was a fundamental dichotomy between the natural ends of the state and the spiritual ends of the church, and that the state, as a purely secular institution, was entitled to exercise complete control over the earthly existence of its members, including the external life of the church.[72] In fact, Munz claims, Hooker was never happy with this solution. While he borrowed heavily from Marsilius, especially in Book VIII, he hesitated to follow his arguments to their logical conclusion. It was for this reason that he left the last three books unfinished at the time of his death, since he was conscious of the contradictions between his Thomism and his Marsilian theory of the state but did not know how to resolve them (pp. 107–11).

Munz's argument, though ingenious, rests on too many unproven assumptions, and it is doubtful whether it will stand up to close examination. In the first place, his description of the alternative theories of church and state open to Hooker is too schematic, and in his efforts to establish a medieval pedigree for Hooker's political ideas he largely ignores the influence of the Reformation on the development of political theory in the sixteenth century. Secondly, his argument is based on a fundamental misinterpretation of the character of Tudor political theory. Like many modern scholars, Munz tends to overestimate the influence of Marsilius of Padua on

English political thought in the sixteenth century, and his use of the term "Tudor Averroism" to describe the philosophy underlying the theory of the Royal Supremacy is seriously misleading.[73] While references to Marsilius are not uncommon in English works of the sixteenth century and it is well known that an English translation of the *Defensor Pacis* was published in 1535 under the auspices of Thomas Cromwell, in general Tudor writers used Marsilius eclectically, as they used other late medieval authors, such as Gerson, and it would be rash to assume that they swallowed his ideas in their entirety. In practice, Marsilius appears to have been quoted chiefly for his historical arguments—in particular, for his attacks on the papacy and his views on episcopacy—and it is significant that the one explicit reference to the *Defensor Pacis* in the *Laws* is to be found not in Book VIII but in Book VII, where Hooker cites him as an exponent of the theory, which he himself had once held but had since abandoned, that bishops were not introduced into the church until after the death of the Apostles.[74] While there are undoubtedly parallels between the arguments used by Tudor writers to justify the Royal Supremacy and the arguments of the *Defensor Pacis*,[75] there is no evidence to support Munz's contention (pp. 89–96) that the Tudor theory of the Royal Supremacy was "Averroistic" in the sense that it was founded on an essentially secular conception of the state. On the contrary, the whole Tudor argument for the Royal Supremacy was based on a fundamentally theocratic conception of kingship. However the Royal Supremacy may have been exercised in practice, in theory, at least, it was taken for granted, as much in Elizabeth's reign as in the reigns of her father and brother, that the monarch was the divinely appointed head of the church, and that he was responsible not merely for the temporal welfare of his subjects but also for the care of their spiritual needs and the advancement of true religion.[76] Given this strong Tudor commitment to the ideal of "the godly prince," much of Munz's argument falls to pieces, for it cannot be maintained that Hooker was under any intellectual pressure to shift his ground because of the need to justify the Royal Supremacy in terms of an essentially secularist philosophy of the state.

Equally, it is difficult to detect any evidence that Hooker did, in fact, shift his ground in the course of writing the *Laws*. Contrary to what Munz contends, a close examination of Hooker's arguments suggests that there is no fundamental inconsistency between the standpoint he adopts in Book VIII and that of the earlier books, but rather that his defense of the Royal Supremacy follows logically from his previous discussions about the nature of the visible church and its character as a "politic society." Thus, while Hooker's treatment of the Royal Supremacy differs in certain important respects from the conventional arguments put forward by Tudor propagandists, these differences stem directly from his conception of the nature of political authority and are a testimony to the internal consistency of his ideas.

The basis of Hooker's justification of the Royal Supremacy lies in his conception of the church as a "politic society," which he had elaborated in the earlier books, especially in Books I and III. As we have seen, this concept formed one of the two main pillars of his defense of the Church of England against the criticisms of the Puritans. Together with the concept of "things indifferent," it provided the theoretical foundation for his claim that every national church was an autonomous institution, which had the right to establish its own laws in relation to the external government and worship of the church. In essence Hooker's theory was not new. It was a refinement of the argument, which had been used in the Henrician formularies of the 1530s and 1540s to justify the breach with Rome and was later employed against the Puritans of the 1560s and 1570s by Parker and Whitgift, that the visible church on earth was divided into a series of local churches, each of which was independent and each of which was free to follow its own customs in matters of external rites and ceremonies.[77] However, Hooker restated this theory in a more sophisticated form by applying to the church some of the political concepts that he had developed in relation to civil societies.

Theologically, Hooker's conception of the church as a "politic society" was founded on the traditional Protestant distinction between the invisible and the visible church. Like most sixteenth-century Protestant theologians, he takes as his starting point the idea that the church is to be defined in two ways. Viewed in its primary sense as Christ's "body mystical," it is a purely spiritual society, whose existence can only be apprehended intellectually and whose membership is known only to God, since God alone knows who truly belongs to Christ's church. However, the church is also to be viewed as a visible society, which has existed on earth since the beginning of the world, and in this sense it is "a sensibly known company" whose members are united by outward profession of faith in Christ (III.i.2–3).

What distinguishes Hooker's doctrine of the church from that of almost all his Protestant contemporaries is his extremely comprehensive definition of the membership of the visible church. For Hooker the visible church must be taken to comprise all those who outwardly profess Christianity, including even heretics and notorious sinners (III.i.7–13; cf. v.lxviii.6). Since men cannot know who is saved, it is not for them to judge who does or who does not belong in Christ's church. As he puts it in Book v, "in the eye of God they are against Christ that are not truly and sincerely with him, in our eyes they must be received as with Christ that are not to outward show against him" (lxviii.8). In Hooker's view only explicit atheism or public denial of Christ excludes one from the church altogether. "That which separateth therefore *utterly*, that which cutteth off *clean* from the visible Church of Christ is plain Apostasy, *direct* denial, utter rejection of the whole Christian faith as far as the same is professedly different from infidelity" (lxviii.6). The importance of this principle was that it enabled Hooker to argue against his Puritan opponents that even Roman Catholics and excommunicated persons were to be regarded as being in some sense members of the visible church, even if it was wrong to communicate with them (III.i.10–13; v.lxviii.9), while it also provided the basis of his claim that in a Christian country such as England all members of the commonwealth were also by definition members of the church (VIII.i.2; Houk, pp. 155–56).

For Hooker the visible church, like the invisible, is a unity in the sense that all Christians on earth are united "in outward profession of those things, which supernaturally appertain to the very essence of Christianity, and are necessarily required in every particular Christian man" (III.i.4). He holds, however, that this unity is purely spiritual, and that for the purposes of external organization the visible church on earth is divided into a series of autonomous local churches, a concept that he illustrates with his famous simile of the sea: "as the main body of the sea being one, yet within divers precincts hath divers names; so the Catholic Church is in like sort divided into a number of distinct Societies, every of which is termed a Church within itself" (i.14). If Hooker's analogy is hardly convincing, the reasoning behind his argument is clear. For Hooker the visible church has two aspects: it is both a spiritual fellowship of all those who profess faith in Christ, in which sense it is a worldwide community that embraces all Christians, and it is also a temporal organization, a group of men joined together for the exercise of Christian religion and worship. In this latter sense it is not one society but many, for as a temporal organization, the church exists wherever a body of men are associated together on a permanent basis for the practice of the Christian religion. "A Church," he writes, "as now we are to understand it, is a Society; that is, a number of men belonging unto some Christian fellowship, the place and limits whereof are certain" (i.14). Hooker's purpose in developing this argument was to justify the autonomy of the Church of England, and it is, therefore, hardly surprising that he applies this definition exclusively to national churches. In Hooker's view, the natural unit which comprises an autonomous church is the entire Christian community in any country or state, and he does not consider the possibility that his definition taken on its own might apply equally well to the "gathered" churches of the Separatists and the Anabaptists.

Apart from enabling him to justify the autonomy of the Church of England, the importance of this definition of a church as "a Society" or "a number of men belonging unto some Christian fellowship" was that it allowed Hooker to apply to the church as an external organization his concept of a "politic society." For Hooker the church as a temporal institution possesses a dual character, "being," as he had put it in Book I, "both a society and a society supernatural" (xv.2). In one sense it is a spiritual community of men who are united with God and with other Christians throughout the world in the fellowship of faith; in this sense it is "a society supernatural," governed by the divine law which God has revealed in Scripture. But it is also a temporal association, a group of men who have joined together for a specific purpose, and viewed in this way it is a human society, not basically different in character from other forms of "politic society."[78] The advantage of claiming that, insofar as it was a temporal association of men, the church constituted a species of "politic society" was that it permitted Hooker to argue that each national church must by definition possess many of the same attributes as other types of "politic society," in particular the power to make laws for its own external government. Thus, while he is careful to insist that the church has no power to alter the laws that God has laid down in Scripture concerning matters of doctrine (I.xv.2; III.x.7), he holds that in the purely temporal sphere of ecclesiastical organization the church has the same powers as other forms of "politic society" to legislate for its external needs. "All things natural," he writes in Book VII, "have in them naturally more or less the power of providing for their own safety: and as each particular man hath this power, so every politic society of men must needs have the same, that thereby the whole may provide for the good of all parts therein. ...The Church therefore being a politic society or body, cannot possibly want the power of providing for itself; and the chiefest part of that power consisteth in the authority of making laws" (xiv.3).

In the first seven books Hooker employed the argument—that the church was a "politic society"—in an extremely comprehensive manner, in order to justify the right of the Church of England not only to determine its own external order of worship but also to retain its episcopal form of church government. Hooker's treatment of the problem of episcopacy is of considerable interest, because in certain respects it foreshadows his justification of the Royal Supremacy in Book VIII. Although in common with a growing number of Anglican divines in the 1580s and 1590s he was prepared to defend episcopacy on historical grounds, arguing consistently, not only in Book VII but also on a number of occasions in the earlier books, that it was the form of government instituted by Christ and the Apostles,[79] the real basis of his defense of episcopacy was quite different. Throughout the *Laws* Hooker always maintained, as a matter of overriding principle, that church polity was by its nature a "thing indifferent" and that every "politic society" possessed an inherent right to determine its own form of government. Thus even in Book VII, where he argued at length in support of Saravia's doctrine that the original institution of bishops could be traced back to Christ himself, through the Apostles, he was careful to qualify this argument by insisting that episcopacy was a matter of positive law. In consequence, bishops could be said to owe their continued existence in the church since the death of the Apostles to the authority of the church that had chosen to retain them, rather than to any immutable command of divine law. On the same principle, he had no hesitation in admitting that the church had power "by universal consent upon urgent cause" to abolish episcopacy at any time, "if thereunto she be constrained through the proud, tyrannical, and unreformable dealings of her bishops, whose regiment she hath thus long delighted in, because she hath found it good and requisite to be so governed" (VII.v.8). In other words, in Hooker's view, the ultimate authority to decide how the church should be governed rested with the church as a whole, which in this respect enjoyed the same powers as other forms of "politic society." In Book VIII he was to employ the same argument in a different fashion in order to justify the Royal Supremacy and the right of Parliament to legislate for the church.

Hooker's problem in Book VIII was that he was faced with the task of defending the Royal Supremacy on two fronts. He not only had to defend it against the claims of the papacy but he had also to answer the implied criticisms of the Puritans, who, without venturing to attack the supremacy openly, maintained that church and state constituted two separate, though related, types of society, each with its own laws and its own form of government. In effect, he met both forms of attack in the same way by developing the argument that in a Christian country such as England church and common-wealth were united to form a single society and that in consequence there was no logical reason why the same person should not possess supreme authority in both ecclesiastical and temporal affairs.

In support of this claim, Hooker put forward two distinct—though complementary—sets of propositions. First, taking his cue, as so often, from Aristotle, he argued that all "politic societies" are by their nature concerned with the care of religion.

For of every politic society that being true which Aristotle hath, namely, "that the scope thereof is not simply to live, nor the duty so much to provide for life, as for means of living well:" and that even as the soul is the worthier part of man, so human societies are much more to care for that which tendeth properly unto the soul's estate, than for such temporal things as this life doth stand in need of: other proof there needs none to shew that as by all men the kingdom of God is first to be sought for, so in all commonwealths things spiritual ought above temporal to be provided for. [VIII.i.4; Houk, p. 158]

What distinguishes a Christian from a heathen commonwealth is that the former upholds "that religion which God hath revealed by Jesus Christ," and in this sense it is not simply a "politic society" but a church (i.2; Houk, p. 156). Secondly, he maintained that where the members of a body politic were Christian, as in England, the same body of people must by definition constitute both church and commonwealth—"seeing there is not any man of the Church of England but the same man is also a member of the commonwealth; nor any man a member of the commonwealth, which is not also of the Church of England" (i.2; Houk, p. 156). On the basis of this principle, he was able to argue in opposition to the Puritans that, although in theory church and commonwealth were distinct, in prac-tice, where the same body of people constituted both, they did not form two societies, but one. "For the truth is," he writes, "that the Church and the commonwealth are names which import things really different; but those things are accidents, and such accidents as may and should always dwell lovingly together in one subject" (i.5; Houk, p. 161). Or again, "the Church and the commonwealth therefore are in this case personally one society, which society being termed a commonwealth as it liveth under whatsoever form of secular law and regiment, a church as it hath the spiritual law of Jesus Christ; forasmuch as these two laws contain so many and so different offices, there must of necessity be appointed in it some to one charge, and some to another, yet without dividing the whole, and making it two several impaled societies." On the same principle, he was able to argue against the Catholics that the use of the term "church" was not to be confined to the clergy, since it embraced the whole body of believers, that is, all the members of a Christian commonwealth (i.4; Houk, p. 160).

Although he treated the idea with much greater sophistication than his predecessors had done, Hooker's theory of the identity of church and commonwealth was not new. The basic concept that church and commonwealth constituted a single society, under the government of one supreme head, had formed one of the standard ingredients of the Tudor theory of the Royal Supremacy since the 1530s, and the actual argument that there was no one in England who was not also by definition a member of the Church of England had first been employed by Stephen Gardiner in his *De Vera Obedientia* of 1535, while Whitgift had also anticipated Hooker by using the same argument to refute the Puritan claim that church and commonwealth formed two separate societies.[80]

Where Hooker departed from the orthodox Tudor theory of the Royal Supremacy was in his refusal to argue that the king enjoyed his position as Supreme Head or Supreme Governor either *ex officio* or by immediate appointment from God. Whereas most Tudor apologists for the Royal Supremacy had taken it for granted, first, that the king's authority in the church was God-given, in the sense that God had entrusted all Christian rulers with the care of the church in their dominions, and, secondly, that the oversight of the church formed an integral part of the office of a king, inseparable from the other duties of kingship, neither of these arguments was compatible with Hooker's theory that the original source of political authority in all "politic societies" was the people and that every "politic society" had the right to determine its own form of government and

to regulate the powers it conferred on its rulers. In consequence—
and there could be no better proof of the overall consistency of his
political ideas than this—Hooker found himself compelled by the
logic of his own arguments to maintain that God had nowhere laid
down that kings either should or should not possess supreme authority
in ecclesiastical affairs, but that it was, in principle, a matter for men
to determine. "As for supreme power in ecclesiastical affairs," he
writes, "the word of God doth no where appoint that all kings
should have it, neither that any should not have it; for which cause
it seemeth to stand altogether by human right, that unto Christian
kings there is such dominion given" (VIII.ii.5; Houk, pp. 171–72).
In other words, for Hooker, the Royal Supremacy, like all forms of
government, belongs to the sphere of positive law. From this it
follows that the Royal Supremacy, like royal authority in general,
must ultimately be derived from the consent of the people. Although
Hooker does not make this point explicitly, the logical implication of
his argument is that in a Christian commonwealth, where church
and commonwealth are one, the people have the undoubted right
to confer such powers on their ruler. At the same time, just as he
maintained that all forms of government were in some sense divine,
so he maintained that in a secondary sense the Royal Supremacy
could also be said to enjoy the sanction of divine law, for "unto
kings by human right, honour by very divine right, is due" (ii.6;
Houk, p. 172).

Hooker's general approach to the defense of the Royal Supremacy
was thus essentially pragmatic. Even when, like other Tudor writers,
he cited the precedents of the Jewish kings of the Old Testament, he
quoted these merely as examples to show that it was lawful for kings
to exercise such authority in the church without drawing the inference that it was necessary that all kings should act in the same way
(iii.1; Houk, pp. 187–88). Instead, he based his main argument for
the Royal Supremacy on the principle of expediency. For Hooker,
just as all government is instituted for the practical purpose of promot-
ing the common good, so the purpose of committing "the supreme
charge of all things" to the care of one man is to avoid the incon-

veniences which are likely to arise in practice, "if men are subject unto sundry supreme authorities."

"No man," saith our Saviour, "can serve two masters:" surely two supreme masters would make any one man's service somewhat uneasy in such cases as might fall out. Suppose that to-morrow the power which hath dominion in justice require thee at the court; that which in war, at the field; that which in religion, at the temple: all have equal authority over thee, and impossible it is, that thou shouldest be in such case obedient to all: by choosing any one whom thou wilt obey, certain thou art for thy disobedience to incur the displeasure of the other two. [ii.18; Houk, pp. 185–86]

Consequently, although God has not laid it down as a necessary law that kings should possess supreme authority in ecclesiastical affairs, reason teaches that this is, in practice, the best system of government for a Christian commonwealth.

The other major point of difference between Hooker's theory and the conventional Tudor doctrine of the Royal Supremacy lies in his emphasis on the principle that the king's authority in the church is limited by law. While it had always been accepted by Tudor theorists that the king's supremacy extended only to the external government of the church, and that he had no power to exercise the spiritual functions of the clergy, much less to command anything in matters of faith which was contrary to God's word,[81] Hooker went considerably further than this by insisting that the same constitutional principles applied in church as in state and that, therefore, even in the sphere of the external government of the church the monarch's authority is, or ought to be, circumscribed by positive law. "It hath been declared already in general," he writes, "how 'the best established dominion is where the law doth most rule the king:' the true effect whereof particularly is found as well in ecclesiastical as in civil affairs." From this he proceeded to argue that just as in the temporal sphere the king is bound to act in accordance with the civil laws of the commonwealth, which he has no power to alter without the consent of his subjects, so equally he is bound to exercise his ecclesiastical supremacy in accordance with the positive laws of the church, which again may only be altered with the consent of the whole:

Whether it be therefore the nature of courts, or the form of pleas, or the kind of governors, or the order of proceedings in whatsoever spiritual businesses; for the received laws and liberties of the Church the king hath supreme authority and power, but against them, none. What such positive laws have appointed to be done by others than the king, or by others with the king, and in what form they have appointed the doing of it, the same of necessity must be kept, neither is the king's sole authority to alter it. [VIII.ii.17; Houk, pp. 182–83]

For Hooker the ultimate authority to make laws for the external government of the church belongs not to the king alone, or even, as the Catholics claimed, to the clergy alone, but to the whole body of the church, including the laity. It is this argument which underlies his claim that in England the authority to make laws for the church is vested in Parliament together with Convocation (VIII.vi). Hooker bases his justification of Parliament's right to legislate for the church on three main principles, which he had already developed at earlier stages of his argument: first, that in all "politic societies" the power of making laws naturally resides in the whole body politic, since laws are only valid if they have the consent of the whole; secondly, that insofar as it is a temporal organization, the church is a "politic society"; and thirdly, that in a Christian commonwealth, church and state constitute a single society. "It is undoubtedly a thing even natural," he states, "that all free and independent societies should themselves make their own laws, and that this power should belong to the whole, not to any certain part of a politic body, though haply some one part may have greater sway in that action than the rest: which thing being generally fit and expedient in the making of all laws, we see no cause why to think otherwise in laws concerning the service of God" (vi.6; Houk, p. 230). From this it follows that in a Christian commonwealth the power of making ecclesiastical laws must by definition belong to the whole body of the people and not simply to the clergy, who constitute only one section of the church, or to the king acting alone, although Hooker is careful to emphasize that the assent of "the highest power" is necessary for all ecclesiastical legislation (vi.6–9; Houk, pp. 230–35). But if this is so, then it is only logical that in England the power of making laws for the church should be exercised by Parliament, interpreted in its widest sense as including both king and Convocation: for "the parliament of England together with the convocation annexed thereunto, is that whereupon the very essence of all government within this kingdom doth depend; it is even the body of the whole realm; it consisteth of the king, and of all that within the land are subject unto him: for they all are there present, either in person or by such as they voluntarily have derived their very personal right unto."[82]

Given his basic assumptions, the logic of Hooker's argument is unimpeachable: since the church is a "politic society" and since, in a Christian commonwealth, church and state are not two societies but one, Parliament must by definition represent the people of the whole realm, not only in their civil capacity as a commonwealth, but also in their ecclesiastical capacity as a church; *ergo*, Parliament has the undoubted right to make laws for the external government of the church. On the other hand, it was not Hooker's intention to exclude the clergy from all share in the making of laws for the church. On the contrary, in accordance with his general principle that "none but wise men" should be admitted to the task of devising laws, he holds that, although the clergy have no power to impose laws on the church by their own authority, it is only proper that where spiritual matters are concerned, the responsibility for drawing up laws for the church should be entrusted to the bishops and clergy. "The most natural and religious course in making of laws is, that the matter of them be taken from the judgment of the wisest in those things which they are to concern. In matters of God, to set down a form of public prayer, a solemn confession of the articles of Christian faith, rites and ceremonies meet for the exercise of religion; it were unnatural not to think the pastors and bishops of our souls a great deal more fit, than men of secular trades and callings." "Howbeit," he continues, "when all which the wisdom of all sorts can do is done for devising of laws in the Church, it is the general consent of all that giveth them the form and vigour of laws, without which they could be no more unto us than the counsels of physicians to the sick: well might they seem as wholesome admonitions and instructions, but laws could they never be without consent of the whole Church, which is the only thing that bindeth each member of the Church, to be guided by them" (VIII.vi.11; Houk, p. 243). It is a comment that reveals very clearly the extent to which Hooker's theory of church and state is rooted in the basic principles of his political philosophy.

In the past forty years a succession of scholars have drawn attention to the parallels that exist between Hooker's ideas and those of Marsilius of Padua.[83] In particular, it has often been pointed out that there are many features of his theory of the church—notably, his emphasis on the autonomy of local churches, his insistence on the principle that in a Christian commonwealth the church is to be identified with the whole body of the people, and his consequent claim that the power of making laws for the church resides in the whole body politic and not in the clergy alone—which bear a striking resemblance to the arguments of the *Defensor Pacis*. However, it would be rash to infer that Hooker must have derived any of these ideas directly from Marsilius, in spite of the fact that he refers to the *Defensor* in Book VII. In practice, although Hooker presented his arguments in a more sophisticated form than many of his contemporaries, the main elements of his doctrine of the Church were commonplaces of sixteenth-century thought. The principle that the visible church was divided into a series of autonomous local churches had been asserted by all the Protestant Reformers, while in England the same argument had been employed since the 1530s to justify the Royal Supremacy and the independence of the *Ecclesia Anglicana*. Similarly, it was a basic maxim of Protestant theology, as it had been of conciliarist thought, that the church was to be identified with the *communio fidelium*, and most of the Protestant Reformers accepted in theory, at least, if not necessarily in practice, that the doctrine of the priesthood of all believers implied that ultimate authority in the church resided in the whole Christian community.

Equally, while Hooker may well have read the *Defensor Pacis*, it is difficult to believe that his political ideas were profoundly influenced by it. Most of the arguments that he puts forward in Book VIII can be paralleled in other Tudor works of political propaganda, and it is unnecessary to posit the influence of Marsilius in order to explain their presence in his thought. On the other hand, if Hooker did borrow from Marsilius, as is possible, it is likely that he regarded him simply as a useful source of polemical arguments, as did many sixteenth-century English writers, and that he paid little attention to the philosophical implications of his thought. In particular, it is impossible to detect in Hooker's thought any traces of the Averroistic leanings that Munz appears to discover in him. At no point does Hooker come close to suggesting that the state is a purely secular institution, which is only concerned with the advancement of man's temporal well-being in this world. On the contrary, his political philosophy is founded on precisely the opposite assumption. For Hooker, it is of the essence of all "politic societies" that they are concerned with the promotion of man's spiritual welfare and, therefore, with the advancement of religion.[84] What distinguishes a Christian from a heathen commonwealth is that the religion maintained in the one is true, in the other, false; in principle, they both exist to serve the same ends (VIII.i.2; Houk, pp. 155–56). Thus Hooker never envisaged the possibility that it could ever be lawful to subordinate religion to the interests of the state, as he showed by his vigorous condemnation in Book v of "these wise malignants" who seek to make what he terms "a politic use of religion" (ii.3–4). Nor is there any evidence to suggest that his views underwent a change in Book VIII, since, in fact, it is in Book VIII that one meets some of his most positive assertions of the principle that "in all commonwealths things spiritual ought above temporal to be provided for" (i.4; Houk, p. 158).

For the same reason it cannot be said that Hooker was an Erastian in the modern sense of the term any more than Thomas Erastus himself was. It was never Hooker's intention to justify the right of the civil magistrate—or of Parliament—to control the church in all circumstances. As he himself makes clear, his theory of the Royal Supremacy only applies in a commonwealth where king and people are both Christian. Where, as in the Roman Empire of the first three centuries, the church exists in the midst of a heathen society and the magistrate is not Christian, the latter can possess no authority in the church, since church and commonwealth have "no mutual dependency" (VIII.i.4; Houk, p. 159). Similarly, he holds that the right of Parliament to legislate for the Church of England derives solely from the fact that in a Christian commonwealth the same people constitute both church and state, so that Parliament represents them in their dual capacity. Like all his contemporaries, Hooker regarded the Christian commonwealth as the summit of political evolution, and he did not foresee the gradual secularization of the state over the following centuries. Had he done so, he would hardly have approved of the continued survival of Parliament's right to make laws for the church long after the conditions which had justified it had ceased to apply.

While Book VIII, as it stands, is incomplete and lacks the final polish of the first five books, it is difficult to accept that there is any fundamental inconsistency between Hooker's treatment of the problem of church and state and the arguments of the rest of the *Laws*. Hooker's defense of the Royal Supremacy, like his justification of Parliament's right to legislate for the church, is firmly grounded on his basic concept that the church is a "politic society" and its corollary, the argument that in a Christian society church and state are one, which is implicit in the earlier books, even if it is worked out in detail only in Book VIII. In fact, one of the most notable features of Book VIII is the extent to which its arguments continually relate back to ideas that Hooker had developed in earlier parts of the *Laws*: his concept of the church as a "politic society" had first been adumbrated in Book I and forms one of the two main pillars of his general defense of the Church of England; his theory of the identity of church and commonwealth follows logically from his definition of the visible church in Book III; his insistence that the Royal Supremacy is based on human rather than divine law reflects his belief that political authority is derived from the people and that no single, uniform system of government is prescribed for all "politic societies." Similarly, his claim that Parliament is the proper authority to legislate for the church is directly related to his general theory that consent is the necessary basis of all laws. The examples could be multiplied endlessly. Thus at every stage in Book VIII one is continually reminded of what Hooker had written at the beginning of Book I.

"I have endeavoured throughout the body of this whole discourse, that every former part might give strength unto all that follow, and every later bring some light unto all before. So that if the judgments of men do but hold themselves in suspense as touching these first more general meditations, till in order they have perused the rest that ensue; what may seem dark at the first will afterwards be found more plain, even as the later particular decisions will appear I doubt not more strong, when the other have been read before" (1.i.2). It is advice that Hooker scholars ignore at their peril.

NOTES

1. J. W. Allen, *A History of Political Thought in the Sixteenth Century*, p. 184.
2. Houk, ed., *Hooker's Ecclesiastical Polity: Book VIII.* Sisson, *The Judicious Marriage of Mr. Hooker and the Birth of "The Laws of Ecclesiastical Polity."* Novarr, *The Making of Walton's "Lives."*
3. Chapter 10, "The Last Years of Elizabeth," *Cambridge Modern History* (Cambridge: Cambridge Univ. Press, 1904), 3:348. In his *Constitutional History of England*, Hallam had written: "Nothing perhaps is more striking to a reader of the Ecclesiastical Polity than the constant and even excessive predilection of Hooker for those liberal principles of civil government, which are sometimes so just and always so attractive. Upon these subjects, his theory absolutely coincides with that of Locke. The origin of government, both in right and in fact, he explicitly derives from a primary contract..." 7th ed. (London: John Murray, 1854), 1:219.
4. Georg Jellinek, *Allgemeine Staatslehre*, 3d ed. (Berlin: Julius Springer, 1916; reprinted Berlin: Julius Springer, 1922), pp. 205–06. Ernst Tröltsch, *The Social Teaching of the Christian Churches* (1911), trans. Olive Wyon (London: Allen and Unwin, 1931), p. 637. Tröltsch mentions Hooker merely as the source of Locke's ideas, and it is not altogether clear that he had read him. On the Continent, Hooker was also beginning to attract attention in the years before the 1914–18 War as a pioneering figure in the Protestant revival of natural law at the end of the sixteenth century and as one of the precursors of Grotius; cf. August Lang's essay, "The Reformation and Natural Law," *Princeton Theological Review* 7 (1909), reprinted in William Park Armstrong, ed., *Calvin and the Reformation: Four Studies by Emile Doumergue, August Lang, Herman Bavinck, Benjamin B. Warfield* (New York: F. H. Revell, 1909), pp. 76–81.
5. Pauck, *Das Reich Gottes auf Erden*, pp. 159–71.
6. Sykes, in *The Social & Political Ideas of Some Great Thinkers of the Sixteenth &*

Seventeenth Centuries, ed. Hearnshaw, pp. 63–89. Murray, *The Political Conse-quences of the Reformation*, esp. pp. 273–81; Allen, pp. 184–98.

7. The main arguments of d'Entrèves' *Riccardo Hooker* are summarized in his Oxford lectures, *The Medieval Contribution to Political Thought*, chs. 5 and 6, some passages being translated almost verbatim.

8. D'Entrèves had already advanced this view in an earlier article, "Hooker e Locke," in *Studi filosofico-giuridici*, 2:228–50; its arguments are summarized in *Riccardo Hooker*, Pt II, ch. 1, pp. 81–102.

9. *Riccardo Hooker*, p. 46.

10. *Medieval Contribution*, pp. 88–89.

11. Michaelis, *Richard Hooker als politischer Denker*, p. 58 (my translation).

12. Previté-Orton, "Marsilius of Padua," *Proceedings of the British Academy* 21 (1935): 165–66. D'Entrèves had noted the parallels between some of Hooker's ideas and those of Marsilius (*Riccardo Hooker*, p. 58, n. 7), but he did not discuss them in such detail as Previté-Orton. See also Michaelis, pp. 54, 70, 97.

13. Kearney, "Richard Hooker: A Reconstruction," *The Cambridge Journal* 5 (1952): 300–11.

14. Munz, *The Place of Hooker in the History of Thought*. See esp. ch. 3, "Hooker and Marsilius of Padua," pp. 68–111.

15. *Journal of the History of Ideas* 24 (1963): 163–82.

16. *Political Thought in England*, ch. 9. Cf. his introduction to the Everyman's Library edition of *The Laws of Ecclesiastical Polity: Books I–V*.

17. Marshall, *Hooker and the Anglican Tradition*. See esp. ch. 8, "Hooker as the Author of a Summa."

18. Marshall, esp. pp. 41 and 66 ff.

19. *Political Thought in England*, p. 176.

20. *The Works of . . . Mr. Richard Hooker*, ed. Keble, 7th ed., rev. 1888. All quota-tions are from this text, by book, chapter, and section; cited below as *Works*.

21. Cf. Paget, *An Introduction to the Fifth Book*, 2d ed., pp. 115–25; Shirley, *Richard Hooker and Contemporary Political Ideas*, ch. 3, pp. 58–70; and Davies, *The Political Ideas of Richard Hooker*, pp. 36–43.

22. This was recognized at the time by the authors of *A Christian Letter* (1599), who complained that "we, happily remembering your *Preface*, that there might be some *other cause*, opened at length our heavy eyes, and casting some more earnest and intentive sight into your manner of fight, it seemed unto us that covertly and underhand you did bend all your skill and force against the present state of our English Church." Bayne, ed., *The Fifth Book* (1902), p. 592. Cf. also pp. 621 ff., where they attacked Hooker's account of Calvin and asked, "what moved you to make choice of that worthy pillar of the Church above all other, to traduce him and make him a spectacle before all Christians!"

23. *Laws* Pref.iv.3. Cf. Richard Bancroft, *A Sermon Preached at Paules Crosse the 9. of Februarie . . . Anno 1588[9]*, pp. 24–25: "for saie they . . . our preachers ought to conforme themselves to the example of Christ and his apostles. Their Mas-

ter had not a house to put his head in. The apostles their predecessors had neither gold nor silver, possessions, riches, goods, nor revenues: and why then should they being in gifts and paines inferior unto them, have greater preferments in the world than they had?...Surelie these advancements which they have do greatlie hinder and hurt them." Although his language is more moderate, Hooker's argument in Pref.iv.3 and 4 is clearly modeled on Bancroft's distinction between "the clergie factious, and the laie factious" (*Sermon*, p. 24). There is another obvious echo of Bancroft's Sermon in Pref.iv.1, where Hooker writes: "A very strange thing sure it were, that such a discipline as ye speak of should be taught by Christ and his apostles in the word of God, and no church ever have found it out, nor received it till this present time." Cf. Bancroft, pp. 10–11: "A verie strange matter if it were true, that Christ should erect a forme of governement for the ruling of his Church to continue from his departure out of the world untill his comming againe: and that the same should never be once thought of or put in practise for the space of 1500. yeers..."

24. *Laws* Pref.viii.6–12. Bancroft also draws an analogy between the Puritans and the Anabaptists in his *Sermon*, pp. 25–26.

25. Cf. esp. *Laws* v.vi–x. In II.vi.4, where he defends Jewel's views on the negative authority of Scripture, Hooker describes Jewel as "the worthiest divine that Christendom hath bred for the space of some hundreds of years."

26. Cf. Hooker's claim that the Apostles were the first bishops (VII.iv, and *passim*) and his admission (VII.xi.8) that he had earlier held the view that bishops were first instituted only after the death of the Apostles. Hooker's conversion to the belief that episcopacy was a dominical institution is almost certainly attributable to the influence of Saravia's *De Diversis Ministrorum Evangelii Gradibus* (1590), which had a profound influence on Anglican attitudes towards episcopacy in the 1590s. Contrary to what Shirley has argued (*Richard Hooker and Contemporary Political Ideas*, pp. 45–57), there is nothing in the views on episcopacy which are expressed in Book VII which would lead one to suspect the authenticity of the book: Hooker's arguments are essentially in accordance with the new theory of the dominical origin of bishops, which was being advanced by a number of Anglican divines, such as Saravia, Bilson, and Bancroft, in the 1590s. For the development of this theory, see W. D. J. Cargill Thompson, "Anthony Marten and the Elizabethan Debate on Episcopacy," in *Essays in Modern English Church History in Memory of Norman Sykes*, ed. G. V. Bennett and J. D. Walsh (London: Adam and Charles Black, 1966), pp. 44–75.

27. *The Works of John Whitgift*, ed. John Ayre, The Parker Society (Cambridge: Cambridge Univ. Press, 1851–53; reprinted New York and London, Johnson Reprint Corp., 1968), 1:363, 6. Cf. also Tract. II, "Of the Authority of the Church in things indifferent," 1:175–295. For a fuller discussion of Whitgift's views, see my article in *Essays in Modern English Church History*, pp. 50–54.

28. Thomas Fuller, *The Church-History of Great Britain* (IX.vii, sub A.D. 1591) quoted by Keble, *Works* 1:79, n. 2.

29. *Laws* Pref.vii, and *Works* 1:196. Houk has argued that the whole work was already complete in some form when the first four books were published in 1593 (*Hooker's Ecclesiastical Polity: Book VIII*, pp. 91–96). While some of Houk's arguments have been criticized by Sisson (*The Judicious Marriage of Mr. Hooker*, pp. 60–64, 88–91), the fact that Hooker twice speaks of Book VIII in the Preface as if it were already in existence (vii.6; viii.2) would appear to lend strong support to Houk's view; cf. W. Speed Hill, "Hooker's *Polity*: The Problem of the 'Three Last Books'," *Huntington Library Quarterly* 34 (1971): 317–36. Whether or not Books VI and VII existed in draft as early as 1593, I am inclined to take the view that Book VIII, in the imperfect form in which it has come down to us, may well have been written by that date.

30. McGrade, *Journal of the History of Ideas* 24 (1963): 165. For a more detailed discussion of this point, see Houk, pp. 72, 79, 87–90.

31. D'Entrèves, *Riccardo Hooker*, p. 74. D'Entrèves has also drawn attention to the significance of the letter from Dr John Rainolds to George Cranmer, printed by Keble in *Works* 1: 106–08 (*Riccardo Hooker*, p. 76). In this letter Rainolds writes: "tamen in Scoto et Aquinate non esse nihil quod inservire possit tuo studio promovendo, libens agnosco. Illud inter meum et tuum judicium discriminis intercedit, quod tu de iis videris honorificentius sentire, quam ego. Nam ego minus tribuo Scoto quam Aquinati, Aquinati quam Scaligero, immo vero pluris unum Scaligerum quam sexcentos Scotos et Aquinates facio." The letter is undated, but presumably belongs to the period when Cranmer was either an undergraduate or a fellow of Corpus Christi.

32. Cf. William T. Costello, *The Scholastic Curriculum at Early Seventeenth-Century Cambridge* (Cambridge: Harvard Univ. Press, 1958); Hugh Kearney, *Scholars and Gentlemen: Universities and Society in Pre-Industrial Britain, 1500–1700* (London: Faber and Faber, 1970), esp. ch. 5. That the scholastics were being read even by Puritans at the beginning of the seventeenth century is illustrated by the well-known story of John Preston, whose enthusiasm for Aquinas was so great that he took his copy along to the barber's and refused to put it down, even while his hair was being cut, but simply blew away the hair as it fell on the pages. Irvonwy Morgan, *Prince Charles's Puritan Chaplain* (London: Allen and Unwin, 1957), pp. 19–20.

33. Paget, *Introduction to the Fifth Book*, pp. 141–45. Cf. Church, ed., *Book I. Of the Laws of Ecclesiastical Polity* (1868), p. xvii.

34. Thomas Cartwright, *A Replye to an Answere made of M. Doctor Whitegift* (n.p., 1574?), cited in Whitgift, *Works* 1: 191 (italics in text mine). Interestingly, Hooker judiciously abridges an earlier section from the same passage in order to underline his own thesis. In his marginal reference to II.i.4, Hooker cites Cartwright as saying, "I say, that the word of God containeth whatsoever things can fall into any part of man's life." In fact, as Keble noted, what Cartwright actually wrote was, "I say that the word of God containeth the direction of all things pertaining to the church, yea, of whatsoever things can

fall into any part of man's life" (*Works* 1:289, n. 1; for the full text of this passage from Cartwright, see Whitgift, *Works* 1: 190–91). For an illustration of Cartwright's views on the differences between the temporal and the spiritual sphere, see Whitgift, *Works* 2:356: "For God hath left a greater liberty in instituting things in the commonwealth than in the church," etc. For Cartwright's readiness to allow a certain degree of authority to philosophy and reason, see Whitgift, *Works* 2:442–43.

35. Whitgift, *Works* 1:195.

36. *Laws* I.xvi.5: "There are in men operations, some natural, some rational, some supernatural, some politic, some finally ecclesiastical: which if we measure not each by his own proper law, whereas the things themselves are so different, there will be in our understanding and judgment of them confusion."

37. For a full discussion of Hooker's debt to Aquinas, see d'Entrèves, *Riccardo Hooker*, Pt I, chs. 2–4, and, more briefly, *Medieval Contribution*, pp. 117–24. Cf. Michaelis, *Richard Hooker als politischer Denker*, pp. 47–49, and Munz, *The Place of Hooker*, ch. 2 and Appendix A, which contains a table of correspondences between Hooker's philosophy and that of Aquinas.

38. *Laws* I.viii.5–8. Cf. Aquinas, *Summa Theologica* II. i.Qu.94, Art. 2.

39. *Laws* I.viii.10–11. Cf. Aquinas, ibid., Art. 4, 6.

40. Cf. d'Entrèves, *Riccardo Hooker*, pp. 44 ff., and *Medieval Contribution*, pp. 117 ff.

41. Hugo Grotius, *Prolegomena to the Law of War and Peace*, trans. Francis W. Kelsey, Library of Liberal Arts (Indianapolis: Bobbs-Merrill, 1957), sections 40 ff.

42. Cf. Lang, "The Reformation and Natural Law," in *Calvin and the Reformation*, ed. Armstrong, pp. 76–81, 93; Georges de Lagarde, *Recherches sur l'esprit politique de la Réforme* (Paris: Auguste Picard, 1926), p. 191; Shirley, *Richard Hooker and Contemporary Political Ideas*, pp. 74 ff.; and Morris, *Everyman Hooker* (1954), p. ix.

43. For a summary of the debate over whether or not Luther held a theory of natural law, see John T. McNeill, "Natural Law in the Thought of Luther," *Church History* 10 (1941): 215 ff.

44. Cf. Martin Luther, *Werke*, Weimar Ausgabe (Weimar: Hermann Böhlau, 1883–) 30 (2): 562. "Aber ynn weltlichem reich, müs man aus der vernunfft (daher die rechte auch komen sind) handeln. Denn Gott hat der vernunfft unterworffen solch zeitlich regiment und leiblich wesen Gen 2."

45. *Laws* I.viii.3. Cf. Luther, W.A. 46: 606; Calvin, *Institutes of the Christian Religion* II.ii.22.

46. *Laws* I.xii.1–2. For Luther's views on the relationship between natural law and the Decalogue, see *Wider die himmlischen Propheten*, W.A. 18: 80–82. Cf. Calvin, *Institutes* II.viii.1.

47. For Hooker's views on human law, see *Laws* I.x, esp. 6–11.

48. *Laws* I.x.8: "That which we spake before concerning the power of government must here be applied unto the power of making laws whereby to govern; which power God hath over all: and by the natural law, whereunto he hath

made all subject, the lawful power of making laws to command whole politic societies of men belongeth so properly unto the same entire societies, that for any prince or potentate of what kind soever upon earth to exercise the same of himself, and not either by express commission immediately and personally received from God, or else by authority derived at the first from their consent upon whose persons they impose laws, it is no better than mere tyranny."

49. Cf. *Laws* Pref.v.2: "A law is the deed of the whole body politic, whereof if ye judge yourselves to be any part, then is the law even your deed also."

50. Since the order of the text of Book VIII in Keble's edition is not always identical with that of the Dublin MS Houk used, in references to Book VIII in this and the following sections I have included page references to Houk in addition to Keble's chapter and section numbers.

51. For the development of these ideas in the late middle ages and the sixteenth century, see Gough, *The Social Contract*, 2d ed., chs. 4–6.

52. Cf. *Laws* VIII.ii.5 (Houk, p. 170): "First, unto me it seemeth almost out of doubt and controversy, that every independent multitude, before any certain form of regiment established, hath, under God's supreme authority, full dominion over itself, even as a man not tied with the bond of subjection as yet unto any other, hath over himself the like power. God creating mankind did endue it naturally with full power to guide itself, in what kind of societies soever it should choose to live. A man which is born lord of himself may be made another's servant: and that power which naturally whole societies have, may be derived into many, few, or one, under whom the rest shall then live in subjection."

53. *Laws* VIII.ii.10 (Houk, pp. 175–76): "May then a body politic at all times withdraw in whole or in part that influence of dominion which passeth from it, if inconvenience doth grow thereby? It must be presumed, that supreme governors will not in such case oppose themselves, and be stiff in detaining that, the use whereof is with public detriment: but surely without their consent I see not how the body should be able by any just means to help itself, saving when dominion doth escheat."

54. *Laws* I.x.5: "The case of man's nature standing therefore as it doth, some kind of regiment the Law of Nature doth require; yet the kinds thereof being many, Nature tieth not to any one, but leaveth the choice as a thing arbitrary."

55. In *Laws* I.x.5, Hooker suggests that in all probability men's first rulers were absolute. "At the first when some certain kind of regiment was once approved, it may be that nothing was then further thought upon for the manner of governing, but all permitted unto their wisdom and discretion which were to rule; till by experience they found this for all parts very inconvenient, so as the thing which they had devised for a remedy did indeed but increase the sore which it should have cured. They saw that to live by one man's will became the cause of all men's misery. This constrained them to come unto laws, wherein all men might see their duties beforehand, and know the penalties of

transgressing them." For a comparison between this passage and the arguments of George Buchanan's *De Jure Regni apud Scotos*, see below, p. 44.

56. Cf. Michaelis, *Richard Hooker als politischer Denker*, p. 58.

57. For an account of the way in which Hooker was used for purposes of Whig propaganda in the late seventeenth and early eighteenth centuries, see d'Entrèves, *Riccardo Hooker*, pp. 9–12.

58. D'Entrèves, *Medieval Contribution*, pp. 127–32; cf. *Riccardo Hooker*, Pt II, ch. 1, pp. 81–102.

59. *Laws* VIII.ii.10 (Houk, p. 176), cited above, n. 53. In this passage Hooker does appear to allow that in the event of a dynasty of hereditary rulers dying out dominion might revert to the people by "escheat."

60. *Laws* VIII.ii.6 (Houk, p. 172): "And therefore of what kind soever the means be whereby governors are lawfully advanced unto their seats, as we by the law of God stand bound meekly to acknowledge them for God's lieutenants, and to confess their power his, so they by the same law are both authorized and required to use that power as far as it may be in any sort available to his honour." Cf. II.i.1, cited below, pp. 49–50.

61. D'Entrèves, *Riccardo Hooker*, pp. 95–97. *Medieval Contribution*, pp. 130–31.

62. *Laws* VIII.ii.11 (Houk, p. 176). The whole passage is as follows: "Touching kings which were first instituted by agreement and composition made with them over whom they reign, how far their power may lawfully extend, the articles of compact between them must shew: not the articles only of compact at the first beginning, which for the most part are either clean worn out of knowledge, or else known unto very few, but whatsoever hath been after in free and voluntary manner condescended unto, whether by express consent, whereof positive laws are witnesses, or else by silent allowance famously notified through custom reaching beyond the memory of man."

63. George Buchanan, *De Jure Regni apud Scotos. or, A Dialogue, Concerning the due Priviledge of Government In the Kingdom of Scotland*, Eng. trans. (London: Richard Baldwin, 1689), pp. 6–7.

64. See above, p. 72, n. 55.

65. *Laws* VIII.ii.5–6 (Houk, p. 171): "By which of these means soever it happen that kings or governors be advanced unto their states, we must acknowledge both their lawful choice to be approved of God, and themselves to be God's lieutenants, and confess their power his. . . .

"Again, on whom the same is bestowed even at men's discretion, they likewise do hold it by divine right. If God in his own revealed word have appointed such power to be, although himself extraordinarily bestow it not, but leave the appointment of the persons unto men. . ."

66. Cf. Houk, pp. 50–51.

67. Cf. Charles Howard McIlwain, *Constitutionalism: Ancient and Modern*, rev. ed. (Ithaca: Cornell Univ. Press, 1947), chs. 4–5.

68. Cf. also *Laws* VIII.vi.1,11 (Houk, pp. 224, 241–42).

69. He cites Bodin's *De Republica* in the fragment which Keble prints as an appendix to Book VIII, "Supposed Fragment of a Sermon on Civil Obedience, hitherto printed as part of the Eighth Book," *Works* 3: 457–58. Houk, p. 237, n. 28.

70. Cf. *Laws*, VIII.ii.2–3; Houk, pp. 168–69.

71. Cf. the "Supposed Fragment of a Sermon on Civil Obedience" (*Works* 3: 456–60), which contains a clear affirmation of the traditional Protestant doctrine of nonresistance. Keble pointed out that this passage did not appear in the first edition (1648) of Book VIII and that the opening paragraph down to "evangelists" is taken verbatim from III.ix.3. He therefore argued that it should be treated "as a separate fragment, probably of a Sermon on Obedience to Governors, annexed by mistake to the eighth book in all the MSS" (*Works* 3: 456, n. 1). Houk, on the other hand, following the text of the Dublin MS, prints it as part of chapter 6 (pp. 235–41). In view of the fact that there are other instances of repetition in Book VIII, which can be accounted for on the assumption that the present text of Book VIII was compiled from Hooker's unpolished first draft, there would appear to be no strong reason why this passage should not be treated, in accordance with the MSS tradition, as forming an authentic part of Book VIII.

72. Munz, *The Place of Hooker*, chs. 1–3, esp. pp. 96–111.

73. See Munz, esp. pp. 89–96 and Appendix C, "Marsilius in the Sixteenth Century," pp. 199–204, which includes a useful list of references to earlier discussions of Marsilius' influence on Tudor thought (p. 199, nn. 1, 2).

74. *Laws* VII.xi.8. For the manner in which Henrician writers used Marsilius as a source of historical arguments against the papacy, see Franklin Le Van Baumer, *The Early Tudor Theory of Kingship*, Yale Historical Publications, 35 (New Haven: Yale Univ. Press, 1940; reprinted New York: Russell and Russell, 1966), p. 43. In the 1560s Bishop Jewel cited Marsilius by name on a number of occasions in his *Apology* and other writings as an exponent of the view that the Pope was Anti-Christ, and also as a historical source for the dealings between the Franks and Pope Stephen in the eighth century; see John Jewel, *Works*, ed. John Ayre, The Parker Society (Cambridge: Cambridge Univ. Press, 1845–50), 3:81; 4:680, 740–42, 1115). It is clear that in the sixteenth century Marsilius was regarded by English Protestants not as a dangerous secularist but as a proto-Reformer along with men like Valla, Hus, and Jerome of Prague. Jewel in his *Defence of the Apology* defends him against the charge of heresy (*Works* 4: 742), while John Philpot in his translation of Curio's *Defence of Christ's Church* (c. 1550) describes him as one of the "trumpets of the Gospel," in *The Examinations and Writings of John Philpot*, ed. Robert Eden, The Parker Society (Cambridge: Cambridge Univ. Press, 1842), p. 393. Cf. John Foxe, preface "To the True and Faithful Congregation of Christ's Universal Church," in *Acts and Monuments*, intro. George Townsend, ed. Stephen Reed Cattley (London: Seeley and Burnside, 1841–43), 1:517.

75. Cf. Baumer, pp. 41–56 *passim*, 67–68; Shirley, *Richard Hooker and Contemporary Political Ideas*, pp. 1–5, 130; Morris, *Political Thought in England*, p. 54. On the other hand, the importance of these parallels should not be exaggerated. While Baumer and others have shown that the *Defensor Pacis* was one of the major sources used by Henrician propagandists in the 1530s, it was not the only one, and many of Marsilius' leading ideas were commonplaces not only of late medieval anti-papal and conciliarist thought but of sixteenth-century Protestant political thought as well (see Morris, p. 35). The evidence suggests that the Henrician pamphleteers of the 1530s used Marsilius as a convenient source of anti-papal propaganda, but that they ignored, and may not even have understood, the philosophical assumptions underlying his political thought.

76. For a classic statement of this doctrine, see Cranmer's Speech at the Coronation of Edward VI, printed in Thomas Cranmer, *Miscellaneous Writings and Letters*, ed. John Edmund Cox, The Parker Society (Cambridge: Cambridge Univ. Press, 1846), pp. 126–27. The same theocratic conception of kingship is to be found in all the leading tracts produced in defense of the Royal Supremacy in the 1530s, such as Stephen Gardiner's *De Vera Obedientia*, Richard Sampson's *Oratio*, and Edward Foxe's *De Vera Differentia*.

77. Cf. the articles on the church in the *Bishops' Book* (1537) and the *King's Book* (1543) in Charles Lloyd, ed., *Formularies of Faith put forth by authority during the Reign of Henry VIII* (Oxford: Clarendon Press, 1825), pp. 52–57 and 243–49.

78. *Laws* I.xv.2. Cf. III.xi.14: "First, so far forth as the Church is the mystical body of Christ and his invisible spouse, it needeth no external polity. That very part of the law divine which teacheth faith and works of righteousness is itself alone sufficient for the Church of God in that respect. But as the Church is a visible society and body politic, laws of polity it cannot want."

79. Cf. *Laws* III.xi.16, 20; V.lxxviii.4, 5, 12. These passages indicate that certainly by the time he wrote Book V, and probably by the time he wrote Book III, Hooker had come to accept the doctrine, put forward by Saravia in his *De Diversis Ministrorum Evangelii Gradibus* (1590), that the origins of episcopacy were to be traced back to the distinction which Christ had made between the Twelve Apostles and the Seventy Disciples (see esp. V.lxxviii.5). In other words, Hooker's conversion from the Jeromian theory, held by most Elizabethan divines, that episcopacy was first introduced into the church after the death of the Apostles (VII.xi.8) to the new theory of Saravia that episcopacy was a dominical institution almost certainly dates back to the period of the early 1590s, when this idea was beginning to be put forward by a number of other Anglican writers, such as Bilson and Bancroft.

80. Pierre Janelle, ed., *Obedience in Church & State: Three Political Tracts by Stephen Gardiner* (Cambridge: Cambridge Univ. Press, 1930), pp. 92–97. Whitgift, *Works* I: 21–22.

81. Cf. "The Injunctions of Elizabeth, A.D. 1559," No. 78, *Documents Illustrative of English Church History Compiled from Original Sources*, ed. Henry Gee and

William John Hardy (London: Macmillan, 1896; reprinted 1910), "An admonition to simple men deceived by malicious," pp. 438–39.

82. *Laws* VIII.vi.11 (Houk, pp. 241–42). The language of this passage bears a striking resemblance to that of Sir Thomas Smith's description of Parliament in *De Republica Anglorum* II.i, and it is likely that Hooker was paraphrasing Smith at this point; see *De Republica Anglorum: A Discourse on the Commonwealth of England*, ed. L. Alston (Cambridge: Cambridge Univ. Press, 1906), pp. 48–49.

83. In addition to those already cited, see also Shirley, *Richard Hooker and Contemporary Political Ideas*, pp. 96, 112; and Morris, *Political Thought in England*, pp. 177, 184.

84. Cf. his remark in VIII.vi.11 (Houk, p. 242): "The parliament is a court not so merely temporal as if it might meddle with nothing but only leather and wool."

HOOKER, THE TUDOR CONSTITUTION, AND THE *VIA MEDIA*

H. C. Porter

I

Within the epic structure of *The Laws of Ecclesiastical Polity*, Richard Hooker was especially successful as a sustained and thoughtful exponent of the balance of prerogative and consent in the Christian commonwealth of Tudor England. His was a work of the scholar's study, which teased into a harmony the ambiguities of the Tudor constitution—for the moment, anyway, and perhaps only for the scholar.

The oath had been taken: Elizabeth was "the only supreme governor of this realm...as well in all spiritual or ecclesiastical things or causes as temporal."[1] In Hooker's words, the Queen's "sacred power matched with incomparable goodness of nature hath hitherto been God's most happy instrument...'By the goodness of Almighty God and his servant Elizabeth we are.'"[2] For Hooker, Thomas More had been mistaken in objecting to the Supreme Headship because "it maketh a lay, or secular person, the head of the state spiritual or ecclesiastical."[3] Was it not true that God himself had named "Saul the head of all the tribes of Israel," including headship of "the state spiritual or ecclesiastical"? (VIII.iv.8). Christ is Head of the church in things spiritual—secret, inward, invisible; the supreme governor is "an Head even subordinated of, and to Christ" (iv.6). But the governor has rightful prerogatives. And Hooker described the subject of Book VIII as the "power of Ecclesiastical Dominion, communicable, as we think, unto persons not ecclesiastical, and most fit to be restrained unto the Prince or Sovereign commander over the whole body politic" (Pref.vii.6). The kings of Israel had "supremacy of power," "dominion," both ecclesiastical and civil—most relevantly, in the "altering of religion" and "the making of ecclesiastical laws" (VIII.i.1). In thus stressing Old Testament precedent in this matter of the Supremacy, Hooker was in a Tudor tradition previously expressed by Stephen Gardiner in the 1530s, John Jewel (Hooker's most important patron) in the 1560s, and John Whitgift in the 1570s.

Hooker was obsessed by the theme of public society: the peace of the community, the "public place" as against "privy conventicles" (v.xii.2), the "public and common good of all" overriding "our own particular, the partial and immoderate desire whereof poisoneth" (Ded.9).

If Walter Travers and his party had their way (and perhaps Hooker was more impressed by the ideals of the discipline than might at first sight appear), there would be in England "as many supremacies as there are parishes and several congregations" (Pref.viii.2). To avoid such proliferation, there must be "an universal power which reacheth over all, importing supreme authority of government over all courts, all judges, all causes." In England there was such a power; it had been taken from Rome in the 1530s "for just considerations by public consent," and "annexed unto the king's royal seat and crown" (VIII.viii.4).

The Headship over the church included the prerogatives of summoning and dissolving the Convocations, assenting to laws concerning ecclesiastical polity, and appointing "principal church-governors to their rooms of prelacy" (ii.1). Here Hooker dealt with the transparent inconvenience of the church having "freedom of elections" (viii.6)—such a freedom, we remember, as John Colet had extolled in his Convocation sermon of 1512[4]—while remarking that the prince must here tread especially carefully: the image is that of a tutor, the church being his pupil, "whom he hath solemnly taken upon him to protect and keep."[5] The supreme governor also has the highest judicial authority, the right of veto, and an exemption from the censures of a "platform of reformation" (ii.1), such censures, no doubt, as those directed at Elizabeth with increasing fervor in the 1580s by some MPs. (Hooker would have been quite aware of the petition of Anthony Cope in 1587 that "all Laws now in force touching ecclesiastical Government should be void," a petition which, against the advice of the Speaker, the House of Commons wished to have read.)[6] On the other hand, the supreme governor could not administer the sacraments, ordain or excommunicate, dictate "how the word shall be taught, how sacraments administered," or "decide the questions which rise about matters of faith and Christian religion" (viii.1). This last was a matter for experts. Hooker presumably meant clerical experts, and here Charles I was to agree with him, in an exposition of his power in 1628: "That we are supreme Governor of the Church of England: and that if any difference arise about the external policy, concerning the injunctions, canons, and other constitutions whatsoever thereto belonging, the Clergy in their Convocation is to order and settle them, having first obtained leave under our broad seal so to do: and we approving their said ordinances and constitutions; provided that none be made contrary to the laws and customs of the land."[7] By 1628, however, the House of Commons had taken it upon itself to be the judge of what was orthodox doctrine.[8] After all, the House had debated and assented to doctrine since the 1530s, and in 1559 the House by statute was given some say in the definition of heresy—a provision of the Act of Supremacy which was to be quoted by Hooker.[9] All this ground was potentially treacherous.

Thomas Cranmer in the late 1530s had been exercised by the puzzle whether a Christian prince in a conquered territory with only laity available could "make and constitute priests." Cranmer decided that he could: history proves that some Christian princes have done so. Nor, mused Cranmer, is it forbidden by God's law for such a Christian prince in his own realm to "make" bishops and priests if all the existing clerics have died. Did he mean consecrate, or merely appoint? Beyond these intellectual puzzles, Cranmer was confirming his conviction that "all christian princes have committed unto them immediately of God the whole cure of all their subjects, as well concerning the administration of God's word for the cure of souls, as concerning the ministration of things political," and that priests should be thought of as "appointed, assigned, and elected in every place by the laws and orders of kings and princes."[10] With this in mind—and remembering also such cravers for royal "absolute power" as Humphrey Gilbert, lecturing the House of Commons in 1571 about "Prerogative Imperial,"[11] thus occasioning the maiden speech of Peter Wentworth—Hooker's exposition of the powers of the supreme governor seems, as one would expect, moderate.

Why—to conclude this summary of Hooker's place in the Tudor traditions of Supreme Headship—are clerical experts needed? Because we need the "judgement of the wisest"; "it were unnatural not to think the pastors and bishops of our souls a great deal more fit, than men of secular trades and callings" (VIII.vi.11). Kings, on the whole, lack "exacter judgement in matters divine," and because of this "personal inability to judge" they should leave such matters to "professors" (iii.3).

Henry VIII would probably not have been amused.

Supreme Head, certainly, but, as G. R. Elton has often reminded us, the king had been made Supreme Head in 1534 "by authority of this present Parliament."[12] Furthermore, as Elton also emphasizes, Elizabeth was supreme governor in 1559 "by virtue of this act."[13] And Hooker was always conscious of the "consent of the lords and commons assembled in parliament" (ii.17)—a Parliament with competent authority in assent and approbation. He warned his readers not to think that MPs have no more right "to give order to the Church and clergy" than they have "to make laws for the hierarchies of angels in heaven" (vi.10). For "the Parliament of England together with the convocation annexed thereunto, is that whereupon the very essence of all government within this kingdom doth depend; it is even the body of the whole realm; it consisteth of the king, and of all that within the land are subject unto him: for they all are there present, either in person or by such as they voluntarily have derived their very personal right unto" (vi.11). Thus ecclesiastical laws in a Christian commonwealth must have the "consent" of the prince, the "consent" of the clergy in Convocation, and "the consent as well of the laity" (vi.8). (The doctrinal Act of Six Articles in 1539 had received the "consent" of the king, the "assent" of the Lords, the "assent" of the Convocation—and the "consent" of the Commons.)[14] In all this, again, there lurked a possible dilemma. In 1589 Christopher Hatton pointed out to the House of Commons that "all authority for dealing in these causes" is "invested into her imperial crown"; but he also pointed out that this investing was "by all your consents (as by right it ought to be)."[15] Stuart Englishmen inherited these ambiguities.

Hooker's treatment was here again controlled by his concern for the entire body of the commonwealth; the whole, not the part. Thus laws, whether ecclesiastical or civil, "do take originally their essence from the power of the whole realm and church of England." Laws have no "form and vigour" without "the general consent of all" (vi.11). In fact, Hooker gave more play to the theme of consent and assent than Whitgift had done, or than Jacobean High Churchmen such as John Overall were to do.[16] We know that John Locke bought a copy of Hooker in 1681, copied out long extracts into his journal, and quoted Hooker sixteen times in his *Second Treatise of Government*.[17] It was basic to Hooker's political thinking that, for the "ordaining" of government—for our yielding ourselves subject to the magistrate—"composition and agreement" are required. Thus lawful power is "granted or consented unto by them over whom they exercise the same." There is, true, another kind of lawful power —that "given extraordinarily from God" (1.x.4). The prince has both kinds: an "authority derived at the first from their consent" and an "express commission immediately and personally received from God" (x.8). It is a traditional but nonetheless typically Hookerian balance of potential opposites. The notion is that the power of the whole politic society is "derived" to the ruler by "consent of the people" (VIII.vi.11,3). There is a reference here to the Roman law, the *lex regia*: "the will of the emperor has the force of law, because the people transfers to him all its own power."[18] The ruler might be one, or few, or many: the choice is arbitrary.[19] But Hooker stressed that both "experience and practice" indicate that "the supreme authority of one" is "commendable" (iii.1). Whether one, few, or many, the magistrates become "God's lieutenants," and so rule by "divine right" (ii.5).

Where do these conceptions of consent apply to the actual working of the Tudor constitution? Most obviously, in the House of Commons, where "our assent is by reason of other agents there on our behalf" (I.x.8). This was a commonplace. Thomas Smith had discussed it in 1565,[20] and in 1595 William Perkins incidentally observed, in a discussion of Adam as "a publike person representing all his posterity," that "in a Parliament whatsoever is done by the Burgesse of the shiere, is done by every person in the shiere."[21] The consent is seen also in custom: "that which hath been received long sithence and is by custom now established." For "we do consent, when that society whereof we are part hath at any time before consented." This was broadened into the idea of the continuity of corporations: "corporations are immortal; we were then alive in our predecessors, and they in their successors do live still" (x.8). Such sections of Hooker were greatly to appeal to Edmund Burke. "The most certain token of evident goodness is, if the general persuasion of all men do so account it"; "the general and perpetual voice of men is as the sentence of God himself" (viii.3).

As these themes were developed in Book VIII, we find that Englishmen "are in no subjection, but such as willingly themselves have condescended unto, for their own most behoof and security" (ii.7). Kings by conquest "make their own charter." Kings "by God's special appointment have also that largeness of power, which he doth assign or permit with approbation." But kings that are "first instituted by agreement" (ii.11), such as are in "this kingdom," have a "dependence upon that whole entire body, over the several parts whereof he hath dominion" (ii.7). The roots of that dependence are "in that first original conveyance, when power was derived by the whole into one" (ii.9). Thereafter, supreme power in England passed by "hereditary birth" (ii.8), succession by blood. In the 1590s, therefore, the crown was not "an estate in condition, by the voluntary deed of the people" (ii.8). The people have expressed their consent in tradition: "silent allowance famously notified through custom reaching beyond the memory of man" (ii.11). One senses the influence of the common lawyers at the Inns of Court.

So, with regard to the existing laws of ecclesiastical polity in the 1590s, men "should be slow and unwilling to change, without very urgent necessity, the ancient ordinances, rites, and long approved customs, of our venerable predecessors" (v.vii.3). The Puritan case, of course, was that in England such time of "urgent necessity" had arrived. Hooker especially insisted on continuity in the church: "the long continued practice of the whole Church" (vii.1), "antiquity, custom, and consent in the Church of God" (vii.3), "from which unnecessarily to swerve, experience hath never as yet found it safe" (vii.1). Those governed by the Puritan imperative would not have laid much store by such "experience."

How far did Hooker recognize a right of resistance—as Aquinas recognized it, albeit rather guardedly?[22] With Hooker, the recognition was, to say the least, *very* guarded. Can the "body politic" withdraw the "dominion" if there be "inconvenience"? Perhaps, but only with the consent of the governor.[23] Laws must be obeyed "unless there be reason shewed which may necessarily enforce that the law of Reason or of God doth enjoin the contrary" (i.xvi.5). *Necessarily*. Hooker did not think it "allowable for men to observe those laws which in their hearts they are steadfastly persuaded to be against the law of God." He asked the Puritans (and perhaps the appeal was not very convincing) to "suspend" their "persuasion" for a time, the rather incomprehending assumption being that Puritan persuasions would in due course (and as a matter of course) be revealed as "mere probabilities only" (Pref.vi.6).

What Hooker feared was an English equivalent of Bernardt Knipperdollinck, Mayor of Münster and Anabaptist, in the 1530s. Hooker felt that the eventual outcome of Puritan victory would be that "all must come by devolution at the length, even as the family of Brown will have it [the reference was to Robert Browne], unto the godly among the people; for confusion unto the wise and the great, the poor and the simple, some Knipperdoling with his retinue, must take the work of the Lord in hand; and the making of church laws and orders must prove to be their right in the end" (VIII.vi.14). It was, in fact, to be a popular theme of London preachers in the 1640s that the "voice of Jesus Christ reigning in his Church comes first from the Multitude, the Common People...God useth the common People and the Multitude to proclaime that the Lord God omnipotent reigneth."[24] So Hooker as a prophet was not too far out—any more than Colet had been in 1512, with his fear that the people might take it upon them to reform the church, if reformation were delayed.[25] This fear of the multitude set limits to Elizabethan whiggery. Hooker felt himself to be living in a time of "strange, untrue, and unnatural conceits, set abroad by seedsmen of rebellion." And one of the marks of rebellion was the "estate in condition" theory, the idea that the powers that be, here and now, are continuously subject to the "voluntary deed of the people." Such a notion was a "defiance unto all law, equity, and reason" (ii.8).

In such moods, the middle-aged, "establishment" Hooker was dominant; many of his readers will find him at his least compelling in this characterization, with his stress on the thesis that "equity and reason, the law of nature, God and man, do all favour that which is in being"; yet he was careful to add a qualifying phrase, "till orderly judgment of decision be given against it" (Pref.vi.5). In the 1590s, when "venturous boldness I see is a thing now general" (v.3), it was especially appropriate to rely on "the wisdom of governors" (viii.1), "them whose gravity and wisdom ought in such cases to overrule" (v.3), "the authorized guides of this church" (vi.1). How could it be stomached that "our English nobility" would "contentedly suffer themselves to be always at the call, and to stand to the sentence of a number of mean persons"? Hooker was especially suspicious of such mean persons when they were "assisted with the presence of their poor teacher" (viii.2). If we look at "the present state of the highest governor placed over us," at "the quality and disposition of our nobles," at "the orders and laws of our famous universities," at "the profession of the civil or the practice of the common law amongst us" (viii.14), it becomes plain that we must beware of the argument that "'God hath chosen the simple'" (iii.14).

Some of such points were borrowed from Whitgift. Whitgift asked Cartwright whether it was his conclusion that "truth, zeal, and godliness, remaineth either only or especially in the simple, rude, and ignorant sort?"[26] Hooker had a similar question: "Touching God himself, hath he anywhere revealed that it is his delight to dwell beggarly? And that he taketh no pleasure to be worshipped saving only in poor cottages?" Typically, and as one would expect, Hooker broadened the mere debating point into a sustained and eloquent defense of "the sumptuous stateliness of houses built unto God's glory" (v.xv.3). The beauty of holiness. But an assumption is there always—that "the aged for the most part are best experienced, least subject to rash and unadvised passions," that "wisdom and youth are seldom joined in one" (vii.1). It is necessary to remind oneself here that Hooker felt that a defense of the powers that be was always difficult, because rebels tend to be believed. "If we maintain things that are established," we are thought to be time-servers, seeking preferment, while the rebel "shall never want attentive and favourable hearers" (1.i.1). And in fact Hooker's establishment tone was usually quite modest and guarded. It was all a question of assuming the *probable* wisdom of the powers that be. Hooker's work might indeed be thought of as an extended essay on probabilities. "The public approbation given by the body of this whole church unto those things which are established, doth make it but probable that they are good." "Of peace and quietness there is not any way possible, unless the probable voice of every entire society or body politic overrule all private of like nature in the same body" (Pref.vi.6). If that probability be assumed, the duty of obedience and alignment follows. "A law is the deed of the whole body politic, whereof if ye judge yourselves to be any part, then is the law even your deed also" (Pref.v.2).

II

There is in the library of Selwyn College, Cambridge, a unique copy (so far as can be ascertained) of a dialogue printed probably in 1532 or 1533: *A dyaloge betwene one Clemente a clerke of the Convocacyuon, and one Bernarde, a burges of the parlyament, dysputynge betwene them what auctoryte the clergye have to make lawes. And howe farre and where theyr power dothe extende.* Some investigators have attributed this (incomplete) item to Christopher Saint-German, for no other reason than that he wrote the same sort of thing at the same sort of time. At any rate, the author was obviously a layman and a common lawyer, expressing the spirit of the Inns of Court—a spirit that was decisively to influence Hooker during his years of residence there in the 1580s. The two characters represent the "spiritualty" and the "temporalty." And the *dyaloge* was timely because of the "Supplication of the Commons against the Ordinaries" of March 1532, and the "Answer" of the clergy, discussed in Convocation and ready by the end of April.[27] The points made in the three publications very nicely overlap.

The second chapter of the dialogue was concerned with "what a lawe is, and howe many lawes there be" (sig. B2ᵛ). The MP began by dividing law into two, the law of God and the law of man, the law of God being in turn divided into the law of Scripture and the law of nature: "The lawe of nature which men call the lawe of naturall reason is that lawe whiche god hathe gyven and put in every soule which sheweth and declareth to every man what thynge is good and what is evyll, and by that lawe man dothe knowe what god wolde have man to do." God acted through this law of nature in pre-New Testament times, as histories and chronicles make manifest, and "ye that be prelates and other of the convocacyons of Englande, have no power to make the lawe nor to chaunge that lawe" (B4ᵛ). The "lawe of holy scripture" (the "posityve lawe divyne") is "but the confyrmacioun of the lawe of nature" (B5ʳ).

The law of man embraces customary law and positive law. Customary law is "that whiche the people use and have used out of tyme of mynde, that is to say, so longe and above that tyme that any man alyve can remembre, and wherof there remayneth no maner of wrytinge to shewe whan and by whome that lawe was made." Positive law is "that whiche is made by the people or els by the pryncies, whose auctoryte is deryvyed and commeth from the people, and they be called actes or statutes made by wrytynge" (B5ᵛ).

The argument followed that the spirituality alone "have no auctoryte to make any suche mans lawe, nother customary lawe nor posityve lawe," no authority over the law of nature or the law of scripture, and no authority over the subjects of the king who break these laws if the "ponysshementes were nat put by god nor Chryste before. For than that order of ponysshement so ordayned by you, shulde be a newe mannes lawe made by you . . . whyche mannes lawes ye have none auctoryte to make, bycause ye have no auctoryte of the people so to do" (B6ʳ). One again remembers Colet's fear of the people in 1512. And G. R. Elton has argued that the Supplication against the Ordinaries, drafted though it may have been by the government in 1532, was based on complaints made to the House of Commons in 1529, especially from the City of London.[28]

The cleric, not surprisingly, was anxious to deny "that all mennes lawes be made only by the pryncies or the people" (B6ʳ⁻ᵛ). For

> the prelates and preests assembled in theyr synodes and convocacyons may make lawes for the orderynge, rulynge and correccyon of them selfes, and for the mynystrynge of the sacramentes and sacramentalles of the churche and sayenge of dyvyne servyce, and for the orderynge of the ceremonyes of the churche, and all those thynges be orders and lawes made by men . . . we of the churche have auctoryte to ordayne correccyon and ponisshement for all them that breke the lawe of god. [B6ᵛ]

The MP here introduced a comparison with the City of London, which could legislate to govern itself but "can nat stretche to governe or to correcte any other of the kynges subjectes beynge no such cytezens" (B7ʳ). (A little like More's idea of the limits of *parliamentary* legislation, as interpreted by William Roper: the House of Commons could not deny God to be God.)[29] So "ye of the spirytualte alone may make no orders nor lawes to extende any correccyon to them that be nat of your owne felyshyppe and communyte" (B7ʳ); because "youre auctoryte stretcheth nat to bynde the lay men therto" (B7ᵛ), it follows that "your lawe can nat extende to gyve any ponysshement or correccyon to them that be nat present at the makynge of your lawes nor never consentynge unto them" (B8ʳ). You "whiche call your selfe of the churche may make none orders nor lawes to ponysshe the kynges subjectes, nother by bodely payne nor losse of theyr goodes, whiche be nat presente nor consentynge to the makynge of those youre lawes" (B8ᵛ). These issues had been the subject of trenchant debate in England since the case of the Londoner Richard Hunne, taken to an ecclesiastical court in 1512 for refusing to pay a burial fee.[30]

Next, the MP was concerned to deny the assumption of the cleric (an assumption that Colet, prime advocate for the spirituality, would have shared) that God has given to the clergy "immedyatly" (C3ʳ) the power of interpretation of the written word of God. He developed his argument into a more general survey of the nature of law and society. England was a realm "politicum" and "regale" (C6ʳ). This notion was taken from Sir John Fortescue (died 1479). In his *De Laudibus Legum Anglie*, written about 1470 and as yet unprinted, Fortescue had defined the French kingdom as absolute (*dominium regale*) and the English kingdom as limited (*dominium politicum et regale*).[31] (Fortescue was to be another of Locke's heroes.) In England, the MP pointed out, "lawes be made bothe by the prynce and the people assembled and present together in counsell or in parlyament" (C5ᵛ), and "they do admytte no order made to have the strengthe of a lawe, excepte it be made bothe by the consente of the prynce and of the people" (C5ᵛ–6ʳ). Furthermore, "I sey that the grounde of all aucthoryte of makynge of mannes lawe commeth pryncypally of the good mynde of the people." And "therfore I sey all you whyche calle youre selfe of the churche, and do take upon you to make any orders or lawes wythout the consente of a ryght mynde of the prynce or of the people whyche shalbe bounde by the same

lawes, ye do it without any auctoryte" (C6ʳ). The cleric protested
against this "newe scole and a newe lernyng" (C6ᵛ). But the MP
reminded him of the examples of godly princes throughout Christian
history, with various especially potent Saxon examples and an appeal
to Lucius, "the fyrst chrystened kyng of Brytayne" (D1ᵛ), whom the
pope in the third century called Vicar of God in England. The
Elizabethans were to be fond of King Lucius.

In May 1532 the clergy agreed not to make any new canons without royal license and assent,[32] and a committee, half lay, half clerical,
was appointed by the king to revise the existing canon law. This was
enacted by authority of Parliament in 1534.[33]

It may be that in considering Hooker's sources, we should look
less to Aquinas than to the "new learning" of common lawyers,
especially as it developed from the 1530s.

In discussing the origins of Anglicanism (if the term be allowed),
we must, again, linger in the 1530s. The first confession of the
ecclesia anglicana was the so-called Ten Articles of 1536, drawn up by
a clerical committee headed by Cranmer and debated in Convocation.[34] Part II of this document was concerned with the visible
technique of piety, customs, and rites which "have been of a long
continuance for a decent order and honest policy" and are therefore
to be retained, "although they be not expressly commanded of God,
nor necessary to our salvation" (p. 796). Abuses must not be destroyed but "moderated" (p. 804)—a word which Hugh Latimer
had been fond of for a decade. Royal injunctions in the same year,
ordering the clergy to explain the Ten Articles to their no doubt
bewildered flocks, spoke in similar vein of "laudable ceremonies,
rites and usages of the Church meet and convenient to be kept and
used for a decent and politic order" (p. 806). Among recent scholars,
J. K. McConica, in his *English Humanists and Reformation Politics under
Henry VIII and Edward VI*,[35] has directed us to put the ideas back
into the 1530s, to pay less attention to historians who have discussed
or "explained" the English Reformation as an act of state by career-
ist politicians, or a by-product of the "divorce," or a chapter in
administrative history, or a series of spontaneous happenings without

intellectual fiber. The line of Cranmer-Cromwell Erasmian reform was to find its most extended expression in Hooker.

Among early statements of the *via media*, Cranmer's 1540 Bible preface must now be considered. The Archbishop was writing for "two sundry sorts of people": "some there are that be too slow, and need the spur: Some other seem too quick, and need more of the bridle: some lose their game by short shooting, some by over-shooting: some walk too much on the left hand, some too much on the right."[36] Both are wrong. The essay owed much to Erasmus. (I am thinking of his essay *Festina Lente*, published in 1508: "Some natures need the spur, other the rein. And so the ancients rightly curled the dolphin round the anchor.")[37] "These two sorts," continued Cranmer, "albeit they be most far unlike the one to the other, yet they both deserve in effect like reproach."[38] He went on to warn that the written word of God must be used and not abused, and he warned Englishmen not to make an idol of Scripture in the way that pagans had made an idol of the sun, the moon, and the stars.[39] Hooker was to develop this theme in his Book II.

Equally relevant was Cranmer's short essay at the end of the Prayer Book of 1549.[40] A Book of Common Prayer—that is, common to the whole realm. This essay went under the title "Of Ceremonies, why some be abolished and some retained." There were in England —even more so than in 1540—two "partyes." First, the ultraconservative, those "so addicted to their olde customes" that they "thynke it a great matter of conscience to departe from a peece of the leaste of theyr Ceremonies." Secondly, the ultraradical, those "so newe fangle that they woulde innovate all thyng, and so doe despyse the olde that nothynge can lyke them, but that is newe." The descendants of the newfangled party were within twenty years to attract (much to their chagrin) the description "puritan"—a word never once used by Hooker. Cranmer's intention was to cater to neither party exclusively, but to "profitte them bothe." Men must serve God "not in bondage of figure or shadowe; but in the free-dome of spirite" (another Erasmian touch). In spite of the radicals, however, it must be observed that there are certain traditional techniques of worship and ritual and symbolism which "serve to a decente ordre and godlye discipline," which "stirre uppe the dulle mynde of manne to the rememberaunce of his duetie to God"; here we must have "reverence unto them for theyr antiquity," even though they are not "to be estemed equal with goddes lawe," being retained mainly for "discipline and ordre," and granted that they may be "altered and chaunged"—"upon just causes." Among the earlier English statements, this, of what was to be a concern of Hooker: "the majesty and holiness" of external worship, as a "sensible help to stir up devotion" (v.xvi.2).

About 1550 there was printed in Canterbury an English version of Erasmus' 1529 Colloquy, *Cyclops, or the Gospel Bearer*, which had as theme the danger of overemphasis on the external Scripture. Some carry the Bible continually in their hand, like friars with their rule or the porters of Paris with their regulations; some quote it constantly, pharisee-like; others (much the best) bear it in their heart. "The true gospel bearer...carries it in hands and mouth *and* heart."[41] Cranmer and Nicholas Ridley were probably responsible for commissioning the translation of this dialogue. They thus continued the tradition, effective in England since 1532, of appealing to specific works of Erasmus as support for the English Reformation.[42]

John Hooper was nominated Bishop of Gloucester in July 1550 at the age of 50. Thereupon Hooper, one of the few Englishmen who had been to Switzerland, made certain points about outward ecclesiastical ceremonies.[43] They "show the pharisaical superstition and priesthood of Aaron" and "may not be used without the breach of God's law." They are not "things indifferent, but very sin, for they be things forbidden by the word of God."[44] "The apostles used it not, *ergo* it is not lawful for us to use it" (2:382). A newfangled prelate indeed! Moreover, Hooper made a significant appeal to "conscience": "ye...do deprive us of our liberty" because "the civil state hath not to meddle with this matter" (2:377–78). These themes had a future. In general: "There is nothing to be done in the church, but is commanded or forbidden by the word of God" (2:390). One is reminded of the assertion of Thomas Wilcox in 1572 that "nothing be don in this or ani other thing, but that which you have the expresse warrant of Gods words for,"[45] an assertion which was greatly to exercise Hooker.

The reply by Ridley, first printed in 1853 but owned in manuscript by Whitgift,[46] contains, when analyzed, seven important points, all to be developed by Whitgift and Hooker. First, concerning use and abuse: "If the right use be profitable, and may be restored, and the abuse more easily taken away than the thing itself, then such are not, because they have been abused, to be taken away, but to be reformed and amended, and so kept still."[47] Secondly, concerning "things indifferent": "It is not necessary that all things necessary have their original and ground" in Scripture, such authority being "required in things to be believed and done of necessity unto salvation," but "not required in all things that be of themselves indifferent" (2:376). In the area of "things...indifferent," lawful authority may legislate. Thirdly, Ridley moved in a mental world of "godly order in the church" (2:376), "godly ecclesiastical polity" (2:379), and "public ordinance," which was not to be broken. "Christian liberty is not a license to do what thou list" (2:377). For instance, ceremonies—in this case, the vestments prescribed in 1549— are "profitable," their abolition would be "harmful"; they have been ordered by "lawful authority" and "agreeable consent" (2: 386) and are necessary in the England of 1550 for the observing of discipline. Fourthly, and following therefrom, Ridley dwelt on the power of the magistrate in the Christian commonwealth; as the princely office is proved both by Scripture and by history, clerics "ought by God's word to maintain the lawful authority of the civil magistrate, and to teach the people due obedience unto the same" (2:378). Vestments are "appointed" by the archbishop and his clerical advisers, who are in turn appointed by the king and "established" by the king and Parliament. Parliament are the "stablishers of the Book of Common Prayer in the church of England" (2:387–88)—a facet of the Tudor constitution which perplexed Martin Bucer, who was at that time living in Cambridge as Regius Professor of Divinity. Ridley maintained that the radical faction had "too vile and too base an estimation of the magistrates" (2:379); generally, he attacked the stubborn obstinacy, "sedition and disobedience of the younger sort against their elders, contrary unto St Paul's doctrine" (2:392). Now, the fifth point: the faction (like the Donatists) was "seditious" and "disobedient," liable to confound a "good order" (2:378). They were "singular"; like the Arians, Ridley said (2:387), or, one might add, like the Lutherans characterized in 1526 by John Fisher.[48] As Lady Russell was to point out in *Persuasion*, "it is singularity which often makes the worst part of our sufferings, as it always does of our conduct." Sixthly, Hooper had no sense of historical development. "I do not a little marvel that he will allow no respect or regard to be had either unto the diversity of times, places, or conditions of the people" (2:389). Finally, in claiming to interpret the written word of God, the radicals add to it: "to forbid and to make that sin which God never forbade" is "bringing in bondage the Christian liberty, and ungodly adding unto God's word" (2:382). "For lack of true understanding of the scriptures all this business doth chance" (2:386). And one must especially beware of ambition, disguised "under the pretence of God's word" (2:380). During the course of the argument (2:393), Ridley quoted from Erasmus' dialogue, *Convivium Fabulosum* ("The Fabulous Feast," 1524).

The policy of Cranmer and Ridley was continued by Archbishop Matthew Parker, with his instinctive feeling for *moderatio* and with the ruling by the Queen that "none should be suffered to decline either on the left or on the right hand from the direct line limited by authority of our said laws and Injunctions."[49] Elizabeth was a curious combination of the impetuous and the inscrutable, and Parker, subject to attacks of melancholia, was never quite at ease: "where the Queen's Highness doth note me to be too soft and easy, I think divers of my brethren will rather note me, if they were asked, too sharp and too earnest in moderation, which towards them I have used, and will still do, till mediocrity shall be received amongst us" (p. 173). When the French ambassador visited the archbishop in 1564, he "noted much and delighted in our mediocrity, charging the Genevans and Scottish of going too far in extremities" (p. 215).

Jewel tells us that a French professor of law had been similarly impressed in 1562, praising *moderatio* "in the late change of religion," as compared with the "preciseness" of Zurich and Geneva.[50] To Jewel in the summer of 1559, a returned Marian exile, this *mediocritas* had seemed a "*leaden*" not a "*golden*" mediocrity—a "crying out, that the half is better than the whole."[51] His nomination to the Bishopric of Salisbury in July somewhat dampened his reforming zeal—and eventually occasioned the bequest to Salisbury of his library, which his protégé Hooker was to use.

There are many points on which Hooker would have sympathized with Parker. He probably shared Parker's rather insular conception of "true Englishmen, not wishing to be subject to the governance of...insolent conquerors": God, wrote Parker, being "so much English as he is,"[52] a notion first expressed by Latimer in 1537.[53] Dr Johnson, Boswell suggests, modeled his style on that of Hooker, among others.[54] And there was sometimes a Johnsonian touch about Parker: "There is a difference betwixt the frailty of man's mutability, and a professing of plain impiety"[55]—one is tempted to add an initial "Sir." Parker had been an agent of government policy under Edward VI, with its aim (the words are Thomas Cromwell's) in "pure sincereness truly to open the word of God" (pp. 5–6) and its insistence (as William May, President of Queens' College, Cambridge, put it) that "all things shall be done moderately and in due order" (p. 38). We also note Parker's praise in 1549 of a moderate conscience—not too narrow, not too broad: "Pity it is that the cause of Christ's religion is thus far hindered by timorous spiced conscience, although too wide conscience in the sinews of Christ's religion is not commendable" (p. 245). Parker's delight in church music—and subsidy of it—echoed an emphasis of Cranmer's and prepared the way for those pages on music as an aid to meditation in which Hooker lauds that "admirable facility which music hath to express and represent to the mind, more inwardly than any other sensible mean, the very standing, rising, and falling, the very steps and inflections every way, the turns and varieties of all passions whereunto the mind is subject" (v.xxxviii.1). Parker certainly would have approved of Hooker's point that "the very majesty and holiness of the place, where God is worshipped, hath *in regard of us* great virtue, force, and efficacy," thus being "a sensible help to stir up devotion" (v.xvi.2), and his insistence that men must seek what is "suitable, decent, and fit for the greatness of Jesus Christ, for the sublimity of his gospel" (xv.3). "Solemn duties of public service to be done unto God, must have their places set and prepared in such sort, as beseemeth actions of that regard" (xi.1)—an argument for the "sumptuous stateliness" (xv.3) of churches which, developed (or exaggerated?), was to inspire John Cosin, William Laud, and the chapel of Peterhouse, Cambridge.

Parker stood for the "reasonableness" of the Elizabethan laws of ecclesiastical polity, for the religion established "by public authority."[56] And so, by 1563, he saw "offence grow by new innovations" (p. 185). "God keep us," he had written to Cecil late in 1559, "from such visitation as Knox have attempted in Scotland; the people to be orderers of things" (p. 105). In 1573 he wrote to Cecil about "puritans"—a word he had first used in November 1572 (p. 409): "if this fond faction be applauded to, or borne with, it will fall out to a popularity, and as wise men think, it will be the overthrow of all the nobility...papists and precisians have one mark to shoot at, plain disobedience; some of simplicity, some of wiliness and stubbornness" (p. 437). The alternative to the Book of Common Prayer was "Muncer's commonwealth" (p. 426). For Parker, as for Hooker (and Elizabeth I), spiritual zeal was more often than not the façade for ambition. "These times are troublesome" (1573) because of "pretensed favourers and false brethren, who under the colour of reformation seek the ruin and subversion both of learning and religion. Neither do they only cut down the ecclesiastical state, but also give a great push at the civil policy. Their colour is sincerity, under the countenance of simplicity, but in very truth they are ambitious spirits, and can abide no superiority." Lamentably, "most plausible are these new devices to a great number of the people, who labour to live in all liberty," led as they are by "these fantastical spirits, which labour to reign in men's consciences." In "the platform set down by these new builders [with this letter Parker enclosed extracts from "Cartwright's book"] we evidently see the spoliation of the patrimony of Christ, a popular state to be sought. The end will be ruin to religion, and confusion to our country." How unattractive to the archbishop, now in his seventieth year, was "this new building, which hitherto, as we think, in no Christian nation hath found any foundation upon the earth, but is now framed upon suppositions, full of absurdities and impossibilities, in the air" (pp. 434–35). So much for the discipline. What Parker most feared, then, was subversion "under the colour of God's word" (p. 445)—here he was talking to Cecil about tyrannicide, a topic that had been on his mind since 1559, when he had seen in London books on sale in its support—subversion of "the Queen's laws, which I trust do not much differ from God's word well understood" (p. 209), which confirm by public authority "that religion which I know in conscience is good" (p. 472). He had outlined his archiepiscopal task in 1560 as "the establishing of God's pure religion again amongst us," with "continuance of sincerity in doctrine, unity in common Christian charity, and safety of realms by godly succession in blood" (p. 131), all phrases that call Cranmer to mind. Such defense of "the state of religion publicly received" (p. 297) involved especially a "diligent watching upon the unruly flock of the English people" (p. 60). One thinks of Hooker's abiding suspicion of the multitude.

From Parker's letters there emerge features of character which would surely have delighted Izaak Walton. (Whatever Walton's defects in detail as a biographer, he remains the best exponent of the Hookerian mood as it was to develop after Hooker's death.) Parker valued sincerity, charity, and peace—as did Erasmus, a portrait of whom Parker owned. He was compassionate: "For pure pity I took home to dinner with me Mr. dean of Paul's" (p. 235)—on the occasion when Dean Alexander Nowell had been interrupted by the Queen in the middle of a sermon. He was not, in the sense typified by Malvolio, puritanical, as in his judging the Dean of Westminster "to be a sad grave man, yet in his own private judgment peradventure too severe" (p. 360). In typically Anglican style, he was allergic to zeal: "I think he were best to be a little colder in his zeal. And, my lord [to the Bishop of Norwich] be you not led with fantastical folk" (pp. 459–60)—all in the context of a constant suspicion that the times were out of joint, that the age was too subtle, "hurly-burly" (p. 392), "brittle" (p. 316). One of his favorite phrases was "Silence and Hope." "I repose myself *in silentio, et in spe*...howsoever the world fawneth or fumeth" (p. 246). "Some things were better put up in silence, than much stirred in" (p. 444).

For in England—and this was the burden of Whitgift's arguments against Cartwright—there had been a *re*formation: not a *trans*formation.

The Elizabethan tone had been caught by Nicholas Bacon—like Parker, a graduate of, and benefactor to, Corpus Christi College, Cambridge—in his speeches to the Parliament of 1559. The things most pressing were "Concord and Unity." The things most to be eschewed were idolatry and irreverence, and the vocation of Englishmen was to run between them a "right and straight course."[57] So there must be "observation of one uniform Order in Religion, according to the Laws now Established" (p. 33), and the burden upon the Parliament was "well making of Laws, for the according, and uniting of these people of the Realm into an uniform order of Religion" (p. 11), "to comprehend, as well those that be too swift, as those that be too slow" (p. 34)—a phrase deliberately based on Cranmer's 1540 Bible preface. The Queen, in a letter of 1563 to the Emperor Ferdinand, argued that the English "follow no novel and strange religions, but that very religion which is ordained by Christ, sanctioned by the primitive and Catholic Church and approved by the consentient mind and voice of the most early Fathers."[58] Ideals, then, of unity, order, and quiet: undisturbed, as Elizabeth insisted in 1565, by "diversity, variety, contention, and vain love of singularity."[59] Such was the social cement. In the last Elizabethan Parliament (1601) the Speaker said that, "If he were asked, what were the first and chiefest thing to be considered, he would say, *Religion*. So Religion is all in all, for Religion breeds Devotion, Devotion breeds Zeal and Piety to God, which breedeth Obedience and Duty to the

Prince, and obedience to the Laws, which breedeth Faithfulness and Honesty and Love. Three necessary and only things to be wished and observed in a well Governed Common-Wealth."[60]

With this background established, it is time to consider the debate in the 1570s about the English church and commonwealth between John Whitgift and Thomas Cartwright.[61]

In this not very sparkling controversy, some very general points were raised: the limitations of schism, the nature of Christian liberty, the distinction between use and abuse, the varieties of legitimate and unnatural zeal, the relationship of the Puritans to the Donatists and the Cathari. The debate embraced also much of seminal importance about political obligation, obedience and consent, individualism, equality and "popularity"; about church and state, conscience and commonwealth, word and sword. The technically theological issues under discussion revealed a clear division. To Cartwright, the Anglicans were unsound on free will, the potentialities of nature, Christian assurance, and (possibly) purgatory. For Whitgift, the Puritans laid too little emphasis on the sacraments and presumed overmuch about election and reprobation (one remembers the seminar on the subject held by a group of Milton's fallen angels). There was dialogue also about the relationship of election and faith, about infant reprobation, the Real Presence, and the nature of the church—Cartwright emphasizing the covenanted church: it was a godly community, not a tavern. (The essence of Puritanism was a conception of the godly community.) But the debate was concerned primarily with the nature and limits of Scripture. Cartwright accused Whitgift of underemphasizing the written word of God: "*it is no small injury which you do unto the word of God, to pin it in so narrow room.*"[62] To Whitgift, following Ridley's dislike of the ungodly adding to the Word of God, the Puritans made of Scripture a nose of wax,[63] by neglecting the distinction (stressed by Ridley, Jewel, and Peter Martyr, sometime Professor at Oxford) between matters of substance, necessary to salvation, and matters indifferent, accidental, or neuter ("accessary," Hooker was to say), neither commanded nor condemned in Scripture, which are to be arranged by the particular national church according to order, authority, and "time, place, persons, and other circumstances."[64] In Whitgift's view, matters of ceremonial and church government came within this territory of the neuter. In the consideration of Scripture, reason must have its place, as must the consent of learned men, remembering that particular texts of Scripture must be seen in relation to the "drift" (3:284), the "general rule" (3:5). Whitgift pointed out to Cartwright, as Fisher had reminded the Lutherans, that a negative argument from Scripture (what is not there is wrong) was absurd. Thus Whitgift set the limits for the appeal to the Scripture and the apostolic church. The key to the debate, as he saw it, was this: "I confess it is no reformation, except it be agreeable to the word of God. The controversy is, what part of it is agreeable to the word of God, and what is not; also, what it is to be agreeable to the word of God" (1:93).

While commending (or at any rate not condemning) a "godly zeal," Whitgift warned his generation to beware of "preposterous and affectionated zeal" (1:36). Hooker was to agree: men must be "sincere, sound, and discreet"; inordinate zeal can be like a mishandled razor or a plucking up of "the corn in the field of God" through a "hatred of tares" (v.iii.1). Beware of "the pang of a furious zeal" (xvii.1). Hooker, like Ibsen, was wary of the Claim of the Ideal. For one thing, evils must be considered inevitable (part of the Anglican negative capability, perhaps, this point). Life is a matter of choosing the lesser evil. In both church and commonwealth "there are and will be always evils which no art of man can cure, breaches and leaks moe than man's wit hath hands to stop" (ix.2). Rather bear the ills we have, than fly to others that we know not of. In "evils that cannot be removed without the manifest danger of greater to succeed in their rooms, wisdom, of necessity, must give place to necessity. All it can do in those cases is to devise how that which must be endured may be mitigated, and the inconveniences thereof countervailed as near as may be; that when the best things are not possible, the best may be made of those that are" (ix.1). There is a kind of gentle pessimism underpinning Hooker's book. An artist—and the thought here goes back at least to Aristotle—may have an Idea; he may have the impetus and the skill; but the execution of the vision is conditioned by the nature of the material. Similarly, men may have general rules and principles, ultimate truths or generalities which have "plainness at the first sight." But in life these plain rules have to be applied with "restraints and limitations" (v.ix.2). A medical doctor may have general rules for a cure, but the rules must be adapted to the need and character of each particular patient.

How can the method of applying ultimate truth in life be prescribed? Well, the task requires uncommon ability; it is not a matter fit for "gross and popular capacities" (ix.2). To "practise general laws according to their right meaning" (ix.3) involves consideration of dispensation and "equity"—a favorite word for Hooker, as it had been for More (the Inns of Court again?). And so Hooker's book was a criticism of what was "inhuman and stern" and of the "rigorous observation of spiritual ordinances," a plea for "relaxation or exception," for "merciful and moderate courses." So long as men avoid what is "absolutely sinful or wicked," they should consider not "necessity" but "public utility" (ix.1).

III

A passage from Hooker concerning nature and the cosmos is justly well known. In it, Hooker pondered a series of six *ifs*:

Now if nature should intermit her course, and leave altogether though it were but for a while the observation of her own laws; if those principal and mother elements of the world, whereof all things in this lower world are made, should lose the qualities which now they have; if the frame of that heavenly arch erected over our heads should loosen and dissolve itself; if celestial spheres should forget their wonted motions, and by irregular volubility turn themselves any way as it might happen; if the prince of the lights of heaven, which now as a giant doth run his unwearied course, should as it were through a languishing faintness begin to stand and to rest himself; if the moon should wander from her beaten way, the times and seasons of the year blend themselves by disordered and confused mixture, the winds breathe out their last gasp, the clouds yield no rain, the earth be defeated of heavenly influence, the fruits of the earth pine away as children at the withered breasts of their mother no longer able to yield them relief: what would become of man himself, whom these things now do all serve? [I.iii.2]

It is a particularly happy example of Hooker's stylistic technique (a technique which, when he was off form, could produce contortions that make one sympathetic to the contemporary complaints about his perverse and untraditional English). And happy in another sense: the passage expresses a rather old-fashioned optimism about the universe and the little world of man. The preoccupation of literary Englishmen at the turn of the century with the theme of the failure and decay of nature needs no emphasis. Many of Hooker's contemporaries and successors consider similar "if"s and achieved only a dusty answer. One thinks of Fulke Greville, of John Donne (who went to the Inns of Court about 1590), and, slightly later, of William Drummond, Laird of Hawthornden near Edinburgh. Drummond's *A Cypress Grove* (1623) is, again, frequently quoted—this time in expositions of how "the new philosophy calls all in doubt." "The element of fire is quite put out" (a pun borrowed from Donne),

the air is but water rarified, the earth is found to move, and is no more the centre of the universe, is turned into a magnet; stars are not fixed, but swim in the ethereal spaces, comets are mounted above the planets. Some affirm there is another world of men and sensitive creatures, with cities and palaces, in the moon: the sun is lost, for it is but a light made of the conjunction of many shining bodies together, a cleft in the lower heavens, through which the rays of the highest diffuse themselves; is observed to have spots. Thus sciences, by the diverse motions of this globe of the brain of man, are become opinions, nay, errors, and leave the imagination in a thousand labyrinths.[65]

How far Donne and Drummond were genuinely tortured by the new astronomy and the new science, and how merely attracted by the rhetoric of literary melancholy, is a matter for discussion. The novelties, one feels, might just as well have been stimulating and exhilarating. But at any rate the theme was there.

Less well known but more relevant is a passage from a sermon preached at Paul's Cross, London, in November 1594, which made specific play with Hooker's words (published in March 1593) and set forth an opposed hypothesis, owing most to the tradition of Christian pessimism. The preacher was John Dove, a graduate of Christ Church, Oxford; a London cleric; and a conforming Calvinist of the William Perkins type.

...nature beginneth generally to intermitte her woonted course, the mother Elements of the worlde, whereof things in this lower world are made, doe loose their qualities and naturall vigour which they had before, the Starres and Planets of heaven waxe dimme and olde, not so well able to preserve our earthly bodies, the celestiall spheres bee almost wearie of their woonted motions and regular volubilitie, the prince of the lightes of Heaven, which before came as a bridegroome trimmed out of his chamber dooth not looke uppon us with so chearefull an aspect, and that giant, which before did runne his unwearied race, dooth as it were by a languishing faintnesse beginne to stand and rest himselfe, the times and seasons of the yeare doe blend themselves with disordered and confused mixture, the windes are in a readinesse to breath out theyr last gaspe, our mother the earth defeated of that aboundance of heavenly influence which at the first shee had, is out of hart, waxeth barren and dead like the wombe of Sara: the herbes and simples which are appointed for medicines for mans bodie, have almost lost their operation and vertue, and man himselfe, whom all these things do serve, is of lower stature, lesse strength, shorter life than at first he was, so that there is a generall decay of nature, and in everie leafe of that booke it is written, that the frame of that heavenly arch erected over our heads must very shortly lose and dissolve it selfe.[66]

A "generall decay of nature," then. Apart from certain homely but ineffective additions, the allusion to Hooker is obvious. Did Dove expect his hearers to grasp it? For those who did not, the passage must have seemed unusually eloquent and rather mystifying.

Hooker discussed the cosmos (how aware was he, one wonders, of contemporary hypotheses on the subject?) because he wished to expound the nature of law in general, "reducing the laws whereof there is present controversy unto their first original causes." The question was, Are the existing laws of ecclesiastical polity "reasonable, just, and righteous, or no"? (i.xvi.i). Hooker assumed himself to be guarding the Tudor constitution against "error," "misconceit," (Pref.i.2) and "opinion" (ii.7), against men "universally bent even against all the orders and laws, wherein this church is found unconformable to the platform of Geneva" (ii.10). Stepping back from the minuter points of controversy, he revivified a conception of the cosmos dominated by two guiding ideas: that "the instrument wherewith God will have the world guided" is "right reason" (v. ix.3), and that "there is nothing more constant, nothing more uniform in all her ways" (ix.1) than nature, within a general supposition of "the harmony of the world" (I.xvi.8). Reason, order, and degree, then, under the "settled stability of divine understanding" (iii.4).

Within this world picture, allowance can be made for "defect in the matter of things natural." Matter can be stubborn; there are "swervings...incident into the course of nature." The cause of these is "divine malediction, laid for the sin of man upon these creatures which God had made for the use of man" (iii.3). Hooker wrote always "presuming the will of man to be inwardly obstinate, rebellious, and averse from all obedience unto the sacred laws of his nature": "in regard of his depraved mind little better than a wild beast" (x.1). Such "corruption of our nature" is "presupposed" (x.4).

Nonetheless, Hooker's critics especially objected to his "position of the light of nature"[67] and his (to them) lack of emphasis on grace and on supernatural knowledge revealed in Scripture. "Reason is highlie sett up against holie scripture" (p. 43). They complained also that Hooker had put himself into a theological tradition which maintained that "there is in the will of man naturallie that freedome, whereby it is apt to take or refuse anie particular object" (p. 11).

They were right. Hooker's conception of the Deity was overtly uncalvinist. "They err therefore who think that of the will of God to do this or that there is no reason besides his will" (I.ii.5). Furthermore—and here again Hooker was in the tradition of More and Fisher—the Deity has endowed his creatures with "sense" and "reason" (xv.4), neither of them meant to fust in us unused. "Capable we are of God both by understanding and will" (xi.3). The Fall of man has certainly "weakened" the will; like other instruments in the search for knowledge, it is "hardly inclinable" to God (vii.7). But "there is in the Will of man naturally that freedom, whereby it is apt to take or refuse any particular object whatsoever being presented unto it" (vii.6). And the whole of Hooker's work, as his critics perceived, was a celebration of "our natural faculty of reason" (vii.5), "the dictates of right Reason," "that light of Reason, whereby good may be known from evil, and which discovering the same rightly is termed right" (vii.4).

In the balance of this conception of the cosmos, the written Word of God in Scripture, the divine law, was given what to Hooker seemed its rightful place. He objected fundamentally to the Puritan thesis that "Scripture is the only rule to frame all our actions by" (Pref.viii.4), that, as Thomas Wilcox put it in the first *Admonition to Parliament* of 1572, "nothing be don in this or ani other thing, but that which you have the expresse warrant of Gods worde for."[68] In Hooker's opinion, men must look not only to Scripture, but to "nature, Scripture, and experience itself" (vi.1). For one thing (and this was the theme of Book III), the state of the apostolic church was not fully described in the New Testament: "so that making their times the rule and canon of church-polity, ye make a rule, which being not possible to be fully known, is as impossible to be kept" (iv.4). Moreover, even if we had fuller details, the orders "which were observed in the Apostles' times, are not to be urged as a rule universally either sufficient or necessary" (iv.5). Scripture—and Cranmer would have agreed here—must not be expected to yield too much. In fact, it is possible to demean the written Word of God by calling upon it to settle "vain and childish trifles": "the meanness of some things is such, that to search the Scripture of God for the ordering of them were to derogate from the reverend authority and dignity of the Scripture" (I.xv.4).

The primacy, and also the limits, of Scripture had been defined in the sixth of the Thirty-Nine Articles: "Holy Scripture containeth all things necessary to salvation: so that whatsoever is not read therein, nor may be proved thereby, is not to be required of any man, that it should be believed as an article of the Faith or be thought requisite or necessary to salvation." For Hooker, elaborating the point, Scripture outlined "the Mystery or secret way of salvation"—the way "supernatural, a way which could never have entered into the heart of man as much as once to conceive or imagine, if God himself had not revealed it extraordinarily" (xi.5). (The resurrection of the body was one such revelation.) Scripture, then, is "a law wherein so many things are laid open, clear, and manifest, as a light which otherwise would have been buried in darkness" (xii.2). Some dogmas, admittedly, such as the Trinity, or infant baptism, are "deduced" from Scripture, not being there "by express literal mention" (xiv.2). But Scripture contains "all things necessary unto salvation" (xiv.1). There is no "revealed law of God" elsewhere, and the *ecclesia anglicana* cannot give to "traditions" the "same obedience and reverence" that it gives to the written word; in other words, it cannot honor Scripture and tradition "equally" (xiii.2), as the Council of Trent had decreed and as More and Fisher had argued.

But nature and Scripture must be considered not "severally" but "jointly." Scripture is an addition, not a substitute; grace comes not to destroy nature but to fulfill it, to perfect it. Scripture is "the evidence of God's own testimony added to the natural assent of reason" (xii.1); man's "light of natural understanding" is by it "perfected" (xiv.5).

Book II—in some ways, nowadays, the most approachable of Hooker's books—was concerned with "the drift, scope, and purpose of Almighty God in Holy Scripture" (II.viii.5). It summarized, refined, and elaborated the points laid down by Cranmer, Ridley, and Whitgift. The Church of Rome errs because papists "imagine the general and main drift of the body of sacred Scripture not to be so large as it is" (viii.5), teaching "Scripture to be so unsufficient, as if, unless traditions were added, it did not contain all revealed and supernatural truth" (viii.7); thus they proceed "dangerously to add to the word of God uncertain tradition" (viii.6). The men of Geneva, on the other hand, have "overshot themselves" (the very image is from Cranmer) by "attributing unto Scripture more than it can have" (viii.7), "racking and stretching" Scripture further than God intended (viii.6), "as if Scripture did not only contain all things in that kind necessary, but all things simply, in such sort that to do anything according to any other law were not only unnecessary but even opposite unto salvation, unlawful and sinful" (viii.7). Thus the Puritans, with their "earnest desire to draw all things unto the determination of bare and naked Scripture" (a phrase which, incidentally, almost echoes Tyndale),[69] make "the bare mandate of sacred Scripture the only rule of all good and evil" (viii.5). In so doing, they make of the Bible "a snare and a torment to weak consciences, filling them with infinite perplexities, scrupulosities, doubts insoluble, and extreme despairs." In teaching that men "put forth their hands to iniquity whatsoever they go about and have not first the sacred Scripture of God for direction; how can it choose but bring the simple a thousand times to their wits' end? how can it choose but vex and amaze them?" (viii.6). So much for Erasmus' vision of the farmer singing portions of Scripture at the plough, the weaver humming parts of it to his shuttle.[70] (Although a more cautious Erasmus was later to emphasize, against Luther, that Scripture is often more like a mysterious grotto than an unclouded heaven.)[71] As Milton was to be in *Christian Doctrine* (ch. 14), Hooker was rather moving on the theme of the silence of Scripture: "Scripture in many things doth neither command nor forbid, but use silence" (v.7). The Puritans had been told for nearly fifty years that "matters of faith, and in general matters necessary unto salvation, are of a different nature from ceremonies, order, and the kind of church government; and that the one is necessary to be expressly contained in the word of God, or else manifestly collected out of the same, the other not so" (III.ii.2). We, said Hooker, put a difference between things necessary and things accessary: they do not. In the category of things accessary—a sphere of freedom—"discretion may teach the Church what is convenient." And "we hold not the Church further tied herein unto Scripture, than that against Scripture nothing be admitted in the Church." Here Hooker used the image of a pathway. The pathway is necessary: whether it is covered with gravel, grass, or stone is accessary (iii.3).

In addition to the Scripture, what do men have to guide them? First, in any "light and common thing" (II.iii.1), there is "the rule of common discretion" (viii.6). Secondly, there is "man's authority," as expressed, for instance, in "the sentences of wise and expert men" (vii.2) or the "orders, laws, and constitutions in the Church" (vii.1). Such "testimony of man" can on occasion be "a ground of infallible assurance" (vii.3). Thirdly, in some cases, "the very light of Nature alone may discover that which is so far forth in the sight of God allowable" (viii.2). Hooker was careful to remind the reader here that "Nature is no sufficient teacher what we should do that we may attain unto life everlasting. The unsufficiency of the light of Nature is by the light of Scripture so fully and so perfectly herein supplied, that further light than this hath added there doth not need unto that end" (viii.3). Nevertheless, the reader has been firmly led to the area of God's "precepts comprehended in the law of nature" (viii.5)— the law of nature being defined as "an infallible knowledge imprinted in the minds of all the children of men, whereby both general principles for directing of human actions are comprehended, and conclusions derived from them; upon which conclusions groweth in particularity the choice of good and evil in the daily affairs of this life" (viii.6). Here Hooker followed St Paul in the letter to the Romans (ch. 2) about "Gentiles" who "do by nature the things contained in the law" and "shew the work of the law written in their hearts, their conscience also bearing witness." It was a passage that was becoming especially relevant in Hooker's England because of its bearing on discussion about the American Indian.

In an especially eloquent section, Hooker, using the figure of Wisdom, outlined "the manifold ways which wisdom hath to teach men by."

As her ways are of sundry kinds, so her manner of teaching is not merely one and the same. Some things she openeth by the sacred books of Scripture; some things by the glorious works of Nature: with some things she inspireth them from above by spiritual influence; in some things she leadeth and traineth them only by worldly experience and practice. We may not so in any one special kind admire her, that we disgrace her in any other; but let all her ways be according to their place and degree adored. [i.4]

Thus the law of Scripture was given its degree and place in the general perspective of Hooker's vision of the cosmos and of the little world of man. Hooker's Elizabethan readers would know the sort of thing to expect. The following passage, for instance, is from a *Briefe Conference of Divers Lawes*, published in 1602 and written by one Ludovic Lloyd, "one of her Majesties Serjeants at Armes."

All creatures of God, as well in heaven as in earth, had lawes given them after they were created, to be governed and ruled by, the Sunne, the Moone, and the

Starres to keepe their perpetuall motions and course in their places and regiments, so the seas have their limits and bounds, how farre they should rule and raigne, and though one starre differeth from an other in glorie, in greatnesse, and in bright-nesse, yet they are governed by one perpetuall lawe; so the seas, though the waves thereof be so loftie and proud, yet are they shut up within doores, and commaunded to keepe in, and not to goe further then the place to them by lawe appointed.

By lawe also the elements are commaunded to staie within their owne regiments, without trespassing one of another....[72]

And so on. Hooker was more detailed, though slightly less elemental. Basic to this great (if frequently challenged) Tudor commonplace was the assumption of "correspondence" (I.xvi.4): that "laws inferior" are "derived" from "supreme or highest law"; that human laws "apparently good" are so because eternal law "worketh in them" (xvi.2). Eternal law is the order, the reason, the will of God. Nature's law is "the natural course of the world," the "manner of working which God hath set for every created thing to keep" (iii.2). (The passage already discussed about nature intermitting its course belongs in this section of the book.) Then there is celestial law, the law of the angels. And so we come to the law affecting man: "Thus much therefore may suffice for angels, the next unto whom in degree are men" (iv.3).

There are three types of law especially affecting men. First, the "Law of Nations," laws affecting relations between states, preventing "violence, injury, and wrong." We might have diplomacy, we might have war: "the one grounded upon sincere, the other built upon depraved nature" (x.13). Secondly, there is the "Law Rational," moral, the law of human nature which men "commonly use to call the Law of Nature." Hooker preferred to call it "the Law of Reason." This is "the Law which human Nature knoweth itself in reason uni-versally bound unto," which "no man can reject...as unreasonable and unjust," which "comprehendeth all those things which men by the light of their natural understanding evidently know, or at least-wise may know, to be beseeming or unbeseeming, virtuous or vic-ious, good or evil for them to do" (viii.9), with a reference here to the *Antigone* of Sophocles. Moreover, the "first principles of the Law of Nature are easy; hard it were to find men ignorant of them" (xii.2);

"the knowledge of them is general, the world hath always been acquainted with them" (viii.9). Here Hooker was, again, on guard against those critics poised to find fault with his exposition of the "Light of Nature." Hooker assumed, and he made the point clearly, that "lewd and wicked custom" can "smother the light of natural understanding" (viii.11), that in some things the "natural understanding even of sundry whole nations hath been darkened" (xii.2), that men need the "perpetual aid and concurrence" of God (viii.11). But is it only "custom" that smothers the light? Is "darkened" all that might happen to the understanding? Does "concurrence" describe the relationship between man and his maker? Hooker gave his critics more than enough material for objections.

The thesis that "men's iniquity is so hardly restrained within any tolerable bounds" (x.13), and that "corrupt and unreasonable custom" has "gotten the upper hand of right reason with the greatest part," leads the argument to the third law—the "Law Human," positive, or civil, necessary to rectify "foul disorder." Human law "generally" is an "affirmation or ratification" of the Law of Reason, in the same way that statute is an "affirmation" of common law. We note Hooker's appeal here to what "the learned in the laws of this land observe." Human law, then, makes specific the teaching of the law of reason, establishing "some duty whereunto all men by the law of reason did before stand bound." Such ratifications Hooker called "mixedly" human. Interpreting Hooker, we might nowadays put in this category the notion that murder is punishable. Some laws, however, are "*merely* human," less immutable, based on what "reason doth but probably teach to be fit and convenient" (x.10). (Hooker's fondness, again, for *probability*.) The custom of murder incurring capital punishment would be such a law, which at certain moments of time has seemed suitable. (Hooker, in fact, used examples from the land law to make this point.) Some human laws, then, "belong for ever," and are "not changeable without cause, neither can they have cause of change, when that which gave them their first instruction remaineth for ever one and the same." Others "may perhaps be clean otherwise a while after" (xv.3).

To apply these concepts of law particularly to England: Hooker was careful to emphasize (with references from Bracton to help him) that the monarch holds his power "of and under the law" (VIII.ii.3)— "not only the law of nature and of God, but very national or municipal law consonant thereto" (ii.12). Thus kingly power in England has been "abridged" and "restrained" (ii.17): "so is the power of the king over all and in all limited, that unto all his proceedings the law itself is a rule" (ii.13). More generally: "It is neither permitted unto prelate nor prince to judge and determine at their own discretion but law hath prescribed what both shall do. What power the king hath he hath it by law, the bounds and limits of it are known; the entire community giveth general order by law how all things publicly are to be done, and the king as head thereof, the highest in authority over all, causeth according to the same law every particular to be framed and ordered thereby" (viii.9). Law is presumed to "speak with all indifferency"—it "hath no side-respect to...persons"; it is "as it were an oracle proceeded from wisdom and understanding" (I.x.7). Law means lawyers, and perhaps Hooker, in using such traditional phrases, meant to give a warning rather than to state a fact. Perhaps the vision of harmony, too, was a warning. "Where the king doth guide the state, and the law the king, that commonwealth is like an harp or melodious instrument, the strings whereof are tuned and handled all by one, following as laws the rules and canons of musical science" (VIII.ii.12).

But laws can be imperfect. And Hooker, like Thomas More, was within a tradition of thinking about equity, the handmaid of reason. There is the "strictness of law," "literal practice"; but above the letter of the law, and conditioning it, is "right reason," "equity and honest meaning," not "against, but above, the law, binding men's consciences in things which law cannot reach unto" (v.ix.3). Thomas More had argued that God himself has his ordinary justice and his absolute justice—of mercy.[73] A similar English common-law distinction applied to the power of the king is familiar from the judgment of Chief Baron Fleming in Bate's Case (1606).[74] In a rather ponderous passage, Hooker introduced equity into his discussion of the law of the church, as "the discretion of the Church in mitigating sometimes with favourable equity that rigour which otherwise the literal generality of ecclesiastical laws hath judged to be more convenient and meet" (v.x.1).

The reader of Hooker becomes accustomed to his reticence. "Of such perfection capable are we not in this life. For while we are in the world, subject we are unto sundry imperfections, griefs of body, defects of mind; yea the best things we do are painful, and the exercise of them grievous" (1.xi.3). In such moods Hooker seems almost overpowered by a sense of the "stain of human frailty" (Pref.iv.8), of the "stains and blemishes found in our state." These, "springing from the root of human frailty and corruption," will exist to the end of the world, "what form of government soever take place" (iii.7). Concerning politics, the citizen should be aware of "the secret lets and difficulties, which in public proceedings are innumerable and inevitable" (1.i.1). Concerning divine truths, men must stand and wait in Parker-like silence and hope, for "of God's extraordinary power without extraordinary warrant we cannot presume" (IV.ix.1). Thus "our safest eloquence concerning him is our silence, when we confess without confession that his glory is inexplicable, his greatness above our capacity and reach. He is above, and we upon earth; therefore it behoveth our words to be wary and few" (1.ii.2). Hooker's work was a plea for endurance.

Dr John Spenser tells us in his 1604 preface to the *Laws*[75] that a work of controversy, attracting opposition, was not really suitable to Hooker's "soft and mild disposition, desirous of a quiet, private life." Hooker was a "true humble man" who "always affected a private state, and neither enjoyed, nor expected any the least dignity in our church." Spenser also tells us how Hooker, in the midst of "the calamities of these our civil wars," worked with such intensity on his epic, fifteen years in the making, that he was increasingly subject to a "great declining of his body, spent out with study." He died revising the final three books, and "hastened death upon himself, by hastening to give them life." The compulsion of the creative artist. One can best think of Hooker as among the heroic poets.

"It sometimes cometh to pass, that the readiest way which a wise man hath to conquer, is to fly" (Pref.ii.6). One wonders how much the words are a key to Hooker's mind. Did the lure of a "private kind of solitary living" (I.x.12) occasion, as compensation, Hooker's constant emphasis on the public rather than the private? The touches in his book of melancholy bewilderment endear him to the modern reader. But beyond the bewilderment there was the vision of order. And that to him was the important thing.

> Without order there is no living in public society, because the want thereof is the mother of confusion, whereupon division of necessity followeth, and out of division, inevitable destruction. The Apostle therefore giving instruction to public societies, requireth that all things be orderly done. Order can have no place in things, unless it be settled amongst the persons that shall by office be conversant about them. And if things or persons be ordered, this doth imply that they are distinguished by degrees. For order is a gradual disposition.
>
> The whole world consisting of parts so many, so different, is by this only thing upheld; he which framed them hath set them in order. Yea, the very Deity itself both keepeth and requireth for ever this to be kept as a law, that wheresoever there is a coagmentation of many, the lowest be knit to the highest by that which being interjacent may cause each to cleave unto other, and so all to continue one.
>
> This order of things and persons in public societies is the work of polity.... [VIII.ii.2]

NOTES

1. Act of Supremacy, 1559, art. ix, in G. R. Elton, ed., *The Tudor Constitution: Documents and Commentary* (Cambridge: Cambridge Univ. Press, 1960), p. 366.
2. *Laws* v.Ded.10. All Hooker references are to *The Works of...Mr. Richard Hooker*, ed. Keble, 7th ed. rev. 1888, by book, chapter, and section.
3. *Laws* VIII.iv.8; Hooker cites *Epistola de Morte D. Thomae Mori et Episcopi Roffensis* (Basle, 1563) by "Gulielmus Courinus" (probably Gilbert Cousin, a former secretary of Erasmus).
4. No. 79, *English Historical Documents, 1485–1558*, ed. C. H. Williams, *English Historical Documents*, 5 (London: Eyre & Spottiswoode, 1967), esp. p. 659.
5. *Laws* VIII.vii.6, 7.
6. Simonds D'Ewes, ed., *A Compleat Journal Of The Votes, Speeches and Debates, Both Of The House of Lords And House of Commons Throughout the whole Reign of Queen Elizabeth* (London: Printed for Jonathan Robinson, 1693), p. 410.
7. "The King's Declaration prefixed to the Articles of Religion," No. 13 in

Samuel Rawson Gardiner, ed., *The Constitutional Documents of the Puritan Revolution 1625–1660*, 3d ed. rev. (Oxford: Clarendon Press, 1906), p. 75.

8. "Resolutions on Religion drawn by a Sub-Committee of the House of Commons," No. 14 in Gardiner, ed., *Constitutional Documents*.

9. Act of Supremacy, art. xx, in Elton, *Tudor Constitution*, p. 368; cf. *Laws* viii.ii.17.

10. Thomas Cranmer, *Miscellaneous Writings and Letters*, ed. John Edmund Cox, The Parker Society (Cambridge: Cambridge Univ. Press, 1846), pp. 116–17.

11. D'Ewes, *Journal*, p. 168. What Gilbert really had in mind was that such power should be delegated to him over North America.

12. 1534 Act of Supremacy, in Elton, ed., *Tudor Constitution*, p. 355.

13. 1559 Act of Supremacy, art. viii, ibid., p. 365.

14. An Act abolishing diversity in opinions, ibid., p. 390.

15. J. E. Neale, *Elizabeth I and her Parliaments*, Vol. 2, *1584–1601* (London: Jonathan Cape, 1957; paperback, 1965), p. 199.

16. I am thinking of *The Convocation Book of M DC VI. Commonly called Bishop Overall's Convocation Book*, Library of Anglo-Catholic Theology (Oxford: John Henry Parker, 1844).

17. *Two Treatises of Government*, ed. Peter Laslett, 2d ed. (Cambridge: Cambridge Univ. Press, 1967), pp. 56–57.

18. *Works* 3: 411, n. 1 (*Laws* viii.vi.11).

19. *Laws* i.x.5.

20. *De Republica Anglorum*, sections 48–49, in Elton, ed., *Tudor Constitution*, pp. 234–35.

21. *An Exposition of the Symbole or Creed Of The Apostles*...in William Perkins, *Works* (London: John Legatt, 1612), 1:161.

22. Aquinas, *De Regimine Principum*, ch. 6, translated in Dino Bigongiari, ed., *The Political Ideas of St. Thomas Aquinas: Representative Selections* (New York: Hafner, 1953), pp. 188–92. Latin text and translation in A. P. d'Entrèves, ed., *Aquinas: Selected Political Writings* (Oxford: Basil Blackwell, 1948), pp. 28–35.

23. *Laws* viii.ii.10.

24. Hanserd Knollys, *A Glimpse of Sions Glory* (1641), quoted by William Haller, *The Rise of Puritanism* (New York: Columbia Univ. Press, 1938; Harper Torchbook, 1957), p. 272.

25. Williams, ed., *English Historical Documents*, p. 659.

26. *The Works of John Whitgift*, ed. John Ayre, The Parker Society (Cambridge: Cambridge Univ. Press, 1851–53; reprinted New York and London: Johnson Reprint Corp., 1968), 1:33.

27. "The Supplication of the commons against the ordinaries, 1532," is in Williams, *English Historical Documents*, No. 94, and also in *Documents Illustrative of English Church History Compiled from Original Sources*, ed. Henry Gee and William John Hardy (London: Macmillan, 1896, reprinted 1910), No. 46; "The Answer of the Ordinaries, A.D. 1532," is in Gee and Hardy, No. 47. See

Michael Kelly, "The Submission of the Clergy," *Transactions of the Royal Historical Society*, 5th series, 15 (1965): 97–119, and Margaret Bowker, "The Commons Supplication against the Ordinaries in the light of some Archidiaconal *Acta*," ibid. 21 (1971): 61–77.

28. "The Commons' Supplication of 1532: Parliamentary Manoeuvres in the Reign of Henry VIII," *English Historical Review* 66 (1951): 507–34.

29. *Two Early Tudor Lives*, ed. Richard S. Sylvester and Davis P. Harding (New Haven and London: Yale Univ. Press, 1962), p. 244.

30. See A. G. Dickens, *The English Reformation* (London: B. T. Batsford, and New York: Schocken Books, 1964), pp. 90–96.

31. Chapter 36; first printed, 1546; English version by Robert Mulcaster, 1567, *A learned commendation of the politique lawes of Englande*, facsimile reprint, Amsterdam and New York: Da Capo Press, 1969. The best edition is that of S. B. Chrimes (Cambridge: Cambridge Univ. Press, 1942). The Mulcaster translation has "politique" and "regall" (or "royall").

32. "The Submission of the Clergy, A.D. 1532," No. 48 in Gee and Hardy, *Documents*, pp. 176–78.

33. An Act for the submission of the clergy to the King's Majesty, No. 175 in Elton, *Tudor Constitution*, pp. 339–41.

34. Williams, *English Historical Documents*, No. 112.

35. J. K. McConica, *English Humanists and Reformation Politics under Henry VIII and Edward VI* (Oxford: Clarendon Press, 1965). See review by G. R. Elton, *Historical Journal* 10 (1967): 137–38.

36. In Carl S. Meyer, ed., *Cranmer's Selected Writings* (London: S.P.C.K. paperback, 1961), p. 1.

37. Margaret Mann Phillips, *The "Adages" of Erasmus: A Study with Translations* (Cambridge: Cambridge Univ. Press, 1964), p. 189; paperback edition of the translations, *Erasmus on his Times* (Cambridge: Cambridge Univ. Press, 1967), p. 17.

38. Meyer, p. 1.

39. Ibid., p. 7.

40. Conveniently available in Everyman's Library, No. 448, *Prayer Books of Edward VI* (London: J. M. Dent, and New York, E. P. Dutton, 1910), pp. 286–88. I have reprinted this essay, with modernized spelling, in my anthology, *Puritanism in Tudor England* (London: Macmillan, 1970), pp. 19–21.

41. *The Colloquies of Erasmus*, trans. Craig R. Thompson (Chicago and London: Univ. of Chicago Press, 1965), p. 419.

42. The essential authority here is E. J. Devereux of the University of Western Ontario, sometime of St Catherine's College, Oxford, whose 1964 D.Phil. thesis was called "A Bibliography of English Translations of Erasmus to 1700." This is unpublished, though some of it has been drawn upon in his essays, such as "English Translators of Erasmus: 1522–1557," in *Editing Sixteenth Century Texts*, ed. R. J. Schoeck (Toronto: Univ. of Toronto Press, 1966), pp. 43–58.

Devereux published a short list of the translations in 1968, *A Checklist of English Translations of Erasmus to 1700* (Oxford Bibliographical Society Occasional Publication 3, Bodleian Library, Oxford).

43. Hooper's statement has been lost and must be reconstructed from the quotations in Ridley's *Reply*. See M. M. Knappen, "Hooper's Lost Argument on the Vestments," in *Tudor Puritanism: A Chapter in the History of Idealism* (Chicago: Univ. of Chicago Press, 1939; reprinted Phoenix Books, 1965), Appendix I. Ridley's *Reply* is in *The Writings of John Bradford*, ed. Aubrey Townsend, The Parker Society (Cambridge: Cambridge Univ. Press, 1848–53; reprinted New York and London: Johnson Reprint Corp., 1968), 2:373–95.

44. *Bradford*, 2:380, 375.

45. "An Admonition to the Parliament," in *Puritan Manifestoes*, ed. W. H. Frere and C. E. Douglas (London: S.P.C.K., 1907; reprinted 1954), p. 15.

46. Whitgift, *Works* 1:64.

47. *Bradford*, 2:378.

48. *A sermon had at Paulis by the commandment of the most reverend father in god my lorde legate | and sayd by John the bysshop of Rochester* . . . (n.p., n.d.), sig. B2ᵛ.

49. *Correspondence of Matthew Parker*, ed. John Bruce and Thomas Thomason Perowne, The Parker Society (Cambridge: Cambridge Univ. Press, 1853; reprinted New York and London: Johnson Reprint Corp., 1968), p. 386.

50. *The Zurich Letters*, 1st series, trans. and ed. Hastings Robinson, The Parker Society (Cambridge: Cambridge Univ. Press, 1842; reprinted New York and London: Johnson Reprint Corp., 1968), 1:118. Latin text, p. 70.

51. Ibid., p. 23.

52. Parker, *Correspondence*, pp. 203, 419.

53. Latimer to Cromwell, 19 Oct [1537]: "God give us all grace to yield due thanks to our Lord God, God of England! for verily he hath shewed himself God of England, or rather an English God, if we consider and ponder well all his proceedings with us from time to time. . . ." In *Sermons and Remains*, ed. George Elwes Corrie, The Parker Society (Cambridge: Cambridge Univ. Press, 1845), p. 385.

54. James Boswell, *The Life of Samuel Johnson*, Everyman's Library, 1 (London: J. M. Dent, and New York, E. P. Dutton, 1906; freq. rpt.), 1:130.

55. Parker, *Correspondence*, p. 252.

56. Ibid., p. 423.

57. D'Ewes, *Journal*, p. 12.

58. Quoted by William P. Haugaard, *Elizabeth and the English Reformation: The Struggle for a Stable Settlement of Religion* (Cambridge: Cambridge Univ. Press, 1968), p. 324.

59. Parker, *Correspondence*, p. 224.

60. D'Ewes, *Journal*, p. 618.

61. Cartwright: *A Replye to an answere made of M. Doctor Whitgifte* ([Wandsworth?], 1573); *The Second replie of T C against Maister Doctor Whitgiftes second*

answer ([Zurich?], 1575); *The rest of the second replie of T Cartwright* ([Antwerp?], 1577). Whitgift: *An answere to a certen Libel intituled, An admonition to the Parliament* (London, 1572); *The Defense of the Aunswere to the Admonition, against the Replie of T. C.* (London, 1574). All are most conveniently found in Whitgift, *Works*. Whitgift reproduced most of the Cartwright material, inserting parts of *A Second Admonition to the Parliament* ([Wandsworth?], 1572), under the probably correct assumption that Cartwright was the author.

62. Whitgift, *Works* 1:187.

63. See H. C. Porter, "The Nose of Wax: Scripture and the Spirit from Erasmus to Milton," *Transactions of the Royal Historical Society*, 5th series, 14 (1964): 155–74.

64. Whitgift, *Works* 1:183.

65. William Drummond, *A Cypress Grove*, ed. A. H. Bullen (Stratford-on-Avon: Shakespeare Head Press, 1907), pp. 14–15.

66. *A Sermon, Preached at Pauls Crosse, the 3. of November 1594....* 2d ed. (London: V[alentine] S[ims] for William Jaggard, n.d.), sig. B5ᵛ-6ʳ. I owe this reference to Mr. Richard Bauckham of Clare College, Cambridge. [Cf. C. A. Patrides, "The 'Universall and Public Manuscript' of Commonplaces," *Neophilogus* 47 (1963): 217–20 —ed.]

67. *A Christian Letter of certaine English Protestants* ([Middleburgh], 1599), p. 8.

68. Frere and Douglas, *Puritan Manifestoes*, p. 15.

69. *Laws* II.vii.1; cf. William Tyndale, "The Obedience of a Christian Man," in *Doctrinal Treatises and Introductions to Different Portions of the Holy Scriptures*, ed. Henry Walter, The Parker Society (Cambridge: Cambridge Univ. Press, 1848): "Paul...exhorteth us to cleave fast unto the naked and pure word of God" (1:277–78).

70. Erasmus, *Paraclesis* (Preface to the New Testament, 1516, 1519), in John C. Olin, ed., *Christian Humanism and the Reformation: Erasmus, Selected Writings* (Harper Torchbook, New York: Harper and Row, 1965), p. 97. The first English translation of this piece, by William Roy, was printed at Antwerp in 1529 and reprinted twice in London late in 1533.

71. *De Libero Arbitrio* (1524), trans. E. Gordon Rupp, in *Luther and Erasmus: Free Will and Salvation*, Library of Christian Classics, 17 (London: SCM Press, and Philadelphia: Westminster Press, 1969), p. 38.

72. Sig. B1ʳ. I owe this reference to Dr James Winny, University of Leicester.

73. *The second parte of the confutacion of Tyndals answere...*(London: William Rastell, 1533), p. clxxviii.

74. J. R. Tanner, ed., *Constitutional Documents of the Reign of James I A.D. 1603–1625 with an historical commentary* (Cambridge: Cambridge Univ. Press, 1930), "Chief Baron Fleming's Judgment," pp. 340–45.

75. Printed in *Works* 1:121–23.

THE EVOLUTION OF HOOKER'S
LAWS OF
ECCLESIASTICAL POLITY

W. Speed Hill

I

It was Izaak Walton who first noted of Hooker's *Laws of Ecclesiastical Polity* that "the foundation of these books was laid in the Temple,"[1] where Hooker was Master from 1585 to 1591, and it was C. J. Sisson whose researches at the Public Record Office enabled us to trace its early printing history in such satisfying detail, once Hooker had completed his manuscript.[2] But the exact moment of conception, as well as the process of gestation, are hidden, as such matters often are, seemingly impervious to historical analysis. Indeed, it is the crucial reticence of history at this point in the evolution of Hooker's treatise that accounts for the ambiguity of his position even today and for the uncertainty with which recent scholarship has viewed the significance of his work. In this essay I will analyze the immediate context of Hooker's *Laws* in as much detail as the surviving documents permit, in order to resolve this uncertainty, to define with some precision the terms in conflict, and to suggest how they arose from the circumstances of the work's appearance and sponsorship.

The earliest account of the "birth of *The Laws of Ecclesiastical Polity*" is, of course, Walton's own, in his *Life* of 1665.[3] In it, Walton quotes the well-known appeal of Hooker to Archbishop Whitgift to release him from his responsibilities as Master of the Temple in order to complete work on "a Treatise, in which I intend a justification of the Laws of our Ecclesiastical Polity."[4] Nothing seems more circumstantial, more definitive. Hooker was writing such a treatise, he did exchange benefices with Nicholas Baldgey, Whitgift was his superior, and the living was in his gift. What could better suggest documentary authenticity? Yet Hooker's "speech" tells us nothing that we, or Walton, could not have inferred from what we already know about Hooker in 1591. It is simply Walton's attempt to map the unknown territory of the mind. When he revised the *Life* in 1670, he revised Hooker's speech as well; comparing the two versions, we can see that no single document lies behind them.[5]

Clearly Walton was working within a thoroughly respectable tradition of humanist biography, and his invention of Hooker's speech was in no way intended to deceive. But the questions it raises bear importantly upon the original impetus for Hooker's treatise. Was it, as Jewel's *Apologia* was, a quasi-official defense of the Church of England as established at the Elizabethan Settlement?[6] Or was it a personal statement of Hooker's own loyalty to his church, his own brief for the authority of its laws, growing out of the attacks that Travers had mounted at the Temple on his teachings—as well as Travers' attempts to presbyterianize his congregation there? Or is it discernibly both—in which case the uncertainty of contemporary scholars would itself seem to have an historical foundation? It was Sisson's thesis, for example, that the *Laws* was, from its inception at the home of Hooker's father-in-law, John Churchman, an officially sponsored, collaborative venture. He dates that sponsorship from Hooker's original appointment to the Mastership of the Temple Church in 1585: "the projected book was to carry with it the full authority, not only of the undisputed learning and persuasive humanity of its author, but also that of the deputed spokesman of the Church, advised and aided by lay notables[Edwin Sandys and George Cranmer], and countenanced by the spiritual heads of the Church, Archbishops Sandys of York [Edwin Sandys' father] and Whitgift of

Canterbury. Hooker's appointment to the Mastership of the Temple, indeed, was an announcement that battle was about to be joined" (pp. 4–5). Sisson's reconstruction is an attractive one, but it is not free from difficulties. Thanks to him, we know that Edwin Sandys was a resident at John Churchman's in the 1580s and that Sandys himself subsidized the publication of the *Laws*. And it is certainly plausible to attribute, as Walton does (*Works* 1:26), to Sandys, who was Hooker's former student and a colleague at Corpus Christi College, Oxford, the suggestion that Hooker's name be put in nomination at the Temple. But it is stretching the evidence to suggest that the *Laws* was in Whitgift's mind at the moment he engineered the appointment in 1585.

That appointment was a minor trial of strength between Whitgift and Burleigh, and it was the fulcrum of Hooker's own career. Before it, his life had been coterminous with two institutions: the Latin School at Exeter and Corpus Christi College, Oxford. The scant evidence we have suggests only what we could have assumed, that he had successfully and uneventfully mastered their highly specialized curricula. By March 1585, the date of his appointment, he was fellow of Corpus, was apparently known for lectures in logic within the College, had given the University lectures in Hebrew, and had been summoned to preach at Paul's Cross.[7] Had he not been nominated for the Temple post, there is little reason to believe that the final third of his life would have materially altered the pattern of its beginning, that of an able, devout cleric and Oxford don who interested himself in theological controversies. But the appointment thrust Hooker into the midst of the ecclesiastical politics of the day, and it led directly to the composition of the *Laws*.

The rival candidates were Walter Travers and Dr Nicholas Bond. Bond, one of the Queen's chaplains and later President of Magdalene College, was the candidate of Archbishop Whitgift. Travers, second only to Thomas Cartwright in the shadow cabinet of Elizabethan Puritanism,[8] had the support of the late Master, Richard Alvey, whom he had served four years as deputy; the Benchers of the two Inns; and Lord Burleigh, whom he had served briefly as chaplain and tutor to his son.[9] The post itself was in the gift of the Queen, for the Temple was not a parish subject to the formal jurisdiction of the Bishop of London, and the Master succeeded to office by virtue of letters patent from the crown.[10] The history of its privileged status is a tangled one, but it had enjoyed its exemption from episcopal control since its foundation in 1185 by the Knights Templars. By the sixteenth century it had become customary to fill the post by nomination of the Benchers of the two Inns, subject to the confirmation of the Queen. Furthermore, such posts had frequently been the only pulpits a preacher with Puritan convictions could secure.[11] Alvey had been sympathetic to the cause of reform, and Travers, with Burleigh's help, had become his deputy in 1581. The larger significance of Hooker's appointment, then, lay less in his personal good fortune —he was sufficiently unknown to be acceptable to both sides—than in Travers' defeat, secured by Whitgift and sanctioned by Elizabeth, on the eve of the Reformers' most concerted push against the Archbishop and his ecclesiastical policies.

Like many Elizabethan Puritans, Walter Travers was a Cambridge man. The son of a Nottingham goldsmith, he entered Trinity College in 1560, age twelve, and was elected junior fellow seven years later— ten years earlier than Hooker's comparable election at Corpus. He was the author of *Ecclesiasticæ Disciplinæ, et Anglicanæ Ecclesiæ ab Illa Aberrationis, Plena è Verbo Dei, & Dilucida Explicatio* (La Rochelle, 1574), in which he expanded and documented the inaugural lectures that Thomas Cartwright had offered as Lady Margaret Professor of Divinity at Cambridge in 1569.[12] The argument was that the discipline of the church, no less than its doctrine, was commanded of men by God in Scripture. "I thincke it plaine and manifest...that the rule and paterne off discipline / is not to be drawne from the ordinaunces and fantasies off men / but from the worde off god. which thing / as it hath long tyme preserved puritie and sinceritie in those churches wherin all thinges are reformed according to goddes worde / So all the corruptions which are in our church this daie / spring from no other heade / then this / that we have followed popishe dreames and fantasies as most sti[n]ckyng syncks and chanells leaving the pure founta[in]es off the worde off God."[13] At one stroke, Travers aligned himself with a whole tradition of reformed thought: diagnosis of present corruption as papistical, prescription of biblical law as corrective and cure. The wedge he drove between the laws of men—"ordinaunces and fantasies"—and the laws of God—"pure fountaines"—was one that Hooker was to struggle to dislodge. Later formulations of Presbyterian polity would spell out in greater detail its familiar pyramidal structure, the upward ascent of ecclesiastical power from consistory (congregational), through classis (local), to synod (regional and national). But no single work so successfully documented the case for its biblical authority. It was published anonymously at Heidelberg in 1574 by Cartwright himself, who translated its Latin into English, contributed a preface of his own, and saw both versions through the press.[14]

In 1578 Travers accepted the call of the English merchant nation at Antwerp. On its authority, he thereafter signed himself "Minister of the Word of God." To Whitgift, Travers' nonepiscopal ordination was a flagrant reassertion of nonconformity. As Vice-chancellor, Whitgift had harried him from Trinity on account of his refusal to take orders, a condition of his fellowship there, and Travers had refused to be ordained lest he so recognize the authority of the Hierarchy. In 1580, when his Antwerp ministry came to an end, Travers returned to England under the protection of Burleigh, who negotiated his substitution for Alvey at the Temple, who was ill and unable to preach. Negotiations continued from November 1580 to February 1581.[15] Travers was to secure "recommendations of his good behavior" from either the Bishop of London (John Aylmer) or from two of the High Commission. He was to "preach in his gown or some other decent apparel and not in a cloak,"[16] associated with Geneva. Through the intervention of Burleigh, Travers secured the necessary credentials. Although notably strict in his defense of conformity, Aylmer apparently did not know Travers well or associate him with the *Explicatio*. "Upon the good report of some of my friends," he wrote the Benchers, "I recommendid Mr Travis unto you to be your reader, a man otherwise unknown to me."[17] A man of learning—he is the "so gentle a schoolmaster" beloved of Lady Jane Grey in Ascham's *Schoolmaster*—Aylmer was known to favor a learned clergy, and Travers could truthfully be so represented by Burleigh.[18]

Once installed, Travers moved to introduce at the Temple the reforms he had advocated in the *Explicatio*. On February 9, 1582, Alvey requested of the Middle Temple "that, in accordance with letters from the Privy Council, they would appoint overseers and collectors for this House and Fellowship, to take the view of all resident and in commons who do not resort to church, or, being there, do not demean themselves according to the laws."[19] By July, the Inner Temple had agreed.[20] As church attendance was a statutory obligation in sixteenth-century England, Alvey was certainly within his rights so to require decency and "good order" in his church. But it is hard not to discern the hand of Travers in the intervention of the Privy Council. In addition, Travers' plan for the Temple was evidently part of a larger one, for in 1583 the "London brethren" had agreed "that the Ministers should by little and little, as much as possibly they might, draw the Discipline into practise, though they concealed the names, eyther of Presbytery, Elder or Deacon, making little account of the names for the time, so their offices might secretly be established." Thus was "a decree" recorded as "an order sette downe, in an assembly... *for the converting of Churchwardens and Collectors into Elders and Deacons*."[21]

Three years after his initial appointment, when Travers had every expectation of succeeding to the Mastership, Whitgift moved to forestall it, suggesting Bond in Travers' stead. Advising the Queen against Travers, Whitgift described him as "one of the chief and principal authors of dissension in this church, a contemner of the book of Prayers...an earnest seeker of innovation; and either in no degree of the ministry at all, or else ordered beyond the seas.... Whose placing in that room, especially by your majesty, would greatly animate the rest of that faction, and do very much harm in sundry respects." He solicited the support of Burleigh for the candidacy of Bond, "such a one...as is known to be conformable to the laws and orders established" (1:29). Burleigh replied that Travers was "well learned, very honest, and well allowed and loved of the generality of that house." He warned that if Bond were not to come "to the place with some applause of the company, he shall be weary thereof," a warning whose melancholy truth Hooker was soon to prove. Whitgift countered with his experience of Travers at Trinity, where "there [was never] any under our government, in whom I found less submission and humility" (1:30). He denied that Travers was generally favored among the lawyers, and he fastened the authorship of the *Explicatio* securely upon him (1:31). Bond's candidacy, however, was faulted because of poor health, and the Queen did not favor it. Hooker's name seems to have been put into nomination by Edwin Sandys, whose father, the Archbishop of York, had succeeded Bishop Jewel as Hooker's patron and who himself was a former student and colleague of Hooker's at Corpus. Hooker was duly installed as Master some seven months after the death of Alvey.[22]

When his own expectations were thus frustrated by the appointment of Hooker, Travers moved immediately to win his rival to the cause of reform. As Hooker tells it, "at the very point of my entering thereinto, the evening before I was first to preach, he came, and two other gentlemen joined with him in the charge of this church, (for so he gave me to understand,) though not in the same kind of charge with [as] him: the effect of his conference then was, that he thought it his duty to advise me not to enter with a strong hand, but to change my purpose of preaching there the next day, and to stay till he had given notice of me to the congregation, that so their allowance might seal my calling" (3:571). By his refusal to "stay" the ratification of the Queen's appointment by the congregation, as arranged by Travers and two overseers (lay elders by another name), Hooker naturally identified himself with the established church. Indeed, with Hooker's appointment, there was every expectation that Travers would simply leave: an able-bodied Master needed no deputy.[23] But again at the intervention of the Privy Council, Travers' pension was continued, and a compromise worked out in which Hooker was to preach Sunday mornings and Travers in the afternoon.[24]

Failing to implicate Hooker in his own attempt to presbyterianize the Temple, Travers next turned its pulpit into a forum from which to challenge the orthodoxy of Hooker's teachings. In his sermons, Hooker had touched on the major doctrinal issues still unresolved within the Elizabethan church: the authority of the pre-Reformation Church of Rome, the continuity between that church and post-Reformation England, the nature of God's grace and its relation to God's will, and the related doctrines of predestination, justification, and assurance. Briefly stated, Hooker's attempt was to define an ethos for the English church that was unambiguously reformed, historically founded, and charitably inclusive. He was willing to submit that God would be merciful to Catholics who had died believing in the efficacy of works, so long as their ignorance of the true faith was innocent, even "to a bishop of the church of Rome, to a cardinal, yea, to the pope himself, acknowledging Christ to be the Saviour of the world...." He was further willing to call Rome "a true Church of Christ...though not a pure and perfect" one.[25] And he set forth an interpretation of the doctrine of predestination at variance with Calvin's—as he had in his Paul's Cross Sermon of 1581—arguing that God was "a permissive, and no positive cause of the evil, which the schoolmen do call *malum culpæ*"; that the will of God was "not absolute but conditional, to save his elect believing, fearing, and obediently serving him"; and that reprobates were rejected of God "not...without a foreseen worthiness of rejection going though not in time yet in order before" (3:592–93). Both aspects of Hooker's teaching were abhorrent to Travers: Rome was an enemy with whom accommodation was unthinkable; predestination, strictly interpreted, the stay of the faithful. When in the spring of 1586, Hooker reiterated his position with particular force on three successive Sunday mornings Travers rose each afternoon to refute him. Twenty-six years later, when Hooker's three sermons were published as *A Discourse of Justification*, his views were still conspicuous for their toleration of Rome; alone of Hooker's works, the *Discourse* seems to have met with immediate public demand, for a new edition was called for within less than a year.[26]

As for Whitgift, now Hooker's patron, the controversy was acutely embarrassing. Fuller remarks that he regarded it as "dangerous" in "person...place...and precedent."[27] Travers was a notorious disciplinarian, the Temple was a public forum, and *any* debate—much less one before half the future lawyers of the realm—compromised the Archbishop's drive for conformity throughout the church. As his biographer remarks, Elizabeth had "committed her establishment to no doctrinal definitions beyond those of the few essential formularies,"[28] steadfastly resisting attempts to define the content of faith more precisely—and more exclusively—than was necessary. Thus when Whitgift moved to silence Travers, he did so with utmost circumspection. The grounds for his action were that Travers was not licensed to preach, that he was not ordained within the English church and had refused to submit to its jurisdiction, and that public correction of erroneous doctrine was contrary to the order of the Bishops, confirmed by the Queen, against public refutation of "erroneous doctrine."[29] Travers replied that in effect he had been licensed to preach by Aylmer's letters on his behalf in 1580–81, that his ordination at Antwerp was as valid as any priest of Rome's who now held cure in the church, and that St Paul had rebuked St Peter himself to his face, "when Peter in this very case which is now between us, had, not in preaching, but in a matter of conversation, not 'gone with a right foot, as was fit for the truth of the Gospel'." St Paul "conferred not privately with him, but, as his own rule required, reproved him openly before all, that others might hear, and fear, and not dare to do the like" (3:562). Travers gathered into a "*short Note*" the fifteen specific points in Hooker's teachings to which he took exception (1:59–60), and he defended his right to preach—or at least not to be deprived of it without due process—in his *Supplication* to the Council.[30]

In it, Travers felicitously compared the Council to that "honourable counsellor" in Mark 15:43 who reproved the Pharisees for "proceeding against our Saviour Christ without having heard him." He cited John 7:51: "Doth our law judge a man before it hear him, and know what he hath done?" (3:550). He reminded the Council that to silence a preacher was to deprive him of his livelihood. He urged his obligation as a Minister of the Gospel to reply to teachings that were "matters...of great moment, and so openly delivered, as there was just cause of fear lest the truth and Church of God should be prejudiced and perilled by it." He made it clear that he regarded their danger "such as the conscience of my duty and calling would not suffer me altogether to pass over." And he claimed that, under the circumstances, he was irresistibly compelled "to deliver, when I should have just cause by my text, the truth of such doctrine as he had otherwise taught" (3:558). Of the Romanism in Hooker's teaching—"sour leaven" Travers called it—he remarked: "I think the like to this...hath not been heard in public places within this land since Queen Mary's days" (3:567).

So public an indictment demanded a public reply. Hooker addressed his *Answer* to the Archbishop.[31] He recounted Travers' initial challenge to his appointment; he detailed the charges of "inconformity," contentiousness, and factionalism; he recalled the accusation that he "had conspired against" Travers, "sought superiority over him," and deviated from the customs of the Temple in his conduct of the service there (3:571–72), and he related the conferences between the two that had ensued. As to the accusation that he was a Romanist in his views of grace and justification—a charge that Travers regarded as "unanswerable"—Hooker stoutly denied it. "Saving only by him," Hooker replied, he had never before been "touched" by such a charge. His intention had been to show more precisely where Rome was in error by indicating where the two churches were in agreement. He did so, he said, in order to rebut their charge, "that when we cannot refute their opinions, we propose to ourselves such instead of theirs, as we can refute." Moreover, he had been at some pains to expose their error on so principal a matter as how the grace of Christ was to be made available to men: "It will not be found, when it cometh to the balance, a light difference when we disagree, as I did acknowledge that we do, about the very essence of the medicine, whereby Christ cureth our disease" (3: 578–79). As for the charge of substituting "school-points and questions, neither of edification, nor of truth," for "the expounding of the Scriptures, and [his] ordinary calling," Hooker called on Calvin himself to authorize the use of "distinctions and helps of schools" (3:585–86).

Hooker saved for last the issues that underlay the entire controversy: the conflict between ecclesiastical law and biblical precedent, and the denial of the authority of reason in matters of religious truth. As to the first, Hooker argued that, even were Travers' impeachments just, he was still under explicit obligation not to challenge him in public: "For the avoiding of schism and disturbance in the Church, which must needs grow if all men might think what they list and speak openly what they think; therefore... it was ordered that erroneous doctrine, if it were taught publickly, should not be publickly refuted.... For breach of which order... all the faults that can be heaped upon me will make but a weak defence for him" (3:587–88). Travers claimed that his rebuke had been temperate and necessary— "charitable, and warrantable in every sort"; he was convinced that a stricter reply was "warranted by the rule and charge of the Apostle" Paul: "Them that offend openly, rebuke openly, that the rest may also fear" (3:562). Thus was the authority of the church, "a decree agreed upon by the Bishops and confirmed by her Majesty's authority" (3:587), poised against the authority of scriptural example, "the rule and charge of the Apostle." In his *Answer*, Hooker treated this issue with due caution, as his Archbishop had done before him, preferring to set forth the inconsistencies of Travers' accusations and to urge the uncharitableness of an offer to confer in private after having rebuked him in public.

But the authority of reason Hooker handled with greater confidence. Travers had challenged his views of predestination: who were his authorities? St Paul, Hooker answered. Travers demanded, what was his authority for a reading of St Paul against that "of all churches and all good writers"? (3:593). Hooker replied, "his own reason." Travers warned him that it was "a matter standing more with Christian modesty and wisdom in a doctrine not received by the Church, not to trust to his own judgment so far as to publish it before he had conferred with others of his profession labouring by daily prayer and study to know the will of God, as he did, to see how they understood such doctrine" (3:559). Hooker replied that he could satisfy Travers' demand for authorities, "mo in number than perhaps he would willingly have heard of" (3:594). What was at issue, however, was not the proper interpretation of Paul, but the authority of reason. His defense of that authority anticipates much of the argument in the first three books of the *Laws*:

I alleged therefore that which might under no pretence in the world be disallowed, namely reason; not meaning thereby mine own reason as now it is reported, but true, sound, divine reason; reason whereby those conclusions might be out of St. Paul demonstrated, and not probably discoursed of only; reason proper to that science whereby the things of God are known; theological reason, which out of principles in Scripture that are plain, soundly deduceth more doubtful inferences, in such sort that being heard they neither can be denied, nor any thing repugnant unto them received, but whatsoever was before otherwise by miscollecting [i.e., misinference] gathered out of darker places, is thereby forced to yield itself, and the true consonant meaning of sentences not understood is brought to light. This is the reason which I intended.... granted by all as the most sure and safe way whereby to resolve things doubted of, in matters appertaining to faith and Christian religion. [3:594–95]

The dispute laid bare the central issue of the English Reformation: in the absence of a single, authoritative tradition (Rome), to what authority was one to appeal when a difference in the interpretation of doctrine arose?[32] To Hooker, it was presumptuous of Travers to assume that, because he differed from him, he had not "conferred with others of his profession." To Travers, it was equally presumptuous of Hooker to substitute the authority of the Roman Aquinas for that of the Genevan Calvin in the interpretation of so principal a tenet of Christian belief as predestination.

In their respective appeals—Travers to the Council, Hooker to Lambeth—the contest was a stand-off. The silenced Travers continued at the Temple, the Councillors still supported him,[33] and his faction remained to harass Hooker as long as he continued in the post. But Hooker's *Answer to Travers* is important for its anticipation of the *Laws*. All that was to become most characteristic of his later work, his patient exposition of complex issues, his faith in the tools of rational inquiry and logical demonstration, his charity and forebearance, his wide reading and keen sense of history, coupled with a deep devotion to his church, are present in the early sermons preached at the Temple and defended in the *Answer*. He had been publicly exposed to the unrelenting and unsympathetic critique of a man of popular eloquence and private piety. He had defended himself ably enough, and Whitgift had silenced his antagonist. But the issues went beyond their occasion, and Whitgift's circumspect vindication was of Hooker's right to preach, not of the substance of his teachings.[34] His peroration conveys the anguish of his situation, his own hunger for peace and unity:

I take no joy in striving, I have not been nuzzled or trained up in it. I would to Christ they which have at this present enforced me hereunto, had so ruled their hands in any reasonable time, that I might never have been constrained to strike so much as in mine own defence....But sith there can come nothing of contention but the mutual waste of the parties contending, till a common enemy dance in the ashes of them both, I do wish heartily that...the strict commandment of Christ unto his [clergy] that they should not be divided at all, may at length...prevail so far at the least in this corner of the Christian world, to the burying and quite forgetting of strife, together with the causes which have either bred it or brought it up; that things of small moment never disjoin them, whom one God, one Lord, one Faith, one Spirit, one Baptism, bands of great force, have linked; that a respective eye towards things wherewith we should not be disquieted make us not...unable to speak peaceably to [our] own brother; finally that no strife may ever be heard of again but this, who shall hate strife most, who shall pursue peace and unity with swiftest paces. [3:596]

II

It may be suggested, then, that the *Laws of Ecclesiastical Polity* came from Hooker with genuine ambivalence. On the one hand, the work reopened debate and contention, abhorrent to him; on the other, it might resolve the contradictions and uncertainties implicit in the authority of the church as it had come to be established. Whether it was explicitly a commission from Whitgift, as Sisson has argued, is open to debate. To Walton's view, seconded by Houk and Craig,[35] that the foundation of the *Laws* was laid at the Temple—the view recapitulated above—Sisson opposed the thesis that the *Laws* was in prospect at the original appointment, that Edwin Sandys was delegated by his own father and by Whitgift to advise and collaborate with Hooker, and that the house of Hooker's own father-in-law, John Churchman, was to be the locus of their collaboration. It is worth while remembering, though, that the evidence provided by the Hooker-Travers controversy—famous in its own day and substantially in the public domain for three and a half centuries—is quite sufficient to account for the origin of the *Laws* in Hooker's own desire to answer to the issues raised by Travers' attacks on him personally, on the authority of the church that was his home, and on the authority of reason itself in matters of faith and doctrine. Whitgift's summons to the Temple had deprived him of an academic career, and with the factionalism at the Temple his new position had clearly turned sour. Could not Hooker, on his own responsibility, have turned inward—to writing—as a way of resolving the issues to his own satisfaction? Such a view of the evolution of the *Laws* is not incompatible with an archiepiscopal commission, but neither does it require one.

Hooker's response to the disciplinarian controversy may be usefully compared to that of one who was indubitably the Archbishop's man: Richard Bancroft, successor to Whitgift in 1604 and Archbishop in everything but name from 1597. When Whitgift became Archbishop in 1583, it fell to Bancroft to answer the Puritans' literary attacks. In the 1570s it had been Whitgift who had replied to the *Admonition to Parliament*, and when Cartwright had risen to defend the Admonitioners, Whitgift had answered him in an eight-hundred page folio that left little ground unturned.[36] Bancroft's methods were different. He culled documents of every sort to discredit the Reformers. As early as 1583 he had prepared the first of his accounts of their principles and practices,[37] and in 1589 his investigations bore fruit in a sermon, preached at Paul's Cross on "the 9. of Februarie, *being the first Sunday in* Parleament, Anno. 1588."[38] He denounced the attacks of Martin Marprelate upon episcopacy—Martin had called them "pettie Popes," not to be tolerated "in a Christian commonwealth"—as a "rebellious argument" (p. 68). He urged that the episcopacy was of apostolic antiquity, if not institution.[39] And he exhorted his hearers to rest in the assurance that "the doctrine of the church of England, is pure and holie: the government thereof... lawfull and godlie: the booke of common praier containeth nothing in it contrarie to the word of God" (pp. 89–90).

Bancroft's documentation of his charges appeared anonymously in 1593, concurrently with the Preface and Books I–IV of the *Laws*, in the well-known *Survay of the Pretended Holy Discipline* and *Daungerous Positions and Proceedings*.[40] Bancroft's aim was frankly to alarm the tolerant to the political menace of the discipline. The first, drawn from published writings, analyzed the contradictions and inconsistencies of their program; the second detailed its revolutionary, seditious, and fanatical character, drawing on letters, minutes of clandestine gatherings, Star Chamber testimony—the gleanings of a decade's resolute pursuit. No longer, Bancroft argued, could right-minded men condone the aims of the Reformers or take seriously their professions of sincerity. The church had here to deal with a revolutionary conspiracy, and Bancroft's evidence was such to prove it so. Hooker's contribution to this literature of denunciation was the Preface to the *Laws*. Here one can find evidence—in the text itself—of lay collaboration and its consequences. But this is anticipating.

In the winter of 1592, when Hooker sought a publisher for his manuscript, he found no bookseller willing to publish it, "for fear of loss." There was apparently little market for an academic treatise on church discipline and none at all for one which took the side of the bishops.[41] As John Spenser, President of Corpus and Hooker's first editor, later related:

I have long since credibly heard and do believe that Mr Richard Hooker having dealt with divers printers for the printing of his Books and finding none that would bear the charge of printing them unless himself would give somewhat towards the charge thereof, because books of that argument and on that part were not saleable, as they alleged, was very much dismayed, and that Sandys who was then daily conversant with him having at length fished out the cause of his melancholy did make him an offer to print them at his own charges and to give him a certain number of copies, which Sandys performed, with adding of certain monies, which offer Mr Hooker did accept very kindly. [p. 52]

The testimony of Nicholas Eveleigh, Sandys' agent, stressed the personal motives behind the offer: it was "principally for the love and good respect wch the sd Sr Edwyne Sandys dyd then bere to the sd Mr Hooker" (p. 138). The contract was eminently fair. Hooker was to see his work in print; upon completion of all eight books, he would receive £50 for his rights to the manuscript. The printer, John Windet, was to be reimbursed for his work and, as Sandys' agent for the sale of the books, might gain additionally from commissions. Sandys' risk was substantial, but, as we shall see, he had a political as well as a personal interest in the venture.

Did Sandys' collaboration in fact antedate his offer to subsidize the publication of the work? There is really no hard evidence one way or the other. He certainly could have, for he was in London throughout the 1580s. He was elected to Parliament in 1586, in 1588–89, and again in 1593. During these years he was a frequent guest of the Churchmans, where Hooker and his wife Joan resided after their marriage in 1588. The two men could scarcely have avoided discussing the work which occupied Hooker's time and attentions during the period in which both shared John Churchman's hospitality. The friendship—indeed, intimacy—of the two men is beyond dispute. But there is no reason to infer from it the kind of formal collaboration that Sisson pictured. Sandys was himself pursuing a career in law—he formally became a student in the Middle Temple in 1589—and in Parliament; and it seems quite as likely that he acquired a personal stake in Hooker's treatise only when he had agreed to subsidize it himself.

The nature and extent of Sandys' involvement prior to 1592–93 is important because, in effect, it dates the point at which we are obliged to regard Hooker's treatise as a quasi-official, collaborative apologia for the Church of England as established. If it was so conceived from the beginning, then its essentially polemical character throughout is undeniable and its pretensions to reconciliation rhetorical.[42] But if it came to be so regarded only with, and to some extent under the pressure of, Sandys' offer of 1592–93 (an offer that in turn necessitated a substantial revision by Hooker of his manuscript and effected a shift in the original conception of the work), then the ambiguities of the work come to have a foundation in the very circumstances of its conception, sponsorship, and publication. I wish to argue the case for the later alternative, for it is precisely the kind of problem to which a critical edition must address itself.

The view that all eight books were complete in the winter of 1592–93, when the manuscript was being considered by the London book trade, was first argued by Ronald Bayne in his edition of Book V (1902). It was refined by R. A. Houk in his edition of Book VIII (1931) and developed by Hardin Craig, in an article published in 1941. The evidence is well known and need be only briefly recapitulated.[43] The title page of the first edition (undated, but demonstrably printed early in 1593)[44] announces eight books, but prints only four. The Stationers' Register entry for January 29, 1593, assigns rights to John Windet for "Eight books, by Richard Hooker," with the notation that they had been "Aucthorised by the lord archbishop of Canterbury his grace under his hand."[45] (These two items amount to the same thing, as Windet would have been responsible for both. In the sixteenth century a title page was a bookseller's advertisement for his wares, equivalent to a modern dust jacket. Together they tell us that Windet, at least, expected the *Laws* to run to eight books when he undertook to print it in January of 1593.) Hooker likewise refers to all eight as complete, once in the Preface (ch. vii), where he abstracts the contents of all eight books to follow, and again in the table of contents following, which notes "What things are Handled in the Bookes Following."[46] Sisson regards this evidence as equivocal, as it could as easily be the *intended* contents of the four published books, but Hooker himself seems unequivocally to refer to the last book as complete, in the text of the Preface: "concerning the supreme power of the Highest, they are no small prerogatives, which now thereunto belonging the form of your discipline will constrain it to resign; as in the last book of this treatise we *have shewed* at large" (Pref.viii.2; italics added). When Hooker acknowledges the hiatus in publication at the end of the volume, it is impossible to tell whether he is covering for himself or for his sponsors: "I have for some causes (gentle Reader) thought it at this time more fit to let goe these first foure bookes by themselves, then to stay both them and the rest, till the whole might together be published. Such generalities of the cause in question as here are handled, it will be perhaps not amisse to consider apart, as by way of introduction unto the bookes that are to followe concerning particulars" (sig. S3ᵛ). Although the evidence is by no means free of ambiguity, it seems to point toward the early completion of all eight books and the unexpected revision of the last four.

As is well known, the fifth book did not appear until late in 1597, when Hooker's last published words were: *"Have patience with me for a small time, and by the helpe of Almightie God I will pay the whole."*[47] Books VI–VIII were not published until the middle of the next century. I have urged the authenticity of the "three last books" in a recent article, and there is no need to reargue the point here. What still needs delineation, however, is the timing and the nature of the collaboration with Sandys, for its effect on the *Laws* is crucial to our view of the very nature of the work itself.

Hardin Craig first argued that "evidence for...collaboration... in the original composition of the work is lacking, although it is abundant for revision."[48] According to this view, Hooker submitted a substantially complete manuscript to Whitgift in 1592–93, but the difficulties in obtaining a printer (one wonders why the church was not forthcoming with a subsidy for a work written in its defense), the consequent entry of Sandys into the project as sponsor and patron, and—as we shall see—the evident need to rush the first four books into print while the 1593 Parliament was sitting, prompted Hooker to release the first four and to withhold the last four pending revision. Judging by the time it took him to revise Book V—it is seven times the average length of the earlier books—it is clear that "revision" was tantamount to entirely rewriting the second half of the work. And from the evident failure of Books VI–VIII to appear in his lifetime, it is clear that the projected revisions were simply beyond Hooker's powers. Craig writes:

There is no reason to think that Sandys was not deeply interested in these books for general as well as personal reasons, but it may be suggested without disrespect that he found the last four books in need of particular amplification in order that they might better fit in with political issues current in the year 1593. The fact that he had paid out his own money in considerable quantity to have the books published would have put him at an advantage in the determination of whether or not the remaining four books would be published in their original forms or undergo revision prior to publication.... Nothing more definite is known about Hooker's attitude toward revision than that he coöperated in the new plan heartily and at once, and received advice as to what should be done. [p. 100]

If we know little of Hooker's own attitude toward the revision of the last four books, we know a good deal about Sandys' and Cranmer's. Each made detailed notes on a manuscript of Book VI which has not come down to us. They show the care with which Hooker's final draft—it was in fair copy and ready for the printer—was read by men who were former students, and they show unmistakably the character of their expectations. Cranmer wrote:

because this question of lay elders and the next of bishops [i.e., Books VI and VII] are the most essentiall points of all this controversy, I could wishe that although in the other bookes you have rather beaten backe their arguments then brought any proof for our assertions, yet in theis two questions if you did deale with them ἀνασκευαστικῶς καὶ κατασκευαστικῶς [constructively, as well as destructively] I thinke it were not amisse. And in the booke of B[ishops] I thinke you have done so....What proofes therefore you can alleage out of Scripture, or antiquity, or reason, to breake the neck of their presbytery, I thinke it were not labour lost to alleage them. [3:125–26]

The most damaging contention of the Puritans was that their proposed system of church government, modeled (according to Hooker) on Calvin's church at Geneva, was uniquely in accord with the Word of God as recorded in Scripture. If it could be refuted on the authority of "Scripture, or antiquity, or reason," the English church would stand acquitted of the charge that it possessed an ungodly discipline, contrary to divine law, nowhere authorized by Scripture, from which the godly were obliged to separate themselves should it refuse to reform itself or else be reformed by others. But Hooker had argued in Book II that a church whose polity was grounded in natural law

135

was no less in accord with the will of God than one putatively raised on scriptural foundations. And in Book IV he had demonstrated to his own satisfaction that the superficial resemblance of the English church to the forms and ceremonies of Rome did not disguise the essential differences between them. What Cranmer sought, however, was a detailed defense of current practice. This explains why Book V grew so long. It was to furnish the pointed defense of the ceremonies and customs of the Church of England which Cranmer and Sandys— and presumably Whitgift—deemed indispensable. Whom it was that Hooker was to answer is clear enough from Sandys' note opposite the rubric "T.C.": "I will here put you in mynd once for all, that you must needes set down Mr. Cartwrights and W[alter] T[ravers'] woords at large in the margent of this booke wheresoever they are impugned. Els will your discourse want much credit of sinceritie: which in your former it hath especially by that meanes" (3:136). From the frequency of this injunction, it is clear that Hooker's lay collaborators envisioned him as engaged in a point-by-point refutation of the charges of Cartwright and Travers, in the traditional manner of sixteenth-century religious polemic,[49] not as composing a self-sustained and self-contained treatise "Of [Latin *de*, "concerning"] the laws," the doctrines, and the ceremonies of the English church.

But, as Coleridge observed, Hooker's mind habitually flew off "to the *General*"; that is, he saw details only as parts of a larger pattern of significance and meaning.[50] Cranmer and Sandys were absorbed in the immediacies of an explosive political situation, and Whitgift's direct and forthright approach was their ideal. They cautioned Hooker to "remember your adversaries," to verify all citations ("A bare narration, unquoted, uncredited"), to be consistent in his terminology, and to qualify all doubtful or uncertain assertions (3:134; 135; 117, 129). They urged Hooker to state succinctly the cause in question and drive home points that tell in their favor. Their concern for clarity—for "perspicuitie"—goes beyond an editor's concern for the niceties of form and expression: it is an admonition to take his controversial responsibilities seriously, to avoid sarcasm, mere "hard wordes" (3:129). Opposite the phrase, "Wholesome Exhortation," Cranmer wrote: "This word may seeme to savour of a scoffe, and therefore I would leave it out" (3:123). Rather, he is urged to lay "open the inconsequence of their argumentes as plainely as may be," and to "not only satisfy yourself and those which are learned, but as farre as may be, even the simplest" (3:129). The text over which Cranmer and Sandys worked has not come down to us, but it is clear that the general topic was the one originally proposed, the ecclesiastical jurisdiction of lay elders. In it, Hooker had apparently argued that no just parallels could be drawn for the Puritans' demand for lay control of the church judiciary from the Sanhedrim of Israel. Cranmer summarizes the point: "whereas the thing is urged as most necessary, and as the absolute ordinaunce of God, yet no direct place can be brought, where any such autority is given to lay elders, but here and there a text is snatcht up by the way, and construed according to their purpose. Bishops and deacons are described, of their elders there is no description, only out of a clause concerning their maintenaunce, a formall distinction is coyned, and an ecclesiasticall court on the suddayne erected" (3:126). From his point of view, Cranmer was thoroughly justified in urging that struggle between the Puritan laity and the established clergy for jurisdictional power within the church—i.e. for disciplinary authority over its members—was "the most essentiall" point of all, for he was concerned with the constitutional implications of the Puritan demands. It was Hooker's erudition and logical acuity, not his spiritual insight, that were being pressed into service.

The role Hooker's lay colleagues played in shaping Hooker's treatise is further suggested by a letter from Cranmer to Hooker, *Concerning the New Church Discipline*, first printed in 1642. Walton used it in 1665 and reprinted it,[51] and since 1666 it has been reprinted with Walton's *Life* in all full-scale editions of Hooker's *Works*. It has been traditionally dated February 1598, on the authority of William Fulman, the seventeenth-century archivist of Corpus.[52] But there is good reason to suppose that it was composed earlier, during the same winter in which the arrangements were concluded for the printing of the first four books of the *Laws*.[53] How much of Hooker's manuscript Cranmer had before him is hard to judge. His first sentence alludes to the opening sentence of Hooker's Preface,[54] and he specifically refers to the discussion of atheism "in the beginning of the fifth book" (2:606), hence the dating of the letter *after* the publication of Book v late in 1597. If impressions may be trusted, the letter reads as if it had been written after reading a manuscript for the first time. Cranmer is less concerned with what Hooker has done than in what he might do; his aim seems to be to point out the immediate relevance of the issues Hooker has raised. He praises Whitgift, attributing to him the preservation of the church against the attacks mounted by the Puritans in the 1580s. He emphasizes the increasingly violent and irresponsible nature of their protests: what began in "some small difference about cap and surplice" has become the pretext for the notorious libels of Martin Marprelate and the fanatical "conspiracy" of Hacket and Coppinger—matters more topical in 1592–93 than in 1597–8. While the Reformers disclaim responsibility for such outrages, their own attacks upon the established church have undermined respect for authority and created an atmosphere of disobedience in which such incidents can take place. Moreover, Cranmer sees the Brownists (separatists) as "lineal descendants" of the Puritans, carrying arguments the more moderate Puritans had broached to their logical conclusions. (Browne urged his followers to withdraw from the established church and to set up a true church themselves; Cartwright's ideal was a reformed state church, on the model of Geneva, in which episcopacy was renovated and replaced by presbyterianism.)

To Cranmer it was all one. If, as Cartwright urged, doctrine and discipline were each equally requisite to individual salvation, and if the Church of England, because of its traditional Hierarchy, was not a true church, then it scarcely mattered if one chose to remedy this by installing presbyters for bishops or by founding a separate communion. The consequences were intolerable in either case, for church and state were coextensive and membership in the one connoted loyalty to the other. "Last of all (which is a point in my opinion of great regard, and which I am desirous to have enlarged) they do not see that for the most part when they strike at the state ecclesiastical, they secretly wound the civil state" (2:609). Advocacy of ecclesiastical reform would lead either to separatism—the denial of the Queen's sovereign power in matters of religion—or to presbyterianism—the subjugation of the sovereign by the church. Under the terms of the Elizabethan Settlement, either was tantamount to treason. The minimum expectation, should the premises of the Reformers be countenanced, would be unchecked sectarianism. In the earlier controversy, Cartwright had vigorously denied the democratic or "popular" implications of reform, and Whitgift had just as vigorously insisted upon them.[55] On this point Cranmer anticipates in Hooker a certain reluctance to thrust home the point—to fasten responsibility for the Brownists on the Puritans—but he is insistent:

What further proofs you can bring out of their [i.e., the Brownists'] high words, magnifying the discipline, I leave to your better remembrance: but above all points, I am desirous this one should be strongly enforced against them, because it wringeth them most of all, and is of all others (for aught I see) the most unanswerable. You may notwithstanding say that you would be heartily glad these their positions might so be salved as the Brownists might not appear to have issued out of their loins; but until that be done, they must give us leave to think that they have cast the seed whereout these tares have grown. [2: 605]

To emphasize the point, Cranmer lists the undesirable elements in society that find succor in the Puritan disturbances. First, there are "godless politics" [i.e. *politiques*], who join forces with the Reformers in order to sabotage their new church discipline and other forms as well. Second, there are atheists who batten upon the disputes among the clergy as occasions for profane scoffing against all religion. Third, there are papists who delight in seeing the enemy's ranks serried by bickering and disputation. Cranmer sums up his advice: Hooker is to bend every effort to separate the "proper and essential points and controversy, from those which are accidental." On this score, Cranmer has no doubts whatsoever: "The most essential and proper are these two: overthrow of episcopal, erection of presbyterial authority" (2:608).

Cranmer's controversial bias is omnipresent, and his praise of Whitgift, whose exertions had earlier turned the tide of victory, pointed an unmistakable moral for Hooker. The insistence that Hooker telescope radical and reformist positions was astute controversial strategy, for the Brownists were viewed with universal disfavor. Cartwright vehemently denied the imputation of radicalism, but it was Whitgift's position that separatism and disobedience could be inferred from the Reformers' principles. Cranmer was thus not bringing to Hooker's attention a hitherto unnoticed facet of the Puritan platform; he was reminding Hooker of what he surely knew but was reluctant to insist upon.

III

There is a second point of interest in Cranmer's letter: its date. If he was writing to Hooker after the fifth book was in print, then his critique could have had no influence on the published text; if earlier, the reverse: it would have directly influenced the revised Book v and the posthumous books as well, insofar as they too were subject to revision. Ronald Bayne first challenged the traditional dating, and Hardin Craig argued convincingly that the letter was written in 1593.[56] In the Parliament that sat from February 19 to April 10, 1593—when the first volume of the *Laws* was being printed in Windet's shop—Edwin Sandys was active in the passage of two bills: "An act to retain the Queen's majesty's subjects in their due obedience" (35 Eliz. c. 1) and "An act for restraining popish recusants to some certain places of abode" (35 Eliz. c. 2). Together, the two constitute the high-water mark of anti-Catholic legislation in Elizabethan England.

The first was of especial interest to Sandys. It was originally drafted to reinforce the legislation of 1581 (23 Eliz. c. 1 and 2), which had been passed to ensure the loyalty of all English Catholics in the face of Pius V's excommunication and deposition of Elizabeth in 1570. Although the new legislation was aimed at recusants, it was the Puritans who opposed it in the session of 1592–93. They did so because, as worded, the bill could be applied to Protestant dissent as well. When reported out of committee—of which Sandys was a member—the bill's penalties were carefully restricted to "Popish recusants." On the floor, Sandys attacked the amended wording, urging "that it might be as it went first for Recusants generally, and not restrained to Popish Recusants only: So that under this Bill there might be included Brownists and Barrowists."[57] In the ensuing discussion all agreed that the Brownists were reprehensible, but there was some disagreement as to how best to deal with them. The legal issue was raised of amending a bill, offered as a clarification of the earlier statute against recusancy, so as to include Protestant sectaries.[58] Puritan members feared that the bill might be subsequently used to stifle loyal criticism of genuine abuses. And Sir Walter Raleigh pointed out that there was the difficulty of committing the judgment of man's intentions to jury trial: "that Law is hard that taketh life and sendeth into banishment, where mens intentions shall be judged by a Jury, and they shall be Judges what another means. But that Law that is against a Fact, is but just; and punish the fact as severeley as you will" (p. 517). It was finally passed on April 7 as a bill "for the Explanation of a branch of a Statute made in the twenty third year of the Queens Majesties Reign," i.e., a bill explaining an earlier statute against Catholic recusancy as now applying to Protestant nonconformity.

For the first time since Queen Mary, the machinery of the secular arm, created to protect the state against the threat of Catholic subversion, was formally enlisted against Protestant dissent. By forcing radical Protestants to choose between conscience and country, and by giving this dilemma the force of law, Whitgift had secured parliamentary sanction for his ecclesiastical policies. With some justice, the Puritans charged that the government was more afraid of sectarian dissent than Catholic recusancy. In their view, the partial reformation of Elizabeth's cautiously Protestant Settlement of 1559 was wholly compromised. Indeed, the exodus of radical Protestants from England dates from the passage of the "conventicle" act of 1593. Thus the years between the Parliaments of 1586 and 1593—

the years of Hooker's work on the *Laws*—belonged to Whitgift, and the passage of the legislation of 1593 symbolized the triumph of his policies.[59]

Sandys saw to it that publication of the first four books of Hooker's *Laws* was timed to coincide with this debate.[60] Writs for election went out on January 4; the contract with Windet was signed on the 26th; on the 29th, the manuscript, licensed for publication by Whitgift, was entered to Windet in the Stationers' Register.[61] Parliament convened on February 19. Within a month the book was printed, "hastened," we are later told, "by such eminente persons whome the cause did moste speciallie concerne."[62]

On March 13, the day Sandys offered his opinion on the "Brownists and Barrowists," Burleigh was dispatched a presentation copy by Hooker, accompanied by a gracious letter acknowledging Burleigh's "painful care to uphold al laws, and especially the ecclesiastical."[63] In the words of Sisson, to whom we are indebted for the recovery of the details of the printing contract, "the Lord Treasurer now had the advantage of being able to consider its clauses in the light of the new and important book awaiting him in his study. He did not need to read far. For Hooker plunged at once, in his Preface, into the very root of the matter then before Parliament, and before Burleigh, for it deals with the errors of the Puritan dissenters" (p. 64).

It is possible to pinpoint exactly the passages to which Sisson refers, for Hooker's Preface is not of a piece. Burleigh would have had to read at least two thirds of it before he came to those chapters, viii and ix, which take up directly the social and political implications of Brownism. The first six (two thirds of the whole), concerned with the legitimacy of Calvin's establishment at Geneva, would not have been immediately germane to the bill under consideration. As Houk was the first to observe (p. 60), Hooker's Preface breaks into two distinct parts. The first comes to a close with a statement of Hooker's fundamentally irenical purpose: "It is no part of my secret meaning to draw you hereby into hatred, or to set upon the face of this cause any fairer glass than the naked truth doth afford; but my whole endeavour is to resolve the conscience, and to shew as near as I can what in this controversy the heart is to think, if it will follow the light of sound and sincere judgment, without either cloud of prejudice, or mist of passionate affection" (vii.1). Abstracts of the eight books follow, and Hooker concludes: "Thus have I laid before you the brief of these my travails, and presented under your view the limbs of that cause litigious between us: the whole entire body whereof being thus compact, it shall be no troublesome thing for any man to find each particular controversy's resting-place, and the coherence it hath with those things, either on which it dependeth, or which depend on it" (vii.7). With chapter viii Hooker forecasts the radical implications of disciplinary reform, "the manifold strange and dangerous innovations which are more than likely to follow, if your discipline should take place" (viii.1), and the theme of the first six chapters—Calvin's enormous prestige among English Puritans—is dropped. The earlier manner had been indirect, for he was addressing an audience for whom Calvin was a very prophet, an oracle of divine truth: "Safer to discuss all the saincts in heaven than M. Calvin," he later noted in a well-known marginal aside.[64] Considering the scriptural basis for presbyterianism, Hooker is gravely ironic: "Wherefore a marvel it were if a man of so great capacity, having such incitements to make him desirous of all kind of furtherances unto his cause, could espy in the whole Scripture of God nothing which might breed at the least a probable opinion of likelihood, that divine authority itself was the same way somewhat inclinable" (ii.7).

But when he turns to the Brownists, he is more direct. He itemizes the degrees of disruption that would ensue: the supremacy of the Queen in her own church would be overthrown and her prerogatives curtailed; university corporations would be dissolved and the universities themselves fall into disorder and disrepute; the practice of civil law would be annulled and the authority of the secular courts subverted; the nobility would be subjected to the arbitrary powers of the church judiciary, free to prosecute whomever they pleased. Fair or not, Hooker's points are uniformly those that would separate conscientious, law-abiding reformers from their potentially radical principles. And the link between the two parts of the Preface is the assertion—supplied Hooker by Cranmer—that the radicalism excoriated in the second half is a necessary consequence of the reform rebutted in the first, that an attack on the authority of the bishops is an invitation to attack all constituted authority whatsoever. On the testimony of a disillusioned Barrowist, who had rebuked his more cautious brethren for refusing to accept the full implications of the principles they themselves have taught, Hooker is able to charge the Reformers with the "schism" of separatism: "Thus the foolish Barrowist deriveth his schism by way of conclusion, as to him it seemeth, directly and plainly out of your principles. Him therefore we leave to be satisfied by you from whom he hath sprung" (viii.1). In his letter to Hooker, Cranmer had argued:

> A third inducement may be to dislike of the discipline, if we consider not only how far the reformers themselves have proceeded, but what others upon their foundations have built. Here come the Brownists in the first rank, their lineal descendants, who have seized upon a number of strange opinions; whereof although their ancestors the reformers were never actually possessed, yet by right and interest from them derived, the Brownists and Barrowists hath taken possession of them. For if the positions of the reformers be true, I cannot see how the main and general conclusions of Brownism should be false. [2: 602–03]

It was of this taunt that Cranmer remarked, "it wringeth them most of all, and is of all others...the most unanswerable" (2:605).

One additional piece of evidence confirms the role Cranmer played in the topical additions to Hooker's Preface and, by extension, the role of Cranmer and Sandys in the revision of the *Laws* proper. Chapters viii and ix were separately printed at Oxford in 1642 by one "W.R." as a treatise with its own paragraphing, together with a fragment of chapter lxxix of Book v, in a 32-page quarto pamphlet, *The Dangers of New Discipline, to the State and Church Discovered, Fit to be Considered By them who seeke (as they tearme it) the Reformation of the Church of England*. How Mr "W.R." secured Hooker's text is a matter of conjecture.[65] The nature of the piece—a portion of Hooker already in print—makes it impossible to trace its descent among Hooker's seventeenth-century editors. We can only assume that an enterprising printer came by it, perhaps in the wake of war plunder,[66] sensed its topicality, and printed it unaware of its provenance. He made no attempt to conceal the author, for the excerpt from the fifth book is headed, "Eccles. Polit. Lib. 5. § 79. ad fin" (p. 28). A comparison of the text of the pamphlet with the 1593 folio (and its derivatives) reveals that it is an earlier draft. The 1593 text is smoother and ampler in its wording, the 1642 text somewhat crisper in its diction and less polished in its word order. That the final two chapters of Hooker's Preface existed in 1642 as a separate text argues that Hooker augmented his treatment of Calvin and the Genevan church at the behest of Sandys and Cranmer. Its germaneness to the parliamentary question at issue (with which its publication was timed to coincide) is unmistakable, and it carried out Cranmer's injunction that Hooker fasten responsibility for the tenets of the separatists upon the disciplinary reforms urged by the Puritans.

IV

In the light of later events, Hooker's decision to publish his treatise under Sandys' sponsorship was a fateful one. As he soon learned, the interests of his sponsors did not necessarily lie upon the same axis as his own. He had originally proposed to set forth the historical and philosophic basis for the doctrines, the ceremonies, and the laws of the English church. His training was in theology, his bias was to the "general," his tone conciliatory. Sandys and Cranmer were apprehensive for the political danger posed by the Puritans. Their concern was for the stability of the established church and the state that supported it, and their controversial posture was uncompromising. Sandys agreed to underwrite the *Laws* out of regard for a former tutor and close friend, but also because he saw in Hooker's treatise a topicality that Hooker could not have seen, one that—adroitly handled—might be turned to good account. Books I–IV, which treat the philosophical background of the controversy, "the generalities of the cause in question," raised no questions with his lay readers. Hooker was clearly in control of his material, and the books were published substantially as Hooker had written them. Cranmer's letter is silent upon the issues they raise. Book V, in which Hooker first treats the "particulars" of the controversy—the extent to which individual ceremonies and practices of the Church of England, and "the manner of bestowing that Power of Order, which enableth men in sundry degrees and callings to execute the same" (1:196), was as yet unregenerate by virtue of its resemblance to Rome—was the first also to raise doubts in the minds of his sponsors. It did not appear for five years after the Preface and Books I–IV. When it did, in December 1597,[67] it was prefaced with a Dedication to Whitgift and a eulogy of his earlier labors on behalf of the church. Finally, with Book VI, the underlying tensions within the collaboration exacted their toll, and the venture collapsed. Hooker's premature death has conventionally been taken to account for the nonappearance in his lifetime of Books VI–VIII, but it is by no means the only reason.[68] In 1599, a year before his death, Hooker composed portions of an answer to his detractors of the *Christian Letter* of that year. These "Fragments of an Answer to the Letter of certain English Protestants"—as Keble, who first printed them, called them—display Hooker at his best, with none of his vital powers impaired. They treat the topics of grace and predestination, which Hooker's sermons of the 1580s had touched on, and taken as a whole, they are comparable in length to Books II, III, or IV of the *Laws*. It was not merely a question of time running out before he could "polish" a manuscript for the press.

The *Laws*, then, had begun as a vindication of Hooker and Hooker's church against the attacks by Travers at the Temple upon his integrity as a scholar and teacher; it took the form of a systematic treatise on the polity and practices of the church as a whole; but it ultimately became subordinate to the demands of an essentially political controversy. By dint of what seems like a threefold amplification of his original manuscript,[69] Hooker had been able in Book V to please all sides: to satisfy his scholar's conscience, to set forth the ethos of his church, and to answer the multiple charges that Cartwright had lodged against its practices and traditions. But the evident collapse of the Puritan threat in the 1590s only increased Hooker's own sense of the futility of "these unpleasant controversies touching ecclesiastical policy" (v.i.1). The Hierarchy had not been forthcoming with aid in publishing a work written in its own defense, and Hooker was dependent on the generosity of Sandys if the work was to get into print at all.[70]

What emerges from the documents that bear on the publication and sponsorship of the *Laws* is, therefore, somewhat at variance with Walton's assertion—itself *ex parte*—that the "presence [of Mr. George Cranmer] added to that of Sir Edwin Sandys, proved very useful in the completing of Mr. Hooker's matchless Books" (1:104), and his emphasis on the "sacred friendship" of tutor and pupils. It was in Walton's own interest to stress the closeness of the tie to Cranmer, because it was from the Cranmer family that he derived much of the material for his biography. For us, then, Cranmer's point of view is doubly reinforced: once as it affected Hooker, again as it shaped Walton's portrait. But it can be suggested, with no disrespect for either Sandys or Cranmer, that their patronage was not an unmixed blessing. Had Sandys not interested himself in Hooker's work, it would never have seen the light of day, but once he and Cranmer were involved, the division of aims and method so added to Hooker's labors that he was unable to sustain the added burden. As a result, the projected defense of his church fell short of his earlier hopes and original intentions. As Sisson tactfully observed, "when the whole story is told it may be questioned whether Hooker was in all respects in harmony with his allies on the controversial ground which it was his function to defend on behalf of the Church" (p. 6).

It is altogether characteristic of Hooker's reticence that we should never have learned from him that disharmony in fact existed; but his failure to bring to completion the revision of a work we have every right to suppose was completed to his own satisfaction seven years before his death is mute testimony of the difficulties under which he worked, the price he had to pay, when he "did accept very kindly" Sandys' offer in the winter of 1592.

V

If we are to learn anything useful about the origin of the *Laws* from the differences that arose between Hooker and his collaborators, we need to draw our inferences with a certain delicacy. We cannot say, for example, that Hooker would never have embarked upon his controversial project had he not been urged by his lay colleagues, for the *Discourse of Justification* is thoroughly controversial in nature, as are the Preface (chs. i–vii as well as viii and ix) and Books ii–iv of the *Laws*, which Hooker issued with a minimum of outside aid. Nor would it be correct simply to see one party to the agreement as simply to the left (or right) of the other along a particular political or doctrinal axis.[71] Rather, the two parties to the collaboration differed in their views of the relevant context for the controversy, what was meant by the issue of "authority." Hooker saw it as inward and individual, Cranmer and Sandys, as social and political. Hooker was far from blind to the subversive implications of the Puritan attack. But he chose not to stress its seditious logic, in the manner of Cranmer,[72] but rather to show the inappropriateness of the program to achieve its desired end. He argued that it was a mistake to identify individual salvation with disciplinary reform. By joining the two, the Puritans were guilty of a confusion of inward substance with outward form. Hooker grounded his treatise upon an investigation of the problem of "assurance," a sifting of the degrees of certainty available to men and the kinds of evidence appropriate to true faith. He held that such doctrine as was requisite for individual salvation was plain and readily available to all sincere and professing Christians, and that faith and doctrine, insofar as they affected individual men, were essentially simple matters—difficult in performance, to be sure, but easy enough to "know." Matters of church polity, however, were intrinsically complex, seldom admitting of clear-cut answers.[73] The administrative organization of the church, the ceremonies and forms of its worship, the nature of its laws and the character of its jurisdiction, and, most importantly, its relation to the state were properly the concern of the church as a corporate body and not of its individual communicants. Could he persuade the Puritans to accept this distinction, Hooker could then argue that individual faith and corporate authority did not, properly speaking, come into conflict at all. That they did—and so conspicuously as in the controversy over church discipline—argued a dislocation of perspective, a failure to see clearly the general problem of faith and the inward nature of "assurance." Only when its nature had been assayed could the problem of human salvation be detached from the passions of factionalism and the complex pressures of political necessity. Once this was done, nonconformity would be seen for what it was, an external symptom of an inward "turbulence of spirit." It need not be condemned outright, as Cranmer urged, as inherently pernicious, the root of every social evil; but neither should it be equated, as was done by the Puritans, with the safety of individual souls. A fixed ground of essentially simple truth had first to be found on which all men could stand in assurance of the adequacy of their faith and the certainty of their salvation. *This* would be the true irenicon, satisfying the tender consciences of individual souls who doubted their "election to grace" and restoring to the church as a corporate body its due sovereignty. It is with this aim in mind that Hooker characteristically raised his argument to the highest permissible pitch of abstraction and generality. Only in the essential simplicity of general truths could a firm reconciliation be affected. "In all parts of knowledge rightly so termed things most general are most strong" (II.i.3).

It may be argued, then, that in his effort to reconcile the disaffected to the laws of the English church, Hooker's most effective weapon was not his philosophical acumen or his logical rigor, but his capacity to speak to the Puritan as a man who appreciated the essential inwardness of his religious experience. Uniquely among the apologists for the Church of England, Hooker recognized that a resolution of the problem of conscience lay at the heart of the question of conformity. Yet it was precisely this recognition that the collaboration, with its parliamentary forcing of consciences and its Whitgiftian sifting of loyalties, compromised. Instead, Hooker offered an argument for obedience that did not deny the validity of that inwardness, but tried rather to see it within the entire range of human history and human aspirations. A genuine empathy with the spiritual needs of the individual in search of "certaintie of faith"—the topic of his first extant sermon—who was deeply fearful of estrangement from God was the ultimate basis for Hooker's attempt to establish grounds for a rational, self-respecting, and affirmative obedience to the laws and sovereign authority of the established church.

No one would deny that Hooker's passion for order and his reverence for the rule of law had its negative component. He shared the fear of his age that the world as men knew it would literally dissolve if the demands of the Reformers were to be taken at face value. The opening words of the Preface strike this note: "That posterity may know we have not loosely through silence permitted things to pass away as in a dream" (i.1), and it resonates as well throughout his most familiar period—quoted in no less than three of the six essays in this volume:

Now if nature should intermit her course, and leave altogether though it were but for a while the observation of her own laws; if those principal and mother elements of the world, whereof all things in this lower world are made, should lose the qualities which now they have; if the frame of that heavenly arch erected over our heads should loosen and dissolve itself; if celestial spheres should forget their wonted motions, and by irregular volubility turn themselves any way as it might happen; if the prince of the lights of heaven, which now as a giant doth run his unwearied course, should as it were through a languishing faintness begin to stand and to rest himself; if the moon should wander from her beaten way, the times and seasons of the year blend themselves by disordered and confused mixture, the winds breathe out their last gasp, the clouds yield no rain, the earth be defeated of heavenly influence, the fruits of the earth pine away as children at the withered breasts of their mother no longer able to yield them relief: what would become of man himself, whom these things now do all serve? [i.iii.2]

The emotional leverage of this apprehension was enormous, as evidenced by the imaginative richness of its utterance. Hooker's distinction, however, was that he did not feel compelled to argue from it. He recognized, as his less introspective colleagues did not, that the inward anxiety of the Puritan was the true source of his political intransigence, and he realized better than they the inexpedience of straightforward controversial rebuttal. No logic, however cogent, could wean a Cartwright or a Travers from his dependence upon Scripture and his concomitant distrust of his own judgment; no forcing of issues could still the Puritan's anguished dialogue with God or resolve the internecine war between his ordinary human needs and the intolerance of a hypertrophied conscience.

But because the *Laws* have been appropriated largely by ecclesiastical historians and political theorists, the inward and intuitive element at the base of Hooker's thought has not always been sufficiently recognized; or, if it has (as by C. S. Lewis), it has been regarded as a distinctive feature of Hooker's non-*Polity* work, scrupulously excluded from the "golden" prose of the *Laws* and uncharacteristic of its "tranquil" philosophy.[74] Hooker himself contributes to this impression by the very impersonality of his style, his air of enunciating age-old truths whose objective validity is not to be questioned, of speaking in an official capacity for the entire history of the church. Nonetheless, the substance of what he has to say can only derive from an intensely held personal conviction, one sufficient to sustain the extraordinary length and detail of the *Laws*. (By the same token, when that conviction is thwarted by the obligation to treat some immediate—and, to Hooker, trivializing—controversial issue, the prose goes flat and the reader becomes uncomfortably aware of just how bored and boring Hooker could become.) But when such convictions are set forth in an objective, abstract, imperturbable prose, an ambiguity of response is inevitable. By his preoccupation with universals, Hooker laid himself open to the charge, then as now, that he "failed to meet some actual issues squarely."[75] Whatever insights hindsight may furnish us, it may be suggested that for Hooker his reluctance to deal directly with the concrete issues in dispute reflected a sincere conviction that these did not in fact constitute the "actual issues." The espousal of a Genevan polity was an outcropping of an "inward turbulence of spirit," and that anxiety was the consequence of a misconstruction of the nature of faith. It had first to be allayed before constructive, "philosophic" thought could go forward.

At the same time, Hooker's appeal to truth at its highest level of

generality and his consequent reluctance to do battle with his adversaries on a point-by-point basis surely constituted his own essentially
inward response to the entrenched absolutisms and vested antagon-
isms that comprised the religious context of post-Reformation England. It was a profoundly personal means of disengaging himself from
conflicts that were irreconcilable, self-destructive both of psyche and
community. It was his way of setting them at arm's length so that
they might be recognized for what they were, "without the cloud
of prejudice, or mist of passionate affection." Whereas Cranmer and
Sandys urged Hooker to push his case the harder, as Whitgift had
done with such evident resolution and political success, Hooker's
reaction was to step backward, to search out some vantage point
from which the partialities and rigidities on each side might finally
come within a single field of vision.[76] If he seemed to them to urge
his case with an inappropriate diffidence, it was because he recognized,
as they did not, that the problems of conscience could not be resolved
by force. The absolute demands of the individual for salvation within
the church of his own making, and of the state for unquestioned
sovereignty within a church deemed coextensive with itself, each
needed tempering with the humanist's sense of the origins of the
controversy and the scholar's sense of the value of evidence. Before
outward obedience could be secured, reason had first to define wherein absolute certainty was legitimately available to man, where relative certainty ("probability") was the best he could expect. Only in
this way could any adversary be detached from an unreasoning,
absolute commitment to his cause.

From our own moment in history, we may argue that Hooker's
terms for reconciliation, however sincere, were nonetheless illusory,
that the forms of thought no less than the forms of political and social
institutions can have a repressive and authoritarian bias. That "intel-
lectualizing" is after all but one kind of "defense mechanism" which
the Puritans were right in their own interests to resist. What Hooker
was in effect offering, with perfectly sincere charity, was to incor-
porate other individuals into *his* view of the laws of nature and the
order of creation. Understandably enough, they might and did feel

threatened by it, not so much in its abstract and philosophical form as in the political and social engines of its practical consequences.

It can come as no great surprise, then, that Hooker is no "set text" in the curricula of universities in the United States, for this country is, after all, the legatee of that view of the relation of church and state which was formally proscribed by Hooker's patrons—and by Hooker himself. For the older and essentially realist view of the state as a corporate reality, the settlers of the new world substituted an essentially nominalist and skeptical view of the state as a human construct, and the assumptions that lie behind Hooker's rationale for incorporation into that body are alien, philosophically and politically, to their descendants. Liberal historians and social analysts have traditionally looked to Hooker's Puritan antagonists as the seed-bed for modern democratic institutions, and Professor Walzer's recent and influential work, *The Revolution of the Saints*,[77] is but the last in a long and honorable scholarly tradition that sees in the process of organized opposition to the "laws of ecclesiastical polity" in sixteenth-century England the roots of twentieth-century political consciousness. If Hooker is to be read nowadays as other than an historical artifact, or, worse still, as the apologist for rigidity, repression, and authoritarianism, I would suggest that his continuing appeal lies in his vision and conviction of the authority of reason as the means by which ideal human values do in fact find their most lasting realization in the imperfect world of men. His essentially humanist heritage—the vision of the ideal orator of Cicero as one who would put into practice in the world of *men* the ideal values of *man* is surely apropos here. Hooker's pertinence and relevance lies in his faith—it can be no more than that, ultimately—in the validity of human reason and the authority of its constructs, social as well as intellectual; its essentially public nature; and its paradoxical harmony with the deepest and most pressing of man's innermost needs: his ultimate sense of individual self-worth.

NOTES

1. *The Works of...Mr. Richard Hooker*, ed. Keble, 7th ed., rev. 1888, 1:66. Cited in the notes as *Works*. Subsequent citations incorporated into the text are either by volume and page number for supplementary texts, or by book, chapter, and section number for quotations from the *Laws*.

2. In *The Judicious Marriage of Mr. Hooker and the Birth of "The Laws of Ecclesiastical Polity."*

3. Thomas Fuller, in his *Church-History of Britain* (1655), gave an account of Hooker's controversy with Travers (ix.vii.59–63), but Walton is the first to link it to the *Laws*.

4. *Works* 1:67.

5. See Novarr, *The Making of Walton's "Lives,"* pp. 286–89. The text quoted above is itself a revision (1670) of Walton's original: "a Treatise in which I intend the satisfaction of others, by a demonstration of the reasonableness of our laws of Ecclesiastical Polity..." (*Works* 1:67, n. 2).

6. Cf. Southgate, *John Jewel and the Problem of Doctrinal Authority*, pp. 55–62.

7. For Hooker's career at Corpus, see Fowler, *The History of Corpus Christi College with Lists of its Members*, pp. 147–52. The authority for his lectures in logic is Daniel Featley's "*The Life and Death of John Reinolds*" in *Abel Redevivus*, ed. Thomas Fuller (London: Thomas Brudenell, for John Stafford, 1651), p. 478; cf. Wood, *Athenæ Oxonienses*, ed. Philip Bliss (London: F. C. & J. Rivington, et al. 1815), 2:13. On his sermon at Paul's Cross in 1581, see Walton's *Life* (*Works* 1:22–23).

8. In Fuller's phrase, "the neck (allowing Mr. Cartwright for the head) of the presbyterian party, second in honour and esteem..." *Church History*, ed. James Nichols (London: Thomas Tegg & Son, 1837), 3:26.

9. For Travers' appointment to the Temple in 1581 and the subsequent controversy with Hooker in 1585–86, see Knox, *Walter Travers*, pp. 54–88.

10. T. Henry Baylis, *The Temple Church...An Historical Guide*, 2d ed. (London: George Philip & Son, 1895), pp. 46, 149.

11. See M. M. Knappen, *Tudor Puritanism: A Chapter in the History of Idealism* (Chicago: Univ. of Chicago Press, 1939; reprinted Phoenix Books, 1965), pp. 220–22.

12. The lectures themselves have not survived, but the following is an abstract of them: "The names and offices of Archbishops and Bishops should be abolished. In their stead the offices of Bishops and Deacons, as described in the New Testament should be established. The Bishop should have a purely spiritual function and the deacon should care for the poor. The government of the Church should not be entrusted to Chancellors of Bishops or Officials of Archdeacons, etc., but to the minister and the Presbytery of the Church. Each minister should be attached to a definite congregation. No one should, like a

candidate, seek the office of a minister and none should be created ministers by the authority of Bishops, but should be elected by a Church. All should promote this reformation according to their several vocations, *i.e.* the magistrate by his authority, the minister by preaching, and all by their prayers." A. F. Scott Pearson, *Thomas Cartwright and Elizabethan Puritanism 1535–1603* (Cambridge: Cambridge Univ. Press, 1925, reprinted Gloucester: Peter Smith, 1966), pp. 28–29; see also John Strype, *The Life and Acts of John Whitgift* (Oxford: Clarendon Press, 1822), 3:19–20.

13. [Walter Travers], *A full and plaine declaration of Ecclesiasticall Discipline owt off the word off God | and off the declininge off the churche off England from the same* ([Heidelberg], 1574; reprinted Ann Arbor, Mich.: Univ. Microfilms, 1966), p. 15.

14. See A. F. Johnson, "Books printed at Heidelberg for Thomas Cartwright," *The Library*, 5th series, 2 (March 1948): 184–86, cited by Knox, *Walter Travers*, p. 30, n. 3.

15. *Middle Temple Records*, ed. Charles Henry Hopwood (London: Butterworth, 1904), 1:239; *A Calendar of the Inner Temple Records*, ed. F. A. Inderwick (London: Henry Sotheran, 1896), 1:311.

16. Inderwick, 1:312.

17. Cited by Knox, *Walter Travers*, p. 57.

18. Although the principal fruit of that learning had been the *Explicatio* of 1574, its authorship had not been fixed on him by 1581. Aylmer's predecessor, Edwin Sandys, had attributed it to Cartwright (Knox, p. 30), and when Archbishop Parker asked Aylmer himself to refute it, the latter declined; see John Strype, *The Life and Acts of. . .John Aylmer* (Oxford: Clarendon Press, 1821), p. 15.

19. Hopwood, 1:248.

20. Inderwick, 1:320–21.

21. [Richard Bancroft], *Daungerous Positions and Proceedings, published and practised within this Iland of Brytaine, under pretence of Reformation, and for the Presbiteriall Discipline* (London: John Wolfe, 1593), pp. 115–16.

22. Alvey died in August 1584 (Inderwick, 1:lvii); Hooker's appointment was confirmed on March 17, 1585 (*Works* 1:27).

23. "Warning shall be given to Mr. Travers that this House mindeth no longer to continue the payment of his yearly pension of 20 *li.*, which was allowed unto him at the request of Mr. Allveye to supply his weakness, who being now dead, Mr. Hooker, now appointed to be master of the Temple, is either in person to preach or else at his charge to furnish the place with a sufficient preacher" (Inderwick, 1:333).

24. Twelve days after the Inner Temple's order for suspension of Travers' pension, the Privy Council intervened to request its continuance (Knox, p. 70 and n. 2). On June 28, 1585, when Hooker had been Master for three months, the Middle Temple allowed Travers continued residence: "Mr. Travers shall have his man in clerk's commons with the Benchers' men, paying what they do" (Hopwood,

1:279). By November both place and pension were secure: "Mr. Travers shall receive his pension and remain in his lodging within the parsonage of the Temple till further order" (ibid., 287).

25. The phrasing is Travers' (*Works* 3:567, 560).

26. A fragment of a letter of Henry Jackson, who edited Hooker's *Tractates* at Oxford and published them in 1612, speaks of the edition's being exhausted within a few days ("ante paucos dies"), but the letter was dated September 1612, and the "*second edition, corrected, and amended*" is dated 1613 (*Works* 1:lii; the original is among the Fulman MSS at Corpus Christi College, Oxford).

27. Fuller, *Church History*, ed. Nichols, 3:130 (IX.vii.60); see Knox, p. 79, and n. 2.

28. Powel Mills Dawley, *John Whitgift and the English Reformation* (New York: Charles Scribner's Sons, 1954), p. 216.

29. *Works* 3:587, n. 1; Fuller, *Church History* 3:129 (IX.vii.56); see also Craig, "Of the laws of Ecclesiastical Polity—First Form," *Journal of the History of Ideas* 5 (1944): 94–95.

30. Reprinted in *Works* 3:548–69.

31. Ibid. 3:570–96.

32. Cf. Southgate, *John Jewel*, pp. vii–viii.

33. See above, n. 24.

34. See Strype, *Whitgift*, 1:452–53, and *Works* 1:64–65.

35. Houk, ed., *Book VIII*, p. 50; see above, n. 29.

36. *The Defense of the Aunswere to the Admonition, against the Replie of T. C.* (London: Henry Binneman, for Humfrey Toye, 1574).

37. *Tracts Ascribed to Richard Bancroft*, ed. Albert Peel (Cambridge: Cambridge Univ. Press, 1953); see Stuart Barton Babbage, *Puritanism and Richard Bancroft* (London: S.P.C.K., 1962), p. 22.

38. *A Sermon Preached at Paules Crosse the 9. of Februarie*...(London: E.B. for Gregorie Seton, 1588 [i.e., 1589]), title page.

39. Ibid., p. 69; Bancroft's claim has usually been taken as the first enunciation of the doctrine of the Apostolic Succession, although his words will scarcely bear the interpretation that the later High Church party was to put on them. His argument is not that episcopacy is of specifically divine institution, only that it is at least as old, and hence as authoritative, as any discipline the Reformers would urge in its place. See W. D. J. Cargill Thompson, "A Reconsideration of Richard Bancroft's Paul's Cross Sermon of 9 February 1588/89," *Journal of Ecclesiastical History* 20 (1969): 253–66, and above, p. 69, n. 26.

40. The *Survay* was entered to John Wolfe on March 5, 1593 (Arber, *Transcript* 2:627); there is no record for *Daungerous Positions*.

41. Sisson, *Judicious Marriage*, pp. 49–50.

42. Cf. Cargill Thompson's remarks, above, pp. 13–15.

43. The following repeats material I have used in "Hooker's *Polity*: The Problem of the 'Three Last Books'," *Huntington Library Quarterly* 34 (1971): 317–36. I argue there that the problem of whether—and when—Hooker finished the

"three last books" is essentially a question of the sponsorship of the *Laws* and its effect on Hooker. Here my concern is to show the evolution of the *Laws* from the controversy at the Temple and the implications for the work as a whole of Sandys' offer. As the subsidy of publication and subsequent collaboration is at the bottom of both problems, the repetition seems inevitable.

44. On the date of the first edition, see Andrew Maunsell, *Catalogue of English Printed Bookes: Which concerneth...matters of Divinitie* (London: John Windet, 1595), p. 59; and Dunkin, "Two Notes on Richard Hooker," *Papers of the Bibliographical Society of America* 41 (1947): 344–46; on its significance, see Sisson, pp. 60–66, and Houk, *Book VIII*, pp. 53–59.

45. Arber, *Transcript* 2:625.

46. *Of the Lawes of Ecclesiasticall Politie. Eyght Bookes.* (London: John Windet, n.d.), sig. D5ᵛ. Cf. above, p. 70, n. 29.

47. *Of the Lawes of Ecclesiasticall Politie. The fift Booke* (London: John Windet, 1597), sig. 2A4ʳ.

48. Craig, "Of the Laws of Ecclesiastical Polity—First Form," *Journal of the History of Ideas* 5 (1944): 93.

49. Cf. Southgate, *John Jewel*, pp. 83–84, and above, p. xiii, 17.

50. See "Richard Hooker" in *Coleridge on the Seventeenth Century*, ed. Brinkley, pp. 148–49; see also d'Entrèves, *The Medieval Contribution to Political Thought*, p. 37; cf. *Laws* II.i.3.

51. See Novarr, *Walton's "Lives,"* pp. 248–49.

52. *Works* 2:598, n. 2.

53. Craig, p. 100; see also Bayne, *The Fifth Book*, p. 578, n. 3.

54. Hooker: "Though for no other cause, yet for this; that posterity may know we have not loosely through silence permitted things to pass away as in a dream, there shall be for men's information extant thus much concerning the present state of the Church of God established amongst us, and their careful endeavour which would have upheld the same" (Pref.i.1).

Cranmer: "What posterity is likely to judge of these matters concerning church discipline, we may better conjecture, if we call to mind what our own age, within few years, upon better experience hath already judged concerning the same" (*Works* 2:598).

55. See A. F. Scott Pearson, *Church & State: Political Aspects of Sixteenth Century Puritanism* (Cambridge: Cambridge Univ. Press, 1928), pp. 45–49.

56. Bayne (p. 578, n. 3) argued for 1596 and saw its influence principally in the Dedication of Book v; cf. Craig, p. 100.

57. *A Compleat Journal Of The Votes, Speeches and Debates, Both Of The House of Lords And House of Commons Throughout the whole Reign of Queen Elizabeth*, ed. Simonds D'Ewes (London: J.S., sold by Jonathan Robinson, 1682), p. 500.

58. See the remarks of Mr Finch, D'Ewes, *Journal*, p. 517.

59. Cf. the discussion of this legislation by J. E. Neale, *Elizabeth I and her Parliaments, 1584–1601* (London: Jonathan Cape, 1957; paperback, 1965), *passim*, pp.

280–97; for the view that "the chief importance of the statute was that it lifted the burden of dealing with refractory Puritans from the bishops and ecclesiastical authorities and made it the concern of ordinary courts," see Dawley, *John Whitgift*, pp. 189–90.

60. First noted by Houk, Book VIII, pp. 44–48; cf. Sisson, *Judicious Marriage*, pp. 12–13, 47, 64.

61. Sisson, p. 52. Arber, *Transcript*, 2:625.

62. Sisson, p. 145.

63. *Works* 1:117; see Sisson, pp. 61–64, 89.

64. *Works* 1:133, n. 2.

65. First noted as Hooker's by Bayne, *The Fifth Book*, p. xxxv; see my note, "Hooker's 'Preface', Chapters VIII and IX," *Notes & Queries*, n.s. 16 (1969): 457–59. Falconer Madan suggested that W.R. was William Raynor; see *Oxford Books* (Oxford: Oxford Univ. Press, 1912), 2:164, 537.

66. Keble noted that in 1640 Jackson's library came into the hands of the Puritans, *Works* 1: xxxii–iii.

67. Sisson, pp. 59, 139.

68. In his letter "to the reader" in the 1604 reprint of the Preface and Books I–IV, John Spenser implied that Hooker died, pen in hand: "For as in the great declining of his body, spent out with study, it was his ordinary petition to Almighty God, that if he might live to see the finishing of these books, *then, Lord, let thy servant depart in peace*, (to use his own words,) so it pleased God to grant him his desire. For he lived till he saw them perfected; and though...he died as it were in the travail of them, and hastened death upon himself, by hastening to give them life: yet he held out to behold with his eyes, these *partus ingenii*, these Benjamins, sons of his right hand..." (*Works* 1: 123). Sisson, however, is skeptical (*passim*, pp. 79–95).

69. Cf. Craig, "Of the Laws of Ecclesiastical Polity—First Form," *Journal of the History of Ideas* 5 (1944): 104.

70. Sisson, p. 52.

71. Cf. Sisson, p. 106.

72. Cf. *Works* 2:604.

73. Cf. *Laws* Pref.iii.2.

74. Lewis, *English Literature in the Sixteenth Century Excluding Drama*, p. 452.

75. Thompson, "Richard Hooker among the Controversialists," *Philologica Quarterly* 20 (1941): 460.

76. Cf. the remarks of Professor Edelen, pp. 273–75, below.

77. Michael Walzer, *The Revolution of the Saints: A Study in the Origins of Radical Politics* (Cambridge: Harvard Univ. Press, 1965; reprinted New York: Atheneum, 1969).

THE
HERMENEUTICAL PROBLEM
IN RICHARD HOOKER

Egil Grislis

I

Hooker's advocacy of consensus as a meaningful route to the discovery of truth lays an obligation on any prospective interpreter of Hooker to consult with his fellow interpreters. This is particularly the case when we propose to investigate two hermeneutical issues in Hooker's thought: the problem of subjectivity and the principles of scriptural interpretation. It is appropriate, then, to begin by surveying earlier attempts to formulate the essence of Hooker's theology.

Hooker research had an unusually slow start. Although the latter part of the nineteenth century was marked by a resurgence of interest, it produced comparatively meager results. Yet, in terms of future developments, they were not entirely insignificant and may be seen as three interrelated but distinctive movements. One group of interpreters sought to discover Hooker's appropriate place within the broad spectrum from High Church to Low Church or even argued that Hooker's thought was spacious enough to include both extremes.[1] Although differing in their conclusions, these interpreters shared the conviction that it was important to think ecclesiologically and liturgically. In an age which had been deeply moved and disturbed by the Oxford movement, such categories appeared to be innately relevant.

A second company of scholars attempted to interpret Hooker in terms of his own major contributions. Within a general upsurge of liberal theology it must have made sense to ask whether Hooker was a rationalist. Unfortunately, the early debates did not proceed beyond rather broad assertions and failed to reach very informative results. Thus, according to Thomas Henry Buckle, Hooker "quotes the ancients, not so much from respect for their authority, as with the view of illustrating his own arguments." Buckle concluded that although Hooker employed both reason and faith, the final "jurisdiction" was accorded reason.[2] John Hunt described Hooker as a "Rationalist"—in contrast with "Scripturalist"—but observed that Hooker had only "vindicated the use of reason within certain limits"; that is, the knowledge that man obtains by natural reason is not salvific.[3] Equally general was Edward Dowden's observation that Hooker "does honour to human reason as a source of truth, yet he has none of the arrogance or the dogmatism of some rationalists." While praising "the audacity of Hooker as a rationalist," Dowden limited his explanation to the observation that Hooker was "tranquil and unaggressive." Only a brief hint suggests in what sense Hooker may be called a "rationalist," in that "Hooker's vindication of the claims of reason prepared the way for Chillingworth and Hales."[4] At the same time other scholars denied that Hooker was a rationalist (for example, Theodore Hunt);[5] some simply emphasized his greatness;[6] and others denied that his theology was in any sense creative.[7] In the end, despite some occasionally valuable insights, the total perspective was blurred because the definition of "rationalism" was far too general to yield meaningful or precise conclusions.

At the same time, when the understanding of Hooker's theology was at a low ebb, there arose a third group of scholars—John Keble, R. W. Church, Francis Paget, and Ronald Bayne—who diligently edited the *Works*, supplying annotations that have contributed to the rise of a far more sophisticated Hooker scholarship in the twentieth century.[8] The intense editorial attention to Hooker's writings and his own footnotes inevitably engendered inquiry into the sources of his thought, which in turn enabled a far more serious assessment of its fundamental shape.

In the nineteenth century, when Hooker's dependence on Calvin was taken for granted, it was argued by E. A. Washburn that Hooker's basic source was St Augustine, appropriated through Calvin.[9] T. F. Henderson expanded this observation to include St Thomas Aquinas, and, above all, "the spirit of Greek thought,"[10] and Bayne's comprehensive evaluation served as a majority report for future decades: "Aristotle and the philosophy of Greece, the Greek and Latin Fathers, and, finally, St. Thomas and the schoolmen, are co-ordinated with the teaching of the Bible...."[11] Several scholars have pursued this line of approach in depth. Lionel Thornton, in the first full-scale presentation of Hooker's theology, showed that Hooker's reliance on St Thomas is consistent and profound and that he had built his entire theological edifice on Thomistic principles. At the same time, he also acknowledged that Hooker had been "brought up as a Calvinist" and continued to employ many Calvinist insights in such a way that "sometimes one influence is dominant and sometimes the other."[12] Christopher Morris, who represents the received orthodoxy on the matter, recognizes Hooker's continued reliance on Calvin but sees Hooker as standing at equal distance from Rome and Geneva.[13] Yet a timely warning—often still overlooked— was made by John T. McNeill, namely that Hooker's "mind has been represented as chiefly under medieval influences. The degree in which this is the case with the Continental reformers renders questionable the sharp contrast drawn by some interpreters between him and them."[14] Hooker's dependence upon medieval thought may have been overstated, but it is of undeniable importance, and it has received detailed attention from such recent scholars as R. W. Carlyle, A. J. Carlyle, Alessandro Passerin d'Entrèves, C. W. Previté-Orton, Robert V. Kavanagh, Peter Munz, John S. Marshall, and Robert K. Faulkner,[15] whereas Hooker's Calvinistic roots have been proclaimed with rather more enthusiasm than investigation.[16]

However indispensable, the inquiry concerning Hooker's sources does not of itself provide us with a complete exposition of his thought. This is particularly true in a more ecumenical age when it can no longer be assumed without question that a Protestant theologian must differ essentially from a Catholic medieval scholar—and also have a monopoly on all truth. Major studies by Otto Herman Pesch and others have taught us that even such theologians as St Thomas and Luther, separated by centuries and historic hostilities, may nevertheless share an essentially similar outlook.[17] Thus along with the inquiry into Hooker's theological heritage it is necessary to reflect on the systematic shape of his thought. Four positions emerge —far from exclusive and showing a significant measure of overlap.

First, the nineteenth-century effort to characterize Hooker as a champion of reason continues. Henderson put it this way: "The leading feature in his system is the high place assigned to reason, for, though affirming that certain truths necessary to salvation could be made known only by special divine revelation, he yet elevates reason into the criterion by which these truths are to be judged, and the standard to determine what in revelation is temporal and what eternal."[18] Such an incisive statement might have satisfied many nineteenth-century interpreters, but their twentieth-century successors have been, as a rule, more circumspect. They have not merely assumed that, in observing Hooker's accent on reason, one has fully understood the essence of his thought. Henderson himself had pointed to St Augustine and St Thomas as the intellectual foundation of Hooker's thought, suggesting that Hooker's appeal to reason might best be understood within a larger perspective. H. O. Taylor took a similar route. Having acknowledged Hooker's indebtedness to St Thomas, he went on to describe Hooker as an "intellectual" like St Thomas. Hooker's "delight is to reason on the things of God and man with sweetness and persuasion."[19] Or, as Dionisio de Lara puts it, Hooker is "an intellectualist."[20] W. M. Southgate's summary may be seen as an attempt to supply the older terminology with a more adequate meaning: "The rationalism of Hooker was a qualified rationalism. He did not dispense with revelation to replace it with reason. Like the reformers before him, he accepted Christian revelation as the primary basis of authority; but his chief interpretative authority was reason, and he insisted furthermore that it be regarded as a valid supplementary authority." Moreover, Southgate makes clear that he is speaking about "a collective reason both in time and place." And the claims to truth that can be made of reason understood in this way are limited: "His was a demand that truth be sought, not a claim that truth had been found...."[21] In other words, Southgate sees the reliance on revelation, the use of historical reason, and even a mild skepticism as all part of a rationalistic position. Yet the nine-teenth-century perspective does not disappear in the twentieth, and some scholars continue to speak of Hooker as a rationalist without further clarification.[22]

A second distinctive way of understanding Hooker is to regard him as a Christian humanist. Dowden, one of the earliest proponents of this view, writes: "The spirit of the Renaissance is brought into harmony by him with the spirit of the Reformation; he is serious, reverent, devout; with seriousness and reverence he does honour to human reason...he is at once humanist and theologian."[23] Dowden was inclined to evaluate Hooker's main contribution as a thrust to-ward rationalism, but he did not think it incompatible with a recog-nition of the fact that Hooker was influenced by both the Renaissance and the Reformation. Hardin Craig similarly sees Hooker as a Chris-tian humanist who generally depends on St Augustine and St Thom-as, who understands that reason must be interpreted with the aid of revelation, but who recognizes that, in the final analysis, the appeal to reason is decisive.[24] Hooker "declares that law can be discovered by the light of reason and thus makes reason coördinate or even, since it is the interpreter, superior to revelation."[25] Herschel Baker speaks of Hooker, Shakespeare, and Bacon as all three "spokesmen of...Renaissance optimism."[26] "A prince among rational theolo-gians," Hooker "did as much as one man could to assert the claims of natural reason...." To Baker, single passages even sound "deis-tic."[27] At the same time, he points to a tradition far more funda-mental in sustaining Hooker during his struggle with the Puritans: "The main lines of Hooker's rebuttal are those laid down by

Aquinas; and although they reach beyond Aquinas to Aristotle and the Stoics, the tone and accent are his own" (p. 93). He thus sees Hooker as a man who "came forward to defend the axiom of knowledge, and to restate, in a different context, the Thomistic claims for human reason" (p. 94). In other words, Hooker's Thomism is to be interpreted in a Neoplatonic manner. Hierarchical order characterizes all existence, and microcosmic order on the human level is congruous with the macrocosmic source of all order (pp. 167, 221). In this way it can be said that "order is reason and reason is God" (p. 74).

Morris shares an everyday version of an otherwise identical perspective. He notes Hooker's dependence on medieval sources and notes his closer proximity to the Renaissance than the Reformation. Yet in his view, Hooker is a well-informed traditionalist: "Hooker had a genuine belief in reason, but in practice what he found reasonable was what tradition, authority, and the majority supported."[28] Other scholars, with variations, have acknowledged Hooker's affinity with the Renaissance, his Thomistic background, his emphasis on reason.[29] Peter Munz, however, provides a significant revision of this view. On the one hand, he presents the most careful documentation of Hooker's indebtedness to St Thomas that we have; on the other, he has distinct reservations vis-à-vis Thomism as a viable base for Hooker's systematic theology and political philosophy. Munz argues that the "incipient naturalism" of Thomism served to undo the Thomistic synthesis employed by Hooker. "Hooker then, evolved in the end a conception of a truly omnipotent reason. The fine and important distinction which he had derived from St. Thomas between reason and faith as two supplementary methods of finding natural and divine law respectively, was wiped out."[30]

Thus, although Hooker is today still regarded as a rationalist, the agreement of contemporary scholars with their nineteenth-century forebears is more verbal than real. Sensitive to the fact that the term "rationalist" does not mean the same thing in the sixteenth and the eighteenth centuries, yet having chosen to call Hooker a rationalist, they suggest that Hooker is to be understood as a Renaissance man who still believes in the reality of God, who serves the church, and who yet thinks of God in rational categories of order and meaning.

A third approach, though closely related, may be distinguished from it insofar as it probes the mind of Hooker with such existential categories as the self, its existence, and its meaning. While E. N. S. Thompson and Ernst Jenssen sketch a basic outline, W. Speed Hill develops a major presentation in distinctively modern categories.[31] He also brings to light several Kantian presuppositions. Hill defines reason as "essentially an instrument of moral choice" and distinguishes "ethical reason" from "scientific reason."[32] It is the former which experiences reality in a total way, and it can only do this on the basis of "self-esteem," defined as "the character of the assumptions he instinctively makes as to the worth of his own existence as a human creature" (pp. 179–80). What further characterizes such self-acceptance is not only the subjective discovery of "human value" as an integral part of the self, but also an awareness of its being "immutably anchored in an objective realm of moral law." As a result, "man's reason is no longer free to serve all values equally and interchangeably," but in obedience to the laws of its own nature, it must "pursue values common to humanity as a whole" (pp. 186–88). Hill sees the continuing relevance of Hooker's thought in its concern with "inward values," which are "peculiar to man as a sentient and a subjective being" and which cannot be supplied from without by scientific reason (p. 193). While primarily interpreting Hooker in secular terms and consistently avoiding God-talk, Hill nevertheless shows a deep regard for Hooker's ultimate concerns and suggests that authentic secularity can be a genuine witness to the sacred.

A fourth approach may be seen as a reaction against the claims that Hooker embodies essentially a Renaissance perspective. The first representative of this movement was Thornton, who called attention to the medieval "balance" between "natural law" and "supernatural grace" and claimed that this balance was restored by Hooker.[33] If Hooker is to be understood rightly, then, reason cannot be exalted at the expense of grace. Yet, having made these important programmatic observations, Thornton himself did not develop them much

further, leaving the task to subsequent interpreters. Although Gottfried Michaelis only warned that Hooker does not think in terms of
an autonomous and individualistic reason of the Enlightenment,[34]
d'Entrèves speaks to the problem with precision:

In what sense can Hooker be termed a rationalist? The implications of the identity
which he asserts between the law of nature and reason, and the great stress which he
lays upon man's power of reason and autonomy of will are as it were neutralized by
his acceptance of the traditional notion of the law of nature as a part of the divinely
appointed order of Creation. The rationalistic bent of his conception of natural law
finds moreover an impediment in his deep historic sense. What divides his theology
from the rationalism of later days are not only the maintenance of the traditional
theological background and the limits which he is careful to assign to the independence of subjective reason, but his idea that rational construction must stand the
test of history and may not contradict the evidence of tradition and historical
development.[35]

Writing as a political scientist, d'Entrèves has not thought in terms
of grace and reason. This needed perspective is finally supplied by
Kavanagh, who specifically points out in what way Hooker's inherited theological perspective both limits *and* enhances his understanding
of reason: "Hooker...makes a place for reason, and for law as a
work of reason, but only in so far as reason is aided by grace. Reason
is competent, as Will is free ONLY WHEN ASSISTED BY SUPERNATURAL
POWER. His apparent confidence in reason is thus qualified and we
may say, therefore, that Hooker has great confidence in supernatural,
but not in natural, reason."[36] Although Kavanagh's brilliant dissertation was not published, other scholars have noted the significance
of reason redeemed by grace independently of him.[37] In this way,
a corrective principle is established which does not deny the significance of reason, yet attempts to subsume it under the overarching
initiative of the saving grace of Christ. At the same time, problems
remain in this view that require further attention. Several have been
pointed out by Gunnar Hillerdal. While often mistaken in fact and
perspective, Hillerdal has made a diligent and occasionally very
perceptive investigation of Hooker's theology. His most important
critique is that Hooker's reasoning is circular.[38] In response, I have
pointed out that Hooker does not introduce reason redeemed by

grace merely in the midcourse of his argument,[39] but rather makes use of such a notion throughout his work. Moreover, I have suggested that the idea of consensus serves as a cogent synthesis of grace and reason.[40] Yet the problems raised by Hillerdal are intrinsically important, and they merit further discussion.

We can only conclude, then, that the interpretation of Hooker's thought is in its beginning stages, that the basic problems have, if not been solved, at least been defined, and that something like an agenda for further study is before us. For the moment, however, we shall direct our attention to the problem of subjectivity; that is, to Hooker's own inquiry as to how one may write with a maximum of objectivity.

II

Although it was written in a polemical setting, Hooker's great defense of the Church of England, *Of the Laws of Ecclesiastical Polity*, is basically an inquiry into the first principles which sustain the structure of the church and inform the system of his Christian theology. Such major areas of inquiry as the problem of subjectivity, the interpretation of Scripture, the nature and activity of God, the created world, the nature of man, the meaning of sin, as well as Christology, grace, salvation, church, and the sacraments are all worked out not only with careful attention to detail, but also in a genuine systematic coherence. And where interpretation of Scripture and tradition fail to supply Hooker with the insight he desires, he does not hesitate to formulate anew or advance by a synthesis of perspectives that in the past have been regarded as contradictory.[41]

At the same time, Hooker is more than an able polemicist and a thoughtful systematician.[42] As a devout believer he is personally involved in the discovery of truth. Precisely because he knows that he has discovered much, he is eager to discover more and is aware of his own shortcomings.[43] Or, to put it another way, just because Hooker is so concerned to record truth as objectively as possible and as fully as he is capable, he must inevitably struggle with the problem of subjectivity. Hence an analysis of Hooker's concern with the problem is an appropriate vantage point from which to approach his entire theology.

In terms of Hooker's overarching intention, he looks to the idea of consensus as a central methodological principle that will guide him.[44] Yet within the history of thought a consensus is never equally obvious to everyone. It must be searched for, interpreted, and constructed from within a stream of often conflicting data. And when finally established, a particular agreement must be able to do battle with other sets of options, also proclaiming to be a "consensus" and speaking for the truth. Thus in his confrontation with the Puritans,[45] Hooker discovered the need to evaluate the basic presuppositions operative in the establishment of a particular consensus. Namely, Hooker saw that the Puritans were indeed consistent, yet narrowly so and in agreement with themselves only. How had they constructed their erroneous perspective? In what way did their personal attitudes shape their insights and determine their conclusions? What was their *modus operandi*? Hooker knew, of course, that there were differences among the Puritans.[46] Yet he had become convinced that there were several major insights which the Puritans shared and which allowed him to construct an overall summary of their position. He recorded it in six basic steps (Pref.iii.6–12).

First of all, as Hooker saw it, the Puritans always presented a vigorous and highly negative critique of society, centering their attention on "the faults...of higher callings." By repeating their accusations, they succeeded in creating an impression of their own "integrity, zeal, and holiness" (iii.6; v, Ded.). In contrast to them, Hooker offers a far better way of responding to the problem of society: "*there will come a time when three words uttered with charity and meekness shall receive a far more blessed reward than three thousand volumes written with disdainful sharpness of wit*" (ii.10).[47] Putting the case this way, Hooker is unmistakably pointing to the objective source of his subjective decision—the Gospel of Christ. The vitriolic words of the Puritans lack such a foundation. At the same time, Hooker is not immediately dismissing the Puritans' case, since he is actually practicing the kind of charity he has preached. He calls attention to the fact that more significant than any style of writing is its actual truth-content (ii.10). Yet the truth itself, and not merely its superficial semblance, is not obtained easily. The first principles of reason, which are the basis of all rational discourse, are self-evident. And the knowledge that is necessary for salvation has been graciously proffered by God. Yet these two sources do not of themselves yield all truth that mankind needs; they only enable a further search which then must be conducted by specialists, with diligent inquiry, over a long period of time: "the Lord hath himself appointed, that 'the priest's lips should preserve knowledge, and that other men should seek the truth at his mouth, *because* he is the messenger of the Lord of hosts.' (Malachi II, 7)" (iii.2). To the Puritan rejoinder that precisely such guidance had not been forthcoming, since the guides themselves lacked the necessary wisdom, Hooker does not yield and proceeds to question the adequacy of the Puritan's own insight (iii.3). His point is that the Puritans are not exempt from criticism but, rather, quite obviously open to it. Their central statement on the correct form of the government of the church which they have claimed to be "altogether necessary" is in fact "collected only by poor and marvellous slight conjectures" (iv.1; cf. viii.5). There is not even "one church upon the face of the whole earth" which would accept the kind of church government they propose (iv.1). To point to the Reformed churches on the Continent really does not help their cause, since it is from these churches that the Puritans have borrowed their ecclesiology in the first place (iv.8). In terms of ultimate origins, there is but one unprecedented model of Puritan church government. Consequently, argues Hooker, "that which you are persuaded of, ye have it no otherwise than by your own only probable collection, and therefore such bold asseverations as in him [i.e., Apostle Paul] were admirable, should in your mouths but argue rashness" (vi.3).[48]

Yet, having so stated his case, Hooker is cautious not to overstate it. He does not suggest that his own interpretation is infallible, thus avoiding the trap in which the Puritans have fallen. He readily admits that even experts can err:

God was not ignorant that the priests and judges, whose sentence in matters of controversy he ordained should stand, both might and oftentimes would be deceived in their judgment. Howbeit, better it was in the eye of His understanding, that sometime an erroneous sentence definitive should prevail, till the same authority perceiving such oversight, might afterwards correct or reverse it, than that strifes should have respite to grow, and not come speedily unto some end. [vi.3; cf. 5–6]

In other words, the kind of church government that Hooker defends is open to change. Within such a church, truth is available and can be recorded with an impressive measure of accuracy, yet it is never possessed in such a way that the process of search could be prematurely ended and the partial insights of one age permanently absolutized. The failure to take such a stand is the weakness of both the Puritans and Rome. As Hooker notes: "Two things there are which trouble greatly these later times: one, that the Church of Rome cannot, another, that Geneva will not erre."[49]

Second, having established their authority with empty rhetoric, the Puritans single out the present form of government in the Church of England as the cause of "all faults and corruptions, wherewith the world aboundeth." They simply overlook "human frailty and corruption" as the continuous source of evil present throughout all human history (iii.7). In response, Hooker elaborates the ways of reaching truth he has proposed; here some of his rejoinders are strikingly deft. For example, his restatement of an insight recorded by John Calvin would have been particularly persuasive—or at least irksome—to the Puritans: "If it be granted a thing unlawful for private men, not called unto public consultation, to dispute which is the best state of civil polity, (with a desire of bringing in some other kind, than that under which they already live, for of such disputes I take it his meaning was); if it be a thing confessed, that of such questions they cannot determine without rashness, inasmuch as a great part of them consisteth in special circumstances, and for one kind as many reasons may be brought as for another; is there any reason in the world, why they should better judge what kind of regiment ecclesiastical is the fittest?" (iii.4).[50] Turning his attention to the relationship between individual and society, he argues that the

Puritans have overlooked the significant fact that the church is a society. Before high ideals can be translated into meaningful reality, the political and social needs—and limitations—of a society have to be recognized. Therefore, in a preliminary agreement with the Puritans, Hooker is prepared to acknowledge that the visible church has its shortcomings. But he is unwilling to conclude that these result from an avoidable fault rather than a necessary finitude (iii.7).

In the third place, Hooker records it as a Puritan habit "to propose their own form of church-government, as the only sovereign remedy of all evils; and to adorn it with all the glorious titles that may be." Two particularly apt comparisons come to his mind. The seriously ill and the almost delirious often imagine that the least known cure will bring them the greatest help (iii.8), and the Anabaptists in their own theorizing aspire to emulate the most positive ideals, yet in actual practice fail to follow any (viii.6–ix.4). In short, while not lacking in idealism, Hooker consistently seeks to be a realist, relating his own proposals to the concrete situations in which the church finds herself. He knows that wishful thinking may attract a following but will not solve any of life's serious problems.

Fourth, Hooker observes that the tragedy is genuine—the Puritans are actually sincere! They have persuaded themselves of the absolute correctness of their own claims. When they consult Scripture, they really think it supports their views. Such self-delusion, of course, is not new. In the ancient world it befell the Pythagoreans and in more recent times the so-called "Family of Love" (iii.9). In response to this situation, Hooker observes that, generally, the best strategy against error is a concerned and objective exegesis of the Scripture that does not lose the truth in the process of searching for it (iii.9).

Fifth, believing themselves to be the only correct interpreters of the Scripture, the Puritans erroneously conclude "that it is the special illumination of the Holy Ghost, whereby they discern those things in the word, which others reading yet discern them not" (iii.10; cf. 7).[51] For Hooker, such a conviction requires further examination in the light of both Scripture and reason, since these are the only two ways by which truth can be reached: "It is not therefore the fervent earnestness of their persuasion, but the soundness of those reasons whereupon the same is built, which must declare their opinions in these things to have been wrought by the Holy Ghost, and not by the fraud of that evil spirit, which is even in his illusions strong" (iii.10).

Sixth, the Puritans insist that precisely because they are guided by such an illumination, they are thereby assured of election to eternal life. In this fashion their particular brand of self-delusion becomes the touchstone of their own authenticity, while all others are branded as "worldlings, time-servers, pleasers of men not of God" (iii.11).

Consequently, forewarned by the Puritan example, Hooker records a profound unwillingness to accept subjective persuasion, however sincere, as a hallmark of truth. Thus when discussing the appropriateness of the particular ceremonies that have been adopted by the Church of England, Hooker challenges the Puritans to "shew some commission, whereby they are authorized to sit as judges, and we required to take their judgment for good in this case. Otherwise their sentences will not be greatly regarded, when they oppose their *methinketh* unto the orders of the Church of England..." (IV.iv.2).[52] And in another passage he writes: "it is but conceit in them to think, that those Romish ceremonies whereof we have hitherto spoken, are like leprous clothes, infectious unto the Church, or like soft and gentle poisons, the venom whereof being insensibly pernicious, worketh death, and yet is never felt working. Thus they say: but because they say it only, and the world hath not as yet had so great experience of their art in curing the diseases of the Church, that the bare authority of their word should persuade in a cause so weighty, they may not think much if it be required at their hands to shew" just why this should be the case (IV.x.2).[53] Moreover, Hooker is convinced that private errors have public consequences: "schism and disturbance in the Church...must needs grow if all men might think what they list and speak openly what they think...." (*Answer to Travers*, 17).

By contrast, Hooker's own theological method is characterized by a genuine passion for objectivity. The manner in which Hooker seeks to sustain it indicates that his concerns are broad, including attitudes toward persons no less than the specific data of research. Thus in regard to the Puritans themselves, with whom "contentions are now at their highest float," Hooker still hopes for a dramatic and profound experience of "unfeignedly reconciled love," as was once felt between Joseph and his brethren (Pref.ix.4). And even before the broken unity has been restored, the debate between Hooker and the Puritans is not to be seen as a contest that would justify a disregard for the opponent. Instead, the entire investigation of the laws of ecclesiastical polity is to be seen as a devout and objective quest for the truth. On more than one occasion Hooker records an eloquent plea that the Puritans should read his writings with the openness and respect that has characterized his own attitude: "Think not that ye read the words of one who bendeth himself as an adversary against the truth which ye have already embraced; but the words of one who desireth even to embrace together with you the self-same truth, if it be the truth; and for that cause (for no other, God he knoweth) hath undertaken the burdensome labour of this painful kind of conference" (Pref.i.3). And again: "read . . . [my writings] with the same mind you read Mr. Calvin's writings, bear yourself as unpartial in the one as in the other: imagine him to speak that which I do: lay aside your unindifferent mind, change but your spectacles, and I assure myself that all will be clearly true . . ." (v.App.i.6).[54]

Having set high standards, Hooker follows them. While there are occasions when Hooker does not hesitate to record his disapproval of Puritan extremes, he expresses at the same time his continuous respect for John Calvin, whom he regards as the father of Puritanism, acknowledging an implicit regard for the Puritans as well. Calvin is "incomparably the wisest man that ever the French Church did enjoy, since the hour it enjoyed him" (Pref.ii.1).[55] In other words, formal concerns with the truth, if they are to be at all successful, must go hand in hand with a desire for maturity on the part of the interpreter. Such an ideal is etched most clearly on those occasions where Hooker reflects on what it means to be a judicious interpreter. Although sometimes Hooker has joined "judicious and wise" (v.lxv.6) or "learned, judicious, and polite" (lxxxi.15) in order to describe a significant though not uncommon accomplishment, most often he employs the term "judicious" as a superlative. Thus when Hooker distinguishes between obeying the law, of which everyone is capable, and evaluating the law, he attributes the latter only to "the wiser and more judicious" (I.xvi.2). Or, as Hooker distinguishes between the wisdom of "the ancient sages of the world" and that of the contemporary sophists who are "turning things that are serious into mockery," he singles out the sages as alone possessing "judicious learning" (v.ii.2). Similarly, a contrast between two exegetes, only one of whom has really grasped the meaning of the text, leads Hooker to describe it as "a more judicious exposition" (lxii.21). A true consensus is upheld by all "judicious men" (xx.5). The consequences of vanity can be foretold by "wise and judicious men," (lxxiv.4) and Aristotle is referred to as "the most judicious philosopher, whose eye scarce any thing did escape which was to be found in the bosom of nature" (VIII.ii.12). If an insight is absolutely correct, then "no judicious man will ever" doubt it (VII.xviii.9). And a "grave and judicious" person will not disagree with what is true (xiv.13; cf. IV.xi.12).[56]

Admittedly, such an exaltation of judicious learning could be but a guise for an underhanded selection of a jury which will then decide in favor of Hooker and against the Puritans. Hooker's rhetorical acumen notwithstanding, he intends no deception and indeed reveals his true character. Though blessed with a sense of humor, he is an utterly serious man who will not dissimulate in order to win an argument. At the same time, his appeal to judicious learning as the ideal for the Christian scholar pays far more attention to fundamental attitudes than to specific formulations. What the truth is in each case still remains to be ferreted out in the light of revelation and reason. When Hooker encounters in Peter Ramus a theological method that promises instant solutions to every problem, he reacts with a scorn appropriate for dilettantes, and his evaluation is swift and devastating:

In the poverty of that other new devised aid two things there are notwithstanding singular. Of marvellous quick despatch it is, and doth shew them that have it as much almost in three days, as if it dwell threescore years with them. Again, because the curiosity of man's wit doth many times with peril wade farther in the search of things than were convenient; the same is thereby restrained unto such generalities as every where offering themselves are apparent unto men of the weakest conceit that need be. So as following the rules and precepts thereof, we may define it to be, an Art which teacheth the way of speedy discourse, and restraineth the mind of man that it may not wax over-wise. [I.vi.4][57]

By contrast, the approach preferred by Hooker presupposes hard and diligent work—a conviction recorded by use of well-chosen epigrams: "The search of knowledge is a thing painful" (vii.7); "but as every thing of price, so this doth require travail" (v.xxi.3). In other words, the kind of truth that Hooker is speaking about does not lie within easy reach (Pref.iii.2). He assumes that once gained, it will not be recognized by those who dislike diligent labor: "He that goeth about to persuade a multitude, that they are not so well governed as they ought to be, shall never want attentive and favourable hearers; because they know the manifold defects whereunto every kind of regiment is subject, but the secret lets and difficulties, which in public proceedings are innumerable and inevitable, they have not ordinarily the judgment to consider" (I.i.i). At the same time, Hooker is fully aware that since he defends a *status quo*, his approach may be mistaken for an essentially selfish act whereby "we either hold or seek preferment" (i.1). Even so, Hooker hopes that his position can be distinguished from the naive subjectivism of the Puritans or from any approach that stresses acceptance without examination and understanding. Although his own reasoning, as he admits, may appear "perhaps tedious, perhaps obscure, dark, and intricate" (i.2), the invitation to examine all evidence and to consider all problems is extended seriously, for it implies the firm belief that there will be judicious men who will follow such an objective route.

In order to appreciate the scope of Hooker's invitation for inquiry, we must remember that he was a sixteenth-century churchman. His pleas for utter objectivity, however precisely stated, are in fact more inclusive than we could expect in comparison to modern demands for the use of the scientific method. He viewed truth in terms of natural and supernatural categories and, therefore, as consisting of data obtained by both reason and revelation. That is to say, while the Continental Reformers attempted to be biblical theologians, Hooker made conscious use of the scholastic method and at the same time worked for a convergence of both traditions. Moreover, Hooker recognized that Scripture does not speak to many important problems of human life and it is necessary to employ insights that have been obtained by right use of man's powers of reasoning. At the moment we cannot follow Hooker's further attempts to correlate faith and reason, but we should note that in speaking about reason, he also thought about man who makes use of his reason: here was occasion for both hope and, sometimes, despair.

For the most part, Hooker exalts the significance of human diligence and judicious perspicuity in the search for truth. While not denying the possibility of effortless creativity and visionary insight, he by and large assumes that the main advances always have been made by pious and intelligent men who have devoted themselves to disciplined prayer and thinking. By such means the precious ore of truth has been gathered out of the depth:

> The stateliness of houses, the goodliness of trees, when we behold them delighteth the eye; but that foundation which beareth up the one, that root which ministereth unto the other nourishment and life, is in the bosom of the earth concealed; and if there be at any time occasions to search into it, such labour is then more necessary than pleasant, both to them which undertake it and for the lookers-on. In like manner, the use and benefit of good laws all that live under them may enjoy with delight and comfort, albeit the grounds and first original causes from whence they have sprung be unknown, as to the greatest part of men they are. But when they who withdraw their obedience pretend that the laws which they should obey are corrupt and vicious; for better examination of their quality, it behoveth the very foundation and root, the highest wellspring and fountain of them to be discovered. [I.i.2]

In other words, Hooker's main thrust is his affirmation that with genuine effort truth can be discovered. This is the foundation of his hope and the rationale for his own diligence. At the same time, he is realistically aware of the necessity to proclaim the need for such an endeavor. He does not doubt that his generation needs such a message, for "this present age [is] full of tongue and weak of brain" (viii.2). Only too often superficial but loud arguments have elicited a better following than the carefully reasoned statements of true worth. Hence it is not surprising that Hooker should show an occasional sense of despair: "Such is naturally our affection, that whom in great things we mightily admire, in them we are not persuaded willingly that any thing should be amiss. The reason whereof is, 'for that as dead flies putrify the ointment of the apothecary, so a little folly him that is in estimation for wisdom' (Eccles., x, 1). This in every profession hath too much authorized the judgment of a few. This with Germans hath caused Luther, and with many other Churches Calvin, to prevail in all things" (Pref.iv.8). But the despair does not overwhelm Hooker. From it he draws one more warning against mere subjectivity, observing that no man except Christ can be always right (iv.8; cf. ix.1). At the same time, his basic thrust is highly positive. He is deeply convinced that truth will not perish from this earth. As he sees it, truth is not a human invention, unique and unrepeatable; it is a subjectively gained insight that has an objective foundation in reality itself. Many judicious observers, their subjectivity notwithstanding, nevertheless acknowledge the same truth. Nor does the presence of truth depend entirely upon the efforts of judicious men alone. All men have been created so as to long ardently for what is true: "the mind of man desireth evermore to know the truth according to the most infallible certainty which the nature of things can yield" (II.vii.5). To be sure, man is no longer in the state of original righteousness. Sin has intervened, and man's soul now "preferreth rest in ignorance before wearisome labour to know." Yet God has not forsaken fallen man: "For a spur of diligence therefore we have a natural thirst after knowledge ingrafted in us" (I.vii.7).

Considered in regard to its ultimate origin, truth has but one source, God himself (xi.5). At the same time, as far as the human approach to truth is concerned, Hooker believes that there are two major avenues open to man: "There are but two ways whereby the

Spirit leadeth men into all truth; the one extraordinary, the other common; the one belonging but unto some few, the other extending itself unto all that are of God; the one, that which we call by a special divine excellency Revelation, the other Reason" (Pref.iii.10).

Although Hooker's full understanding of reason cannot be elaborated at this point, a significant aspect of his total perspective may be noted—that is, the reason which Hooker places alongside with revelation is not the general capacity for thinking present in all men, but only the special kind of judicious reasoning present in all those who "are of God" (iii.10). By contrast, those who are not redeemed by grace possess only a perverted reason that cannot function properly. Moreover, in speaking about reason redeemed by grace, Hooker thinks in terms of three interrelated yet distinct levels. In this way he erects a safeguard against its too superficial use. The first level consists of intuitive knowledge, whereby the first principles of reason are recognized as self-evidently true (II.vii.5). Here the certainty is absolute, "free from all possibility of error, clear and manifest without proof" (I.viii.5), but such principles are not numerous. The second level of knowledge is established by "strong and invincible demonstration," yet truth is not necessarily more accessible here than on the preceding level. Although "it is not by any way possible to be deceived," this assurance holds true only insofar as specific proofs are actually presented and duly examined. At the same time, the presentation of proofs is a rather complicated undertaking that requires diligence, insight, and caution. Finally, where the first two levels have failed, there remains a third, the level of "greatest probability" which men prefer when more certain knowledge is not available (II.vii.5). Thus while it is possible to discover truth through reason on all three levels, men's actual success is never as high as when they are dealing with the Scripture as the source of truth. Therefore, whenever Hooker exalts the significance of grace-redeemed reason, he is mainly considering a principle rather than recording what in fact most often happens in human life. In practice the kind of truth that has been revealed in Scripture does possess a unique advantage, for it is incontrovertible: "that for which we have probable, yea, that which we have necessary reason for, yea, that which we see with our eyes, is not thought so sure as that which the Scripture of God teacheth; because we hold that his speech revealeth there what himself seeth, and therefore the strongest proof of all, and the most necessarily assented unto by us (which do thus receive the Scripture) is the Scripture" (II.vii.5).

Though he has come close to the Puritan position, Hooker has not sided with it. Two significant reservations remain. First, there are problems in life for which Scripture provides no specific answers and where reason must be employed. Second, even Scripture itself is understood with the help of reason and may be misunderstood or applied quite inappropriately (vii.9). Thus at no time is it possible to escape the problem of subjectivity. Although the approaches are not the same, whether we are dealing with reason or with Scripture, we always obtain truth discursively, and the possibility of error cannot be ruled out in advance. To put it in another way, Hooker recognizes that a mere appeal—be it to reason or to Scripture—does not automatically produce truth. There simply is no theological method, however correct, that can itself ensure its own infallibility. Even when the best method is most judiciously employed, it yields, at the very best, only the highest probability that can be humanly achieved and is never beyond further debate.

However, such a recognition of human finitude does not force Hooker into theological inactivity. If the highest probability is the best that can be achieved, then it is important to make certain that it is actually gained. Here the best route is not by independent research but in close dependence on the most judicious men that have preceded us. A good case in point is provided by the discovery of the best human laws: "Laws, as all other things human, are many times full of imperfection; and that which is supposed behoveful unto men, proveth oftentimes most pernicious. The wisdom which is learned by tract of time, findeth the laws that have been in former ages established, needful in later to be abrogated" (IV.xiv.1). Understanding "laws" as basic principles for right action, he suggests that the correspondence between reality and the laws that describe it must be thought of in dynamic terms. That is to say, he knows that there have been many laws which at one time have been written with great thoughtfulness. When examined at the time of their codification, they seemed to correspond to the existing structures of reality and human need. Yet it was subsequently recognized that such laws were "true" only on the surface. Their correspondence to reality was partial, not complete, and they were later found to be inadequate. These laws became outdated because they did not allow continuous application to new situations. Hooker's point is that such an inadequacy could be recognized only through their use in changing situations, that the truth of a given law can be fully perceived only through experience. Only in the light of many such experiences could genuine wisdom be obtained (v.i.2). So it is with all truth. Even apart from native ability and diligence in formulation, the finite scope of human life does not allow one individual to grasp all truth with the same degree of probability as is possible through the cumulative experience of many judicious men over many centuries. Wisdom—in the true sense of that word—is proclaimed not by individual men but by whole nations living through centuries. This is the best available vantage point from which to obtain the highest measure of truth: "The general and perpetual voice of men is as the sentence of God himself. For that which all men have at all times learned, Nature herself must needs have taught; and God being the author of Nature, her voice is but his instrument" (I.viii.3). And again, "That which all men's experience teacheth them may not in any wise be denied" (III.viii.14).

By pointing to such a universality of agreement, Hooker is not suggesting some concrete and formally reached agreement. He is aware that what this agreement might be in any specific case still remains to be stated. Even so, he has recognized a principle of significant usefulness. Intrinsically rational, objectively grounded in reality itself, the consensus principle allows an important reduction of the daily present danger of the error that arises through subjectivity. Understood in this way, the truth has not been offered for a popular vote. The *consensus gentium* remains an aristocratic rather than a democratic principle.[58] It suggests what the best minds can come to recognize, rather than what all minds have in fact already recognized. Most certainly, the appeal to a universal consensus does not in itself ensure that he who has made use of it has done it well. Rather, it invites further discussion and nurtures a climate of deliberation with seriousness and diligence. It is the kind of theological stance which Hooker thought best for any man genuinely interested in truth, and he proposed it as a means of furthering theological thinking in his own generation. In this way, right reason is not viewed as a mere abstraction but will have been embodied in the judicious thinkers of the church. These men will look at the complexities of their contemporary world in the broader perspective of truth. As occasion arises, they will draw upon wisdom, either as discovered by reason and refined through the centuries, or as revealed by God in the Holy Scripture.

At the same time Hooker can foresee situations—and here he is reflecting on his own encounters with the Puritans—in which neither time nor occasion permits a detailed explanation. Or it can happen that the individual to whom a specific explanation has been offered does not succeed in comprehending it. Then the leaders must nevertheless be followed. Yet such an obedience, strictly speaking, is not arbitrary, because it takes place in response to truth, however implicit: "It is therefore the voice both of God and nature, not of learning only, that especially in matters of action and policy, 'The sentences and judgments of men experienced, aged and wise, yea though they speak without any proof or demonstration, are no less to be hearkened unto, than as being demonstrations in themselves; because such men's long observation is as an eye, wherewith they presently and plainly behold those principles which sway over all actions'" (v.vii.2). Hooker firmly believes that unless such a course of action is followed, chaos will ensue, and in chaos truth is ordinarily lost. Thus where we discover "singularity"—that is, a unilateral course of action that claims to follow the guidance of the Holy Spirit—there it is in order to reflect: if this particular insight is true, why did not God give it to other men as well? Hooker never appeals to reason as the only touchstone for truth, he consistently preserves the traditional twofold understanding of truth as both natural and supernatural, and he does not prejudge which means God should employ in disclosing a truth more widely than to one individual only. Truth may be obtained "either with miraculous operation, or with strong and invincible remonstrance of sound Reason" (v.x.1). Moreover, the test of truth always consists in its success in persuading others: "God hath not moved their hearts to think such things as he hath not enabled them to prove" (x.1). In this way he is once more pointing to the methodological role of the consensus rather than merely proposing the credulity of many as the norm for individual piety. Genuine authority is never arbitrary. That no authority had ever any right to contradict Scripture was such an obvious Protestant insight of his own day that Hooker does not even try to defend it. He simply assumes it, focusing his attention on the principle that every authoritative demand must be rational: "that authority of men should prevail with men either against or above Reason, is no part of our belief" (II.vii.6). In short, "Be it in matter of the one kind or of the other, what Scripture doth plainly deliver, to that the first place both of credit and obedience is due; the next whereunto is whatsoever any man can necessarily conclude by force of reason; after these the voice of the Church succeedeth. That which the Church by her ecclesiastical authority shall probably think and define to be true or good, must in congruity of reason overrule all other inferior judgments whatsoever" (v.viii.2).

When such guidelines are judiciously followed, an entire theological system can emerge. It will be neither exclusively a biblical theology nor merely a rational construct, but will have made use of both. Most important, while written by one man, it will not be narrowly his subjectivistic theology, but a devout offering to the church to accept and to remold it, should it so choose, for its own.

III

As part of the general thrust of his theology, Hooker has also thought about the methodology of scriptural interpretation. Although he wrote no commentaries on the Scripture—his preaching was more concerned with particular theological problems than with the detailed exposition of specific texts—he interpreted Scripture with notable skill.[59] Moreover, he recorded his presuppositions, described his method of exegesis, and made some overall observations concerning the larger issue of hermeneutic. Once assessed, his contribution is substantial and of considerable originality.

The larger context of Hooker's theological labors nurtured a conservative outlook. He sees himself as wedged in between two powerful extremes.[60] One is Roman Catholicism, which, in Hooker's day, regarded Scripture as a partial source of "all revealed and supernatural truth" that must be supplemented by tradition, if salvation is to be obtained (II.viii.7).[61] The other, Puritanism, believed that Scripture contains absolutely all directives that are mandatory for a Christian life. As a result, "to do any thing according to any other law were not only unnecessary but even opposite unto salvation, unlawful and sinful" (viii.7; cf. iii.1). Although Hooker's basic position remains constant, his accent varies depending on whether he is addressing Rome or Geneva.

Thus, over against Roman Catholics, Hooker repeatedly underscores the "absolute perfection of Scripture" in regard to its ultimate purpose: "the testimonies of God are all sufficient unto that end for which they were given. Therefore accordingly we do receive them, we do not think that in them God hath omitted any thing needful unto his purpose, and left his intent to be accomplished by our devisings. What the Scripture purposeth, the same in all points it doth perform. Howbeit that here we swerve not in judgment, one thing especially we must observe, namely that the absolute perfection of Scripture is seen by relation unto that end whereto it tendeth" (viii. 5).[62] Yet such an outspoken defense of the perfection of Scripture is not to be mistaken for a simple dismissal of the entire extrabiblical

Christian heritage. Rather, at this point, Hooker is only concerned to preserve the so-called "sufficiency" of the Scripture in regard to those purposes for which it was given to mankind.[63] Hooker believes that any other stand would jeopardize the Scripture as a supernaturally given revelation. At the same time, he does not deny that for those spheres of life where Scripture is silent, human reason must gain knowledge in addition to revelation. Therefore, he always correlates "sufficiency" with the "appointed use." As such, scriptural sufficiency is not viewed as absolute but only as valid in regard to specific goals: "We count those things perfect which want nothing requisite for the end whereto they were instituted. As therefore God created every part and particle of man exactly perfect, that is to say in all points sufficient unto that use for which he appointed it; so the Scripture, yea, every sentence thereof, is perfect, and wanteth nothing requisite unto that purpose for which God delivered the same" (II.viii.5). Therefore, Roman Catholics must be challenged whenever they rely on sources outside the Scripture and treat them as Scripture. This includes appeals to church councils (vii.5) and to oral tradition (I.xiii.2; xiv.5; Serm.II.11). Consequently, it should not be surprising that in opposing Rome, Hooker can sound as outspoken as any good Puritan. For example, Hooker can proclaim: "God himself can neither possibly err, nor lead into error. For this cause his testimonies, whatsoever he affirmeth, are always truth and most infallible certainty." Yet Hooker is not a Puritan; hence the qualification remains intact: "Yea further, because the things that proceed from him are perfect without any manner of deficit or maim; it cannot be but that the words of his mouth are absolute, and lack nothing which they should have for performance of that thing whereunto they tend" (II.vi.1).

As Hooker sees it, the Puritans have not recognized the need for such caution and have asserted the perfection of Scripture without the attention to its "appointed use." He sees the Puritans as "racking and stretching it further than by him was meant," proclaiming "that in Scripture all things lawful to be done must needs be contained" (viii.5; cf. I.xvi.5). In contrast, Hooker believes that it is wrong to imagine that "God in delivering Scripture to his Church should clean have abrogated amongst them the law of nature..." (II.viii.6; cf. iv.7). The moment we think that revelation abrogates the valid conclusions reached by judicious reasoning, Scripture becomes merely "a snare and a torment to weak consciences, filling them with infinite perplexities, scrupulosities, doubts insoluble, and extreme despairs" (viii.6). Moreover, the Puritans demand the impossible, since there are innumerable situations for which no revealed insight is given but human reason must wisely supply it:

> For in every action of common life to find out some sentence clearly and infallibly setting before our eyes what we ought to do, (seem we in Scripture never so expert,) would trouble us more than we are aware. In weak and tender minds we little know what misery this strict opinion would breed, besides the stops it would make in the whole course of all men's lives and actions. Make all things sin which we do by direction of nature's light, and by the rule of common discretion, without thinking at all upon Scripture; admit this position, and parents shall cause their children to sin, as oft as they cause them to do any thing, before they come to years of capacity and be ripe for knowledge in the Scripture: admit this, and it shall not be with masters as it was with him in the Gospel, but servants being commanded to go shall stand still, till they have their errand warranted unto them by Scripture. [II.viii.6][64]

If taken indiscriminately, the Reformation call of *sola Scriptura* is completely subverted.[65] Of course, unlike the Puritans, neither Luther nor Zwingli nor Calvin ever meant it in such a narrow sense; they were prepared to acknowledge the useful role of reason in its appropriate domain. Hence in opposing the hermeneutical presuppositions of the Puritans, Hooker is not abandoning the basic perspective of the magisterial Reformers. He is merely pointing to a rather obvious failing among the Puritans. And in so doing, he uncovers the deeper roots of the Puritan error, that their argument is circular. Assuming that their church discipline is thoroughly scriptural, they insist that the very finding of their discipline in the Scripture has been the direct result of "the illumination of the Spirit" (Pref.iii.16).[66] But actually they have proceeded "only by poor and marvellous slight conjectures" (iv.1). Thus they end by ascribing "divine authority" to what is but their "own erroneous collections" (viii.5; cf. II.vii.9).

Since neither the church nor the faithful individual can be assumed to receive infallible guidance by the Holy Spirit, the task of the interpreter of the Scripture becomes especially significant. He must weigh all the available evidence, seek the best insight possible, and finally exercise very cautious judgment. Before he proclaims, he must have probed deeply. In the end, though a measure of truth can be obtained by the judicious searcher, he must acknowledge that the best insights are only relatively true.

Such an approach, which Hooker adopted for his own, rests on three important presuppositions. First, that Scripture is the Word of God and absolutely necessary for salvation. He restates this basic conviction in several ways: "Nature is no sufficient teacher what we should do that we may attain unto life everlasting" (II.viii.3; cf. III.iii.3); Scripture "teacheth things above nature, things which our reason by itself could not reach unto" (III.viii.12; cf. I.xv.4); Scripture contains "supernatural truths which cannot otherwise be demonstrated" (v.App.I.14). Such a formulation is essentially Thomistic. St Thomas had customarily distinguished between revealed knowledge and that obtained by human reasoning, and taught that revelation is above reason and must be accepted in faith: "If our opponent believes nothing of divine revelation, there is no longer any means of proving the article of faith by reasoning, but only of answering his objections—if he has any—against faith."[67] In a similar vein, Hooker contrasts the role of reason in the natural sciences with the discovery of the truth of the Christian faith that is revealed. Here he can say that "the things which we properly believe be only such as are received upon the credit of divine testimony" (v.xxii.5), as well as to note that "the simplicity of faith which is in Christ taketh the naked promise of God, his bare word, and on that it resteth" (Serm.I).

The second presupposition is that Scripture does not consist exclusively of supernatural laws, but contains numerous laws of nature as well. Although a discussion of Hooker's understanding of law belongs in another context, we may suggest here why it is that he finds the presence of natural laws within Scripture of such significance.

While supernatural laws are given by revelation only, cannot be established by human reasoning, and must be accepted on faith, natural laws are structures of reality that can be recognized by human reason. Hence it is important to consider for what purpose natural laws have been included in the Scripture among revealed laws. Hooker suggests a threefold rationale: (1) Men are induced to believe in supernatural laws when they discover them alongside natural laws in the same Scripture; the truth of natural laws is provable by reason; hence, it is possible for men to recognize that Scripture is at least partially trustworthy and to transfer this trust to supernatural laws, also contained in Scripture but beyond rational proof. (2) Although through close association in the same Scripture natural laws can enhance the credibility of the divine laws, the reverse is also true and needs to be acknowledged (I.xii.1). (3) Finally, although "the first principles of the Law of Nature are easy; hard it were to find men ignorant of them" (xii.2), in practice human sin and subsequent ignorance have altered the situation. Men can no longer grasp natural laws with ease. Yet once they are revealed and recorded in Scripture, men have been given considerable assistance toward better obtaining of truth (xii.2-3).

Such a Thomistic distinction between natural and supernatural knowledge, as well as reason and faith, allows Hooker to establish what might be loosely designated as the human dimension of Scripture. God is its author, yet it contains wisdom both divine and human. The notion of human wisdom allows Scripture to participate in the same class of wisdom that is discovered by right reason outside it. Or, as Hooker puts it, with the Puritans in mind, just because an insight is reached by way of right reasoning, it does not necessarily follow that it must be opposed to Scripture (II.i.4).

Third, Hooker presupposes the divine authorship of Scripture. Yet while he seems to accept a verbal inspiration,[68] he is circumspect in its use and at times qualifies it to a considerable extent. Thus when reflecting upon the origins of Scripture, he distinguishes between revelation and inspiration: "In the first age of the world God gave laws unto our fathers, and by reason of the number of their days their

memories served instead of books; whereof the manifold imperfections and defects being known to God, he mercifully relieved the
same by often putting them in mind of that whereof it behoved them
to be specially mindful. In which respect we see how many times one
thing has been iterated unto sundry even of the best and wisest among
them" (I.xiii.1). In one of his sermons he puts it this way:

But God himself was their instructor, he himself taught them, partially by dreams
and visions in the night, partly by revelations in the day, taking them aside from
amongst their brethren, and talking with them as a man would talk with his
neighbour in the way. Thus they became acquainted even with the secret and
hidden counsels of God. They saw things which themselves were not able to utter,
they beheld that whereat men and angels are astonished. They understood in the
beginning, what should come to pass in the last days. [Ser.v.3]

Although Hooker does not say that in the days of revelation men
were actually preserved from all error, he seems to assume it. His
exuberant description of the repetition of revelation for the sake of
remembrance and the acknowledged and continued nearness of God
to these patriarchs suggest a kind of supernatural saturation with
revelatory insight. No occasion seems to be left for any misunderstanding or even partial grasp.

At the same time, Hooker is convinced that revelation, once received, is preserved intact. He notes that when "the lives of men were
shortened," it was necessary to prevent "oblivion and corruption"
(I.xiii.1). God achieved this goal by actually directing the process
of recording Scripture itself: "First therefor of Moyses it is said, that
he 'wrote all the words of God;' not by his own private motion and
device: for God taketh this act to himself, 'I have written.' Furthermore, were not the Prophets following commanded also to do the
like? Unto the holy evangelist St. John, how often express charge is
given, 'Scribe,' 'Write these things'" (I.xiii.2). That here some kind
of verbal inspiration is meant seems beyond reasonable doubt. Convinced of the absolute perfection of God, Hooker finds it appropriate
that the divine handiwork should share in the same divine attributes:
"All those venerable books of Scripture...are with such absolute
perfection framed, that in them there neither wanteth any thing the

lack whereof might deprive us of life, nor any thing in such wise aboundeth, that as being superfluous, unfruitful, and altogether needless, we should think it no loss or danger at all if we did want it" (I.xiii.3; cf. I.xv.4; II.vi.1). Admittedly, the context of such a statement is polemical, directed as it is against the Roman Catholic reliance on tradition as an extrascriptural channel for the transmission of revelation; as Hooker warns, "What hazard the truth is in when it passeth through the hands of report, how maimed and deformed it becometh, they are not, they cannot possibly be ignorant"(I.xiii.2). Yet he is not merely polemicizing, he is also spelling out his own deeper presuppositions. Only because he is convinced that Scripture is *sui generis* and differs from all other literary documents does he find it necessary to oppose anyone who will place beside Scripture other writings that have not been divinely inspired. Moreover, when he speaks of the inspiration of Scripture in a clearly nonpolemical context, he continues to affirm its divine authorship. Describing the miracle of divine inspiration in a sermon, he contrasts it with those more ordinary occasions where a scriptural insight is to be communicated. Then it is first of all necessary to grasp the inner meaning of the text that one desires to explain to others. But when this has happened, thorough and prolonged deliberation is still in order: "how great, how long, how earnest meditation are we forced to use!" The right selection of words as well as clarity of expression are no easy tasks. Even so, an automatic projection of what we want to communicate is in no way assured: "And after much travail and much pains, when we open our lips to speak of the wonderful works of God, our tongues do falter within our mouths, yea many times we disgrace the dreadful mysteries of our faith, and grieve the spirit of our hearers by words unsavoury, and unseemly speeches...." In speaking about God, even the "wisest" among men do so "as if the children which are carried in arms should speak of the greatest matters of state" (Serm.v.4).

By contrast, when the prophets proclaim the truth of God, they are guided "by the secret inspiration of God" (Serm.v.2). "God, which lightened thus the eyes of their understanding, giving them knowledge by unusual and extraordinary means, did also miraculously himself frame and fashion their words and writings…" (Serm. v.4). And again:

so oft as he employed them in this heavenly work, they neither spake nor wrote any word of their own, but uttered syllable by syllable as the Spirit put it into their mouths, no otherwise than the harp or the lute doth give a sound according to the discretion of his hands that holdeth and striketh it with skill. The difference is only this: an instrument, whether it be a pipe or a harp, maketh a distinction in the times and sounds, which distinction is well perceived of the hearer, the instrument itself understanding not what is piped or harped. The prophets and holy men of God not so…they felt the power and strength of their own words. When they spake of our peace, every corner of their hearts was filled with joy. When they prophesied of mourning, lamentations, and woes, to fall upon us, they wept in the bitterness and indignation of spirit, the arm of the Lord being mighty and strong upon them. [Serm.v.4]

Here Hooker is unmistakably recording his conviction that revelation is a divinely guided process. Its outcome is predetermined and allows no variables. Such a conviction, of course, was rather the rule in his age. Historically considered, it is less remarkable that Hooker should have affirmed a verbal inspiration of Scripture than that, in the course of subsequent reflection, he sought to introduce several qualifications.[69] Two of the more significant ones may be noted.

First, within the larger discussion of the inspiration of Scripture, Hooker has introduced two contrasting sets of scriptural quotation. One serves to document the anguishing lack of insight which the writers of Scripture experienced and confessed when they spoke merely "as men" and thus without divine guidance (Serm.v.4; cf. Wisdom 9:6, Job 42:3, and II Macc. 15:38). The other set of passages, which acknowledge the reception of inspiration, do so only vis-à-vis a particular situation, without suggesting that all the rest of Scripture is similarly inspired (Serm.v.4; cf. Isa. 49:3, I Cor. 2:12–13). Nowhere does Hooker ever quote II Tim. 3:16 in its entirety ("All scripture is inspired by God and profitable for teaching, for reproof, for correction, and for training in righteousness"). On the two occasions when he actually refers to this passage, he makes use of the second half without underscoring that "all scripture is inspired by

God" (II.i.4; v.xxii.10). An implicit distinction between uninspired and inspired Scripture may therefore suggest that Hooker ignores the message of a key verse in order to qualify the blanket affirmation of total inspiration customary in his day. His view of Scripture is thus rather more reflective than could have been assumed at a rapid glance, and the balanced vantage point that results is in accord with his general theological perspective. For the belief in the reality of inspiration of some but not all of Scripture allows him to appeal to such revealed truth as is absolutely certain and unquestionable. At the same time, his distinction between two levels of Scripture leads him to make use of judicious reasoning in dealing with verses that are not inspired. In this way, his exegetical endeavors are no longer limited to a pedestrian interpretation of Scripture, a restatement of its contents passage by passage (III.viii.16), but on the grounds of specific exegesis of selected texts and judicious reasoning, he can build a systematic theology that is truly overarching and encompasses all wisdom available to man.

Second, an expression of basically the same concern may be seen in Hooker's distinction between central and peripheral ideas of Scripture. Here the principle of selectivity is spelled out as Christocentric:

The main drift of the whole New Testament is that which St. John setteth down a[5] the purpose of his own history; "These things are written, that ye might believe that Jesus is Christ the Son of God, and that in believing ye might have life through his name." The drift of the Old that which the Apostle mentioneth to Timothy, "The Holy Scriptures are able to make thee wise unto salvation." So that the general end both of Old and New is one; the difference between them consisting in this, that the Old did make wise by teaching salvation through Christ that should come, the New by teaching that Christ the Saviour is come, and that Jesus whom the Jews did crucify, and whom God did raise again from the dead, is he. [I.xiv.4]

And in a sermon Hooker writes: "prophecies, although they contain nothing which is not profitable for our instruction, yet as one star differeth from another in glory, so every word of prophecy hath a treasure of matter in it, but all matters are not of like importance, as all treasures are not of equal price. The chief and principal matter of prophecy is the promise of righteousness, peace, holiness, glory, victory, immortality, unto 'every soul which believeth that Jesus is

Christ, of the Jew first, and of the Gentile'" (Serm.v.5; cf. Serm.
II.16, 23). Precisely because Scripture has a Christocentric shape, it
is of essential importance that in interpreting individual passages the
overarching design be carefully kept in mind.[70] At the same time,
any arrangement of scriptural passages which is blind to the overall
concerns of Scripture as a whole will fail to be a truly faithful interpretation of God's word. In short, while the inspiration of Scripture
assures the interpreter that divinely revealed and genuine truth is indeed available, the need for human wisdom and diligent effort is
never denied and even explicitly demanded.

Here Hooker turns his attention to reason as an interpreter of
Scripture. He recognizes two major concerns: the problem of whether
human reason can recognize Scripture as the Word of God and the
role of reason in the actual task of exegesis. The point of departure
is the common ground shared by all Christians that "we all believe
that the Scriptures of God are sacred, and that they have proceeded
from God" (II.iv.2), a belief Hooker himself shares. Yet he recognizes
that such a belief rests on an assumption that has not been so far
examined. To this he now turns. Particularly in Protestant circles,
Scripture has been viewed as teaching its own authority. But can one
really testify in his own favor? Hooker does not think so:

For if any one book of Scripture did give testimony to all, yet still that Scripture
which giveth credit to the rest would require another Scripture to give credit unto
it, neither could we ever come unto any pause whereon to rest our assurance this
way; so that unless beside Scripture there were something which might assure us
that we do well, we could not think we do well, no not in being assured that
Scripture is a sacred and holy rule of well-doing. [iv.2][71]

But even if the truth of Scripture cannot be established by an appeal
to its extrinsic authority, can we not look at the content of it, recognize from it its intrinsically divine character, and deduce thereby its
divine authority? Having thought of such a possibility, Hooker
nevertheless rejects it. For the sake of a clear illustration, he records
such a self-evident proposition as "every whole is more than any
part of that whole" (III.viii.13). If the divine character of Scripture
were self-evident, all men would necessarily accept it as revealed,

but that is patently not the case! To say this, however, does not close the inquiry, since Hooker does not think that self-evident propositions are the only kind of statements that yield truth. His remedy is to propose another approach, which would assess the role of human initiative and wisdom in understanding the true character of Scripture.[72]

The Puritans need to be reminded of this human dimension, because they are inclined to overlook it. The purpose here, of course, is not to disparage the revealed character of Scripture, but rather to discover a genuinely persuasive avenue that does not beg the very question it seeks to prove. Hooker's proposal is as follows. Though indeed often fallible, human testimony can nevertheless serve "as a ground of infallible assurance." The following examples illustrate it: "That there is a city of Rome, that Pius Quintus and Gregory the Thirteenth and others have been Popes of Rome, I suppose we are certainly enough persuaded. The ground of our persuasion, who never saw the place nor persons beforenamed, can be nothing but man's testimony. Will any man here notwithstanding allege those mentioned human infirmities, as reasons why these things should be mistrusted or doubted of?" (II.vii.3). A similar case, and closer to the point at issue, is the actual meaning of the words used in Scripture. "The Scripture could not teach us the things that are of God, unless we did credit men who have taught us that the words of Scripture do signify those things." Consequently, he suggests, we may recognize human authority as "the key which openeth the door of entrance into the knowledge of the Scripture" (vii.3). To be sure, he does not assign such authority indiscriminately to all men, but restricts it to the truly wise. And when such men make use of human authority, they are not autonomous but are assisted by the grace of God. Even so, the content of Scripture is grasped by the instrumentality of reason. And although the ultimate value of Scripture is not proven, man is at least made ready for the last step.[73]

Before we describe just how such a step is to be taken, we may note that Hooker is prepared to arrive at this same point by yet another route. Hooker observes that our first attention to Scripture is not drawn by Scripture itself but by human authority. This is, of course, the familiar argument of St Augustine, now toned down: "by experience we all know, that the first outward motive leading men so to esteem of the Scripture is the authority of God's Church. For when we know the whole Church of God hath that opinion of the Scripture, we judge it even at the first an impudent thing for any man bred and brought up in the Church to be of a contrary mind without cause" (III.viii.14).[74] That is, the testimony of judicious men that Scripture is the Word of God supplies us with the greatest probability of the truth of their claim and thus induces us to become personally acquainted with Scripture. When, in the process of seeking truth, the truth is actually discovered and probability replaced by certainty, the final step has taken place. Hooker describes the sequence in this way: "Afterwards the more we bestow our labour in reading or hearing the mysteries thereof, the more we find that the thing itself doth answer our received opinion concerning it. So that the former inducement prevailing somewhat with us before, doth now much more prevail, when the very thing hath ministered farther reason" (viii.14). Put another way, the inward conviction of the certainty of Scripture as revelation takes place by a kind of dialectical process. Human reason supplies the meaning of scriptural words; highly reputable human authority from within the church enhances the probability that the Scripture is in fact revelatory; yet such a witness does not in itself suffice to bring about an immediate acceptance of the truth. Deliberation continues, more questions are raised, and further acquaintance with the Scripture takes place. All the while the witness of the wise is taken in account. The fruition of this process is complete when man finally recognizes the complete correspondence between the church's witness about Scripture and his own personal discovery of what Scripture means to him. Thus when a tradition of faith and personal understanding concur, the individual is assured of the objective dimension of his subjectively held belief. Then it becomes possible to say that the discovery has taken place by the assistance of grace (viii.15; II.vii.4), yet not without the exclusion of the instrumental role of human reason.

Unfortunately, Hooker does not indicate which specific arguments of the church Fathers he has had in mind. Perhaps he was not thinking about any particular sets of proofs, but merely referred to the general tendency to collect rational arguments in support of the divine character of Scripture.[75] This at least would be in accord with Hooker's basic preference not to cling to simplistic formulas but to suggest a process of reasoning that can take place under the assistance of grace. Which is to say that while Hooker certainly does not exclude the assistance of the Holy Spirit, he refuses to regard the work of the Holy Spirit as an irrational miracle that must bypass every use of reason:

> Neither can I think that when grave and learned men do sometime hold, that of this principle there is no proof but by the testimony of the Spirit, which assureth our hearts therein, it is their meaning to exclude utterly all force which any kind of reason may have in that behalf; but I rather incline to interpret such their speeches, as if they had more expressly set down, that other motives and inducements, be they never so strong and consonant unto reason, are notwithstanding uneffectual of themselves to work faith concerning this principle, if the special grace of the Holy Ghost concur not to the enlightening of our minds. [III.viii.15]

On account of the particular historical situation in which Hooker found himself pitted against the Puritans, it is understandable that, without belittling personal piety or the decisive significance of grace, he nevertheless sought to underscore the learned use of reason. Not a rationalist, nor dispensing with reliance on grace essential for the purification of reason, he seeks to retain a careful balance. By contrast, when the Puritans begin to view reason as a servant of sin (viii.4), they necessarily lose their rationality in both thought and deed. Betraying his outrage and admitting that in the last resort the use of force is legitimate, Hooker exclaims:

> Thus much we see, it hath already made thousands so headstrong even in gross and palpable errors, that a man whose capacity will scarce serve him to utter five words in sensible manner blusheth not in any doubt concerning matter of Scripture to think his own bare *Yea* as good as the *Nay* of all the wise, grave, and learned judgments that are in the whole world: which insolency must be repressed, or it will be the very bane of Christian religion. [II.vii.6]

On another occasion, following Guy de Brès's account of the rise of Anabaptism, he suggests clear parallels between the obscurantism of the Anabaptists and the attitudes of the Puritans, for the Anabaptists had literally burned all books except their Bibles. But by reading the Bible alone and setting all reason and learning aside, did the Anabaptists really come to grasp the meaning of revelation more clearly? Hooker does not think so: "when they and their Bibles were alone together, what strange fantastical opinion soever at any time entered into their heads, their use was to think the Spirit taught it to them" (Pref.viii.7).[76] In addition, their morals soon disintegrated: "These men, in whose mouths at the first sounded nothing but only mortification of the flesh, were come at the length to think they might lawfully have their six or seven wives apiece; they which at first thought judgment and justice itself to be merciless cruelty, accounted at the length their own hands sanctified with being embrued in Christian blood..." (viii.12). The implication is clear—Hooker suspects that the Puritans might soon do likewise. Similarly, Hooker records his grave distrust in a subjectivistic piety that purports to revere Scripture yet exhibits "open contempt" toward well-established ceremonies of the church (v.viii.4). The question here is the same as it was above: is it possible to practice piety on a narrow and subjectively selected range? Does one accept Scripture as he prefers to interpret it, or must he always take into account the corporate wisdom and witness of the entire church? Hooker opts for the latter.

At the same time, the prior commitment to a consensus does not obviate the need for exegesis. Though briefly, Hooker outlines what he considers to be the best exegetical approach: "I hold it for a most infallible rule in expositions of sacred Scripture, that where a literal construction will stand, the farthest from the letter is commonly the worst. There is nothing more dangerous than this licentious and deluding art, which changeth the meaning of words, as alchymy doth or would do the substance of metals, maketh of any thing what it listeth, and bringeth in the end all truth to nothing" (lix.2). Such advice appears to rest on Hooker's assumption that interpretation consists of three steps: encounter with reality, conceptualization, and final expression by word image. Consequently, in order to understand the meaning of anyone's word, we must not only hear what they have said but also observe the reality about which they have been speaking (ix.3, xxii.10). A good illustration of Hooker's own exegesis may be seen in regard to John 3:5, "Unless a man is born again of water and the Spirit, he cannot enter into the kingdom of heaven." It has been at times suggested, Hooker notes, that the word "water" is but a metaphor for "Spirit." Such a reading claims that the text does not point to actual water but argues that the real meaning of the passage is "that unless a man be born again of the Spirit, he cannot enter into the kingdom of heaven." Should this be the case, the text would teach direct regeneration by the Holy Spirit and thus reject the doctrine of baptismal regeneration. When Hooker censures such an interpretation, he does so on the grounds that the word "water" is perfectly clear. A literal interpretation is therefore in order and with it the doctrine of baptismal regeneration (v.lix.1).

Yet Hooker's plea for a literal interpretation, insofar as he is consistent, does not apply to all Scripture but, as we have noted, stands in clear subordination to an overarching Christocentric principle. When the Puritans merely "quote by-speeches in some historical narration or other" and regard them as a "most exact form of law" (III.v.1), their literal interpretation is out of order. Like Luther, Hooker appears to believe that within Scripture there is a central and Christocentric core. Only within this essential sphere is literal interpretation and strict obedience in order. Elsewhere we deal with peripheral statements, which need to be understood in accord with the Christocentric essence of the Scripture and not vice versa. It is the duty of grace-redeemed reason, relying on a consensus established within the church, to distinguish between the two levels of Scripture and to indicate what kind of exegetical method is in order (cf. III. viii.16).

In this way the faithful exegete must be a judicious theologian and not merely a diligent proof-text hunter. Although Hooker does not claim that he will always accomplish the great task of interpreting

Scripture faultlessly, he is clearly concerned that the basic Christo-centric thrust of the Scripture not be missed. Thus both in his reflections on the problem of subjectivity and in the discussion of the interpretation of the Scripture, Hooker acknowledges the difficulties and the dangers of the task. Yet successful accomplishment does not depend on mere chance. The redeeming presence of God in Jesus Christ, dwelling within the church, assures men that reason and revelation have not lost their power and will inform as well as transform the seeker.

NOTES

1. For the High Church view, see Barry, in *Masters in English Theology*, p. 35, and especially Keble, ed., *The Works of...Mr. Richard Hooker*, 7th ed., 1888, 1 : xcix. For the Low Church position, see Nash, "A Statesman of the English Church," *American Journal of Theology* 7 (1903): 564–65. For the view that he encompassed both, see John Hunt, *Religious Thought in England from the Reformation to the End of the Last Century*, 1:57.

2. Henry Thomas Buckle, *History of Civilization in England* (New York: Appleton, 1875), 1:247, 249.

3. John Hunt, pp. 60–61.

4. Dowden, in *Puritan and Anglican*, pp. 81, 89, 96.

5. Theodore W. Hunt, "Richard Hooker, The Elizabethan Ecclesiastic," *Homiletic Review* 28 (1894): 492.

6. Lecky, *History of the Rise and Influence of the Spirit of Rationalism in Europe*, rev. ed., p. 178.

7. Nash, p. 564.

8. Church, ed., *Of the Laws of Ecclesiastical Polity: Book I*, 1866; Paget, *An Introduction to the Fifth Book of Hooker's Treatise of the Laws of Ecclesiastical Polity*; Bayne, ed., *Of the Laws of Ecclesiastical Polity: The Fifth Book*, 1902.

9. Washburn, in *Epochs in Church History and Other Essays*, ed. Tiffany, pp. 209–10.

10. Henderson, in *The Encyclopaedia Britannica*, 11th ed., 13:673.

11. Bayne, in *Encyclopedia of Religion and Ethics*, ed. Hastings, 6:776.

12. Thornton, *Richard Hooker*, pp. 26–27, 74.

13. Christopher Morris, in *The Great Tudors*, ed. Garvin, p. 283.

14. McNeill, in *Books of Faith and Power*, p. 70.

15. See Carlyle and Carlyle, *A History of Mediaeval Political Theory in the West*, Vol. 6; Previté-Orton, in *Proceedings of the British Academy*, Vol. 21; Faulkner, "The Natural Law Theory of Richard Hooker," dissertation, Chicago, 1960;

and Faulkner, "Reason and Revelation in Hooker's Ethics," *American Political Science Review* 59 (1965): 680–90.

16. For example, by J. W. Allen, *A History of Political Thought in the Sixteenth Century*, p. 185; Paul Schütz, *Richard Hooker*, p. 23; and Hughes, *The Reformation in England*, Vol. 3, pp. 224–25.

17. Otto Hermann Pesch, O.P., *Theologie der Rechtfertigung bei Martin Luther und Thomas von Aquin: Versuch eines systematisch-theologischen Dialogs*, Walberberger Studien der Albertus Magnus Akademie, 4 (Mainz: Matthias Grünewald, 1967). Jared Wicks, S.J., ed., *Catholic Scholars Dialogue with Luther* (Chicago: Loyola Univ. Press, 1970).

18. Henderson, in *The Encyclopaedia Britannica*, 11th ed., 13:673.

19. Taylor, in *Thought and Expression in the Sixteenth Century*, 2:161.

20. De Lara, "Richard Hooker's Concept of Law," *Anglican Theological Review* 44 (1962): 382.

21. Southgate, *John Jewel and the Problem of Doctrinal Authority*, pp. 136, 138, 139.

22. See, for example, J. W. Allen, p. 240; Jordan, *The Development of Religious Toleration in England*, 1:229, 232; Dirksen, *A Critical Analysis of Richard Hooker's Theory of the Relation of Church and State*, p. vi; Schütz, *Richard Hooker*, pp. 46, 49, 53, 57, 58; and B. M. G. Reardon, "Richard Hooker's Apology for Anglicanism," *Hibbert Journal* 52 (1954): 282.

23. Dowden, in *Puritan and Anglican*, p. 69.

24. Craig, *The Enchanted Glass*, pp. 24, 28.

25. Craig, "Of the Laws of Ecclesiastical Polity—First Form," *Journal of the History of Ideas* 5 (1944): 94.

26. Herschel Baker, *The Dignity of Man: Studies in the Persistence of an Idea* (Cambridge: Harvard Univ. Press, 1947, and Gloucester: Peter Smith, 1961), reprinted as *The Image of Man: A Study of the Idea of Human Dignity in Classical Antiquity, the Middle Ages, and the Renaissance* (New York: Harper and Row, Harper Torchbooks, 1961), p. 290. Cf. its sequel, *The Wars of Truth*, p. 28.

27. Baker, *Wars of Truth*, pp. 32, 117.

28. Christopher Morris, *Political Thought in England*, pp. 177, 195.

29. See Kearney, "Richard Hooker," *Cambridge Journal* 5 (1952): 305; Lewis, *English Literature in the Sixteenth Century Excluding Drama*, p. 454; Stueber, "The Balanced Diction of Hooker's *Polity*," *PMLA* 71 (1956): 826; and Bush, *English Literature in the Earlier Seventeenth Century 1600–1660*, 2d rev. ed., p. 326.

30. Munz, *The Place of Hooker in the History of Thought*, pp. 98, 61, 62.

31. Thompson, "Richard Hooker among the Controversialists," *Philological Quarterly* 29 (1941): 457. Jenssen, in *Solange es "heute" heisst*, p. 150. Hill, "The Doctrinal Background of Richard Hooker's *Laws of Ecclesiastical Polity*."

32. Hill, pp. 167, 175, n. 5.

33. Thornton, *Richard Hooker*, p. 36.

34. Michaelis, *Richard Hooker als politischer Denker*, p. 38.

35. D'Entrèves, "Richard Hooker," in *Abstracts of Dissertations for the Degree of*

Doctor of Philosophy, 6 (1934): 33. See also *Riccardo Hooker*, pp. 50, 51; *The Medieval Contribution to Political Thought*, p. 120; and *Natural Law: An Historical Survey* (London: Hutchinson, 1951; reprinted New York: Harper & Row, Harper Torchbooks, 1965), pp. 46, 47. A similar view is held by Southgate (see above, n. 21) and Wolin, "Richard Hooker and English Conservatism," *Western Political Quarterly*, 6 (1953): 36.

36. Kavanagh, "Reason and Nature in Hooker's *Polity*," p. 101.

37. See, *i.a.*, Lewis, *English Literature in the Sixteenth Century Excluding Drama*, p. 456; Grislis, "Richard Hooker's Method of Theological Inquiry," *Anglican Theological Review* 45 (1963):202; essay in *Renaissance Papers 1963*, ed. Heninger, et al., pp. 82–84; and essay in *The Heritage of Christian Thought*, ed. Cushman and Grislis, p. 72; Marshall, *Hooker and the Anglican Tradition*, pp. 112–13; McGrade, "The Coherence of Hooker's *Polity*," *Journal of the History of Ideas* 24 (1963): 166, 167; Hill, "Doctrinal Background," pp. 134, 142, 143, 146, and 163; Willey, in *The English Moralists* (Garden City, N.Y.: Doubleday, Anchor Books, 1967), pp. 90, 99–101; Faulkner, "Reason and Revelation in Hooker's Ethics," *American Political Science Review* 59 (1965): 680; Booty, "The Quest for the Historical Hooker," *The Churchman* 80 (1966): 190; and Morrel, *The Systematic Theology of Richard Hooker*, pp. 26, 79, 151.

38. Hillerdal, *Reason and Revelation in Richard Hooker*, p. 97.

39. Ibid., p. 117. Grislis, in *Renaissance Papers 1963*, ed. Heninger, et al., p. 82.

40. Grislis, in *The Heritage of Christian Thought*, ed. Cushman and Grislis, pp. 85–88.

41. Murray, *The Political Consequences of the Reformation*, observes that "there was in Hooker an instinctive faith in the power of truth, and he possessed the gift of enabling others to feel this power" (p. 278). Cf. Dowden in *Puritan and Anglican*, p. 82.

42. Paget, *An Introduction to the Fifth Book*, admirably sums up Hooker's character: "He never handles truths like chessmen with which his adversary's pieces may be got into a corner, or like weapons with which an assailant may be driven in discredit from the field. There is in him a reverent chivalry towards the teaching for which he contends; and so he makes his readers think far more of the truth than of its champion, far more of its greatness than of his skill, and the truth is only gaining vividness and splendour and authority while he is fighting for it; —he shows its beauty as he proves its strength" (p. 4); cf. Hughes, *The Reformation in England*, 3: 218; Dowden, p. 72; and H. F. Woodhouse, "Permanent Features of Hooker's Polity," *Anglican Theological Review* 42 (1960): 165. At the same time it is not to be overlooked that Hooker was in control of the techniques of polemic and followed Aristotle's *Rhetoric* rather closely. Cf. Yoder, "The Prose Style of Richard Hooker's *Of the Laws of Ecclesiastical Polity*."

43. Rowse, *The England of Elizabeth*, pp. 483, 484.

44. Cf. my study in *The Heritage of Christian Thought*, ed. Cushman and Grislis.

45. Hooker's controversy with Travers has been discussed by Knox, *Walter*

Travers. See also A. F. Scott Pearson, *Thomas Cartwright and Elizabethan Puritanism 1535–1603* (Cambridge: Cambridge Univ. Press, 1925; reprinted Gloucester: Peter Smith, 1966). New, *Anglican and Puritan*, pays greater attention to disagreement, while John D. Eusden, *Puritans, Lawyers, and Politics in Early Seventeenth Century England*, Yale Studies in Religious Education, 23 (New Haven: Yale Univ. Press, 1958; reprinted Hamden: Archon, 1968) observes the genuine continuity of thought between the two groups. Other important studies are Perry Miller, *Orthodoxy in Massachusetts, 1630–1650: A Genetic Study* (Cambridge: Harvard Univ. Press, 1933; reprinted New York: Harper & Row, Harper Torchbooks, 1970, and Gloucester: Peter Smith, 1970); Perry Miller and Thomas H. Johnson, *The Puritans* (New York: The American Book Co. [et al.], 1938; reprinted New York: Harper & Row, Harper Torchbooks, 1963); Perry Miller, *The New England Mind: The Seventeenth Century* (Cambridge: Harvard Univ. Press, 1939 and Boston: Beacon Press, 1961); M. M. Knappen, *Tudor Puritanism: A Chapter in the History of Idealism* (Chicago: Univ. of Chicago Press, 1939; reprinted Phoenix Books, 1965); Collinson, *The Elizabethan Puritan Movement*; H. C. Porter, ed., *Puritanism in Tudor England*, History in Depth (London: Macmillan, 1970); and Leonard J. Trinterud, ed., *Elizabethan Puritanism*, A Library of Protestant Thought (New York and London: Oxford Univ. Press, 1971).

46. Cf. Scott Pearson, p. 311; Knappen, pp. 212–14, 152, 157; E. T. Davies, *The Political Ideas of Richard Hooker*, pp. 37, 38; McNeill, in *Books of Faith and Power*, p. 69; Shirley, *Richard Hooker and Contemporary Political Ideas*, pp. 67, 68; and Munz, *Place of Hooker*, pp. 29–39, 88.

47. Cf. *Laws* Pref.ix.4; i.3; also Murray, *Political Consequences*, p. 273.

48. "*Probable, —ly*, with us is said of the *positive effect* of proof, and means generally that it is convincing and satisfactory—that the balance is clearly on one side. In Hooker it is generally used of the *nature* of the proof, and means that it falls short of being conclusive" (Church, ed., *Book I: Of the Laws of Ecclesiastical Polity*, 1866, p. 152). Hooker himself uses the term "probable" in the following ways. First, he is convinced that a probable proof is better than none at all: "in defect of proof infallible...the mind doth rather follow probable persuasions than approve the things that have in them no likelihood of truth at all..." (II.vii.5). And by "proof" Hooker means not only a cogent argument but also an appeal to legitimate authority; he continues: "surely if a question concerning matter of doctrine were proposed, and on the one side no kind of proof appearing, there should on the other be alleged and shewed that so a number of the learnedest divines in the world have ever thought; although it did not appear what reason or what Scripture led them to be of that judgment, yet to their very bare judgment somewhat a reasonable man would attribute, notwithstanding the common imbecilities which are incident into our nature" (II.vii.5). Second, Hooker makes clear that a probable argument of common men is always inferior to public law; should this not be the case, the collapse of

social order would follow: "Because except our own private and but probable resolutions be by the law of public determinations overruled, we take away all possibility of sociable life in the world" (i.xvi.5). Finally, from such principles Hooker draws the conclusion that the probable proofs of the church are always to be accepted in obedience: "That which the Church by her ecclesiastical authority shall probably think and define to be true or good, must in congruity of reason overrule all other inferior judgments whatsoever" (v.viii.2). Therefore when the Puritans propose what is but a probable argument against the authority of Church, their argument is, by definition, invalid; cf. Pref.vi.6; also Paget, *Introduction to the Fifth Book*, p. 97; and Kavanagh, "Reason and Nature in Hooker's *Polity*," pp. 63–70, 162.

49. *Works* 1:140, n. 1.

50. Cf. Joannis Calvini, *Opera Selecta*, ed. Peter Barth and Wilhelm Niesel, 2d rev. ed. (Munich: Chr. Kaiser, 1957–62), 5 : 478 (IV.xx.8); Calvin, *Institutes of the Christian Religion*, ed. John T. McNeill, tr. Ford Lewis Battles, Library of Christian Classics, Vol. 21 (Philadelphia: Westminster Press, 1960), p. 1493.

51. Calvini, *Opera Selecta* (1957–62), 3 : 70–71 (I.vii.5); Calvin, *Institutes* 20 : 80–81. Cf. Werner Krusche, *Das Wirken des Heiligen Geistes nach Calvin* (Göttingen: Vandenhoeck & Ruprecht, 1957); and Gottfried W. Locher, *Testimonium internum: Calvins Lehre vom Heiligen Geist und das hermeneutische Problem*, Theologische Studien, 81 (Zürich: E. V. Z. Verlag, 1964).

52. Paget observes that Hooker overlooks the fact that some Puritan criticisms of the Church of England expressed a widely shared sentiment and were to the point (p. 97).

53. Hooker also notes that "insolent and proud wits would always seem to be their own guides" (v.lxiii.13) and remarks of Walter Travers: "his opinion is no canon" (*Answer to Travers*, 16).

54. *Works* 2:542.

55. Scholars are divided as to the real meaning of this expression. According to Maurice, *Moral and Metaphysical Philosophy* (London: Macmillan, 1873), 2: 191: "The caution and hesitancy of Hooker in finding fault with the foreign Reformer, when he was most disposed to be severe upon his English imitators, show how much the metaphysics of the Institutes governed his mind." A similar opinion was expressed by the nineteenth-century scholars John Hunt, *Religious Thought in England*, p. 57; Washburn, in *Epochs in Church History and Other Essays*, ed. Tiffany, p. 209; and Sidney Lee, in *The Dictionary of National Biography* (1891), 27:290; and in this century—without, however, claiming Hooker's theological dependence on Calvin—by Taylor, in *Thought and Expression in the Sixteenth Century*, p. 167; Sykes, in *The Social & Political Ideas of Some Great Thinkers of the Sixteenth & Seventeenth Centuries*, ed. Hearnshaw, p. 70; Dirksen, *Hooker's Theory of Church and State*, p. 60; McNeill, in *Books of Faith and Power*, p. 69; and H. F. Woodhouse, "Permanent Features of Hooker's Polity," *Anglican Theological Review* 42 (1960): 166. Others have

suggested that Hooker was rather critical of Calvin: for example, Foakes-Jackson, in *The Cambridge History of English Literature*, 3:457; Thornton, *Richard Hooker*, p. 23; Dimond, "Richard Hooker and the Twentieth Century," *Church Quarterly Review* 108 (1929): 8; Yoder, *Prose Style of Hooker*, p. 165; and E. T. Davies, *The Political Ideas of Richard Hooker*, p. 38. The following generalization may be in order. If it is assumed that Hooker is significantly influenced by Calvin's thought, then it is stated that Hooker is sympathetic and respectful to Calvin. If, however, it is believed that Hooker was primarily influenced by St Thomas, then Hooker's attitude toward Calvin is evaluated as critical or even hostile. Following McNeill, I think it is necessary to see Hooker's thought as dependent on both St Thomas and Calvin. Hooker's attitude toward Calvin therefore may reflect both respect and censure.

56. In view of Hooker's predilection for the term "judicious" it is not surprising that he has been praised by use of this expression. Sir William Cooper's monument included "judicious" in the epitaph (*Works* 1:86, n. 5). Despite Maurice's ridicule (p. 190), "judicious" has been used by Keble in the full title of the *Works* (a tradition dating from Gauden's edition of 1662); cf. Theodore W. Hunt, "Richard Hooker, The Elizabethan Ecclesiastic," *Homiletic Review* 28 (1894): 492, 493; J. W. Allen, *History of Political Thought*, p. 184; Munz, *Place of Hooker*, p. 14; and Sisson, *The Judicious Marriage of Mr. Hooker and the Birth of "The Laws of Ecclesiastical Polity."*

57. Hooker's attitude toward Ramus is discussed briefly by Baker, *Wars of Truth*, p. 103; Munz, *Place of Hooker*, pp. 151–55, 166, 167; and in *The Encyclopedia of Philosophy*, ed. Edwards, 4:65. The best monograph on Ramus' thought is by Walter J. Ong, S.J., *Ramus, Method, and the Decay of Dialogue: From the Art of Discourse to the Art of Reason* (Cambridge: Harvard Univ. Press, 1958). The significance of Ramus for Calvinism is explicitly discussed by Jürgen Moltmann, "Zur Bedeutung des Petrus Ramus für Philosophie und Theologie im Calvinismus," *Zeitschrift für Kirchengeschichte*, fourth series, VI, 68 (1957): 296–318; and Keith L. Sprunger, "Ames, Ramus, and the Method of Puritan Theology," *Harvard Theological Review* 59 (1966): 133–51.

58. See Kavanagh, "Reason and Nature in Hooker's *Polity*," pp. 64–67, 163–64; and Talbert, *The Problem of Order*, p. 41.

59. The significance of exegesis for Hooker may be also observed from the subtitles of Books II and III of the *Laws*.

60. Cf. Thornton, p. 24, and Dimond, p. 3; the most colorful account appears in the 1662 ed. of Hooker's *Works*, p. 38, in the *Life* written by John Gauden. The first two lines of a poem "The Character of Mr. *Richard Hooker*" proclaim as follows:

> The Painted Whore *and* Naked Matron *he*
> Dislik'd, *both* Rome *and her quite contrary....*

They are quoted and translated into French by Rémusat, *Histoire de le Philosophie en Angleterre depuis Bacon jusqu'à Locke*, 1:127.

61. Heiko A. Oberman, "Quo Vadis? Tradition from Irenaeus to Humani Generis," *Scottish Journal of Theology* 16 (September 1963): 225–55, provides a brilliant outline of the basic doctrinal issues at hand. A more detailed study, Yves M.-J. Congar, O.P., *Tradition and Traditions: An Historical and a Theological Essay* (New York: Macmillan, 1967), refers briefly to Hooker (pp. 516, 517). Hooker himself denied a two-source theory of revelation: "we therefore have no *word* of God but the Scripture" (v.xxi.2); cf. Serm. II, 11 and Serm. v, 7.

62. Cf. *Laws* II.viii.5 and v.xxi.3.

63. Morrel, *Systematic Theology of Hooker*, p. 120.

64. Cf. *Laws* Pref.viii.4; II.i.3; iii.1; and iv.3–4, 6.

65. Cf. *Laws* v.xx.9; Hill interprets Hooker's position as follows: "If we demand for our every action the unequivocal sanction of Scripture, we debase its genuine authority in matters of salvation; and by seeking in it the surcease of merely temporal anxiety, we jeopardize the assurance it offers us of eternal life. The danger of Cartwright's scripturalism, then, was that it achieved an effect precisely opposite to the one sought: men look to Scripture for faith and find despair instead" (pp. 265–66); cf. Hill, "Doctrine and Polity in Hooker's *Laws*," *English Literary Renaissance* 2(1972):187. John S. Coolidge, *The Pauline Renaissance in England: Puritanism and the Bible* (Oxford: Clarendon Press, 1970), pp. 9–14, acknowledges that Hooker won the argument but claims that the Puritans nevertheless had a rationale for Christian norms which went beyond Scripture.

66. Cf. *Laws* Pref.viii.12, and II.vii.5.

67. Aquinas, *Summa Theologica*, trans. Fathers of the English Dominican Province (New York: Benzinger Brothers, 1947), I,Q I, Art. 1 and 8 (vol. 1:1, 5).

68. Schütz, *Richard Hooker*, p. 47, claims that Hooker has overcome the view of verbal inspiration; Morrel, p. 125, cautiously suggests that "it would appear that he did" accept "verbal inspiration."

69. The definition of "verbal inspiration" and "literal interpretation" is by no means a simple task. In Calvin scholarship, as noted by J. K. S. Reid, *The Authority of Scripture* (New York: Harper & Bros, n.d.), pp. 54–55, and Edward A. Dowey, Jr, *The Knowledge of God in Calvin's Theology* (New York: Columbia Univ. Press, 1952), pp. 100–03, there are major divisions among the better-known Calvin scholars. Werner Krusche, *Wirken des Heiligen Geistes nach Calvin*, pp. 163–84, and, recently, H. Jackson Forstmann, *Word and Spirit: Calvin's Doctrine of Biblical Authority* (Stanford: Stanford Univ. Press, 1962), have further elucidated the complexity of the problem. Hooker's attempts to qualify the infallibility of a verbally inspired text therefore are not to be seen as unique, but as an undertaking rather familiar in Calvinist circles.

70. Cf. "The end of the word of God is *to save*, and therefore we term it *the word of life*" (v.xxi.3). Hillerdal mainly emphasizes the differences between Luther and Hooker and neglects to observe a genuine similarity as well (*Reason and Revelation*, p. 91).

71. Here Hooker's main point is clear; elsewhere he is less precise. For example, the statement "Scripture indeed teacheth things above nature, things which our reason by itself could not reach unto. Yet those things also we believe, knowing by reason that the Scripture is the word of God" (III.viii.12) has been interpreted by Dirksen to mean: "In fact, 'knowing by reason that the Scripture is the word of God,' one might be tempted to say that reason is the foundation of inspiration" (p. 66). To do justice to Hooker, the above passage needs to be read in conjunction with II.vii.5, which appeals to the eventual coincidence between the scriptural claim of divine authorship and our human experience of it. The phrase "Scripture is a sacred and holy rule of well-doing" may reflect Ramist terminology. Cf. Sprunger, above, n. 57.

72. Cf. Paget, *Introduction to the Fifth Book*, pp. 111–12: "But this revelation does not efface the conditions, dispense with the efforts, preclude or forestall the operations of human faculties and human life. It comes among men as a transcendent manifestation of God's care and goodness; it uses, it crowns, it advances and illuminates the powers of men, the processes by which men move towards the knowledge of truth; it does not overbear them, or drive them from the fields where God meant them to be exercised."

73. Apart from the assistance of reason, asks Hooker, "what warrant have they, that any one of them doth mean the thing for which it is alleged?" (II.vii.9). When Hooker ascribes credibility to the Scripture on the grounds of intrinsic authority, he is referring exclusively to believers who have gone through the dialectical process of quest and conversion and therefore recognize that Scripture is the Word of God. Insofar as this recognition is a divine gift, its certainty is beyond doubt, cf. *Laws* v.xxi.3, and xxii.8.

74. St Augustine's famous statement is this: "But should you meet with a person not yet believing the gospel, how would you reply to him were he to say, I do not believe? For my part, I should not believe the gospel except as moved by the authority of the Catholic Church." *Against the Epistle of Manichaeus*, ch. 5, *A Select Library of the Nicene and Post-Nicene Fathers of the Christian Church*, ed. Philip Schaff, Vol. 4, *St. Augustine, The Writings against the Manichaeans and against the Donatists* (reprinted Grand Rapids, Mich.: Wm. B. Eerdmans, 1956), p. 131. Calvin quotes that passage and then offers his Protestant interpretation: "Augustine is not...teaching that the faith of godly men is founded on the authority of the church; nor does he hold the view that the certainty of the gospel depends upon it. He is simply teaching that there would be no certainty of the gospel for unbelievers to win them to Christ if the consensus of the church did not impel them." *Institutes*, 20 : 77 (I.vii.3); Calvini, *Opera Selecta*, 3 : 67.

75. Cf. *Institutes*, 20 : 81–92 (I.viii.1–13), and *Opera Selecta*, 3 : 71–81.

76. William Echard Keeney, *The Development of Dutch Anabaptist Thought and Practice from 1539–1564* (Nieuwkoop: B. De Graaf, 1968), offers a modern assessment: "Guy de Bres was an important Reformed leader in Belgium from

about 1545 until his martyrdom on May 31, 1567. Although he was antagonistic towards the Anabaptists and one must accept his description of them with caution, his facts are generally reliable so we can assume that the reports contain a considerable element of truth. He tells of some Anabaptists who wandered about the country without weapons, girdle (*ceinture*), or money, saying on the basis of Matthew 10:9, 10, that they were divinely sent. Others preached from the roof because Jesus had said, '. . . and what you hear whispered, proclaim upon the housetops.' (Matthew 10:27.) Still others played as little children because of the saying that you must become as children to enter the kingdom of heaven. (Matthew 10:2–4.)" (p. 33). It is, of course, incorrect to imagine that such were all Anabaptists, and that naiveté necessarily led to violence.

HOOKER AND ANGLICANISM

John E. Booty

I

Thomas Babington Macaulay echoed the opinion of many when he asserted that the Church of England came into being as a result of compromise and is marked by that in its constitution, doctrines, and services. This church, he believed, stood midway between Rome and Geneva. In her articles of religion, homilies, and other official doctrinal statements, all composed by professed Protestants, she "set forth principles of theology in which Calvin or Knox would have found scarcely a word to disapprove," whereas her liturgical formularies, "her prayers and thanksgivings derived from ancient Breviaries," Macaulay considered "such that Cardinal Fisher or Cardinal Pole might have heartily joined in them."[1] Frederick Denison Maurice, a nineteenth-century Anglican theologian, rejected Macaulay's notion. The Elizabethan reign could not be explained in terms of a compromise between two parties, a compromise that would seem to indicate that the Queen was "pledged to the defence of an ecclesiastical system which had not the courage to ally itself with the thorough Reformers of Knox's type, or with the bold reactionaries of the Council of Trent." Maurice believed that the success of the Elizabethan Settlement rested upon the Queen's ability as the ruler of the nation to unite "in herself the Calvinistic and the Catholic elements" abroad in the land. This was her goal, but its achievement was not at all assured in the early years of her reign. "The alkali and the acid produced a healthy effervescence; no neutral salt had as yet resulted from their combination."[2] Of the theologians serving the Queen, Maurice singled out Richard Hooker as exemplifying "that union of opposites in which we have contended that the strength of the Elizabethan period lay, whatever seeds of weakness it might leave for the succeeding time. In him, as little as in his royal mistress, was there any inclination to a mere balance of opinions. Circumstances compelled both, for the defence of that which they held, to resist aggressions proceeding from two opposite quarters. But both were sure that that which they were fighting for was a real substantial possession—a trust from God, not to be abandoned for any clever and ingenious conceptions of men." Both Queen and theologian acknowledged that they were bound to law, which might be corrupted but which protected the nation from coercion by extremists of the right or the left, Rome or Geneva, "an instrument for preventing truth from being mangled and extinguished by them all" (p. 192). In brief, their aim was not compromise, but comprehension. Comprehension differed from compromise in that it was not a matter of steering between two fierce and foreign powers, but rather of understanding God's will for men in accordance with Scripture, tradition, and reason. This implied the rejection of error whatever its source and the affirmation of truth wherever it might be found. The national church was to comprehend in a settlement of religion whatever was true and beneficial according to the tests of Scripture, tradition, and reason, and to exclude all to the contrary.

Writing of Anglican theology in the period of its first emergence, Paul Elmer More has said that its distinguishing feature was not the pursuit of a middle way devised to avoid conflict, but rather a commitment to a principle of positive importance, "aiming to introduce into religion, and to base upon the 'light of reason,' that love of balance, restraint, moderation, measure, which from sources beyond our reckoning appears to be innate in the English temper." More referred to Joseph Hall, Bishop of Norwich, and his discussion of measure as the ruling force which maintains the heavenly bodies in their courses and is the center for all that is good, "the silken string that runs through the pearl-chain of all virtues, the very ecliptic-line under which reason and religion move without any deviation."[3] But it is Hooker, whose work came at the opening of the greatest age of Anglican theology, who most clearly sets the tone and lights the way. Hooker it was who exalted measure, beginning with the first law eternal, the law of God for himself, extending thence down as a precious chain through the second eternal law to man and his governments, secular and sacred. More cited Hooker:

If therefore it be demanded why, God having power and ability infinite, the effects notwithstanding of that power are all so limited as we see they are, the reason hereof is the end which He hath proposed, and the law whereby His wisdom hath stinted the effects of His power, in such sort that it doth not work infinitely, but correspondently unto that end for which it worketh, even "in all things χρηστῶς, in most decent and comely sort," in all things in Measure, Number and Weight.[4]

This could have resulted in a narrowing kind of compromise. But in Hooker's theology it did not. More compared what happened in the seventeenth century to the results of the Christological conflict in the early church. There two widely divergent positions were opposed concerning the nature of the person of Christ, the one accenting his humanity, the other his divinity. Both, in and of themselves, were deficient, affirming only a part of the truth. Taken together they approximated the truth. And so, More said, "the Church, by the Definition of Chalcedon, simply thrust its way through the middle by making the personality of the Incarnate so large as to carry with it *both* natures." Here measure and restraint did not diminish the truth but rather acted to prevent either of the two positions from excluding the other. "Nor," said More, "is the middle way here a mean of compromise, but a mean of comprehension" (p. xxiv).

The "love of balance, restraint, moderation, measure" was a keynote of seventeenth-century Anglicanism and of Hooker, who contributed to its genesis. H. R. McAdoo sees the paradox of Anglican theological method as the assertion of the freedom of reason alongside an affirmation of the visible church, of continuity with the first five centuries of the church's history.[5] There is a basic liberalism and a basic conservatism involved, sometimes uneasy in tandem but in fact coexisting through the history of Anglicanism from the seventeenth century to the present. Indeed, McAdoo points to a native theological tradition. "Side by side through their thought from Hooker to *Lux Mundi* ran this vivid sense of the present reality of continuity with the past, and the sense of the necessity of the freedom of reason to differentiate and assess, a combination which came to be known later as liberal Catholicism but which for the seventeenth century was the accepted theological method of Anglicanism" (p. 336). The method produced ecclesiastics who represented this combination. For example, Archbishop Laud's views of ecclesiastical polity were conservative and his actions often reactionary, but in matters of doctrine, and at least in some policy, he has been considered liberal.[6] Hooker, whom McAdoo views as establishing a liberal method based upon a concept of reason as competent to deal with polity, is labeled a conservative by Norman Sykes for turning "back deliberately to seek the old paths and to walk in them."[7]

Another point of view was expressed by Richard Church, the nineteenth-century Dean of St Paul's Cathedral, London, who worked with Francis Paget to revise Keble's edition of Hooker's *Works*. In seeking for Hooker's basic principle, Church rejected Hallam's view that it was "the mutability of ecclesiastical government"[8] and asserted that he found it in the doctrine of "the *concurrence and co-operation*, each in its due place, of all possible means of knowledge for man's direction. Take which you please, reason or Scripture, your own reason or that of others, private judgment or general consent, nature or grace, one *presupposes*—it is a favourite word for him—the existence of others, and is not intended to do its work of illumination and guidance without them: and the man who elects to go by one alone, will assuredly find in the end that he has gone wrong."[9] In another place Church wrote of a certain tentativeness in Anglicanism and openness to manifold possibilities, both divine and human.[10] For Hooker this tentativeness and concurrent openness result from the realization of the many ways by which God makes himself known to his creatures.

If we put these various points of view together, we obtain, I believe, a fairly accurate description of seventeenth-century Anglican theology and of Hooker's contribution toward its beginnings. Most deeply at work, theologically, was the conviction that at both extremes, Protestant and Catholic, only a part of the truth was being affirmed. The extreme Protestant emphasized Scripture to the neglect or condemnation of church, tradition, and reason. The extreme Catholic emphasized church and tradition to the neglect of Scripture and reason. True Christianity was broader and higher and deeper than either extreme could or would admit. To know the truth the theologian must be governed by that measure and restraint which is the opposite of extremism. So governed he would be in tune with the universe and available to all of the ways, Scripture, church, tradition, and reason, by which to know God's saving grace and His will for man. It is not simply a matter of all ways being possible; they are all necessary. The result for the Church of England is that the theologian condemns the falsities of the extremists while accepting and affirming the truths that the extremists hold. Thus Hooker decried the Puritan view of Scripture while embracing the Protestant doctrine of justification. And he decried the Roman Catholic view of the church and the papacy while defending his use of the schoolmen and claiming salvation for all of those Roman Catholics who adhered to the fundamental belief in Christ. His stance was thus comprehensive in terms of the history of the church. As McAdoo attests, Hooker maintained continuity with the past, looked to the old ways as preferable, would maintain the historic episcopate and traditional worship, but with his views of the freedom of reason he opened a door to the future— a crack perhaps—but nevertheless a way by which others might proceed in time to come.

II

Hooker's influence upon the development of this position or attitude is difficult to assess. It cannot be said that he created it, for that would ignore its development in the theology of such men as Cranmer, Jewel, Whitgift, Andrewes, and Bancroft. Furthermore, there is no overwhelming evidence that Hooker was widely read in his own time or in the years immediately following his death, when his works seemingly did not sell well.[11] But there is at least some evidence that he was read. No great counterattack was launched by the Puritans against the first five books of his *Ecclesiastical Polity*, the books published during his lifetime, but in 1599 *A Christian Letter* was published against him. At his death Hooker was preparing a response that in time might have led to something approximating the "Great Controversy" of the 1560s, which had involved John Jewel and English recusants at Louvain.[12] Roman Catholic polemicists, such as Lawrence Anderton (writing under the name of John Brereley), Richard Broughton, Edward Maihew, Sylvester Norris, and Edward Knott, cited Hooker at the beginning of the seventeenth century as one of a number of prominent and representative Anglican divines, usually to demonstrate that there were those among the English Protestants who tended toward papist positions on vital issues. Anglican divines under the early Stuarts, such as William Laud, Christopher Potter, Thomas Morton, and William Chillingworth, were acquainted with Hooker and acknowledged his importance. In addition, there was a brief exchange between Job Throckmorton, the Puritan, and Matthew Sutcliffe, Dean of Exeter, concerning Hooker specifically.[13] Others read and felt the weight of his influence. Among these were Lancelot Andrewes, Richard Field, Joseph Hall, John Cosin, George Bull, Robert Sanderson, and Jeremy Taylor.[14] All mentioned Hooker specifically, but there were others who mentioned him not at all whose writings reflect the point of view to which he adhered.[15] This is not to say that such persons were directly influenced by Hooker, for such a commonplace idea as that of right reason was abroad, the influence of the humanists was still very much felt, and the works of the schoolmen were still read in the universities.[16]

Michael Walzer cites the Anglican preacher Anthony Fawkner, for instance, as one "who restated in popular fashion Hooker's view of natural law,"[17] in a work entitled *Nicodemus for Christ, or the Religious Moote of an Honest Lawyer*. This was a sermon delivered at the assize in Okeham, Rutlandshire, March 10, 1627, by one who received his B.A. from Oxford in 1620.[18] The sermon displays Fawkner's intellectual accomplishments and seems to reflect Hooker's teachings, but it nowhere mentions Hooker by name, and it expresses ideas derived from the Fathers and schoolmen (Aquinas is specifically cited). Nevertheless, one attuned to Hooker can detect his ideas in such a passage as this:

> Now though all things are, and are guided by this eternall Law, yet this *Summa ratio*, (so S. *Augustine* stiles it) this supreme directive rule, though it bee *aliqualiter* (as the Schooleman limits) in some sort in all creatures subject to the Divine providence; yet I say more especially, more eminently it shines in man. So that by this more excellent impression of the eternall Law, there followes a participation of that Rule in man; by which hee hath an inbred inclination to the accomplishment of his proper acts and ends. Which participation of the eternall Law is defined to be the Law of Nature. By the light of which wee may easily view what should be done, by our naturall inclination to what wee would doe.[19]

The problem here is that there was a common body of thought abroad. As Father Costello said, "Cambridge in the early seventeenth century was orthodoxly Protestant and scholastic,"[20] a statement that might well be applied to the sister institution as well. It is thus an orthodox Protestant scholasticism which is in evidence in Fawkner, as in Hooker and many others at the time. Thomas Taylor, the Puritan, fellow of Christ's College, Cambridge, 1599–1604, was minister of St Mary Aldermanbury, London, 1625–30. While in London he preached a sermon against "the pestiferous sect of Libertines, Antinomians, and sonnes of Belial," in which he explained the "*substance of the Law perpetuall.*" Amongst other things, he had this to say:

> The Law in the substance is the expresse idea or representation of the Law of nature written in our hearts in the time and state of innocency, and the naturall principles of it cannot be quite extinct, or shaken out of the heart of the worst man; for the very Heathens had it written in their hearts, *Rom.* 2. 15. and much lesse can it be shaken out of the beleever, in whom it is renewed and rewritten in their spirits by the finger of Gods spirit, *Jer.* 31.33.[21]

As Taylor shows, the idea here of law "as the expresse idea or representation of the Law of nature" can be based on Scripture, it can be derived from the works of the schoolmen, and it can be seen as in tune with the humanist concept of right reason. Hooker was not the only one thinking and writing as he did.

But Walzer provides another example,[22] Robert Bolton, M.A. Oxford, 1602, fellow of Brasenose College, made rector of Broughton, Northamptonshire, in 1610. Wood says that Bolton was "a most religious and learned Puritan," and that at Brasenose he was made a "reader of Natural Philosophy in the public Schools." Afterward, Wood tells us, "he grew well studied in the Metaphysics, Mathematics, and in all School Divinity, especially in *Thomas Aquinas*; some of whose works he read over once or twice."[23] In a sermon preached before the judges of assize at Northampton in 1621, Bolton cited Hooker; like Hooker he reflected upon the necessity of government and the grief which comes when it breaks down:

Government is the prop and pillar of all States and Kingdomes, the cement and soule of humane affaires, the life of society and order, the very vitall spirit whereby so many millions of men, doe breath the life of comfort and peace; and the whole nature of things subsist. Let the heart in a man surcease from the exercise of its principality and prime motion, and the whole body would presently grow pale, bloudles and livelesse. If that glorious Giant in the sky, should retire his light into himselfe, and through a languishing faintnesse stay his course, and the Moone should wander from her beaten way, whom GOD hath appointed rulers over day and night; the times; and seasons of the yeare would blend themselves, by disordered and confused mixture. This goodly frame of the world would dissolve, and fall into confusion and darknesse. Proportionably, take Soveraignety from the face of the earth, and you turne it into a Cockpit. Men would become cut-throats and Canibals one unto another. Murder, adulteries, incests, rapes, roberies, perjuries, witchcrafts, blasphemies, all kinds of villanies, outrages and savage cruelty, would overflow all Countries. We should have a very hell upon earth, and the face of it covered with blood, as it was once with water.[24]

There is a passage in Hooker which comes very close to this:

Now if nature should intermit her course, and leave altogether though it were but for a while the observation of her own laws; if those principal and mother elements of the world, whereof all things in this lower world are made, should lose the qualities which now they have, if the frame of that heavenly arch erected over our heads should loosen and dissolve itself; if celestial spheres should forget their wonted motions, and by irregular volubility turn themselves any way as it might happen; if the prince of the lights of heaven, which now as a giant doth run his unwearied course, should as it were through a languishing faintness begin to stand and to rest himself; if the moon should wander from her beaten way, the times and seasons of the year blend themselves by disordered and confused mixture, the winds breathe out their last gasp, the clouds yield no rain, the earth be defeated of heavenly influence, the fruits of the earth pine away as children at the withered breasts of their mother no longer able to yield them relief....[25]

Besides the fact that both writers depended in one place upon a passage from the Psalms, there are two other points worth noting. One is the assertion on the part of Hooker's editor that he seems to have had in mind a passage from Arnobius.[26] While it is evident that neither Hooker nor Bolton directly quoted Arnobius, it is possible that both, quite independently, were inspired by it and other similar dissertations on disorder. The other point is that men of learning in that age were obsessed with considerations of order and disorder in the heavens and on earth, among the inanimate and the animate.[27] Hooker and Bolton were men of their time. There is no need to say that Bolton "virtually quoted from Hooker." And yet it would seem, in the order of things presented and in the very language used, that Bolton was in fact mindful of the impressive passage in Hooker when he was writing his sermon.[28] Indeed, Bolton, though Wood called him "a most religious and learned Puritan," shared, along with most Puritans, what I would call a central Anglican concern, the concern for order, for measure, for restraint.

III

Turning now to more definite evidence, we note that the eighth chapter of Book III was a matter of concern for Puritans, Roman Catholics, and Anglican divines, each group for its own reasons. It was certainly not the only such passage, but it was an important one and it illustrates something of Hooker's relation to and influence upon nascent Anglicanism in the seventeenth century. In it, Hooker confronted the proposition put forth by Thomas Cartwright on behalf of the Puritans, that "Nothing ought to be established in the Church, but that which is commanded in the word of God."[29] Over against this, Hooker set a rule, "that sundry things may be lawfully done in the Church, so as they be not done against the Scripture, although no Scripture do command them, but the Church only following the light of reason judge them to be in discretion meet" (III.vii.2). Here Hooker was not only refuting the Puritan understanding of Scripture but protesting against their treatment of reason as pernicious and not to be used in guiding the church. Hooker concluded, "we have endeavoured to make it appear, how in the nature of reason itself there is no impediment, but that the selfsame Spirit, which revealeth the things that God hath set down in his law, may also be thought to aid and direct men in finding out by the light of reason what laws are expedient to be made for the guiding of his Church, over and besides them that are in Scripture" (viii.18).

In chapter ix of Book III, Hooker wrote of the polity of the church as largely composed of laws that give it its structure and force. Working by means of reason, man makes such laws in accord with God's will for his church as this is expressed in both Scripture and natural law. It is important to note that reason is operative even when Scripture is applicable and in force. Hooker wrote:

Scripture comprehending examples and laws, laws some natural and some positive: examples there neither are for all cases which require laws to be made, and when there are, they can but direct as precedents only. Natural laws direct in such sort, that in all things we must for ever do according unto them; Positive so, that against them in no case we may do any thing, as long as the will of God is that they should remain in force. Howbeit when Scripture doth yield us precedents, how far forth they are to be followed; when it giveth natural laws, what particular order is thereunto most agreeable; when positive, which way to make laws unrepugnant unto them; yea though all these should want, yet what kind of ordinances would be most for that good of the Church which is aimed at, all this must be by reason found out. [III.ix.1]

The church is governed, by and large, by human laws, created by man through the instrumentality of reason, but these laws are under firm control. Hooker followed Aquinas in insisting that such laws of man be conformable to higher laws, that is "made according to the general laws of nature, and without contradiction unto any positive law in Scripture."[30] Thus in more than one sense, the laws of the church, though they be human, are accounted divine and must be acknowledged as ultimately derived from God—a point stressed by Hooker in the light of his conviction that the Puritans seemingly opposed God in opposing the godly laws of the Church of England. Hooker asserted that the laws which guided the heathen proceeded from God, who is the author of that light of nature by which they were led: "How much more then he the author of those laws, which have been made by his saints, endued further with the heavenly grace of his Spirit, and directed as much as might be with such instructions as his sacred word doth yield!" (ix.3).

In the eighth chapter, Hooker set forth the limits of Scripture, limits that may be summarized under four heads.[31] (1) Scripture presupposes in men the operation or knowledge of the law of nature which is the law of reason. (2) Scripture presupposes the operation of the legislative power with which societies of men have been endowed by nature to make human, positive laws. (3) Scripture presupposes the activity of human authority and reason for the confirmation of Scripture itself. (4) Scripture presupposes the operation of human authority and reason for the interpretation of Scripture. What Hooker had to say about the attestation of Scripture as the Word of God was of considerable importance for his understanding of the authority of the church. The Christian bases his belief in Jesus Christ on Scripture and believes Scripture true. But that Scripture is true is not self-evident. "Scripture teacheth us that saving truth which God hath discovered unto the world by revelation, and it presumeth us taught otherwise that itself is divine and sacred" (viii. 13). By what means is the Christian taught? Some may answer tradition: our fathers believed it so and thus we believe. From them we have received the Scripture as true. But Hooker pointed to another way, and this he arrived at by reference to experience:

by experience we all know, that the first outward motive leading men so to esteem of the Scripture is the authority of God's Church. For when we know the whole Church of God hath that opinion of the Scripture, we judge it even at the first an impudent thing for any man bred and brought up in the Church to be of a contrary mind without cause. Afterwards the more we bestow our labour in reading or hearing the mysteries thereof, the more we find that the thing itself doth answer our received opinion concerning it. So that the former inducement prevailing somewhat with us before, doth now much more prevail, when the very thing hath ministered farther reason. [viii.14]

He went on to argue that if "infidels or atheists" should question Scripture and its authority, then the Christian uses the "occasion to sift what reason there is, whereby the testimony of the Church concerning Scripture, and our own persuasion which Scripture itself hath confirmed, may be proved a truth infallible. In which case the ancient Fathers being often constrained to shew, what warrant they had so much to rely upon the Scriptures, endeavoured still to maintain the authority of the books of God by arguments such as unbelievers themselves must needs think reasonable. . . ." Reason has its place, "for that it confirmeth me in this my belief the more"; and if I do not believe it, reason is an instrument of God to persuade me to believe the Gospel.[32]

This, predictably, angered the Puritans, who believed that the Scriptures themselves attest to their own validity as the Word of God and that it is necessary to call upon Scripture to discern the true church from the false. How then can the church attest to the Scripture? Referring to Hooker's teaching, the Puritan authors of the *Christian Letter* asked: "Have we not here good cause to suspect the underpropping of a popish principle concerning the churches authoritie above the holy Scripture, to the disgrace of the English church? If not, then reconcile your assertions unto theirs, and shew mercie and trueth unto our reverend Fathers" of the Church of England who affirm the supremacy of Scripture.[33] To the accusation that he placed the church above Scripture, Hooker retorted: "You have already done your best to make a jarre between nature and scripture. Your next endevour is to do the like between scripture and the Church. Your delight in conflicts doth make you dreame of them where they are not."[34] His adversaries challenged him "to expound either by experience or otherwise; Whether the worde of God was receaved in the world, and beleeved by men, by virtue and authoritie of the witnesses, either Prophets or Apostles, or the holy church, or that such witnesses were not esteemed for the wordes sake: and the Church always approved both by God and faithfull men, as the same was described, commended, and ordered by the rule of holy scripture" (p. 10). To this Hooker replied, "I am sorrie to see you in the groundes and elements of your religion so sclenderly instructed."[35]

We have no way of telling how Hooker might have elaborated these particular notes. They were composed on the spur of the moment as he read the Puritan tract. But he could not have done better than to repeat, perhaps in different ways, his earlier arguments. In effect, this is what William Covel did in *A Just and Temperate Defence*, his response to the *Christian Letter*. Covel, made fellow of Queens' College, Cambridge, in 1589, was a parish clergyman, but he was also chaplain to Archbishop Abbot.[36] In support of Hooker and against the Puritans, he wrote:

For as there is no salvation without religion; no religion without faith; so there is no faith without a promise, nor promise without a word: for God desirous to make an union betwixt us and himselfe, hath so linked his word and his Church, that neither can stand, where both are not. The Church for her part, in her choice allowance testifying, as well that it is the scripture; as the scripture, from an absolute authority, doth assure us that it is the Church. For as those, who are con-verted, have no reason to beleeve, that to be the Church, where there is no scripture; so those who are not converted, have no great reason, to admit that for scripture, for which they have not the Churches warrant. So that in my opinion, the contention is unnaturall and unfit, to make a variance by comparison, betwixt these two, who are in reason and nature, to support each other.[37]

Covel went on to speak of four offices of the church in relation to Scripture: (1) to be the witness and keeper of them, (2) to discern between false and true in Scripture, (3) to publish them, and (4) to be an interpreter or expositor of their meaning. He concluded:

Touching therfore the authoritie of the Church, and the scriptures, though we graunt (as you say) that the Church is truly distinguished by the scriptures; that the scriptures (which is a strange phrase) warrant the trial of Gods word; and that it was ever beleeved for the words sake; yet without feare of underpropping anie popish principle (as you tearme it) we say, that we are taught to receive it, from the authoritie of the Church; we see her judgement; we heare her voice; and in humilitie subscribe unto all this; ever acknowledging the Scriptures to direct the Church, and yet the Church to afford (as she is bound) her true testimony of the Scripture.[38]

Hooker did not say that the church possessed an absolute authority with regard to Scripture. The mature Christian passes beyond the bare authority of the church. Reason is no infallible authority in itself, but reason operating in relation to church and Scripture is an instrument testifying to the truth of Scripture, aiding in the apprehension and interpretation of Scripture.[39] The point here is that Scripture presupposes the existence of a living, thinking recipient of revelation, a person capable of reaction and interaction, indeed a being whose nature it is to accumulate experience and to reason. Furthermore, he lives in relation to other experiencing, reasoning beings in society, most importantly in the context of the faithful who testify to the truth out of their accumulated and communal experience. Revelation is thus given in a mode befitting the recipient, as well as the giver. Revelation presupposes man in the context in which he has been created and is being recreated.

In all, Covel accepted and defended Hooker's position. Here as elsewhere he was forced by the adversary to defend Hooker's doctrinal teachings rather than his views of church discipline, which the authors of A Christian Letter chose to ignore or perhaps accepted. Covel was convinced that Hooker's teaching was in accord with the doctrine of the Church of England, its theologians, and its formularies, concerning Scripture and all else.[40] For him, Hooker's understanding of the relation between Scripture and nature and between Scripture and the church, and his defense of the place of reason and tradition in relation to Scripture, were those of the Church of England and were fundamentally right.

IV

In 1604, one year later, there appeared a book by one John Brereley in which Hooker was cited, with others, as a spokesman for the Protestant party in England.[41] The author was in fact Lawrence Anderton, B.A. Christ's College, Cambridge, 1596/7, a convert to Roman Catholicism who proceeded to Rome and entered the Society of Jesus in 1604.[42] Returning to England, he became Superior of the

Lancashire District of the Jesuits.[43] In *The Apologie*, Anderton cited Hooker and Covel in defense of Roman Catholics as Christians and the Church of Rome as a true church.[44] He further cited Hooker as accusing the Puritans of having "*many Supremacies*" (or "many domesticke Popes," as he put it) and as acknowledging "the lawfullnes of Christian vowes."[45] But most importantly, Anderton cited Hooker, along with Rainolds, Whitaker, and Bilson, as admitting the necessity of having "a certaine visible Judge," as well as Scripture, for the determining of controversies (p. 33). And in discussing the necessity, in addition to Scripture, for "the Churches true Pastours" to "*evermore continew* and *withstand* all innovation of false doctrine even *with open reprehension*," he wrote: "The answerable performance wherof in perticuler being matter of fact, can be to us at this day, no otherwise made knowen, then upon the onely credite of humane testimonie commended to us by historie, the force of which testimonie our very adversaries acknowledge that there fore the Same SCRIPTURES do therein most evidently perforce reduce them to this foresaid triall by historie and Fathers: whereto if they stand, their overthrow (they see) is certaine, and in refusing the same, their flight is shamefull."[46] What is interesting is exactly how Anderton drew on Hooker for support in his argument. He quoted him as saying: "*The strength of mans authoritie is affirmatively such, that the weightiest affaires in the world depend there-upon.*" "*Whatso-ever we beleeve concerning salvation by Christ, although the scripture be therin, the grounde of our beleefe, yet is mans authoritie the keye that openeth the dore etc. The scripture coulde not teach us these thinges, unlesse wee beleeved men: etc.*" "*Of thinges necessarie the very cheefest is to knowe what bookes we are bound to esteeme holy, which point is confessed impossible for the scripture it selfe to teach.*" "*For if any one booke of scripture did give testimonie to all, yet still that scripture which giveth credit to the rest would require an other scripture to give creditt unto it, neither coulde we ever come to any pause whereon to rest our assurance unlesse besides scripture there were some thinge which might assure us. etc.*" And finally he cited the following as proceeding from these quotations: "*We all knowe that the first out-ward motive leading men so to esteeme of the scripture, is the authority of Gods Church.*"[47] The last two of these quotations were cited by the authors of the *Christian Letter* as proving Hooker's heresy; here they are cited by the Jesuit as demonstrating Protestant agreement with Roman Catholic teaching.

In 1608 Anderton published another work, *The Protestants Apologie For The Roman Church*, in which he cited the quotations concerning Scripture given above (except the first) and added a reference from the eighth chapter of Book III concerning the testimony of the Spirit in relation to Scripture.[48] He did this with the assertion "that Protestants are not able to determyne by Scripture which is Scripture, is in it selfe evident, and by them selves confessed."[49] It was this passage in Anderton's work which then commanded the attention of William Laud in his *Conference with Fisher*. Indeed, Laud considered what Hooker had to say concerning Scripture, tradition, church and reason in III.viii to be of such importance that he returned to it more than once.[50] In the most important place, Laud argued that it was not in God's nature to demand of his creatures that they be able to demonstrate rationally that Scripture is what it claims to be. Rather *faith* is the basic requirement, with such rational demonstration as may support faith. "Now God doth not require a full *Demonstrative Knowledge* in us, that the Scripture is his Word, and therefore in his Providence hath kindled in it no Light for that, but he requires our Faith of it, and such a *certain Demonstration*, as may fit that." For this purpose, God has "left sufficient Light in Scripture to Reason and Grace meeting, where the Soul is *morally* prepared by the *Tradition of the Church*" (p. 56). Against this, in what appears to be a contrived dialogue, "Fisher" brought forth Hooker's statement (I.xiv.1) that Scripture is not self-authenticating. Indeed, Scripture cannot possibly attest to the truth that it is God's word, for if one book of Scripture were to yield such demonstration concerning the rest, it would itself require some other book to attest to its own authenticity. Something external to Scripture is thus needed, and this, Laud noted, Anderton had found in Hooker to be "*the Authority of Gods Church.*"[51] Laud then stated that Hooker's demonstration was indeed valid but that Anderton had twisted his words:

For in the first place, *Hooker's* speech is, *Scripture it self cannot teach this*; nor can the Truth say, that Scripture it self can. It must needs *ordinarily* have *Tradition*, to prepare the mind of a man to receive it. And in the next place, where he speaks so sensibly, That *Scripture* cannot bear witness to it self, nor one part of it to another; that is grounded upon *Nature*, which admits no created thing to be witness to it self; and is acknowledged by our Saviour, *If I bear witness to my self, my witness is not true*, that is, *is not of force to be reasonably accepted for Truth*. But then it is more than manifest, that Hooker delivers his Demonstration of *Scripture alone*. For if Scripture hath another proof, nay many other proofs to usher it, and lead it in, then no Question, it can both prove, and approve it self.

Laud's point was that Hooker had maintained the proper supremacy of Scripture and that when he asserted the necessity for some external authority, he was referring to the first introduction to Scripture as God's Word. Laud pointed out that Hooker did not deny the ultimate authority of Scripture: "His words are, *So that unless, besides Scripture, there be*, etc. *Besides Scripture*; therefore he excludes not *Scripture*, though he call for another Proof to lead it in, and help in assurance, namely *Tradition*, which no man, that hath his brains about him, denies" (p. 57).

Laud sought to set the record straight concerning what Hooker had to say in II.vii of the *Laws*: the authority of man, or tradition, is "the *Key* that lets us in," but the ground, the house, is Scripture. The authority of man is clearly subservient, a useful tool. And as regards Anderton's citation from III.viii, Laud emphasized that Hooker's words were these:

The first outward Motive, leading men so to esteem of the Scripture, is the Authority of Gods Church, etc. But afterwards, the more we bestow our Labour in reading or learning the Mysteries thereof, the more we find that the thing it self doth answer our received opinion concerning it: so that the former inducement prevailing somewhat with us before, doth now much more prevail, when the very thing hath ministred farther Reason. Here then again, in his Judgment, Tradition is the first Inducement; but the farther Reason, and Ground, is the Scripture. And Resolution of Faith ever settles upon the Farthest Reason it can, not upon the First Inducement. So that the State of the Question is firm, and yet plain enough to him that will not shut his eyes.[52]

For Laud, as for Hooker, Scripture contained all things necessary for salvation and was thus supreme. But Scripture presupposes the operation of tradition, reason, and church authority, each in its proper place. There is a confluence of God-given instruments and means contributing toward that certainty concerning salvation which is attested by Scripture. Against the Jesuit, Laud emphasized Hooker's high estimation of the authority of Scripture. Against the Puritans he might very well have emphasized the limits of the Scripture's authority. Fundamentally, the results would not greatly differ.[53]

<h1 style="text-align:center">V</h1>

There were other Roman Catholic polemicists who, like Anderton, cited Hooker's teaching on Scripture and the church. Edward Maihew used Hooker's contention that we cannot know Scripture to be canonical by means of its own testimony and must claim the authority of the church to do so as grounds for claiming that Hooker, Zanchius, Brentius, and Kemnitius "flie from Scriptures unto tradition for the proofe of this matter."[54] Sylvester Norris cited Hooker as casting doubt upon those who claim to interpret Scripture by the power of the Holy Spirit: they are deluded, following their own conjectures and grounding *"themselves on humane authority."*[55] He expanded this in a later edition of the *Antidote*, concluding that Hooker had argued "that the outward letter sealed with the inward witnesse of the spirit, is not a sufficient warrant for every particuler man, to judg, and approve the Scripture to be Canonicall; the ghospel itself to be the ghospell of Christ; but the authority of gods Church (as he acknowledgeth) is necessarily required thereunto."[56]

Of greater importance was the emergence of one Matthew Wilson, who wrote under his adopted name, Edward Knott.[57] Knott studied at St Omer and at Rome, was ordained priest in 1606, entered the Society of Jesus, and served as a missionary priest in England, becoming provincial of the English Province of the Jesuits in 1643. In 1630 he wrote a treatise entitled *Charity Mistaken*, which was answered by Christopher Potter, fellow of Queen's College, Oxford, 1614–15.[58] Potter was at one time a Puritan opponent of Laud's, but on becoming provost of Queen's in 1626, he attached himself to Laud, became known to the Puritans as an Arminian, and wrote with

Laud against the Roman Catholics, chiefly Knott. Knott countered with his treatise, *Charity Mayntayned*, in 1634. It was in this latter work that Knott cited Hooker on the subject of Scripture and the church:

That Scripture cannot assure us, that it selfe is Canonicall Scripture, is acknowledged by some Protestants in expresse *words*, and by all of them in deeds. *M. Hooker* whome *D. Potter* ranketh among men of great learning and judgement, sayth: *Of thinges necessary, the very chiefest is to know what bookes we are to esteeme holy; which point is confessed impossible for the Scripture it selfe to teach.* And this he proveth by the same argument, which we lately used, saying thus: *It is not the word of God which doth, or possibly can, assure us, that we doe well to thinke it his word. For if any one Booke of Scripture did give testimony of all, yet still that Scripture which giveth testimony to the rest, would require another Scripture to give credit unto it. Neyther could we come to any pause whereon to rest, unless besids Scripture, there were something which might assure us etc.* And this he acknowledgeth to be the Church.[59]

William Chillingworth prepared an answer to Knott, *The Religion of Protestants. A Safeway to Salvation*, which was perused by Potter at Laud's request and published in 1638. Remembered as an early champion of toleration and a latitudinarian,[60] Chillingworth was an Oxford man and fellow of Trinity College. A godson of Laud, he debated with the Jesuit John Fisher, was himself converted to Roman Catholicism, and went to Douay in 1630. In 1631 he was back at Oxford, though he did not immediately associate himself with the Church of England. Having failed to find satisfaction in the Church of Rome and doubting that all of the Thirty-Nine Articles of Religion of the Church of England could be proved by Scripture, he then sought for a reasonable basis of belief, relying upon Scripture as interpreted by reason and no longer expecting to find any perfect system of doctrine or practice. Chillingworth's reply to Knott was written while he was a guest in the house of his friend, Sir Lucius Cary, Viscount Falkland, at Great Tew in Oxfordshire. Indeed, Chillingworth (along with John Hales, Henry Hammond, Gilbert Sheldon, George Morley, Edmund Waller, and Lord Clarendon) was considered a member of the Falkland group, opposed to Calvinism, espousing free investigation, the use of reason in the interpretation of Scripture, and the separation of saving truth from "correct" theology. As Bishop McAdoo says, "it is in their almost exaggerated reaction in this direction, in their spirit of free investigation, and in their view of Biblical authority, that they may be seen to be the first wave of that tide of thought which, by the end of the century, had swept past the breakwaters of traditional orthodoxy."[61] It was in this context that Chillingworth, writing against Knott, sought to correct his misinterpretation of Hooker. He concentrated on matters which most accorded with his own current concerns. Thus he did not cite sections 2 and 3 of II.vii, where the authority of man in things divine is defended, but its subsequent qualification in sections 5 and 6. Furthermore, he ended with a quotation from Hooker that was very much to his liking:

> *That authority of men should prevail with men either against or above reason, is no part o* *our belief. Companies of learned men, be they never so great and reverend, are to yield unto* *reason, the weight whereof, is no whit prejudiced by the simplicity of his person which doth* *alledge it, but being found to be sound and good, the bare opinion of men to the contrary,* *must of necessity stoop and give place.*[62]

Here, as elsewhere, Chillingworth interpreted Hooker as supporting his views against infallibility, certainty, and for toleration, whether justified or not.[63] Against Knott, he protested: "It is vain for you to tell us what M. *Hooker* says at all. For M. *Hooker*, though an excellent man, was but a man" (p. 238). Yet he felt that papists and Puritans alike misused Hooker in asserting that he required "a blind and an unlimited obedience, to Ecclesiastical decisions universally and in all cases, even when plain Texts or Reason seems to controul them." To the contrary, Hooker "is as far from making such an Idol of Ecclesiastical Authority, as the Puritans whom he writes against" (pp. 238–39).

Referring to both Knott and Brereley's use of Hooker's statement, "*That whereon we must rest our assurance that the Scripture is God's Word, is the Church,*"[64] Chillingworth asserts that Hooker has been abused. Quoting the entire passage, he argues that, read in context, it does not support the papist position. "M. *Hooker* hath not one syllable to your pretended purpose, but very much to the contrary. There he tells us indeed, *That, ordinarily the first Introduction and probable Motive to the belief of the verity, is the Authority of the Church*; but that it is the last Foundation whereon our belief hereof is rationally grounded, that in the same place he plainly denies" (pp. 49–50). Thus, at the outset, Chillingworth is intent upon undermining Hooker's emphasis upon the church. This he does in a series of marginal notes on the quotation from III.viii of the *Laws*. Where Hooker asserts that the whole church acknowledges the verity of Scripture ("*For when we know the whole Church of God hath that opinion of the Scripture, we judge it at the first an impudent thing for any man, bred and brought up in the Church to be of a contrary mind without cause*"), Chillingworth takes this to mean the national church in which a man has been brought up: "The whole Church that he speaks of, seems to be that particular Church wherein a man is bred and brought up; and the Authority of this he makes an Argument which presseth a man's modesty more than his reason." And where Hooker states that it would be an impudent thing to disagree with the whole church on such a matter, Chillingworth rejoins: "In saying, It seems impudent to be of a contrary mind, without cause, he implies; There may be a just cause to be of a contrary mind, and that then it were no impudence to be so." Hooker goes on to say that once having received the Scripture on the authority of the church, "*the more we bestow our labour upon reading or hearing the mysteries thereof, the more we find that the thing it self doth answer our received opinion concerning it.*" To this Chillingworth counters, in an attempt to interpret Hooker in a manner suited to his own convictions and contrary to the teachings of the papists: "Therefore the Authority of the Church is not the pause whereon we rest: we had need of more assurance, and the intrinsecal Arguments afford it." He pushes even farther when he plays down Hooker's subsequent argument that church authority "*prevailing somewhat with us before, doth now much more prevail, when the very thing hath ministred farther reason.*" Chillingworth, not in his best form, writes: "Somewhat, but not much, until it be backed and inforced by farther reason: it self therefore is not the farthest reason and the last resolution." He then leaps upon Hooker's statement that when "*Infidels or Atheists*" question the truth of Scripture, the Christian looks for reason—for rational proof—that what the church presents as true and what Scripture itself has taught us is true may be proven to be so. He is not simply protecting the authority of Scripture over against the church when he notes in the margin: "Observe, I pray; Our perswasion, and the testimony of the Church concerning Scripture, may be proved true; Therefore neither of them was in his account the farthest proof" (p. 50).

Finally, Hooker points to the example of the Fathers of the early church who, in order to defend their reliance upon Scripture in the face of opposition, were forced to argue in a reasonable way. "*Neither is it,*" wrote Hooker, "*a thing impossible or greatly hard, even by such kind of proofs, so to manifest and clear that Point, that no man living shall be able to deny it, without denying some apparent Principle, such as all men acknowledge to be true.*" Here Chillingworth rejoined, noting: "Natural reason then built on principles common to all men, is the last resolution; unto which the Churches Authority is but the first inducement" (p. 50).

It is clear, then, that however appreciative Chillingworth may have been of Hooker, he did not altogether agree with him. The notes made by Chillingworth were inserted to make sure that the reader understood Hooker rightly—that is, in accordance with Chillingworth's own views. Hooker saw no good reason why a person should question the interpretation of Scripture made by the church and the ancient Fathers. His view of the church and its authority was high without being idolatrous. The church not only introduced the Christian to the authority of Scripture as the Word of God, but it provided as well a foundation for the maintenance of this truth throughout life, a foundation that would be confirmed in its testimony by the internal evidence of Scripture, understood by reason. Where necessary, the verity of Scripture could be defended by rational proofs, but this was not necessary for all Christians. For Hooker, the rational understanding of Christianity did not necessarily involve doubt concerning the church's witness nor any close investigation of its teachings. But to Chillingworth, the church provided simply the first introduction; it was "the first outward motive, not the last assurance where we rest"; the church's testimony was to yield to the individual scrutiny of Scripture and its claims. Faith was to be arrived at by the individual on the basis of Scripture, to which the church had initially testified. Over against Hooker's belief in passive consent to the church's teaching concerning Scripture by those born into the company of believers, Chillingworth argued for the strivings of rational men: "Natural reason then built on principles common to all men, is the last resolution; unto which the Churches Authority is but the first inducement."[65] It is no wonder that Laud was disturbed and had his godson's book perused and revised by others before it was published.

It is true, as McLachlan says, that Chillingworth, in a sense a disciple of Hooker's, "stood upon his shoulders and saw farther."[66] But it must not be forgotten that Hooker had opened the door. He was intolerant for the sake of order, and yet his teaching led toward the development of toleration by those who followed after him.[67] His philosophy was scholastic, but it opened the way toward the new philosophy. "The flexibility associated with the idea of reason and law as an implanted directive in the universe" seemingly "predisposed Anglican theological method to accept and assimilate the work of the scientists and naturalists."[68] It is not surprising, then, that Chillingworth could argue on the basis of Hooker's teaching and go beyond him. The line of development, in fact, can be traced from Hooker to the Falkland group, thence to the Cambridge Platonists, beyond them to the eighteenth-century Latitudinarians, on to Coleridge and Maurice, to liberal Catholicism of the *Lux Mundi* type in the nineteenth century, and so into our own times. This is not to deny, however, that High Churchmen of the seventeenth century and Anglo-Catholics of the Tractarian era before *Lux Mundi* could and did cite Hooker as an authority with whom they could agree. But the line of development does not rest with them. A hint—and no more than that is possible here—that the line reaches beyond Chillingworth to the Cambridge Platonists is provided by a glance at Benjamin Whichcote, whose teacher, Tuckney, complained that his student had been reading Hooker and Chillingworth. In his reply to Tuckney, Whichcote set forth three arguments by which scriptural authority can be proved. The first is that Scriptures make their own witness, the second is that the Holy Spirit testifies, and the third is that tradition yields proof. On the latter, Whichcote had the same high regard for the church's testimony and the same concern to avoid the pitfalls of Roman Catholicism with respect to the visible church as did Hooker.[69]

VI

Francis Paget, Bishop of Oxford and a reviser of Keble, summarized the important eighth chapter of Hooker's Book III in this way: "The tradition and authority with which a man finds himself encompassed; the witness of his own heart and conscience, recognizing and responding to the Spirit which meets him in the Bible; the scrutiny and appraising of the credentials which it offers to his reason: such is the threefold process which a man may use, and which the Bible presupposes for the warrant of its claim to teach in God's Name, and with His authority, the means whereby men now must reach the end for which they were created."[70] Here we have the famous three strands of Anglican authority, Scripture, tradition (in the church), and reason. The insistence upon all three and the giving of just weight to each in relation to the others was a keynote of Hooker's work. His classic statement of it in his first four books, together with his application of it in the last four (especially the fifth), were known and influential in theological debate of the early seventeenth century, as we have seen in our perusal of one small segment of it.

The results were many and important. For one thing, there was an emphasis upon measure and restraint, balance and coherence. Scripture presupposes tradition and reason, and each is necessary to the other. Upset the balance and truth is lost in falsehood. Furthermore, comprehension results. More than twenty years ago the then Archbishop of Canterbury, Geoffrey Fisher, asked the Evangelical and Anglo-Catholic parties of the Church of England and the English Free Churchmen to present their views. In doing so, both Evangelicals and Anglo-Catholics emphasized the comprehensiveness of the Church of England as it had emerged from the era of the Reformation. Furthermore, both discerned the fact that this initial comprehensiveness of pre-Reformation, Reformation, and humanistic elements was succeeded by the development of three post-Reformation movements: Anglo-Catholicism, Evangelicalism, and Liberalism.[71] It is not difficult to see that each of these movements is related to one of the strands of authority: the Reformation and Evangelicalism emphasized the authority of Scripture; the pre-Reformation and Anglo-Catholicism emphasized the authority of tradition (in the church); and humanism and Liberalism emphasized individual conscience and the use of reason. As the Anglo-Catholic report put it:

The Anglican Reformation embodied principles from which some degree of return to the fulness of the Christian Tradition might be made. There was the appeal to the ancient Tradition of the undivided Church to which the "Catholic Fathers and ancient Bishops" bore witness. There was also a freedom to learn from Protestantism and from the Renaissance, without falling under the domination of any contemporary dogmatic system. Hence there has been a true Anglican witness to the fulness of Christian tradition; and the history of Anglican theology shows that it possesses a power of construction which has made for synthesis rather than for division.

We may perhaps discern more than a little wishful thinking in this, but I would not wish to debate their further conclusion that "the power of construction in Anglican divinity comes from theologians who, recognising loyally the limits laid down by our formularies, were able to combine the appeal to Scripture and to sound learning with the appeal to ancient Tradition in its fulness and, as a result, could escape from the blinkers of sixteenth century systems and controversies. With Hooker this power of construction made its first significant appearance."[72]

VII

It is in the development of a certain method and attitude rather than in the details of his teaching that Hooker is important, that he came to represent a vital turning in the history of Anglicanism. It can be seen time and again where Hooker deals with practical matters of concern in the theological controversies of the day, in relation to ecclesiastical law, teaching about sacraments, episcopacy and the relation of church and state. The threefold authority, maintained in balance, is everywhere present. Scripture, tradition (church), and reason are brought to bear in such ways that truth is accented, truth which comprehends differing points of view as well as may be, given the exigencies of the time.

One final example must suffice: Hooker's treatment of the controversy over Christ's presence in the Lord's Supper. For him it was the end in view, participation in Christ, that mattered, rather than any particular definition of the mode of Christ's presence. Thus at one point, when he confronted the statement "This is my body," he defined it first in terms of consubstantiation, then in terms of transubstantiation, and lastly as the "Sacramentaries" would define it—this last being representative of his own understanding of the matter. Of these three definitions or interpretations Hooker wrote:

the last hath in it nothing but what the rest do all approve and acknowledge to be most true, nothing but that which the words of Christ are on all sides confessed to enforce, nothing but that which the Church of God hath always thought necessary, nothing but that which alone is sufficient for every Christian man to believe concerning the use and force of this sacrament, finally nothing but that wherewith the writings of all antiquity are consonant and all Christian confessions agreeable. And as truth in what kind soever is by no kind of truth gainsayed, so the mind which resteth itself on this is never troubled with those perplexities which the other do both find, by means of so great contradiction between their opinions and true principles of reason grounded upon experience, nature and sense. [v.lxvii.12]

In the course of his argument, Scripture, tradition (in the church and in the testimony of the early church Fathers), and reason were each used, but they were used in such a way that they emphasized what is most true in each, most common to all. Thus Hooker shifted attention away from a change in the elements toward their use by the faithful: "Is there any thing more expedite, clear, and easy, than that as Christ is termed our life because through him we obtain life, so the parts of this sacrament are his body and blood for that they are so to us who receiving them receive that by them which they are termed? The bread and cup are his body and blood because they are causes instrumental upon the receipt whereof the *participation* of his body and blood ensueth" (lxvii.5).

Since this was the position followed by some of Hooker's successors, C. W. Dugmore has identified Hooker as the precursor of what he terms the central school of those who wrote concerning Eucharistic doctrine.[73] Archbishop Ussher, identified with the central school, stated firmly that the elements

are not changed in nature, but in use (I *Cor.* 10.16). For the words of eating and drinking do properly belong to the outward elements of bread and wine, and by a borrowed speech do improperly belong to the body and blood of Christ: to note unto us the communion we have with our Saviour Christ, of whom we are verily partakers by a lively faith, as of the bread and wine, by eating and drinking them. And thus we say that these elements are changed in use; because being separated from a common use they are consecrate to sign and seal unto us our spiritual nourishment and growth by the body and bloud of Christ Jesus (*Luke* 22.19. I *Cor.* 3.4.)[74]

Here the attempt was to hold fast to Scripture regarded as supreme in matters pertaining to salvation and to the witness of the church in its formularies, the teachings of the Fathers, and the councils of the undivided church, while at the same time not running contrary to reason—reason whereby the devout believer apprehends the truth in Scripture and tradition. All of these elements of understanding were at work in this treatment of Eucharistic doctrine. But with Hooker there was—over and above these elements—an attitude of devotion, appropriate to the Christian worshiper, which qualified the claims of reason, as of all human authority. At the end of his discussion of Christ's presence, he passed beyond rational argument to prayer: "what these elements are in themselves it skilleth not, it is enough that to me which take them they are the body and blood of Christ, his promise in witness hereof sufficeth, his word he knoweth which way to accomplish; why should any cogitation possess the mind of a faithful communicant but this, O my God thou art true, O my Soul thou art happy!" (v.lxvii.12). Reason was not unbridled. In this respect, Chillingworth and his successors represent a trend that moved beyond Hooker and came more nearly in accord with the rationalism that was to come with the deists and the Enlightenment. But for Hooker, reason was primarily the receptacle of divine truth, not a scrutinizing, critical faculty of the mind.

There is, admittedly, very much that remains to be done in tracing Hooker's relation to and influence upon Anglicanism as it developed and was transformed in the seventeenth century and beyond. But that he was a part of that development, and a vital part, and that he was influential, cannot, it seems to me, be denied. As Norman Sykes, with his customary accuracy, wrote: "It was the good fortune of the Church of England that from the midst of controversy and of the controversialists there arose an apologist, in the person of Richard Hooker, whose defence of its position was based upon lines so broad and deep that his work was not only effective as a refutation of his opponent's contentions, but has won a recognised place as a classic of English theological literature."[75]

NOTES

1. Thomas Babington Macaulay, *The History of England from the Accession of James II* (Boston: Houghton Mifflin, 1882), 1:56–58.
2. Maurice, *Moral and Metaphysical Philosophy* (1872), 2:138–39. Cf. Stephen Neill, *Anglicanism*, 3d ed. (Harmondsworth, Middlesex: Penguin Books, 1965), p. 119. Neill denies that Anglicanism represents a compromise or a "middle-way" which means neither this nor that. "Anglicanism is a very positive form of Christian belief; it affirms that it teaches the whole of catholic faith, free from the distortions, the exaggerations, the over-definitions both of the Protestant left wing and of the right wing of Tridentine Catholicism."
3. More and Cross, *Anglicanism*, pp. xxii–xxiii.
4. Ibid. Cf. *Laws* I.ii.3, citing Sapientia [Wisdom of Solomon] 8:1, 11:20. All Hooker references are to *The Works of...Mr. Richard Hooker*, ed. Keble, 7th ed., rev., 1888, by book, chapter, and section.
5. McAdoo, *The Spirit of Anglicanism*, p. 22.
6. McLachlan, *Socinianism in Seventeenth Century England*, pp. 52–53. On Laud's theological liberalism and political conservatism, see H. R. Trevor-Roper, *Archbishop Laud 1573–1645* (London: Macmillan, 1940; 2d ed., 1962), p. 338. On Laud as a liberal, see Gladstone's comment in John Morley, *The Life of William Ewart Gladstone* (London: Macmillan, 1903), 3:480.
7. McAdoo, p. 5. Sykes, in *The Social & Political Ideas of Some Great Thinkers of the Sixteenth & Seventeenth Centuries*, ed. Hearnshaw, p. 88. Cf. Little, *Religion, Order, and Law*, pp. 147–50.
8. Henry Hallam, *Introduction to the Literature of Europe in the Fifteenth, Sixteenth, and Seventeenth Centuries* (London: Ward, Lock, n.d.), p. 289 (II.iv.1, 3).

9. Church, "Introduction," in *Book I: Of the Laws of Ecclesiastical Polity*, 1882, p. xvii.

10. For a discussion of Hooker and the English Reformation in relation to Lancelot Andrewes, see R. W. Church, *Pascal and Other Sermons* (London: Macmillan, 1895), pp. 52–96.

11. Cf. Sisson, *The Judicious Marriage of Mr. Hooker and the Birth of "The Laws of Ecclesiastical Polity*," p. 71; on the publication and sale of Hooker's first five books, cf. pp. 66–78. [See below, p. 239 —ed.]

12. Covel, *A Just and Temperate Defence Of The Five Books of Ecclesiastical Policie*, sig. A 4. Corpus Christi College, Oxford, MS 215b.

13. Job Throckmorton, *The Defence of Job Throckmorton, against the Slaunders of Maister Sutcliffe* (n.p., 1594), sig. C4; Matthew Sutcliffe, *An Answere unto a Certaine Calumnious Letter* (London: Christopher Barker, 1595), pp. 43^{r-v}, 51^{v}, 53^{r}–57^{r}.

14. Lancelot Andrewes, *A Pattern of Catechistical Doctrine, and Other Minor Works* (Oxford: John Henry Parker, 1846), pp. 366–67, where Hooker is quoted with regard to the use of pagan ceremonies. Richard Field, *Of the Church, Five Books* (Cambridge: Cambridge Univ. Press, 1852), 4 : 403, where he cites Hooker on the ubiquity of Christ against Theopilus Higgons. Joseph Hall, *A Recollection of Such Treatises as have bene heretofore severally published* (London: Henry Fetherstone, 1621), 1 : 502, where Hooker is cited in defense of the English settlement of religion; 511, where Hooker is cited concerning the ministry and cure of souls by law ordered; 2, where Hooker's fourth book is cited concerning the Church of Rome; 52, where Hooker's third book is cited concerning church membership. John Cosin, *Works* (Oxford: John Henry Parker, 1843–51), 1 : 101 n., 103 n., where the editor believes Cosin was relying upon Hooker (p. vii); 4 : 24, where Hooker's fifth book is specifically cited in a discussion of Christ's presence in the Eucharist; 405, where Hooker is cited in a letter to Mr Cordel; and 459, where Hooker is cited in a discussion of the sabbath. George Bull, *Works*, ed. Edward Burton (Oxford: Oxford Univ. Press, 1846), 4 : 377, citing Hooker's *Discourse of Justification*. Robert Sanderson, *Works* (Oxford: Oxford Univ. Press, 1854), 2 : 117, who cites Hooker as one having dealt with Puritan contentions, and one whose works were "written with singular learning, wisdom, godliness, and moderation." Jeremy Taylor, *The Whole Works* (London: Frederick Westley and A. H. Davis, 1835), 2 : 52, where he cites the *Discourse of Justification*; 3 : 23, where he cites Hooker on confirmation (*Laws* v.lxvi), and 46, where he refers to the lost Books VII and VIII. This list is but an indication of the use of Hooker by Anglican writers.

Other than Anglican theologians, one might mention Samuel Hieron, the Puritan, and his *A Defence Of The Ministers Reasons, For Refusall Of Subscription To The Booke of Common Prayer, and of Conformitie* (n.p., 1607), p. 4, citing *Laws* Pref.ix, and John Locke, *Two Tracts on Government*, ed. Philip Abrams (Cambridge: Cambridge Univ. Press, 1967), pp. 170–71, 193. On Hooker and

Locke, see also Munz, *The Place of Hooker in the History of Thought*, App. D., pp. 205–08; and Bull, "What did Locke Borrow from Hooker?", *Thought* 7 (1932): 122–35. [Cf. above, pp. 4–5, 40–42 —*ed.*]

15. For instance, there is seemingly no direct reference in *The Sermons of John Donne*, ed. Evelyn M. Simpson and George R. Potter, 10 vols. (Berkeley and Los Angeles: Univ. of California Press, 1953–62). But William R. Mueller in *John Donne: Preacher* (Princeton: Princeton Univ. Press, 1962), writes, p. 149: "John Donne was an early seventeenth-century Anglican to the core. If the *Divine Comedy* is a literary monument to Thomism and *The Pilgrim's Progress* the dramatic embodiment of Puritanism, then the Sermons of Donne are the most compelling presentation of that *Summa* of Anglicanism: Richard Hooker's *Of the Laws of Ecclesiastical Polity*." Cf. pp. 49, 52–53, 58, 64, 65, 79, 106, 156, 213–14, and 240. See also Richard E. Hughes, *The Progress of the Soul: The Interior Career of John Donne* (New York: Morrow, 1968), pp. 168–69.

16. Cf. William T. Costello, *The Scholastic Curriculum at Early Seventeenth-Century Cambridge* (Cambridge: Harvard Univ. Press, 1958).

17. Michael Walzer, *The Revolution of the Saints: A Study in the Origins of Radical Politics* (Cambridge: Harvard Univ. Press, 1965; reprinted New York: Atheneum, 1969), p. 159.

18. Wood, *Athenæ Oxonienses* (London: R. Knaplock, D. Midwinter, and J. Tonson, 1721), 1 : 607, and the appended *Fasti Oxonienses*, 1:215.

19. Anthony Fawkner, *Nicodemus for Christ, or The Religious Moote of an Honest Lawyer* (London: Felix Kyngston for Robert Allott, 1630), p. 6, citing "*S. August. de lib. arb. c. 6*" and "*Aquin. 12. q. 92. Art. 2.*" For other references to nature, see Fawkner's sermon delivered at Paul's Cross on May 21, 1626, *Comfort to the Afflicted* (London: Robert Milbourne, 1626), sig. A 2 and pp. 16–17, and a sermon delivered at the assize in Okeham, Rutlandshire, July 31, 1629, entitled ΕΙΡΗΝΟΓΟΝΙΑ; *Or The Pedigree of Peace* (London: Felix Kyngston for Robert Allott, 1630), pp. 1–2, 5, 6, and esp. 15–18. Nowhere in Fawkner's writings do I find any direct reference to Hooker.

20. Costello, p. 121.

21. Thomas Taylor, *Regula Vitæ, The Rule Of The Law Under The Gospel* (London: W.I. for Robert Dawlman, 1631), pp. 21–22.

22. Walzer, p. 159 n.

23. Wood, *Athenæ Oxonienses*, 1:560.

24. Robert Bolton, *Two Sermons Preached at Northampton at Two Severall Assisses There* (London: George Miller for E[dw.] B[agshawe], 1635), p. 10; see also p. 51.

25. *Works* 1:207–08 (I.iii.2); cf. Psalm 19:5.

26. Ibid., p. 208 n. Cf. Arnobii, *Adversus Nationes: Libri VII*, ed. Augustus Reifferscheid, Corpus Scriptorum Ecclesiasticorum Latinorum (Vienna: C. Geroldi filium, 1875), 4:4; Arnobius of Sicca, *The Case Against the Pagans*, trans. George E. McCracken, Ancient Christian Writers, 7 (Westminster, Md.: Newman Press, 1949–52), 1:59–60.

27. Cf. Tillyard, *The Elizabethan World Picture*, pp. 7–15. On the Puritan concern for order and especially disorder, see Walzer, ch. 6. For a discussion of the difference between Anglican and Puritan views of order, see Little, *Religion, Order, and Law*, esp. pp. 149–53.

28. See also Bolton's use of the concept of "participation" in connection with the Eucharist, in *A Three-fold Treatise* (London: E. Purslow for R. Harford, 1634), pp. 35, 41–42. This concept was central to Hooker's understanding; cf. *Laws* v.i.1–3; lv.1; lvii.1; lxvii.2, 5, 7, 12.

29. *Laws* III.viii.1, citing Thomas Cartwright, *A Replye to an Answere made of M. Doctor Whitegift* (n.p., 1574?), 2: 56–57.

30. *Laws* III.ix.2. Aquinas, *Summa Theologica* I.ii.91(3).

31. Paget, *An Introduction to the Fifth Book of Hooker's Treatise of the Laws of Ecclesiastical Polity*, pp. 111–15.

32. *Laws* III.viii.14. Cf. Paget, p. 145. On Hooker and reason in this place, see Bethell, *The Cultural Revolution of the Seventeenth Century*, pp. 19–23.

33. *A Christian Letter of certaine English Protestants* ([Middleburg: R. Schilders], 1599), pp. 9–10. See also pp. 7–8.

34. Corpus Christi College, Oxford, MS 215b, in the margin of p. 8 of this copy of *A Christian Letter*. In the previous section (p. 7), the Puritans attacked Hooker for saying, "*It sufficeth that nature and scripture doe serve in such full sorte, that they both jointlie and not severallie eyther of them be so compleate, that unto everlasting felicities we need not the knowledge of anie thing more than these two. etc.*" (cf. *Laws* I.xiv.5).

35. Oxford, MS 215b, in the margin of p. 10. Hooker noted a passage from Tertullian, *Contra Gentiles*, in his *Opera* (Paris, 1566), 2: 637. Hooker's transcription ran: "Fides nititur authoritate docentis. Docens autem confirmatam habet authoritatem personae virtute miraculorum. Id quod omnino necessarium est propter ea quae docet supra et praeter naturalem rationem quo omnis probatio argumentosa nititur quae fidem facit. Atque hoc Apostolus de se testatur cum efficacem fuisse sermonem suum asserit non vi humanae persuasionis sed assistentis spiritus ad opera miraculosa perficienda."

36. Cf. *DNB*, *sub* William Covell; also, John Venn and J. A. Venn, *Alumni Cantabrigienses* (Cambridge: Cambridge Univ. Press, 1922), 1: 406. Covel was a fellow of King James's College, Chelsea, an institution devised for the maintenance of scholars writing against Roman Catholics.

37. Covel, *A Just and Temperate Defence Of The Five Books of Ecclesiastical Policie*, p. 29.

38. Ibid., pp. 33–34. Richard Broughton, *The First Part of Protestants Proofes for Catholikes religion and recusancy* (Paris: François Gueffier, 1607), p. 18, quoted Covel in this place at great length in support of the Roman Catholic position on Scripture. In citing Covel, Broughton was citing teaching which was essentially that of Hooker. Covel was engaged in much literary controversy at the time, and Hooker's influence was thus felt through his defender.

39. Cf. Grislis, in *The Heritage of Christian Thought*, ed. Cushman and Grislis, p. 80.

40. Cf. Covel, p. 12.

41. John Brereley, *The Apologie of the Romane Church* ([Douay?: J. Mogar?], 1604). This treatise was answered by Thomas Morton in *A Catholike Appeale for Protestants* (London: George Bishop and John Norton, 1609).

42. The authority for this is Joseph Gillow, *A Literary and Biographical History, or Bibliographical Dictionary of the English Catholics* (London: Burns & Oates, [1885]), 1:32–37. The *DNB* wrongly identifies Brereley as James Anderton, Lawrence's uncle.

43. Ibid., pp. 34–35, and *DNB*, *sub* Lawrence Anderton.

44. Brereley, *Apologie*, pp. 40, 154–55. See Morton's *Catholike Appeale*, pp. 441–42.

45. Brereley, pp. 168, 29–30.

46. Ibid., pp. 71–72. See also p. 184.

47. Ibid., p. 72 n.; cf. *Laws* II.vii.2, 3; I.xiv.1; II.iv.2; and III.viii.14.

48. Specifically, and in this order: I.xiv.1, II.iv.2, III.viii.14, II.vii.3, III.viii.15.

49. Brereley, *The Protestants Apologie for the Roman Church* ([St Omer: Eng. Coll. Press], 1608), Trac. 1, no. 10, n. 3, pp. 254–55. William Whitaker was also cited and found to agree with Hooker.

50. William Laud, *A Relation Of The Conference between William Laud...and Mr. Fisher...* 3d ed. rev. (London: J. C. for Tho. Basset, et al., 1673), pp. 42, 45, 49–50, 55, 56–58, 76. This book was first published in 1639.

51. Laud, pp. 56–57, citing *Laws* II.vii.3 and III.viii.14.

52. Ibid., p. 58, citing *Laws* III.viii.14. For other references to Hooker in Laud, see pp. 24, 90, 160, 161, 205.

53. On Laud and Hooker concerning Scripture, cf. McLachlan, *Socinianism*, pp. 53–54, and Orr, *Reason and Authority*, p. 112.

54. Edward Maihew, *A Treatise of the Groundes Of The Old And Newe Religion* (n.p., 1608), Part II, p. 49, citing *Laws* III.viii.14. For other citations of Hooker, see Part I, pp. 50, 57, 60, 102, 103–04, 117, 133–34, and Part II, pp. 2, 18, 45, 77–78, 160.

55. Sylvester Norris, *An Antidote Or Soveraigne Remedie Against The Pestiferous Writings Of All English Sectaries* ([St Omer: Eng. Coll. Press], 1615), p. 20.

56. Norris, *An Antidote Or Treatise of Thirty Controversies: With a large Discourse of the Church* ([St Omer: Eng. Coll. Press], 1622), Part I, p. 20.

57. Cf. Wood, *Athenæ*, 2:86, *sub* Christopher Potter, where we find that he was "known sometimes by the Name of *Edw. Knott*, and sometimes by that of *Nich. Smith*, and at other times by *Matthew Wilson* (which was his true Name)." According to the *DNB* (*sub* Knott), he took the name Edward Knott upon leaving England and retained it as his name from then on. For this reason it is customary to refer to him by his later name.

58. Christopher Potter, *Want of Charitie Justly charged* (Oxford: for William Webb, 1633). For references to Hooker, see sig. a3ᵛ–4ʳ, G8ʳ⁻ᵛ, H2ʳ. On sig. a3ᵛ–4ʳ, Potter wrote: "The testimony of the present Church, though it be not the last

resolution of our faith, yet it is the first externall motive to it. It is the *key,* or *doore* which lets men in to the knowledge of the divine mysteries...But the faith of a Christian findes not in all this any sure ground whereon finally to rest or settle itselfe; till it arise to greater assurance then the present Church alone can give."

59. Edward Knott [Matthew Wilson], *Mercy & Truth. Or Charity Mayntayned by Catholiques* ([St Omer: Eng. Coll. Press], 1634), p. 42, referring to *Laws* I.xiv.1, II.iv.2, III.viii.14. For other citations of Hooker, see pp. 61, 103, 104, 211.

60. G. R. Cragg, *From Puritanism to the Age of Reason: A Study of Changes in Religious Thought within the Church of England 1660 to 1700* (Cambridge: Cambridge Univ. Press, 1950; reprinted 1966), pp. 190, 226.

61. McAdoo, *Spirit of Anglicanism,* p. 13.

62. William Chillingworth, *The Religion of Protestants. A Safeway to Salvation,* 4th ed. (London: Andrew Clark for Richard Chiswell, 1674), p. 239, citing *Laws* II.vii.6. Cf. pp. 192, 237–39.

63. Ibid., pp. 37, 64, 250.

64. Ibid., p. 49. Cf. *Laws* III.viii.14.

65. Ibid., p. 50 n. For a more complete discussion, see Orr, *Reason and Authority,* pp. 108–13, 147–54.

66. McLachlan, *Socinianism,* p. 54.

67. Cf. Lecler, *Toleration and the Reformation,* 2:400–03, and Jordan, *The Development of Religious Toleration in England,* 1:222–32.

68. McAdoo, *Spirit of Anglicanism,* p. 5.

69. Cf. W. C. de Pauley, *The Candle of the Lord: Studies in the Cambridge Platonists* (London: S.P.C.K., 1937), pp. 27–31.

70. Paget, *Introduction to the Fifth Book,* p. 114.

71. *Fullness of Christ: The Church's Growth in Catholicity* (London: S.P.C.K., 1950), pp. 51–52 (the Evangelical contribution), and *Catholicity: A Study in the Conflict of Christian Traditions in the West* (Westminster: Dacre, 1947), pp. 49–50 (the Anglo-Catholic contribution).

72. *Catholicity,* pp. 49–50.

73. Dugmore, *Eucharistic Doctrine in England from Hooker to Waterland,* p. 17; cf. ch. 3. On Hooker, see pp. 9–22.

74. James Ussher, *The Principles of Christian Religion,* 7th ed. (London: Ranew, 1678), p. 400. For the identity of Ussher, Field, Hall, and Morton as moderate or "central" churchmen, see Dugmore, p. 56.

75. Sykes, in *The Social & Political Ideas,* pp. 63–64.

HOOKER'S STYLE

Georges Edelen

I

The most significant elements of Hooker's style in the *Laws of Ecclesiastical Polity* are the length of his sentences and the complexity of their structure. Even for his contemporaries it was these aspects of Hooker's prose that drew immediate attention. George Cranmer, in his notes on a preliminary manuscript of Book VI, urges Hooker at a number of points to abbreviate his sentences. A Puritan attack complains of his "cunningly framed sentences, to blind and entangle the simple." Thomas Fuller describes his style as "long and pithy, drawing on a whole flock of several clauses before he came to the close of a sentence."[1]

In an analysis of sentence length, summary statistics are of limited value, since they fail to take into account the range of an author's effects.[2] Far more revealing than any average figures (which, after all, are an addition and a division away from the text) is the extraordinary freedom with which Hooker varies his sentence length. Taking only the extremes from Book I, the range is from 2 to 267 words. Of the 723 sentences in that book, 83 fall into the rather arbitrary category of short (15 words and under), 302 may be considered long (40 words and over), and 71 are very long (80 words and over). The sensitive reader is likely to share the view of Hooker's contemporaries that the longer sentences are more representative. They call attention to themselves, partly for the obvious reason that they take more space and require a greater span of attention, partly because they are rarer in English prose, especially when organized as true grammatical units. Shorter sentences are less likely to impress a reader as a distinguishing note in an author's style, no matter what average statistics may indicate.

Hooker is thus distinctively a writer of copious sentences, but far from exclusively so; he remains aware of the usefulness of occasional brief, even aphoristic, statement. Cicero had recommended diversifying one's style with these "little daggers," although he seems to have had only the rhetorical virtue of variety in mind. Typically, Hooker uses the technique with a firm sense of the expressive values inherent in syntactical form. Often his short sentences will come in clusters for specific effects. In the following passage, for example, the epigrams help to preserve the tone of kindly, ironic wisdom with which Hooker analyzes the career of John Calvin:

But wise men are men, and the truth is truth. That which Calvin did for establishment of his discipline, seemeth more commendable then that which he taught for the countenancing of it established. Nature worketh in us all a love to our owne Counsels. The contradiction of others is a fanne to inflame that love. Our love set on fire to maintaine that which once we have done, sharpneth the wit to dispute, to argue, and by all meanes to reason for it. Wherefore a marvaile it were if a man of so great capacitie, having such incitements to make him desirous of all kind of furtherances unto his cause, could espie in the whole Scripture of God nothing which might breed at the least a probable opinion of likelihood, that divine authoritie it selfe was the same way somewhat inclinable. [Pref.ii.7][3]

I quote the passage at length, not only to indicate the context from which the aphorisms derive their avuncular force, but also to suggest a side of Hooker little known to the general reader. The last sentence of the passage is a fine sample of ironic diction. "At the least a probable opinion of likelihood" deftly iterates to dilute the concession Hooker seems to be making, and verbs like "espie" and "breed" are particularly wicked. Nor is the rather awkward, lumpy movement of this sentence without pejorative effect in suggesting the strain with which Calvin, in Hooker's view, inclined Scripture to his purpose.

In more sober moods Hooker sometimes uses his clusters of short sentences with what might be called axiomatic force. The following passage begins his discussion of the nature of law: "All things that are have some operation not violent or casuall. Neither doth any thing ever begin to exercise the same without some foreconceaved ende for which it worketh. And the ende which it worketh for is not obteined, unlesse the worke be also fit to obteine it by. For unto every ende every operation will not serve" (I.ii.I). Here the relative brevity of the sentences reflects Hooker's realization that he is enunciating the axioms of his philosophic system. As with any first principles, these teleological assumptions are not susceptible of formal proof. As starting points they are accorded the careful enunciation and syntactical simplicity of Euclidian definitions. A similar use of short sentences occurs in Hooker's Thomistic analysis of human will: "To choose is to will one thing before another. And to will is to bend our soules to the having or doing of that which they see to be good. Goodnesse is seene with the eye of the understanding. And the light of that eye, is reason" (vii.2). Sometimes the short sentences are used to emphasize the logical force of the reasoning: "Now if men had not naturally this desire to be happie, how were it possible that all men shoulde have it? All men have. Therefore this desire in man is naturall" (xi.4). The extreme brevity of the sentences, as well as the repetition of terms and the use of "therefore," call attention to the syllogism. The major premise is somewhat extended as a rhetorical question, but the minor and the conclusion are cast into the abrupt simplicity of the scholastic mode, conveying a tone of logical finality.

Hooker's brief sentences have far greater effect in context, of course, since the contrast with his elaborate constructions is more emphatic. Any clear deviation from an author's normal syntactical patterns can be used to focus attention at key points, and the technique is too common an aspect of all good prose to warrant special comment. What does distinguish Hooker from lesser stylists is the superb sense of decorum with which he uses these contrasts of syntactical form, not simply for emphasis, but with acute sensitivity to the expressive values implicit in the form itself. As these examples suggest, the forms of Hooker's sentences grow organically out of the thought processes they embody. Whatever typical patterns can be discerned are the result not of preconceived or inherited syntactical molds into which thought is poured, but rather of the recurrent patterns of Hooker's own cognitive processes.

Of far greater importance in Hooker's prose style than mere sentence length is sentence structure, although the two elements are related. Structure, after all, is a question of word order, of the arrangement of phrases and clauses, and of syntactical ligatures, all of which, in English at least, admit of diverse shaping in direct proportion to the copiousness of the sentence. Indeed, it may be questioned whether one can speak meaningfully of sentence structure in analyzing English plain styles, since the organization of the individual sentence often seems more a question of grammatical inevitability than of individual pattern. Generally speaking, in English, the longer the sentence, the greater the possibilities of expressive structure.

II

The normal principle of structural organization in Hooker's longer sentences is logical subordination. Around an independent clause the remaining elements are carefully ordered, customarily by the use of subordinating conjunctions, to indicate their logical relationships within the thought of the sentence. Cause and effect, condition and concession, definition and distinction—all find their explicit functions within the structure of his grammatical units. For Hooker the complex sentence is the reflection of rational process.

Often the main clause will come toward the middle of the sentence, the first members grammatically suspended in preparation, the later members walking backward. As a relatively simple example, here is one of the many passages in which Hooker analyzes the psychology behind Puritan obstinacy in error:

1   But so easie it is for every man living to erre,

2   and so hard to wrest from any mans mouth the playne
                       acknowledgement of error,

3   that what hath beene once inconsiderately defended,

4 *the same is commonly persisted in,*

5   as long as wit by whetting it selfe is able to finde out
                    any shift,

6   be it never so sleight,

7   whereby to escape out of the handes of present
                  contradiction.

                [III.v.I][4]

The sentence is not grammatically complete until the end of the main clause, the first three members being subordinated and held in suspension by the conjunction "so...so...that," the third member operating as the antecedent for the pronoun "the same" and hence as the subject of the main verb. The last three members are grammatically complex, but the use of the introductory conjunction "as long as" restrains them from grammatical independence. Since, taken together, they function as an adverb modifying the "is...persisted in" of the main clause, they look back to the core of the sentence as pointedly as the earlier members had looked ahead. The passage is, in fact, a prime example of the centripetal tendency characteristic of much Ciceronian prose.

Hooker's structure here is completely organic. The syntactical organization of the sentence exactly reflects the movement of the thought. The heart of the idea, given in the main and only independent clause, is the fact of Puritan obduracy, even in the face of proven error. But no fact is a self-sustaining entity for Hooker, with his strong orientation to Aristotelian logic and metaphysics. A fact, insofar as it represents an empirical observation, can only be understood within the context of the rational patterns of an ordered cosmos. In the coherent procession of events, a fact is a point defined by the intersection of lines of cause and effect. Thus the first two members of the sentence investigate the reasons for Puritan obstinacy; the last three define the results, as Hooker's adversaries whet their wits, seeking any shift in their attempt to escape "present contradiction." The grammatical suspension of the earlier part of the sentence stresses this movement from cause to central fact, just as the subordination of the latter part emphasizes the derivation of the effects from that same fact. The syntactical cohesiveness of the sentence thus embodies the integrity of a logical analysis.

A striking example of Hooker's sensitivity to the expressive possibilities of syntactical form occurs in the first two members of this sentence. An antithetical figure is created and emphasized by a slightly unidiomatic inversion ("so easie it is...so hard"); we might expect in the second member little more than an elaboration, in parallel syntax, of the thought in the first. Such static devices of aural elegance appear rarely in Hooker's prose. The two members are notably asymmetrical since, as a matter of fact, the idea is not simply elaborated. A sequence of causality occurs even within the early members of the sentence. The ease with which the Puritans, like all men, fall into error is the subject of the first clause, and the idea is embodied in easy, flowing syntax. The second member calls attention to what is psychologically and temporally a succeeding step. After an implicit stage in which the Puritans become at least semiconscious of error, they fall guilty of the intellectual pride that prevents their acknowledging their mistakes and makes them difficult antagonists. The initial symmetry is justified by the close relationship between the thought in these members (a relationship that is further echoed in the "inconsiderately defended" of the third member), but since the thought is progressive, Hooker deliberately rejects the invitation to extended symmetry. Furthermore, just as the emphasis has changed from a common flaw to the more culpable and less docile vice of intellectual hypocrisy, the syntax of the second member becomes thicker and less fluent. The effect is achieved most obviously by the greater length of the second member and by suppressing the active verb, but also important is the use of an inflected genitive, a form surprisingly rare in the *Laws*. A comparison in context of "any mans mouth" with Hooker's usual phrasal form, "the mouth of any man," is instructive in suggesting the accuracy of his ear for syntactical effects.

Hooker's strong tendency to avoid obvious formal symmetries has been misunderstood. One critic, noting this phenomenon, has even called Hooker a "baroque" stylist.[5] But this is to apply arbitrary criteria mechanically. The asymmetrical quality of the sentence structure in the *Laws* is better understood as Hooker's implicit realization that the figures of parallelism and antithesis are essentially static. His is rather a style of rational thrust, constantly pushing along the chains of logical relationships. "I have endevoured," Hooker writes, "throughout the bodie of this whole discourse, that every former part might give strength unto all that followe, and every later bring some light unto all before" (1.i.2). He is writing of the plan of the *Laws*, but the words apply equally to the structure of his individual sentences.

The mere presence of hypotactic constructions is hardly likely to impress a contemporary reader as a distinguishing note in a prose style. The proper use of syntactical ligatures and the correct subordination of sentence elements to indicate their relative importance is a constant theme in modern handbooks of rhetoric. What makes Hooker's prose distinctive is partly the elaborateness of his sentence structure, partly the order in which he places his syntactical elements. The following passage is a useful example of both points:

1	Now whether it be that through an earnest longing desire
2	to see things brought to a peaceable end,
3	I do but imagin the matters, whereof we contend,
4	to be fewer then indeed they are,
5	or els for that in truth they are fewer
6	when they come to be discust by reason,
7	then otherwise they seeme, when by heat of contention
8	they are devided into many slipps,
9	and of every branch an heape is made:
10	surely, as now we have drawne them together,
11	choosing out those thinges which are requisite
12	to be severally all discust,
13	and omitting such meane specialties as are likely

14	(without any great labour)
15	to fall afterwardes of themselves;
16	*I knowe no cause why either the number or the length of these controversies should diminish our hope*
17	of seeing them end with concord and love on all sides;
18	which of his infinite love and goodnes the father of all peace and unitie graunt.

[II.i.1]

As in the previous example, there is but one independent clause, conveying the heart of the thought, and the other members are arranged to point either ahead or back to the core of the sentence. In this case, however, the main clause comes so late that far more attention is directed to the grammatical suspension of the first fifteen members, which carefully explain why Hooker eventually asserts his conviction that a reconciliation with the Puritans is possible, always assuming that they are willing to discuss their differences "by reason." He begins with the disarming admission that his own rational perceptions may be colored by his "earnest longing desire" for a peaceable settlement. Although, for persuasive purposes, he gives only coordinate grammatical value to the alternative—that the number of questions at issue has been unduly magnified "by heat of contention"—he clearly subscribes to this latter view. Accordingly, he lays down in members 10–15 the conditions that will permit fruitful discussion. Only after this chain of argument, considering the reasons, both subjective and objective, on which his conclusion is based and the necessary procedure which is a consequent, does Hooker announce his message of hope.

The expressive value of such an extended grammatical suspension is to be found in Hooker's insistence on an exploration of all the relevant arguments before adopting a controversial position. The syntactical order reflects the temporal and logical priority given to premise, evidence, condition, and cause over conclusion. By first exploring the reasons for his position, even to the extent of admitting a subjective bias, Hooker suggests that his conclusion comes only as the result of a rational process of investigation; by treating each element in the argument with syntactic discursiveness, he implies that he has scrupulously examined each link in the chain; by casting the entire chain as a single sentence, he emphasizes the logical coherence of his thought. The structure of Hooker's sentences has much to do with his reputation for judiciousness.

Any attempt to recast this sentence into syntactical patterns that sound more familiar quickly defines the quality of Hooker's effects. In such a reworking, the concession of bias might still open the sentence, but the main clause would be strongly attracted to the second position. The remainder of the thought would, in all likelihood, be appended as an explanation of the grounds for the stand taken. In such an ordering, the syntax inevitably connotes rationalization for a conviction that has been previously adopted, perhaps for reasons of dubious objectivity. A stylist like Bacon will write, typically:

But farther, it is an assured truth and a conclusion of experience that a little or superficial knowledge of philosophy may incline the mind of man to atheism, but a farther proceeding therein doth bring the mind back again to religion, for in the entrance of philosophy, when the second causes, which are next unto the senses, do offer themselves to the mind of man, if it dwell and stay there, it may induce some oblivion of the highest cause, but when a man passeth on farther, and seeth the dependence of causes and the works of Providence, then, according to the allegory of the poets, he will easily believe that the highest link of nature's chain must needs be tied to the foot of Jupiter's chair.[6]

The syntax here is as expressive as Hooker's, but the gulf between is wide indeed. Bacon opens his sentence with his conviction; no attempt is made to soften the dogmatic tone by admitting an element of opinion (compare Hooker's "I knowe no cause..."). To the contrary, Bacon's position is "an assured truth and a conclusion of experience." Doubtless it is an assured truth precisely because it is a conclusion of experience, possibly only Bacon's own; later ages might question whether experience assures anything of the sort. The remainder of the sentence investigates the reasons for the observed phenomenon. As the syntactical ordering implies, Bacon's explanation is offered less as the logical grounds for his assertion than as a way of accounting for an empirical observation. The investigative process comes after, not before the fact. The failure of his explanation to carry logical force in supporting the original proposition is further echoed in the comparatively loose ligatures of Bacon's sentence. Where Hooker integrates the major elements of his thought by correlative and subordinating conjunctions ("whether...or else," "as now"), Bacon prefers the weaker coordinating links ("but" twice; although "for" is probably subordinating as used here, it is a weak hinge on which to swing two thirds of the sentence). Hooker thus invites us, syntactically, to think along with him and, hopefully, to reach the same conclusion. Bacon's assertion, although subject to control by our own experience, stands at the head of his sentence as a summary pronouncement. Judicious Hooker; judicial Bacon.

The use of these extended grammatical suspensions, or periodicity, is often cited as one of the most important characteristics of Hooker's prose. Critics, by and large, have been content to label such suspensions Latinisms, common in those English styles under heavy Ciceronian influence but essentially unidiomatic and foreign to the genius of the English language. The attempt to recreate in English this syntactical pattern borrowed from the Romans was—so the argument goes—almost as much of a dead end as the Elizabethan experiments with quantitative meter. Brief grammatical suspensions are common, almost inevitable, even in relatively plain styles, but true periodicity, the withholding of grammatical completion until the end of a complex hypotactic sentence, was never successfully acclimated in English.

The analysis, so far as it goes, is sound. Hooker's grammatical suspensions have a distinctly archaic or unidiomatic ring to most modern ears; at the least they seem overelaborate. Like any unusual feature in a prose style, they are apt to be taken as a defining feature, independent of frequency. But the explanation of grammatical suspension in terms of a classical tradition has had the unfortunate effect of obscuring whatever expressive values the syntactical pattern may have. Whether Hooker felt freer to retard his main clauses because of his intimate familiarity with classical and patristic Latin is a question irrelevant to his meaningful use of such sentence structure. An author's slavery to a tradition may explain his stylistic vices but not his triumphs.

In fact, Hooker's classical training doubtless had a crucial effect upon his English prose style. He belonged to that transitional generation of educated men whose English and Latin were virtually in balance, and, as Dr Johnson self-consciously put it, "he that has long cultivated another language, will find its words and combinations croud upon his memory."[7] The Latin influence on Hooker is better understood, however, as a liberation than as a restraint. It freed him from both the rambling formlessness of a native tradition and the overly obvious, semimechanical formalism of the Euphuistic school, and it freed him to adapt the Ciceronian patterns as they suited his expressive purposes. No doubt his grammatical suspensions and inversions of normal English word order seemed less unusual to that part of his audience as well versed in their classics as he. The tyranny of a native idiom had yet to be strongly felt.

Tyranny is exactly what English idiom has become, and later structural habits in the language stand as a barrier between us and Hooker. The periodic sentence is an excellent case in point. The language is perfectly capable of handling even protracted suspensions with clarity, as Hooker demonstrates. The failure of such suspensions to achieve an idiomatic foothold in English (except, perhaps, for special uses) can hardly be accounted for on purely linguistic grounds. Only in the expressive connotations can an adequate reason be sought. Perhaps, as the passage from the *Advancement of Learning* suggests, one explanation for the unidiomatic ring of the period may lie in the incurably empirical thought patterns of the English-speaking peoples.

In turning our backs on the suspended sentence, however, we have lost a valuable construction, as Hooker proves in almost every chapter of the *Laws*. The period has certain obvious structural advantages, for example, as a means of unifying a long sentence when the thought involves a number of elements of coordinate value, all in approximately the same relationship to the central idea. In the following example Hooker organizes a series of distinctions on this principle. He is defending here his position that "the scripture of God leaveth unto the Churches discretion" some aspects of ecclesiastical polity, against the Puritan charge that such a stand can only "impaire the honour which the Church of God yeeldeth to the sacred scriptures perfection":

1   Wherein seeing that no more is by us mainteyned,

2   then onely that scripture must needes teach the Church

3   whatsoever is in such sort necessarie, as hath beene set downe,

———

4   and that it is no more disgrace for scripture

5   to have left a number of other thinges free

6   to be ordered at the discretion of the Church,

7   then for nature to have left it unto the wit of man

8   to devise his owne attyre,

9   and not to looke for it

10   as the beastes of the field have theirs:

———

11   if neyther this can import,

12   nor any other proofe sufficient bee brought foorth

13   that wee eyther will at any time or ever did affirme

14   the sacred Scripture to comprehende no more then onely those bare necessaries;

———

15   if we acknowledge that

16   as well for particular application to speciall occasions,

17   as also in other manifolde respectes

18   infinite treasures of wisedome are over and besides aboundantly to be found in the holy scripture;

———

19   yea that scarcely there is anye noble parte of knowledge,

20   woorthy the minde of man,

21   but from thence it may have some direction and
light;

---

22   yea, that although there be no necessitie

23   it should of purpose prescribe any one particular
forme of Church-governement,

24   yet touching the manner of governing in generall

25   the precepts that scripture setteth downe are not
fewe.

26   and the examples manie which it proposeth

27   for all Church-governors, even in particularities
to followe;

---

28   yea, that those thinges finally which are of principall
waight

29   in the verie particular forme of Church-politie

30   (although not that forme which they imagine,

31   but that which we against them upholde)

32   are in the selfe same scriptures conteyned:

---

33   if all this be willingly graunted by us

34   which are accused to pinne the worde of God in so
narrowe roome,

35   as that it should be able to direct us but in
principall poyntes of our religion,

36   or as though the substance of religion

37   or some rude and unfashioned matter of building
the Church were uttered in them,

38   and those thinges left out,

39   that should pertaine to the forme and fashion of it;

---

40   *let the cause of the accused bee referred to the accusors owne
conscience,*

41   *and let that judge whether this accusation be deserved*

42   *where it hath beene layd.*

[III.iv.1]

The structure of the sentence is worth close examination as an
example of Hooker's genius in ordering heavy masses of thought.

The passage opens with an absolute participial construction; "seeing" governs and suspends the first ten members, which in turn are broken into two groupings, both integrated around the same correlative conjunction, "no more...then." Typically, Hooker avoids any more obvious or extended symmetries. He uses his first grouping (members 1-3) to restate and delimit his position on the all-sufficiency of Scripture. The second element (4–10) summarizes the parallel between Nature and Scripture which he has developed at greater length in the preceding sentence. This initial suspension is not resolved but leads into the major one, which begins at member 11 and continues to 39. These 29 members are further subdivided into 6 sections, each introduced by the subordinating conjunction "if" or its equivalent. The first grouping (11–14) cautions against drawing unfounded inferences from the premise announced in the earlier part of the sentence. The next four sections (15–18, 19–21, 22–27, 28–32) explain, in a series of admissions, why such inferences are invalid. The series opens with the concessive clause, "if we acknowledge that...", which is implicitly repeated in the opening "yea, that..." of the next three sections to indicate the parallelisms of thought through this part of the sentence. Since the substitution also has intensive force, implying "if we even acknowledge that...", the series of *yea*'s directs attention to the progressive movement of the thought as Hooker spirals down from the most general concession closer and closer to the Puritans' specific stand on this question. The section beginning at member 33 is summary, setting in juxtaposition the concessions made ("if all this be willingly graunted by us...") with the Puritan charges ("which are accused..."). The discrepancy is too obvious to need belaboring, and Hooker finally resolves his suspension with legal metaphor of members 40–42. Interestingly, he ends with a rather unusual doubling of the independent clause, where the idea is statically elaborated, probably on purely formal grounds: the tremendous weight of the sentence pressing on the final members requires two legs for stability.

The expressive value of Hooker's suspension in this sentence is less obvious than in the previous example. The syntactical pattern still follows the movement of Hooker's mind along a chain of argument, each section of the sentence developing logically out of what has preceded, but the final clauses are less a rational consequent than a rhetorical elaboration. While the validity of the metaphor in the last three members depends upon the argument that has been unfolded, the suspension is not resolved by a final thrust of the thought into a logical conclusion. Rather, Hooker ends with a more explicit and emotive restatement of the position that has already been reached in members 33–39. In other words, the suspension seems at the end more a deliberate artifice than an organic reflection of rational process, and it would, in fact, be easier to reconstruct a large part of this sentence into nonperiodic syntax without destroying the logical patterns on which it is built.

The grammatical suspension here has, nonetheless, strong expressive values. Hooker's purpose in this sentence is basically one of definition. His contention that Scripture contains what is necessary to salvation and leaves many unessential details of ecclesiastical government to the judgment of men has been misinterpreted by the Puritans to mean that Scripture contains only what is necessary to salvation. Distinctions are clearly necessary. Hooker begins, appropriately, with the restatement of his position that has caused the confusion, but, unlike Bacon, he does not allow it to assume the finality of grammatical independence. The suspension forces the reader ahead into the distinctions and concessions that are necessary to an understanding of the proposition. The structure of the sentence demands, as in the previous case, that all relevant information be absorbed before a grammatical or logical stopping-place is reached.

III

These sentences provide sufficient evidence to attempt some generalizations on the expressive value of the period. Insofar as the true period is an extended sentence, it emphasizes the cohesiveness of the complex thought that it embodies, since no intermediate segment is allowed to detach itself as grammatically and logically independent.

Insofar as all but the final parts of the sentence are explicitly sub-ordinated to the principal thought, the period also emphasizes the articulation of the various segments, the logical relationships existing among the elements of the sentence. Yet neither of these qualities sufficiently defines the value of grammatical suspension. Even though cohesiveness and logical articulation find an appropriate home in the period, it still cannot be denied that these virtues are common in prose styles dominated by short and thoroughly unsuspended sentences. And, after all, neither length nor explicit subordination is the exclusive property of the suspended construction. The essential expressive value of the periodic sentence must be sought in the dis-tinguishing characteristic of that pattern—that is, in the suspension itself.

In a sense, virtually every literate sentence is suspended. The open-ing word excites an expectation of that eventual grammatical com-pletion which will reflect a coherent thought. Each new element in the sentence is related by the reader to what has gone before, and the segment thus produced is held in suspension to await further modi-fications until the grammatical completion reveals the entire pattern. Even the so-called "loose" construction, where the sentence is grammatically complete early but trails on in a series of further ele-ments, has the same pattern of suspension, the reader's expectation being reopened with each new relative pronoun or conjunction. This pattern of a grammatical expectation, which invites mental suspension and is eventually satisfied or resolved, is as true of simple declarative syntax as it is of Hooker's most involved periods, al-though in curt sentences the process may seem instantaneous. The difference is one of degree. The extended period makes more pro-longed and emphatic use of what might be called the natural rhythm of grammar, substituting larger blocks of thought for the simpler meanings represented by single words or brief phrases.

The expressive value of extended periods can thus be viewed as a tapping of a psychological process inherent in the very structure of language, that process of holding subsidiary elements in mental sus-pension until the developing form of the thought absorbs them into a larger pattern. In philosophical or apologetic writing, the period is a natural vehicle for the mind that insists that no conclusions can be validly reached prior to a discursive and open-minded examination of all the relevant premises, causes, evidence, arguments, distinctions, or effects. The sudden intuition, the imaginative lunge, the emotional stance, the dogmatic pronouncement—all are alien to the genius of the period. Extended suspensions reflect the methodological tentativeness of a rational process whose conclusions are finally validated by their position in a logical pattern.

Periodicity is, therefore, not simply a favorite grammatical construction for Hooker, but a cast of mind which is reflected everywhere in the *Laws*. Not only the syntax of individual sentences but the plan of the entire work is periodic. Hooker "suspends" to the last four books the specific questions of ecclesiastical polity at issue with the Puritans, insisting that it is first necessary to examine in detail the more general principles on which valid particular judgments must be based.

But when they who withdraw their obedience pretend that the lawes which they should obey are corrupt and vitious; for better examination of their qualitie, it behooveth the very foundation and root, the highest welspring and fountaine of them to be discovered.... So that if the judgements of men doe but holde themselves in suspence as touching these first more generall meditations, till in order they have perused the rest that ensue: what may seeme darke at the first will afterwardes be founde more plaine, even as the later particular decisions will appeare, I doubt not more strong, when the other have beene read before. [1.i.2]

In two suspended sentences Hooker gives the rationale underlying the structure of both his entire work and his individual periods.

Suspension is thus to be understood not simply as a syntactical or organizational principle in the *Laws* but as an expressive embodiment of Hooker's understanding of the rational processes by which men must seek truth. The entire force of his attack upon the Puritans lies in his conviction that they have failed to suspend their judgments, that they have leapt to conclusions that are not rationally tenable, precisely because they have failed to take into previous account all of the relevant considerations. The long historical account in the Preface

of the Puritan triumph in Geneva, for example, is expressly designed
to prove that Calvin's theories of ecclesiastical discipline were an
ex post facto attempt to justify and elevate to the dignity of principles the church laws he had been forced to adopt by the exigencies
of a single, particular situation: "that which once they had done, they
became for ever after resolute to maintaine" (Pref.ii.2). In other
words, the Puritan position was reached not by suspended judgment
and rational process but by historical accident; what is offered as
rational foundation is, in fact, rationalization. In like manner Hooker
twits Calvin for a reversal of logical priority: "We should be injuri-
ous unto vertue it selfe, if wee did derogate from them whome their
industrie hath made great. Two thinges of principall moment there
are which have deservedly procured him honour throughout the
worlde: the one his exceeding paynes in composing the Institutions
of Christian religion; the other his no lesse industrious travailes for
exposition of holy Scripture according unto the same institutions"
(ii.8). For Hooker, Calvin's thought processes were anything but
periodic.

One final, famous, and somewhat atypical period of Hooker's
should be examined:

1	Now if nature should intermit her course, and leave altogether,
2	though it were but for a while,
3	the observation of her own lawes:
4	if those principall and mother elements of the world,
5	wherof all things in this lower world are made,
6	should loose the qualities which now they have,
7	if the frame of that heavenly arch erected over our heads
8	should loosen and dissolve it selfe:
9	if celestiall spheres should forget their wonted motions
10	and by irregular volubilitie, turne themselves any way
11	as it might happen:
12	if the prince of the lightes of heaven

13	which now as a Giant doth runne his unwearied course,
14	should as it were through a languishing faintnes
15	begin to stand and to rest himselfe:
16	if the Moone should wander from her beaten way,
17	the times and seasons of the yeare blend themselves by disordered and confused mixture,
18	the winds breath out their last gaspe,
19	the cloudes yeeld no rayne,
20	the earth be defeated of heavenly influence,
21	the fruites of the earth pine away
22	as children at the withered breasts of their mother
23	no longer able to yeeld them reliefe,
24	*what would become of man himselfe,*
25	whom these things now do all serve? [I.iii.2]

This elaborate period is probably the best-known passage in the *Laws*, since it has become, together with Ulysses' speech in *Troilus and Cressida*, a classic citation to illustrate the Elizabethan sense of an ordered cosmos. Frequent excerpting of the sentence has done some disservice to Hooker and the popular conception of his style. He is at his best in the exposition of logical relationships or in moments of quiet eloquence rather than in such dazzling rhetorical amplification.

The sentence is organized around a series of hypothetical conditions, grammatically suspended until the consequent is finally enunciated in member 24 as a rhetorical question. Each succeeding "if" heightens expectation, impelling the reader toward the resolution, an effect reinforced by the increasing brevity and swiftness of the parallel elements and the omission of the conjunction (18–20), until the rubato of members 21–23 prepares for the conclusion. The tension in this case is accompanied by no corresponding logical thrust: the thought of the period is complete if members 4–23 are omitted. True, there is an orderly progression of the coordinate hypotheticals. After the most general statement of the condition (1–3), Hooker defines the total scope of natural order, from the "mother elements" of this "lower world" (4–6) to the "heavenly arch" (7–8). The remaining sections of the suspension trace the hierarchy between these poles, beginning with the highest "celestiall spheres" and moving progressively down a chain of physical being to the "fruites of the earth," until the whole is related to man in the final clauses. Yet this orderly development of the amplifications, reflecting the natural order which is their subject, does not conceal their essentially static quality as elaboration by example of what was explicit from the opening of the sentence.

Doubtless the rhetorical quality[8] of this period derives from Hooker's implicit realization that he is dealing with a subject not susceptible of logical demonstration. Alfred North Whitehead speaks of the "instinctive faith that there is an Order of Nature." The formation of such a general idea, he suggests, and "the grasp of its importance, and the observation of its exemplification in a variety of occasions are by no means the necessary consequences of the truth of the idea in question." Nonetheless, in the long tradition of Western thought, "we all share in this faith, and we therefore believe that the reason for the faith is our apprehension of its truth."[9] It is precisely to this faith, this consensus, this traditional assumption, that Hooker appeals by his rhetorical amplification, as well as by the interrogative mood of the resolving clause. He does not attempt the impossible task of logical proof. Even he is forced to admit the existence of "swarvings" in the course of nature, and the biblically learned of his day could protest that if nature should intermit her course, nothing more calamitous might happen to man than the winning of a battle. Furthermore, Hooker can recognize that the physical order "hath in it more then men have as yet attained to know, or perhaps ever shall attaine" (I.iii.2). All such difficulties vanish for Hooker, however, before the general and perpetual voice of men: "so constantly the lawes of nature are by naturall agents observed, that no man denieth but those things which nature worketh, are wrought either alwaies or for the most part after one and the same manner" (iii.3). The rhetorical force of his static amplification is essentially an appeal to what "no man denieth."

In this connection, one rhetorical value of the period should be noted, a value that derives from the grammatical tensions of that construction. Since a kind of syntactic spring is stretched tauter with each succeeding element of the suspension, the swift release of the tension in the terminal clauses has the effect of snapping the spring back to a position of rest. Here, I think, the psychic effect of the extended suspension differs so much in degree from that of simpler constructions that it might almost seem a difference in kind. The whip-crack of the resolution in the periodic sentence produces a radically stronger impression of release than the gradual relaxation of tension in the more common forms of English sentence structure. Because the resolution has been postponed so long, the grammatical expectations have become correspondingly more intense; the climactic fulfillment of those expectations at the end of the sentence seems quintessentially right. This emotion is translatable into persuasive force. The strong feeling of syntactical inevitability in the resolution impels the reader into a state of rest, both grammatical and conceptual.

A discussion of Hooker's use of the period in the *Laws* cannot end without an even more general consideration of the expressive nature of the construction, abstracted from any particular example. Syntax can be analyzed as expressive in representative sentences, as I have done above, where the question becomes the extent to which the grammatical structure reflects the author's premises and the movement of his mind within the area of thought he is specifically treating. Such an analysis deals with what might be called immediate or contextual expressiveness. Insofar as the sentences chosen for dissection are representative, such a discussion leads naturally to broader considerations of the author's habitual modes of thought. Yet there remains another aspect of structural expressiveness, more abstract and more tenuous. In default of a less clumsy term, it might be called ontological expressiveness. A favorite syntactical construction may embody not only the forms emanating from the immediate movement of the author's mind but also from those ultimate patterns that he assumes to lie at the heart of a meaningful cosmos. In other words, syntax may be understood as reflecting cosmological as well as psychic order.

In Hooker's case, the ontological expressiveness of the period can be seen as an embodiment of his profoundly teleological assumptions. The concept of final cause dominates the *Laws*: "the nature of everie lawe must be judged of by the ende for which it was made, and by the aptnes of thinges therein prescribed unto the same end" (III.x.1). For Hooker the world is the creation of a rational God, and reason is defined as the purposive choice of the best means for a pre-conceived end. Standing firmly in the Aristotelian-scholastic tradition, Hooker rejects the Puritan insistence on an inscrutable God of will. On the other hand, he carefully avoids the opposite extreme into which eighteenth-century rationalism happily leaped. God's reason is analogous, not identical, to man's. No less than Browne (and, for that matter, Bacon) Hooker has his "O, altitudo!" (I.ii.5) and he concedes, "Dangerous it were for the feeble braine of man to wade farre into the doings of the most High" (ii.2). Nonetheless, whatever the limitations on man's actual ability to understand the ways of God, those ways are rationally meaningful because they are purposive. The flux of the world is, in reality, an orderly pattern of movement toward divinely known and appointed ends, a pattern hierarchically arranged in a chain of causality reaching ultimately to the Final Cause, God Himself. Thus, for example, the unintermitting order of nature is to be understood not in Newtonian terms as an embodiment of physical laws that are expressible mathematically, but rather as a purposive order, the final cause being man, "whom these things now do all serve."

The periodic sentence is itself a syntactical embodiment of this same teleological pattern. The "final cause" of the grammatical structure is the terminal resolution which exerts an attractive force on the preceding elements, rationally ordering and justifying them as means to a preconceived end. There is surely significance in the fact that the stylistic revolt in the seventeenth century against the periodic construction as overly formal and inexpressive almost exactly coincided with the supplanting of teleological premises by a new scientific interest in proximate, material, and efficient causes.

IV

Although the centripetal and periodic sentences are favorite and significant constructions with Hooker, examples of which can be culled from almost every page of the *Laws*, they by no means represent his only syntactical forms. Indeed, it is precisely because he uses them occasionally, often reserving them for crucial moments of argumentation or eloquence, that they retain their expressive force unsmudged.

Variety of syntactical form can be understood as expressive of a writer's flexibility of mind. Yet it may be doubted if sufficient diversity can be achieved on purely expressive principles. The very uniqueness and force of an author's vision is apt to lead him into monotonous patterns unless he has a simultaneous respect for the rhetorical virtue of variety as a means of holding the sympathetic attention of his reader. Even when diversity of form is pursued on such rhetorical grounds, however, it has an important function in maintaining expressive values. The expressive edge of any form can be blunted by insistent repetition. Patterns that are meaningful will come by overuse to seem ornamental and mannered. The classic case of such syntactical wolf-crying is provided by Lyly's Euphuism. Professor Jonas Barish has suggested that Lyly's steady stream of antithetical constructions is his "way of expressing the perpetual ambiguities of human sentiment, and above all, the most ambiguous of all human sentiments, love."[10] Without denying the validity of Professor Barish's argument, a reader of *Euphues* might protest that Lyly's bag of tricks is too limited and too obvious. The structure of his prose may be meaningful, but the reader's sensitivities in that direction are quickly dulled, and the antitheses come to seem no more expressive than a facial tic. The real trouble with Lyly's prose style, leaving to one side his second-rate mind, is that he is too little, rather than too much, concerned with rhetoric.

The rhetorical virtue of syntactical variety is thus a condition for sharpness of expressive force at the moments that count. Few prose stylists in the language have grasped that principle more clearly than

Hooker. The true value of his more carefully formed sentences can only be appreciated in the context of his normal flow. Here, for example, is a longer passage representing Hooker in an expository mood:

1   Now besides that lawe which simplie concerneth men as men, and that which belongeth unto them as they are men linked with others in some forme of politique societie; there is a third kinde of lawe which toucheth all such severall bodies politique, so far forth as one of them hath publique commerce with another.

2   And this third is the *Lawe of nations*.

3   Betweene men and beastes there is no possibilitie of sociable communion, because the welspring of that communion is a naturall delight which man hath to transfuse from him selfe into others, and to receyve from others into himselfe especially those thinges wherein the excellencie of his kind doth most consist.

4   The chiefest instrument of humaine communion therefore is speech, because thereby we impart mutuallie one to another the conceiptes of our reasonable understanding.

5   And for that cause seing beastes are not hereof capable, for as much as with them we can use no such conference, they being in degree, although above other creatures on earth to whome nature hath denied sense, yet lower then to be sociable companions of man to whome nature hath given reason; it is of Adam said that amongst the beastes *He found not for him selfe any meete companion*.

6   Civill society doth more content the nature of man then any private kind of solitarie living, because in societie this good of mutuall participation is so much larger then otherwise.

7   Here with notwithstanding we are not satisfied, but we

264

covet (if it might be) to have a kind of societie and fellowship even with al mankind.

8   Which thing Socrates intending to signifie professed him self a Citizen, not of this or that common-welth, but of the world.

9   And an effect of that very natural desire in us, (a manifest token that we wish after a sort an universall fellowship with all men) appeareth by the wounderful delight men have, some to visit forrein countries, some to discover nations not heard of in former ages, we all to know the affaires and dealings of other people, yea to be in league of amitie with them: and this not onely for trafiques sake, or to the end that when many are confederated each may make other the more strong, but for such cause also as moved the Queene of Saba to visit Salomon; and in a word because nature doth presume that how many men ther are in the world, so many Gods as it were ther are, or at least wise such they should be towards men. [I.x.12]

The first, fifth, and ninth sentences of this passage, with the main clauses medial, terminal, and initial, provide good examples of expressive syntactical patterns. The opening centripetal sentence is used for transition, the initial suspension glancing back at the subjects of the previous chapters; the central clause turns to the new topic of international law, whose scope is defined in the concluding members. The fifth sentence gathers the arguments that have been expounded in the third and fourth sentences into a typical periodic construction. Since the ninth sentence explicitly deals with effects of man's natural desire for international amity, the principal clause is placed first. The expressive force of these three sentences is dependent, however, on the context of more casually patterned transitional sentences, whose structure is determined by the logical continuum within which they occur.

To this point I have concentrated upon Hooker's tendency to

subordinate the less important elements of a sentence to a single main clause. Coordinate elements within the subordinations are common, of course, but in most of the longer sentences only the principal thought is allowed grammatical independence. Nonetheless, in a stylist as conscious of the value of syntactical variation as Hooker, it is hardly surprising to find occasional sentences with multiple independent clauses. Even such infrequent constructions are used with expressive force. For example, in a passage where Hooker attempts to refute the Puritan contention that "no way is good in any kind of action, unlesse wisedom do by scripture leade unto it," he insists that "wisdom hath diversly imparted her treasures unto the world":

1   Some things she openeth by the sacred bookes of Scripture;

2   some things by the glorious works of nature:

3   with some things she inspireth them from above by spirituall influence,

4   in some thinges she leadeth and trayneth them onely by worldly experience and practise.

[II.i.4]

Here the coordinate syntax clearly reflects Hooker's position that the Book of Nature has, within its proper sphere, the same dignity and validity as Scripture. The Puritan insistence on a total subordination of natural reason to divine revelation is tacitly resisted even by Hooker's syntactical structure; it is entirely significant that of the ten sentences in the section from which the quotation is taken, six have more than one independent clause. The parallelism in the two pairs of clauses quoted above also has expressive value, reflecting Hooker's view that Nature and Scripture are congruent modes of attaining wisdom, since both emanate from the same rational God.

V

The distinctive structure of any prose style is defined not only by the placement and relationship of sentence elements but also by the internal character of those elements. The individual members of Hooker's sentences are notable for their syntactical discursiveness. Nouns and verbs tend to double, adjectives and adverbs to expand into phrases, phrases into clauses. The typical copiousness of the Ciceronian is achieved largely by this expansive tendency in which every aspect of the thought is made explicit by full grammatical development. The historical movement of the English sentence toward greater conciseness has been achieved in part by contraction of the sentence elements into a kind of syntactical shorthand; Hooker belonged to an earlier, more discursive tradition.

Here, for example, is a typical expansive period from the *Laws*:

1   Albeit therefore every cause admit not such infallible evidence of profe,
2   as leaveth no possibilitie of doubt or scruple behind it;
3   yet *they* who claime the generall assent of the whole world
4   unto that which they teach,
5   and doe not feare to give very hard and heavy sentence
6   upon as many as refuse to embrace the same,
7   *must have speciall regard*
8   that their first foundations and grounds be more then sclender probabilities.
[II.1.3]

It will be noted that the periodic form is characteristically used to give logical precedence to the opening concession and, in members 3–6, the aspects of the Puritan position that justify the conclusion.

The expansive tendencies at work in the sentence can be shown by compressing the thought to essentials, preserving Hooker's order and diction (with one exception): Albeit therefore every cause admit not infallible evidence, yet they who demand general assent unto that which they teach must have special regard that their foundations be more than slender probabilities. The substitution of the stronger verb "demand" for the original "claim" absorbs the relative clauses in members 5 and 6. A further change of diction, replacing the pronominal subject of member 3 with "Puritans" or, to preserve the abstractive tone, with "dogmatists," would remove any strict necessity for the clause "unto that which they teach." The entire central part of the sentence could be reduced to half a dozen words without radically affecting the conceptual content.

Such recastings are useful in revealing structural traits. The original sentence displays, in fact, the principal syntactical techniques used by Hooker for expansion. Occasionally he will adopt nearly tautological constructions: the doublings of "hard and heavy sentence" or of "first foundations and grounds" seem to fall within this category. More often the tautology will be used for clearly emphatic purposes. In the opening members, "such infallible evidence of profe, as leaveth no possibilitie of doubt or scruple behind it" seems, on strictly logical grounds, redundant. The repetition helps, however, to emphasize the limits of Hooker's concession. If he is willing to admit that the Anglicans cannot claim strict or absolute infallibility, so that no possibility of doubt remains; nonetheless, his entire argument is designed to show that for practical purposes his position attains as much certainty as can reasonably be expected in the disputed areas of ecclesiastical polity. A somewhat similar use of redundancy occurs in "the generall assent of the whole world," which serves to emphasize the sweeping claims of the Puritans.

The most common expansive device in the *Laws* appears through the central part of the sentence. In such key grammatical positions as the subject of the main clause, Hooker will often use a weak abstraction, most frequently a pronoun, which he can later expand with relative or appositional clauses. The *Laws* begins, in fact, with such a construction: "He that goeth about to perswade a multitude ..." In a similar manner, Hooker may prefer a weaker or less precise verb, which he can define more precisely in later expansions: in the sentence above, the exact form of the Puritan "claime" to general assent is explained in the clauses "and doe not feare to give very hard and heavy sentence upon as many as refuse to embrace the same." Indeed, the second half of this expansion itself illustrates the pattern of pronoun and defining clause.

As an expressive technique this form of elaboration is probably to be interpreted as a quest for precision of meaning, the explanatory clauses determining the connotational overtones with greater accuracy than a single word is likely to achieve. For instance, can any substitution of "demand," or "insist upon," or "enforce" for the original "claime" reproduce exactly the effect of "doe not feare to give very hard and heavy sentence," with its connotations of temerity and ruthlessness? More generally, the syntactical discursiveness of the individual member can express, particularly in passages of controversy, a meticulous attention to detail, a sense that every aspect of the opponents' position and every step in the author's own argument has received his full and deliberate consideration. Nor can any consideration of the expressive value of this copiousness of development avoid noticing the manner in which it reinforces other forms of structural expressiveness. A suspended construction of ten members is twice as periodic as one of five.

VI

One final aspect of Hooker's prose structure remains to be treated: the nature of his syntactical ligatures, the mortar of his style, so to speak. The question is closely related to Hooker's expansive inclinations, since the heavier the weight of individual segments of the sentence, or of the sentences themselves, the stronger must be the bonds that join them if the stylistic edifice is to cohere.

Hooker uses many means to bind his logical chains, most obviously his heavy sprinkling of conjunctions, but his most revealing technique is his characteristic dependence on pronouns for linkage. I have mentioned his fondness for a pronoun followed by a relative clause as a typical expansive movement, but the extraordinary frequency of pronominal forms in the *Laws* cannot be explained only as a method of inducing natural elaborations.

The pronoun is a widespread linguistic device, of course, whose primary function is to render unnecessary the clumsy repetition of nouns or a harried search for synonyms. Generally speaking, the more sensitive a prose stylist to the connotational aura of words, the more unhappy he will be in the quest for exact synonyms, and the stronger will be his attraction to pronominal constructions, particularly in passages of careful argument. Or a fondness for pronouns may reflect a strong bias in favor of formal logic, since the syllogism is based on an identity of terms which renders suspect the use of synonyms. The syllogism is stylistically awkward in itself, but it may be absorbed into the flow of prose without loss of force by substituting pronouns for the repeated terms. Both explanations can be used to account for the frequency of pronouns in the *Laws*. Yet when all these justifications are taken into account, Hooker's pronominal supply remains far in excess of need.

The most basic explanation for the ubiquity of pronouns in the *Laws* lies in their function as a method of linkage. The cohesion of Hooker's style is, to a great extent, dependent upon this technique. In the following illustration he is disclaiming those flaws in the Anglican position which are attributable to human failings rather than to the system itself:

1	Wherefore all these abuses being severed and set apart,
2	which rise from the corruption of men
3	and not from the lawes themselves:
4	*come we to those things*
5	which in the very whole intier forme of our Church- politie have beene
6	(as we perswade our selves)
7	injuriously blamed by them,
8	who endevour to overthrow the same,
9	and in stead therof to establish a much worse;

10	onely through a strong misconceipt they have,
11	that the same is grounded on divine authoritie.

[II.i.1]

The sentence has the typical centripetal structure Hooker often employs for transition; the opening suspension summarizes the previous argument, the main clause indicates a change of direction, and the trailing elements define the new area of investigation. Characteristic expansive devices are present: the doublings of "severed and set apart" (which is neither tautological nor conceptually necessary) or "whole intier," the explicit development of an antithesis in two members (2 and 3), and the patterns of pronoun and relative clause ("those things which...", "blamed by them, who..."). Typical, also, is the linkage of this sentence to the previous one by an initial conjunction.

The sentence supplies a rather striking example of the use of pronominal forms for linkage in the two occurrences of "the same" (8 and 11). It will be noted that both appear in that part of the sentence which is grammatically "loose" or unsuspended and thus has the greater tendency to fragment. The interlocking strength provided by the pronouns comes, of course, from the necessity of recalling the antecedent and substituting the more specific noun for the vaguer pronoun, a process that involves the reader in a simultaneous consideration of two parts of the sentence. When the pronoun immediately follows the antecedent, as it does in most relative constructions, the act of substitution is so instantaneous that it could scarcely be called a process, and the linking force is limited to the point of contact, in the manner of a hinge. The greater the syntactical distance between a pronoun and its antecedent, the larger is the area the reader must scan before making the necessary substitution. The mental processes involved in this determination of meaning, no matter how low the level of consciousness at which they operate, will thus require the interrelating of two quite separate syntactical points. If the linkage is less strong than that provided by conjunctions or immediately relative pronouns, it embraces a larger portion of the sentence. In the passage quoted above, both occurrences of "the same" are separated from their antecedents by at least two clauses. In more extreme cases, the antecedents for Hooker's pronouns are found three or four sentences earlier.

The use of pronouns for linkage is not without attendant dangers. One far from uncommon aspect of Hooker's pronominal forms is an ambiguity of reference. In the sentence under discussion, identical pronouns are used for different antecedents. In member 8 "the same" refers to "our Church-politie" in 5, whereas in 11 it substitutes for "a much worse" in 9. The possibility for confusion is strong, and only the general context of Hooker's argument provides an adequate clue to the correct antecedent. In fact, such an overly casual approach to the pronoun represents Hooker's major stylistic vice. Often the problem is one of diction rather than syntax; the simple substitution of "theirs" for "the same" in member 11 would remove the confusion. But Hooker is not careful in his choice of pronouns, and the reader is sometimes brought to a halt in a conscious search for the correct referent. Yet devotion to pronominal forms for linkage, whatever the occasional difficulties that may be entailed, is a key element in his style. When a reader enters upon a search for the correct referent, he does not, except in cases of confusion, actually reread the previous part of the sentence. Instead, he scans his memory for a substitution that will be meaningful in the context of the new clause. Thus a heavy use of linking pronouns trains the reader to hold in immediately available suspension the sentence members, or even whole sentences, he has already absorbed, even when they have been grammatically completed. No previous element must be allowed to escape the immediate consciousness lest it be required for pronominal reference. Such an analysis reduces, of course, to mechanical terms a swift and perhaps partly intuitive mental process, but it is nonetheless useful in describing the cohesive effect Hooker thus achieves. As an expressive tendency, therefore, pronominal linkage is similar to grammatical suspension. Both embody a refusal to pigeonhole, an insistence upon examining all the evidence in a rationally tentative manner without precipitate judgments.

My own experience in reading Hooker with students has been revealing. Influenced as most of them have been by modern prose styles, their absorption of written meaning seems analogous to the manner in which they would count the cars of a train entering a tunnel. Each element of the thought passes before them on its own syntactical gondola. Coherence depends on an unobtrusive head-to-tail linkage and a general unity of direction as all the cars move along the same track. Each car is inexorably displaced by the succeeding one, each disappears in turn into the darker recesses of the memory. Reading Hooker for the first time, these students seem to find that, because of his complicated and expansive sentence structure, particularly the periodic construction, and his heavy use of pronominal linkage, they are constantly losing count. The train has to be backed up, the passages reread. After a period of vocal suffering they learn to adapt to this unaccustomed mode of prose. To pursue the analogy a little further, they learn not to count cars just before they enter a tunnel. In a sense, they learn not to count at all, but to remove themselves to a nearby hilltop from which they can simultaneously see the whole train and estimate its length, the nature of its freight, and its true direction, even when some cars are still rounding a curve. Some losses are entailed in the more distant perspective. The individual cars, the syntactical elements, are less immediately exciting. From afar the colors are weaker, the details of individual pieces of freight less precise, the noise of passage less internally vibrating. The corresponding gain is in a more comprehensive outlook, which is never distracted from embracing the whole by the immediacy of the present part.

The analogy has obvious limitations, but I think it instructive in revealing some essential qualities of Hooker's prose structure. Distinctions are often made between prose styles on the basis of coherency. As Coleridge put it, in stylists like Hooker, the unity "is produced by the unity of the subject, and the perpetual growth and evolution of the thoughts, one generating, and explaining, and justifying, the place of another, not, as it is in Seneca, where the thoughts, striking as they are, are merely strung together like beads, without any causation or progression."[11]

Throughout the previous discussion I have emphasized the syntactical forms by which Hooker expresses this logically coherent movement. Yet such a proximate analysis as Coleridge's is far from satisfying. What, exactly, is meant by logical coherence? What is incoherent about Senecan beads on a string? Does not a necklace have unity, cohesiveness, progression, even a kind of structural causality? In short, how does the progression of a Ciceronian passage really differ from that of a Senecan? I am inclined to think that too much emphasis can be placed on this distinction between a causally unified, logically progressive style and one that proceeds more atomistically by a series of striking thoughts. The distinction is valid for descriptive purposes, but it deals only in effects and leaves untouched more essential questions.

No readable style can be incoherent or lack all progressive movement. A glance at a Bacon essay in the Senecan "curt" mode will invariably reveal an underlying development. "Of Riches," for example, opens with Coleridge's beads on a string: "I cannot call Riches better than the baggage of virtue. The Roman word is better, *impedimenta*. For as baggage is to an army, so is riches to virtue. It cannot be spared nor left behind, but it hindreth the march; yea and the care of it sometimes loseth or disturbeth the victory. Of great riches there is no real use, except it be in the distribution; the rest is but conceit." Structurally, Bacon's prose is almost at the opposite extreme from Hooker's here. Typically, he begins the passage with the conclusion, and the explanation follows. Notable is his use of the pronoun in the fourth sentence. Some linking force is present, but Bacon is less interested in structural coherence than in the value of the indefinite pronoun for reinforcement of his metaphor: "it" has a double antecedent, both baggage and riches. Elsewhere Bacon prefers to repeat such key nouns.

Although the passage moves in the staccato bursts of the *stile coupé*, it hardly seems accurate to say that it is "without causation or progression." The introduction of the metaphor, the development of its relevance, the explicit application in a moral epigram surely represents a "growth and evolution of the thoughts, one generating, and explaining, and justifying, the place of another." The difference between the Ciceronian and Senecan modes, of course, lies in structural emphasis. Were Hooker to rework Bacon's passage into one of his characteristic periods, we would be made much more conscious of rational progression, much more aware, for example, of the change of subject from "riches" to "great riches." Doubtless there are degrees of logical coherence in all good English prose styles, but the poles are not widely separated. A train remains a train, regardless of our perspective. The crucial difference is the extent to which an author impresses his coherence upon our attention.

In short, one gets closer to an essential definition of Hooker's prose structure by thinking less of logical coherence as an absolute quality in itself. What matters is rather an author's syntactical emphasis on coherence, which in turn is symptomatic of a more basic perspective, which I can only call syntactical distance. The writer views his train from the hilltop. Less metaphorically, syntactical distance can be defined as an emphasizing of larger structural patterns in place of individual elements. The syntactical whole is more important than the parts, or, more accurately, the parts are significant only as they contribute to the whole. Coleridge explains this aspect of style as "that prospectiveness of mind, that surview, which enables a man to foresee the whole of what he is to convey, appertaining to any one point; and by this means so to subordinate and arrange the different parts according to their relative importance, as to convey it at once, and as an organized whole."[12] Thus the reader is required to perceive simultaneously much greater quantities of prose embracing a larger area of thought. Reading remains, of course, a process. The reader cannot, in practice, grasp a long sentence or a chapter immediately; he must proceed element by element. But by such devices as involved subordinating constructions, a heavy incidence of conjunctions, and pronominal linkage, Hooker requires his reader to exercise more fully the suspending powers of memory until the whole argument has taken form.

The negative side of this integrating perspective has already been mentioned. No syntactical part may be allowed to become so immediately vivid that it usurps the attention. A striking metaphor, a self-sufficient epigram, the magical rhythm of a happy phrase, in fact all the partial virtues of a Senecan style are deliberately avoided by Hooker, not because he is incapable of managing them, but because they have the effect of lessening syntactical distance, of involving the reader too deeply with the present segment. Like his contemporary, Spenser, with whom he has great stylistic affinities, Hooker is continually dissolving his imagery, his wit, his epigrams in his discursive syntax and in the expansive movement of his style. The generally low density of his prose results from a deliberate emphasis on the whole rather than the part. Like Spenser, Hooker seeks his effects by the page, not the line.

NOTES

1. Cranmer's notes are included in *The Works of...Mr. Richard Hooker*, ed. Keble, 7th ed., rev., 1888, 3:108–30. The Puritan pamphlet, *A Christian Letter of certain English Protestants...* (1599), is included in Bayne's edition of *The Fifth Book* (1902), pp. 589–635; for the attack on Hooker's style and his replies see pp. 630–33. Fuller's comment is reprinted in *Works* 1:79.

2. The average length of Hooker's sentences is high, but not extreme: a little over 41 words in Book 1 of the *Laws*. Edwin Herbert Lewis, *The History of the English Paragraph* (Chicago: Univ. of Chicago Press, 1894), pp. 40–41, gives a tabulation of average sentence length for 69 writers from Tyndale to Herbert Spencer, in which Hooker ranks 22nd. But the count in this instance is purely mechanical, from period to period, taking no cognizance of the distinction between indicated sentences and grammatically complete units. Since Hooker's sentences normally contain but one independent clause, he would stand appreciably higher in a tabulation that called the authors to a stricter grammatical accounting.

3. All citations to the *Laws* in my text are identified by the book, chapter, and section numbers in the Keble editions, but I follow the text of the 1593 edition.

4. In analyzing the structure of Hooker's more complicated sentences I reproduce them schematically, using indentations to suggest degrees of subordination and italics for the main independent clause. I am uncomfortably aware that such orderings are often moot.

5. Munz, *The Place of Hooker in the History of Thought*, pp. 173–74.
6. *Of the Advancement of Learning*, in Francis Bacon, *Works*, ed. James Spedding, Robert Leslie Ellis, and Douglas Denon Heath (Boston: Brown and Taggard, 1860–64), 6:96–97.
7. Samuel Johnson, *A Dictionary of the English Language* (London: J. and P. Knapton, etc., 1755; reprinted New York: A.M.S. Press, 1967), "Preface," Vol. I, sig. C2ᵛ.
8. I should make clear my implicit distinction between expressive and rhetorical (or impressive) values in stylistic analysis. The critic, standing so to speak on the written word, can look back to the writer and describe how *precisely* the text expresses the author's meaning, or he can look forward toward the reader and analyze how *effectively* the author's meaning is communicated. The theoretical implications of this distinction are too complex to be investigated here, but I think the critic unwilling to admit the discreteness of these perspectives and the validity of each is in trouble.
9. Alfred North Whitehead, *Science and the Modern World* (New York: Macmillan, 1927), p. 6.
10. Jonas Barish, "The Prose Style of John Lyly," *ELH* 23 (1956): 24.
11. *Coleridge's Miscellaneous Criticism*, ed. Thomas Middleton Raysor (Cambridge: Harvard Univ. Press, 1936), p. 217.
12. Coleridge, *Biographia Literaria*, ed. J. Shawcross (London: Oxford Univ. Press, 1907), 2:44.

RICHARD HOOKER

AN

ANNOTATED BIBLIOGRAPHY

Egil Grislis and W. Speed Hill

This Bibliography is both selective and representative. It includes all items that have come to the attention of its compilers as of June 1, 1971, whose stated subject is Hooker or in which Hooker receives more than passing notice. Excluded, as a class, are routine notices in encyclopedias—with some exceptions, as where the contributor has elsewhere written on Hooker—excerpts in textbooks, and paraphrases. Not all of the items in section v, naturally, are of equal interest or scholarly merit, and a number of these items are included because they testify to a substantial popular or semipopular interest in Hooker. A special effort has been made to locate foreign items and unpublished dissertations. Each item has been seen by at least one of the compilers, unless otherwise noted. Where the item is not readily available, a library location has been given. Sections I–IV are the responsibility of the editor, section v the joint responsibility of the compilers; contributed annotations have been initialed. A fuller version of this Bibliography, unannotated but with an additional section of works of more general interest to students of Hooker and his period, appears in *Bibliographia Tripotamopolitana*, edited by Dikran Y. Hadidian and published by the Clifford E. Barbour Library of the Pittsburgh Theological Seminary.

I. BIBLIOGRAPHY AND REFERENCE

BATESON, F. W., ed. *The Cambridge Bibliography of English Litera-ture.* Cambridge: Cambridge Univ. Press, 1940. 1:685–88. *Supplement.* Cambridge: Cambridge Univ. Press, 1957. 5:321–22. The most complete to date; a revision, prepared by P. G. Stan-wood, is in press.

BRITISH MUSEUM. *General Catalogue of Printed Books: Photolitho-graphic Edition to 1955.* London: The Trustees of the British Museum, 1961. 106:519–25. *Ten-Year Supplement.* 1968. 21:349.

COXE, HENRY O., ed. *Catalogus Codicum MSS. qui in Collegiis aulisque Oxoniensibus hodie adservantur,* Pars II. Oxford: Oxford Univ. Press, 1852. Locates MSS at Corpus Christi, Hooker's College at Oxford; excerpted by Keble, *Works* (1888), 1:106–17, cited below.

———— "Episcopal and Anglican History: An Annotated Biblio-graphy." June issue, 1966–, *Historical Magazine of the Protestant Episcopal Church.*

GREG, W. W., ed. *English Literary Autographs 1550–1650.* Oxford: Oxford Univ. Press, 1932; rpt. Nendeln, Liechtenstein: Kraus, 1968. Facsimiles and transcriptions of portions of folios 78^r, 111^r, and 212^r of Bodleian MS Add. C. 165, the printer's copy of Book v, with Hooker's corrections.

HILL, W. SPEED. *Richard Hooker, A Descriptive Bibliography of the Early Editions: 1593–1724.* Cleveland and London: The Press of Case Western Reserve University, 1970. A formal, descriptive bibliography of all recorded editions, issues, and states of Hooker's printed works, based on first-hand analysis of examples from the Folger, Yale, McAlpin, and Newberry collections; here issued in a trial edition, prior to inclusion in revised form in final volume of *Complete Works.*

[JACKSON, WILLIAM A.] *The Carl H. Pforzheimer Library: English Literature, 1475–1700.* New York: privately printed, 1940. 2:502–08. Authoritative descriptions of important early editions.

KEBLE, JOHN, ed. *The Works of That Learned and Judicious Divine,*

Mr. Richard Hooker: With an Account of His Life and Death by Isaac Walton. Revised by R. W. Church and F. Paget. 7th ed. 3 vols. Oxford: Clarendon Press, 1888; reprinted New York: Burt Franklin, 1970. The Church and Paget rescension of Keble's *Works* is a mine of useful information, much of it buried in footnotes to Keble's original Preface and to Walton's *Life.*

LEVINE, MORTIMER, ed. *Tudor England 1485–1603.* Conference on British Studies: Bibliographical Handbooks. Cambridge: Cambridge Univ. Press, 1968. A selective updating of Read (see below); lists items through September 1, 1966; useful annotations, with an emphasis on historical scholarship.

LIEVSAY, JOHN L., ed. *The Sixteenth Century: Skelton through Hooker.* Goldentree Bibliographies in Language and Literature. New York: Appleton-Century-Crofts, 1968. Complements Levine as a guide to scholarship in "Renaissance English literature and culture"; selective, with an emphasis on work of "the past three or four decades."

———— "Literature of the Renaissance." Annual compilation, April issue (through 1969) of *Studies in Philology.* An invaluable resource, wide-ranging, which has been discontinued in favor of the *MLA International Bibliography of Books and Articles on the Modern Languages and Literatures,* ed. Harrison T. Meserole; indexes book reviews.

PEEL, ALBERT, ed. *The Seconde Parte of a Register: Being a Calendar of Manuscripts under that title intended for publication by the Puritans about 1593, and now in Dr. Williams's Library, London.* 2 vols. Cambridge: Cambridge Univ. Press, 1915. Peel calendars a major collection of documents exactly contemporary with the *Laws;* Hooker himself noted as one who, at the Temple, "preacheth but now and then" (2:184).

POLLARD, A. W. and REDGRAVE, G. R., eds. *A Short-title Catalogue of Books Printed in England, Scotland, and Ireland...1475–1640.* London: The Bibliographical Society, 1926; frequently reprinted. Revision in progress.

READ, CONYERS, ed. *Bibliography of British History: Tudor Period,*

1485–1603. 2d ed. Oxford: Clarendon Press, 1959. The standard, comprehensive bibliography of the period; lists items through January 1, 1957; cf. Levine, above.

———— *The Year's Work in English Studies.* London: The English Association, John Murray.

II. BIOGRAPHY

BERNARD, J. H. "The Father of Richard Hooker." *The Irish Church Quarterly* 6 (1913): 265–70. Supplements Maclean (below) on Irish career of Hooker's father.

BUTT, JOHN, and URE, PETER. Review of Novarr (below). *Modern Language Review* 54 (1959): 588–91. Cites evidence in the Lincolnshire archives that Hooker held the benefice of Drayton Beauchamp from October 1584 to October 1585; Sisson (below) argued that Hooker was nonresident.

FLETCHER, C. R. L. "Richard Hooker." In *Historical Portraits: Richard II to Henry Wriothesley 1400–1600.* The Lives by C. R. L. Fletcher; the portraits chosen by Emery Walker. Oxford: Clarendon Press, 1909. A note, dependent upon Walton, with a portrait by an unknown painter from the National Portrait Gallery. (EG)

FOWLER, THOMAS. *The History of Corpus Christi College with Lists of its Members.* Oxford: Oxford Historical Society, Clarendon Press, 1893. The major source of our knowledge of Hooker's college career.

FULLER, THOMAS. *The Church-History of Britain from the Birth of Jesus Christ until the Year MDCXLVII.* London: John Williams, 1655. IX.vii.49–63; viii.40. Early account of Hooker's controversy with Walter Travers at the Temple.

———— *The History of the Worthies of England.* London: J.G.W.L. and W.G., 1662. A brief notice.

GAUDEN, JOHN. *The Life & Death of Mr. Richard Hooker...* In *Works,* 1662 (see below). Chiefly important because its inaccuracy provoked Walton's *Life* (see below).

HOOKER, RICHARD. *The Answere of Mʳ Richard Hooker to a Supplica-*

tion Preferred by Mr Walter Travers to the HH. Lords of the Privie Counsell. Oxford: Joseph Barnes, sold by John Barnes, 1612. Hooker's own account of the controversy with Travers.

KEEN, ROSEMARY. "Inventory of Richard Hooker, 1601." *Archeologia Cantiana* 70 (1956): 231–36. Reprints inventory of Hooker's possessions made at his death (Kent Archives Office PRC 11/1).

KNOX, S. J. *Walter Travers: Paragon of Elizabethan Puritanism.* London: Methuen, 1962. The fullest account of the Hooker-Travers controversy (pp. 70–88).

LEE, SIDNEY. "Hooker, Richard." In *The Dictionary of National Biography* (New York: Macmillan, 1891, 27:289–95; reprinted London: Oxford Univ. Press, 1945–50, 9:1183–89). A largely uncritical rescension of Walton.

MACLEAN, JOHN, ed. John Hooker, *The Life and Times of Sir Peter Carew.* London: Bell & Daldy, 1857. Maclean's notes provide important information on the Irish career of Hooker's father, who was Carew's steward (John Hooker was Richard's uncle).

NOVARR, DAVID. *The Making of Walton's "Lives."* Cornell Studies in English, 41. Ithaca, N.Y.: Cornell Univ. Press, 1958. An indispensable critique of Walton's sources, biases, and literary art as they shaped his classic biography of Hooker and through it Hooker's subsequent reputation.

PAMP, FREDERICK E., Jr. "Walton's Redaction of Hooker." *Church History* 17 (1948): 95–116. Pamp sees Walton as the "unconscious spokesman" of the Restoration Episcopate; cf. Novarr, above.

SISSON, C. J. *The Judicious Marriage of Mr. Hooker and the Birth of "The Laws of Ecclesiastical Polity."* Sandars Lectures in Bibliography, University of Cambridge, 1938. Cambridge: Cambridge Univ. Press, 1940. An indispensable addition to Walton; especially important for its reconstruction of the publishing history of the *Laws* and for an unbiased portrait of Hooker's marriage; prints extensive new documentary evidence (pp. 112–90).

SMITH, ELSIE. "Hooker at Salisbury." *Times Literary Supplement* (March 30, 1962), p. 223. Furnishes documentary evidence that Hooker was in residence at Salisbury Cathedral as of 1591.

STALEY, VERNON. *Richard Hooker*. The Great Churchmen Series. London: Masters, 1907. A popular biography. (EG)

TRAVERS, WALTER. *A Supplication Made to the Privy Counsel*. Oxford: Joseph Barnes, sold by John Barnes, 1612. Travers' version of the controversy with Hooker; cf. Hooker's *Answere*, above.

WALTON, IZAAK. *The Life of Mr. Rich. Hooker, The Author of those Learned Books of the Laws of Ecclesiastical Polity*. London: Richard Marriott, 1665; reprinted 1666, 1670, 1675. Walton's famous *Life* remains the major seventeenth-century source; it replaced Gauden's *Life* (1662) in the 1666 edition of the *Works* and was reprinted in all subsequent editions throughout the nineteenth century. Walton revised his text in 1670 and again in 1675; John Strype supplemented it in *Works* (1705). For Walton's limitations as a biographer, see Novarr, Pamp, and Sisson, above.

WOOD, ANTHONY À. "Richard Hooker." In *Athenæ Oxonienses*. 2 vols. London: Thomas Bennet, 1691–92. Wood's notice is based mainly on Walton.

III. MANUSCRIPTS

Archiepiscopal Library, Lambeth

MS 711, No. 2, Tenison Collection. Book VIII.

MS Fairhurst 2006, fols. 6–15. Original documents of Hooker-Travers controversy at the Temple, March 1585, as adjudicated by Whitgift (cf. *Works* 1:59–65).

MS Fairhurst 2014, fols. 1–46, Book VIII.

Bodleian Library, Oxford

MS Add. C. 165. Printer's copy of Book V; corrections in Hooker's hand.

MS e. Mus. 55, fols. 83^r–92^r. Travers' *Supplication* and Hooker's *Answer*.

MS Rawlinson D. 843, fols. 20^r–24^r. Book VIII.

The British Museum

MS Burney 362, fols. 96–115. Hooker's *Answer to Travers*.

MS Harleian 291 (81), fols. 183^r–184^r. "Propositions taught and maynteined by Mr Hooker. The same breefly confuted by L. T. [Laurence Tomson] in a private letter."

MS Harleian 291 (82), fols. 184^v–185^v. "Doctrin preached by Mr Hooker in the Temple the fyrst of Marche 1585."

MS Harleian 980 (p. 49). Citations from Hooker by Gybbons.

MS Harleian 4888/215, No. 7. Travers' *Supplication.*

MS Lansdowne 96 (14), fols. 50–51. "A shorte note of sundrie unsounde pointes of Doctrine at divers times delivered by Mr Hooker in his publick sermons. (30. Martij. 1585)"

MS Lansdowne L., No. 79, fols. 171–77. Anonymous account of the Hooker-Travers controversy.

MS Sloane 2750. Book VIII.

Corpus Christi College, Oxford

MS 215b. Hooker's copy of *A Christian Letter,* with marginalia.

MS 215a. Transcript of notes in 215b, above.

MS 288. Sermon on Matthew 7:7, "Certaintie and Perpetuitie."

MS 295. Notes of Cranmer and Sandys on lost draft of Book VI.

MS 303, fols. 208, 210. Letters of Hooker to John Rainolds; printed, *Works* (1888), 1: 109–14.

——, fol. 214. Letter of G. Bishop to Rainolds with reference to Hooker.

Dr. Williams's Library, London

MSS Morrice A, Part I, fols. 109–16. Travers' *Supplication.*

MSS Morrice A, Part II, pp. 64–78. Transcript of the above.

MSS Morrice A, fols. 178–83. Sir Hew Herbert's treatise against Hooker.

MSS Morrice, fol. 35. Laurence Tomson's description of the Hooker-Travers controversy.

Gonville and Caius College, Cambridge

MS 291/274. Book VIII.

Folger Shakespeare Library, Washington, D.C.

MS X. d. 74. Travers' *Supplication.*

MS V. b. 314. John Earle's Latin translation of Books I–V (see Novarr, p. 207 and n. 72).

Public Record Office, London

MSS C. 24/390/100; C. 24/394/73. Hooker vs. Sandys (transcribed by Sisson, pp. 127–56).

MS SP. 12/188 (5). April 6, 1586. "To the godlie and his lovinge brother in Christe Mr Houldesworth preacher of gods holie woord at Newcastle." By Christopher Tayler; discusses Hooker-Travers debate at Temple.

MS 12/246 (112). Notes from Hooker's *Polity* (1593?).

MS SP. 38/4. vij° die January 1594/5. Appointment of Hooker to Bishopsbourne.

Queen's College, Oxford

MS 292. Book VIII.

Trinity College, Dublin

MS 118, fols. 1-22. *A Discourse of Justification*. [old A. 5. 6.]

MS 119, fols. 1-70. Hooker's *Answer to Travers*; transcript of Hooker's notes in Corpus Christi College, Oxford, MS 215b (above), *A Christian Letter*. [old A. 5. 22.]

MS 120. Book VIII (printed by Houk). [old C. 3. 11.]

MS 121. Book VI (fols. 1-32); *Sermon of Pride* (fols. 33-41), in Hooker's autograph; *Sermon of Pride* (fols. 43-50, incomplete); draft of reply to *A Christian Letter*. [old B. 1. 13.]

MS 774. "The Causes of the Continuance of contentions concerning church government" (fols. 56^{r-v}); Ussher notes relating to Book VIII (fols. 68^{v}-71). [old D. 3. 3.]

IV. EDITIONS

HOOKER, RICHARD. *Of the Lawes of Ecclesiasticall Politie. Eyght Bookes*. London: John Windet, n.d. Editio Princeps of Preface and Books I-IV; entered to Windet January 29, 1593 (*A Transcript of the Registers of the Company of Stationers of London; 1554-1640 A.D.*, ed. Edward Arber [London: privately printed, 1875-94], 2:295); rarely extant as separate volume; usually bound with the next item.

—— *Of the Lawes of Ecclesiasticall Politie. The fift Booke*. London: John Windet, 1597. Editio Princeps of Book V, the last book of the *Polity* to be printed in Hooker's lifetime. Printer's copy (Bodleian MS Add. C. 165), with corrections in Hooker's hand, survives; see *Works* (1888), 2:v-xvii.

—— *Of the Lawes of Ecclesiasticall Politie, Eight bookes*. London:

John Windet, 1604. A reprint of Books I–IV, bound with unused sheets of 1597 edition of Book V. Spenser's address "to the Reader" (reprinted *Works*, 1888, I:121–23) announces his intention of printing the last three books (VI–VIII).

—— *Of the Lawes of Ecclesiastical Politie, Eight Bookes*. London: William Stansby, sold by Matthew Lownes, 1611. A reprint of Books I–V; the basis for numerous reprints of mixed dates in the early seventeenth century (1616–17, 1622, 1632, 1638–39).

—— *The Answere of M*ʳ *Richard Hooker to a Supplication Preferred by M*ʳ. *Walter Travers to the HH. Lords of the Privie Counsell*. Oxford: Joseph Barnes, sold by John Barnes, 1612. Edited by Spenser's assistant, Henry Jackson; reprinted *Works* (1888), 3:570–96.

—— *A Learned and Comfortable Sermon of the certaintie and perpetuitie of faith in the Elect; especially of the Prophet Habakkuks faith*. Oxford: Joseph Barnes, sold by John Barnes, 1612. Edited by Jackson; reprinted *Works* (1888), 3:469–81.

—— *A Learned Discourse of Justification, Workes, and how the foundation of faith is overthrowne*. Oxford: Joseph Barnes, sold by John Barnes, 1612; 2d ed., 1613. Edited by Jackson; reprinted *Works* (1888), 3:482–547.

—— *A Learned Sermon of the Nature of Pride*. Oxford: Joseph Barnes, sold by John Barnes, 1612. Edited by Jackson; reprinted *Works* (1888), 3: 597–642, with a substantial addition from MS 121 (old B. 1. 13.), Trinity College, Dublin.

—— *A Remedie against Sorrow and Feare, delivered in a funerall Sermon*. Oxford: Joseph Barnes, sold by John Barnes, 1612. Edited by Jackson; reprinted *Works* (1888), 3:643–53.

—— *Two Sermons upon Part of S. Judes Epistle*. Oxford: Joseph Barnes, 1614. Facsimile, Amsterdam and New York: Da Capo Press, 1969 (No. 195, The English Experience); reprinted *Works* (1888), 3:654–99. Authenticity questioned by Keble, ibid., I: lvi–lviii, but confirmed by Sisson, *Judicious Marriage*, pp. 109–11.

—— *Certayne Divine Tractates, and other Godly Sermons*. London:

[William Stansby] for Henrie Fetherstone, 1618. First collected edition of *Tractates*; issued with 1616–17 reprint of Books I–V; reprinted 1622, 1632, 1635–36, 1639.

——— "A discovery of the Causes of the continuance of these Contentions touching Church-government: out of the fragments of Richard Hooker." In *Certain Briefe Treatises...concerning the... government of the Church*. Oxford: Leonard Lichfield, 1641. Perhaps a sermon; descended through Andrewes and Ussher; Keble doubts its authenticity (*Works*, 1888, 3:460, n. 2) and reprints it as Appendix ii, Book VIII (3:460–65).

——— *Of the Lawes of Ecclesiasticall Politie; The Sixth and Eighth Books...now published according to the most Authentique Copies*. London: Richard Bishop, sold by John Crook, 1648 [variant imprints: "LONDON, Printed by *Richard Bishop* 1648."; "LONDON, Printed in the Year, 1648."]; reissued, 1651, with imprint: "*LONDON*, Printed by *R.B.* and are to be sold by *George Badger...*" First edition of Books VI and VIII, the latter incomplete (omits chs. vii and ix); Bishop's text from British Museum MS Sloane 2570 (see Houk, ed., *Book VIII*, pp. 119–21, 137–40).

——— "Mr. Hookers Judgment of the Kings Power in matters of Religion, advancement of Bishops &c." In *Clavi Trabales*, edited by Nicholas Bernard. London: R. Hodgkinson, sold by R. Marriot, 1661. Fragments of Book VIII of the *Laws* from MSS of Ussher; used by Walton to discredit Gauden's edition of *Works*; see next item.

——— *The Works of Mr. Richard Hooker...in Eight Books of Ecclesiastical Polity. Now Compleated, as with the Sixth and Eighth, so with the Seventh...out of his own Manuscripts, never before Published*. London: J. Best, for Andrew Crook, 1662. First edition of all eight books of the *Laws*; first edition of Book VII. Authenticity of posthumous books, claimed by Gauden (the compiler of the edition), challenged by Walton; but Gauden's text, prefaced by Walton's famous *Life*, was reprinted in 1666 (London: Thomas Newcomb for Andrew Crook), 1676, 1682, with corrections to

Walton by Strype in 1705 and 1723, and in Dublin in 1721 (reissued, 1724).

—— *A Sermon of Richard Hooker...Found in the Study of the late Learned Bishop Andrews.* In Izaak Walton, *The Life of Dr. Sanderson, Late Bishop of Lincoln.* London: Richard Marriott, 1678. Reprinted *Works* (1888), 3: 700–09.

—— *Works*...3 vols. Oxford: Clarendon Press, 1793. The first Clarendon Press edition, and the first in octavo; reprinted 1807, 1820.

—— *Works*...2 vols. Edited by W. S. Dobson. London: G. Cowle, 1825.

—— *The Ecclesiastical Polity and other works.* Edited by Benjamin Hanbury. 3 vols. London: Holdsworth and Ball, 1830. Reprints *A Christian Letter* (1599) and Covel's *Just and Temperate Defense* (1603).

—— *The Works of...Mr. Richard Hooker: With an Account of His Life and Death by Isaac Walton.* Edited by John Keble. 3 vols. Oxford: Clarendon Press, 1836 (see above, section 1). First critical edition; much new material; reprinted frequently, both with Keble's apparatus (1841, 1845, 1863, 1874) and without (1850, 1875, 1890); the 7th ed., revised by R. W. Church and F. Paget (1888) and reprinted by Burt Franklin (New York, 1970), is the standard reference text.

—— *Book I: Of the Laws of Ecclesiastical Polity.* Edited by R. W. Church. Clarendon Press Series: English Classics. Oxford: Clarendon Press, 1866; reprinted 1868, 1873, 1882, 1896, 1905. Especially important for Richard Church's introduction, in which Church as an Anglican theologian and historian discusses Hooker's importance and the meaning of his work. (JB)

—— *Confession and Absolution: Being the Sixth Book of the Laws of Ecclesiastical Polity by that Learned and Judicious Divine Mr. Richard Hooker.* Edited by John Harding. London: Charles Murray, 1901. Based on Keble's text; accepts the view that Book VI is, in the main, not written for the *Laws*; analysis, notes, appendix of proper names.

———— *Of the Laws of Ecclesiastical Polity: The Fifth Book.* Edited by Ronald Bayne. The English Theological Library. London: Macmillan, 1902. Based on Keble's text; Bayne's apparatus is notably full, including a translation of Hooker's Greek citations; reprints *A Christian Letter,* Hooker's MS replies, and Cranmer's *Letter* (Oxford, 1642).

———— *Of the Laws of Ecclesiastical Polity: Books I–V.* Edited by Ronald Bayne; revised introduction by Christopher Morris. Everyman's Library, 201–2. 2 vols. London: J. M. Dent & Sons, and New York: E. P. Dutton & Co., 1907; rev. ed., 1954; frequently reprinted. Reprints Keble's text of the first five books of the *Laws* and Sermons I and II.

———— *Hooker's Ecclesiastical Polity: Book VIII.* Edited by Raymond Aaron Houk. New York: Columbia Univ. Press, 1931. An important study, arguing the authenticity of the posthumous books. Houk's views were qualified by Sisson (*Judicious Marriage,* cited above, section II) and Craig ("First Form," cited below, section V). He prints the text of the Dublin MS of Book VIII.

———— *Of the Lawes of Ecclesiasticall Politie: Books I–V,* [1594]–1597. Menston, England: Scolar Press, 1969. A facsimile of the first editions of Books I–V.

V. COMMENTARY

ADDISON, JAMES T. "Early Anglican Thought, 1559–1667." *Historical Magazine of the Protestant Episcopal Church* 22 (1953): 247–369. A discussion of authority, the church, episcopacy, and the eucharist with many quotations from the sources and a minimum of interpretation. (EG)

ALLEN, J. W. *A History of Political Thought in the Sixteenth Century.* London: Methuen, and New York: Dial Press, 1928; reprinted with new bibliographies, New York: Barnes & Noble, 1957. An important early treatment of Hooker's political thought under the rubric "The Question of Toleration" (pp. 231–46). (WSH)

ALLEN, WARD. "Hooker and the Utopians." *English Studies* 51 (1970): 37–39. A brief introduction to the statements (*Laws* v.xxxvi.4) in which the Puritans are identified as doctrinaire Utopians. (EG)

ALLISON, CHRISTOPHER F. *The Rise of Moralism: The Proclamation of the Gospel from Hooker to Baxter.* New York: Seabury, and London: S.P.C.K., 1966. A succinct analysis of the essence of Hooker's soteriology. (EG)

AMELUNXEN, C. R. *Die staatskirchenrechtlichen Ideen Richard Hookers in der Entwicklung des Establishment.* Dissertation, Westfälische Landes-Universität zu Münster, Germany, 1950 [film, Hartford Seminary Foundation]. An interpretation of Hooker's understanding of church and state which emphasizes its originality, Elizabethan character, and the influence of the middle ages rather than the anticipation of rationalism. A critique of Schütz. (EG)

BAKER, HERSCHEL. *The Wars of Truth: Studies in the Decay of Christian Humanism in the Earlier Seventeenth Century.* Cambridge: Harvard Univ. Press, 1952; reprinted Gloucester: Peter Smith, 1969. Chapter 5, "Anglican and Puritan," succinctly analyzes the intellectual background of Hooker's thought in the light of its fate in the century of Thomas Hobbes. (WSH)

BARRY, ALFRED. "Richard Hooker." In *Masters in English Theology: Being the King's College Lectures for 1877,* pp. 1–60. London: John Murray, and New York: E. P. Dutton, 1877. An eloquent but uncritical summary of Hooker's theology. (EG)

BAYNE, RONALD, ed. *The Fifth Book.* See above, section IV.

——— "Hooker." In *Encyclopedia of Religion and Ethics,* edited by James Hastings, 6:772–76. New York: Charles Scribner's Sons, 1914. An older but still valuable summation, scholarly and detailed. (WSH)

BETHELL, S. L. *The Cultural Revolution of the Seventeenth Century.* London: D. Dobson, and New York: Roy, 1951. Hooker is dealt with especially in ch. 2, "The doctrinal treatment of faith and reason in seventeenth-century Anglican theology." (JB)

BÉVENOT, MAURICE. "The Catholicism of Richard Hooker—Does

It Point to a Reunion?" *The Hibbert Journal* 41 (1942): 73–80. A review of Augustus H. Rees, *The Faith in England*, Signposts, No. 12 (Westminster: Dacre, 1941), and a claim that Hooker shared Whitgift's Protestant understanding of the eucharistic presence of Christ. (EG)

BLENCH, J. W. *Preaching in England in the late Fifteenth and Sixteenth Centuries: A Study of English Sermons 1450–c. 1600.* Oxford: Basil Blackwell, 1964. General comment on Hooker's style (pp. 188–92) and his "wholesome" spirituality (pp. 319–20). (WSH)

BOOTY, JOHN. "The Quest for the Historical Hooker." *The Churchman* 80 (1966): 185–93. A thoughtful sketch by a wise Anglican scholar emphasizing the contemporary need to recognize the developmental and relational dimensions of Hooker's life and thought. (EG)

BOUGHNER, DANIEL C. "Notes on Hooker's Prose." *Review of English Studies* 15 (1939): 194–200. Emphasizes Hooker's use of the traditional rhetorical devices, although always with restraint and in subordination to graver matters. (GE)

BROMILEY, G. W. *Baptism and the Anglican Reformers.* London: Lutterworth, 1953. A major study that pays detailed attention to Hooker; it concludes that the Anglican view of the doctrinal foundations of baptism was historically consistent with that of the Reformed churches on the Continent. (WSH)

BULL, GEORGE. "What did Locke Borrow from Hooker?" *Thought* 7 (1932): 122–35. A brief discussion of piecemeal resemblances and overall differences of intent. (EG)

BUSH, DOUGLAS. *English Literature in the Earlier Seventeenth Century 1600–1660.* Vol. 5, The Oxford History of English Literature. Oxford: Clarendon Press, 1945; 2d rev. ed., 1962. A critical glimpse of Walton with a few but memorable characterizations of Hooker's Christian humanism. (EG)

CAMERON, ALAN L. "The Eucharistic Teaching of Hooker and Calvin." B.D. thesis, McGill University Divinity School, Montreal, 1963. A beginner's interpretation of some Eucharistic problems that needs to be supplemented by other scholarly works. (EG)

CARLYLE, R. W. and CARLYLE, A. J. *A History of Mediæval Political Theory in the West*. Vol. 6, *Political Theory from 1300 to 1600*. Edinburgh & London: William Blackwood & Sons, and New York: G. P. Putnam's Sons, 1903–1936; reprinted New York: Barnes & Noble, n.d. A brief statement (pp. 350–57) of Hooker's importance as a legal thinker, emphasizing his Thomism and his debt to the medieval revival of Roman law. (WSH)

CARPENTER, S. C. "Master Richard Hooker Concerning the Lambeth Conference." *Spectator* 145 (July 12, 1930): 43–44. A sermonic message to the Lambeth conference, 1930. (EG)

CARTER, C. SYDNEY. "Richard Hooker." *Church Quarterly Review* 139 (1945): 218–27. A popular and charming summary of Hooker's life and thought without benefit of scholarly insight. (EG)

———— *Richard Hooker*. Great Churchmen. London: Church Book Room Press, 1947. [Not seen.]

CATTERMOLE, RICHARD. *The Literature of the Church of England Indicated in Selections from the Writings of Eminent Divines: With Memoirs of their Lives, and Historical Sketches of the Times in which they Lived*, 1:15–24. London: John W. Parker, 1844. A popular sketch. (EG)

CHIASSON, ELIAS J. "Swift's Clothes Philosophy in the *Tale* [*of a Tub*] and Hooker's Concept of Law." *Studies in Philology* 59 (1962): 64–82. Finds "close, if ironic, affinities between the philosophy of clothes ["sartorism"], which is central to Swift's religious allegory, and the concept of Law formulated in Hooker's *Laws*" (p. 64). (WSH)

CHURCH, R. W., ed. *Book I*. See above, section IV.

CLARK, R. A. D. "The Doctrine of the Church in the Writings of Jewel, Cartwright, Whitgift, Hooker." B. Litt. thesis, Oxford, St. Catherine's Society, 1952. [Not seen.]

COLERIDGE, SAMUEL T. "Richard Hooker." In *Coleridge on the Seventeenth Century*, edited by Roberta Florence Brinkley, pp. 140–52. Durham, N.C.: Duke Univ. Press, 1955. Assembles Coleridge's scattered comments and marginalia. (WSH)

COLLINSON, J. *An Analysis of Hooker's 8th Book of Ecclesiastical Polity.* London, 1810. [Not seen.]

COLLINSON, PATRICK. *The Elizabethan Puritan Movement.* London: Jonathan Cape, and Berkeley & Los Angeles: Univ. of California Press, 1967. A carefully done scholarly study which explores the broad spectrum of Puritanism with particular attention to politics and a marginal mention of Hooker. (EG)

CONGAR, YVES M.-J., O.P. "Richard Hooker." In *Catholicisme Hier–Aujourd'hui–Demain.* Paris: Letouzey, 1962. A compact and lucid statement by a famous French Dominican. (EG)

COPLESTON, FREDERICK. *A History of Philosophy.* Vol. 3, *Ockham to Suarez.* London: Burns & Oates, and Westminster, Md.: Newman Press, 1953; reprinted Garden City, N.Y.: Doubleday, Image Books, 1963. A standard history of philosophy with a brief reference to Hooker (pp. 322–24). (EG)

COSTELLO, SISTER MARY CLEOPHAS. "The *Cursus* Forms in the Prose of Richard Hooker." M.A. dissertation, Catholic University of America, 1939. Notes the "simplicity of vocabulary, the prevalence of native cadences, and the characteristic balancing of phrases" (p. 53) in Hooker's prose. (WSH)

COVEL, WILLIAM. *A Just and Temperate Defence of the Five Books of Ecclesiastical Policie: Against an uncharitable Letter of certain English Protestants*...London: P. Short for Clement Knight, 1603; reprinted *Works* (1830), ed. Hanbury (see above, section IV). The one book wholly devoted to a defense of Hooker against the Puritan *Christian Letter.* (JB)

CRAIG, HARDIN. *The Enchanted Glass: The Elizabethan Mind in Literature.* New York: Oxford Univ. Press, 1936. Craig has frequent occasion to cite Hooker's views as representative of the climate of opinion in Elizabethan England. (WSH)

—— "Of the Laws of Ecclesiastical Polity—First Form." *Journal of the History of Ideas* 5 (1944): 91–104. An important study of the genesis of the *Laws* and the revision of the last four books; takes issue with Sisson. (WSH)

CRANEY, EDWARD J. "Richard Hooker: A Study of His View of the

Rule of Faith." Thesis, Gregorian University, Rome, 1934. [film, Hartford Seminary Foundation.] A sympathetic but pre-ecumenical first Roman Catholic study of Hooker's view of the Bible, tradition, and the church. (EG)

CRANMER, GEORGE. *Concerning the New Church Discipline, An Excellent Letter...* n.p. [Oxford], 1642. An important commentary by Hooker's collaborator and former student; probably written in 1592–93 (see Craig, *Journal of the History of Ideas* 5, above); reprinted by Walton in 1665 and subsequently by Keble (*Works*, 1888, 2:598–610). (WSH)

DAVIES, E. T. *The Political Ideas of Richard Hooker.* London: S.P.C.K., 1946; reprinted 1948. Essentially a work of popularization, designed to present Hooker's ideas to the intelligent layman. (WDJCT)

———— *Episcopacy and the Royal Supremacy in the Church of England in the XVI Century.* Oxford: Basil Blackwell, 1950. A scholarly study of Anglican formularies which pays detailed attention to Hooker (pp. 41–58), particularly his stand in the *Laws* on episcopacy. (EG)

DAVIES, HORTON. *Worship and Theology in England.* Vol. 1, *From Cranmer to Hooker, 1534–1603.* Princeton: Princeton Univ. Press, 1970. A learned and detailed work stressing the differences between Anglican and Puritan with numerous significant references to Hooker's major insights. (EG)

DAVIES, J. G. "Richard Hooker and the Rites of Burial." *Theology* 52 (1949): 406–10. A good description of the burial practices in the early church with a note that Hooker apparently did not possess this information. (EG)

DE LARA, DIONISIO. "Richard Hooker's Concept of Law." *Anglican Theological Review* 44 (1962): 380–89. An enthusiastic précis of Book 1. (WSH)

D'ENTRÈVES, ALESSANDRO PASSERIN. "Hooker e Locke: Un contributo alla storia del contratto sociale." In *Studi filosofico-giuridici, dedicati a Giorgio Del Vecchio nel XXV anno di insegnamento (1904–1929)*, 2:228–50. Modena: Società Tipografica Modenese, 1930–31. [Univ. of Michigan Law Library.] Examines the relationship between Hooker and Locke, and argues that it is anachronistic to interpret Hooker's political thought in terms of Locke's doctrine of social contract. Its arguments are developed in *Riccardo Hooker*, especially pp. 81–102; see next item. (WDJCT)

—— *Riccardo Hooker: Contributo alla teoria e alla storia del diritto naturale*. R. Università di Torino, Memorie dell'Istituto Giuridico, series 2, No. 22. Turin: Presso L'Istituto Giuridico della R. Università, 1932. [Library of the Harvard Law School.] A landmark in the modern study of Hooker; the first full-scale monograph devoted to the study of his political philosophy. D'Entrèves emphasizes Hooker's importance in the history of the theory of natural law and examines his debt to his medieval predecessors, especially Aquinas. He also attacks the traditional conception of Hooker as a social-contract thinker and emphasizes the differences between his position and that of Locke. (WDJCT)

—— "Richard Hooker: A Study in the History of Political Philosophy." *Abstracts of Dissertations for the Degree of Doctor of Philosophy*. Oxford University, Committee for Advanced Studies, 6 (1934): 31–37.

—— *The Medieval Contribution to Political Thought: Thomas Aquinas, Marsilius of Padua, Richard Hooker*. Oxford: Oxford Univ. Press, 1939; reprinted New York: Humanities Press, 1959. Chapters 5 and 6 summarize the main arguments of *Riccardo Hooker* and reinforce the view that Hooker's political thought is essentially medieval in character. (WDJCT)

DIMOND, S. G. "Richard Hooker and the Twentieth Century." *Church Quarterly Review* 108 (1929): 1–18. A popular statement. (EG)

DIRKSEN, CLETUS F. *A Critical Analysis of Richard Hooker's Theory of the Relation of Church and State*. Notre Dame, Ind.: University of Notre Dame, 1947. Argues that "it was Hooker's role to give a theoretical foundation to the politically expedient Establishment" (p. 137) of Queen Elizabeth. (WSH)

DISRAELI, ISAAC. *Amenities of Literature: Consisting of Sketches and Characters of English Literature*. Edited by B. Disraeli, 2:86–98. New York: W. J. Widdleton, 1870. A bombastic account. (EG)

DOWDEN, EDWARD. "Richard Hooker." In *Puritan and Anglican: Studies in Literature*, pp. 69–96. London: Kegan Paul, 1900; New York, Henry Holt, 1901. A sensitive interpretation of Hooker's personality as well as an outline of the *via media* character of his theology, taking into account both method and temper. (EG)

DRURY, T. W. *Confession and Absolution: The Teaching of the Church of England as Interpreted and Illustrated by the Writings of the Reformers of the Sixteenth Century*. London: Hodder & Stoughton, 1903. An older scholarly study. (EG)

DUGMORE, C. W. *Eucharistic Doctrine in England from Hooker to Waterland*. London: S.P.C.K., and New York: Macmillan, 1942. An interpretation of Hooker's Eucharistic thought in its immediate historical context as affirming a real participation in the body and blood of Christ which occurs unexplainably in the soul of the believer. (EG)[See above, p. 233 —*ed.*]

DUNKIN, PAUL S. "Two Notes on Richard Hooker: Date of the 'Ecclesiastical Polity,' First Edition; The Oxford Tracts of 1612." *Papers of the Bibliographical Society of America* 41 (1947): 344–46. Supplies bibliographical evidence for the 1593 dating of Books I–IV; shows that the *Tractates'* title pages, printed at Oxford in 1612, share a common setting. (WSH)

FACIO MORENO, ANGEL. "Dos notas en torno a la idea de derecho natural en Locke: Hooker en el segundo tratado de gobierno civil." *Revista de Estudios Políticos*, No. 190 (1960): 159–64. Despite some sixteen citations of Hooker in the *Second Treatise*, Facio Moreno finds Locke's political philosophy essentially incompatible with Hooker's, although Locke clearly thought of himself as continuing the tradition Hooker represented. (WSH)

FAULKNER, ROBERT K. "The Natural Law Theory of Richard Hooker—A Comparison with St. Thomas Aquinas." M.A. dissertation, University of Chicago, 1960. A provocative essay that argues that Hooker's natural law theory differs radically from that of Aquinas and implies that it cannot stand comparison with the classic formulation in Aristotle. (WSH)

——— "Reason and Revelation in Hooker's Ethics," *American*

Political Science Review 59 (1965): 680–90. A discriminating and closely reasoned comparison of the differing assumptions that lie behind the political thought of Hooker and of Aristotle. Faulkner concludes that "Hooker's ethics is given its decisive tone by his Christian understanding of man as finally a spiritual animal, not simply a rational and political animal" (p. 690). (WSH)

FIELD, GEORGE C. "Donne and Hooker." *Anglican Theological Review* 48 (1966): 307–09. Provides evidence that Donne was acquainted with the *Laws,* in the form of a Latin couplet on Donne's copy of Covel's *Just and Temperate Defense.* (WSH)

FLESSEMAN–VAN LEER, E. "Richard Hooker, Anglicanisme en Protestantisme." *Kerk en Theologie* 6 (1955): 234–42. A scholarly discussion of episcopacy as it relates to the ecumenical role of contemporary Anglicanism. (EG)

FLOTHOW, RUDOLPH C. "The Ecclesiastical Polity of Richard Hooker and Samuel Taylor Coleridge: A Study in the Continuity of Historical Issues." Ph.D. dissertation, University of Southern California, 1959. A comparison with the major focus on Coleridge which gives only a surface portrait of Hooker's thought. Its strength is the wide consultation of secondary sources on social and political issues. (EG)

FOAKES-JACKSON, F. J. "Of the Laws of Ecclesiastical Polity." In *The Cambridge History of English Literature*, Vol. 3, ch. 18. Cambridge: Cambridge Univ. Press, and New York: G. P. Putnam's, 1909. An older survey of the *Laws* against a background of the Elizabethan Settlement and subsequent Puritan attacks upon it. (WSH).

FORRESTER, DUNCAN B. "Richard Hooker." In *History of Political Philosophy*, edited by Leo Strauss and Joseph Cropsey, pp. 314–23. Chicago: Rand McNally, 1963. A succinct exposition of Hooker's political philosophy, emphasizing his defense of reason and natural law against the "biblical radicalism" of his Puritan opponents. (WSH)

FRIEDRICH, CARL JOACHIM. "Sir Thomas Smith and Richard Hooker." In *The Philosophy of Law in Historical Perspective*, pp. 67–76. Chicago and London: Univ. of Chicago Press, 1958;

2d ed., 1963. A defense of the thesis that "Hooker is among the most important legal philosophers of the English-speaking world." (EG)

FRY, ROLAND M. *Shakespeare and Christian Doctrine*. Princeton: Princeton Univ. Press, 1963. Fry uses Hooker, along with Luther and Calvin, as representative sources of Protestant theology in this critique of Christian allegorical readings of Shakespeare's plays. (WSH)

FULLER, THOMAS. *Church-History*. See above, section II.

FUSSNER, F. SMITH. *Tudor History and the Historians*. New York and London: Basic Books, 1970. A useful study that contains a short and incisive assessment of Hooker's historical thought. (EG)

GALANTE, ANDREA. "La teoria della relazione fra lo Stato e la Chiesa secondo Riccardo Hooker (1554–1600)." In *Festschrift Emil Friedberg zum siebzigsten Geburtstag gewidmet von seinen Schülern Francesco Brandileone...*, pp. 229–44. Leipzig: Veit, 1908. A brief outline of Hooker's understanding of church and state. (EG)

GAUTIER, CARL DIDIER. "Verdensorden og Evangelium i Richard Hooker's Theologi." In *Festskrift til Jens Nørregaard*, pp. 51–75. Copenhagen: G. E. C. Gads Forlag, 1947. A learned discussion of world order and the Gospel in Hooker. (EG)

GAYLEY, CHARLES MILLS. *Shakespeare and the Founders of Liberty in America*. New York: Macmillan, 1917. Chapter 5, "Richard Hooker, and the Principles of American Liberty," uncritically assumes a continuity between Hooker, Locke ("As Hooker thought, so Locke," p. 113), and the authors of the American Constitution. (EG)

GEORGE, CHARLES H. and KATHERINE. *The Protestant Mind of the English Reformation 1570–1640*. Princeton: Princeton Univ. Press, 1961. An introduction that restates Hooker's position on numerous issues. (EG)

GORLE, J[ames]. *An Analysis of the Fifth Book of Hooker's Ecclesiastical Polity: with Examination Questions*. Cambridge: J. Hall, 1858. [Krauth Memorial Library, Lutheran Theological Seminary, Philadelphia.] A catechetical work. (WSH)

GOUGH, J. W. *The Social Contract: A Critical Study of its Develop-*

ment. Oxford: Clarendon Press, 1936; 2d ed., 1957; reprinted 1963. A standard work; Hooker receives a brief notice (pp. 71–75, 131–32). (WSH)

GREEN, V[ivian] H. H. "Richard Hooker." In *From St. Augustine to William Temple: Eight Studies in Christian Leadership*, pp. 103–25. London: Latimer House, 1948. A popular account by a noted historian, placing Hooker in the context of the entire sixteenth century. (EG)

GREENLEAF, W. H. *Order, Empiricism and Politics: Two Traditions of English Political Thought 1500–1700.* University of Hull Publications. London: Oxford Univ. Press, 1964. A study of the climate of opinion of English political thought, 1500–1700; Hooker notably exemplifies "the political theory of order" in ch. 2, "Order and Politics." (WSH)

GRISLIS, EGIL. "Richard Hooker's Method of Theological Inquiry." *Anglican Theological Review* 45 (1963): 190–203. An analysis of objectivity, Scripture, tradition, and church in reference to the problem of authority. (EG)

—— "Richard Hooker's Image of Man." In *Renaissance Papers 1963*, edited by S. K. Heninger, Jr., *et al.*, pp. 73–84. The Southeastern Renaissance Conference, 1964. A critique of Hillerdal's claim that Hooker's use of reason and grace resulted in a circular argument. (EG)

—— "The Role of *Consensus* in Richard Hooker's Method of Theological Inquiry." In *The Heritage of Christian Thought: Essays in Honor of Robert Lowry Calhoun*, edited by Robert E. Cushman and Egil Grislis, pp. 64–88. New York: Harper & Row, 1965. An important discussion of Hooker's general theological position. (JB)

HALLAM, HENRY. *The Constitutional History of England from the Accession of Henry VII to the Death of George II.* 2 vols. 5th ed., London: John Murray, 1846 (originally published, 1827). Hallam's is the classic statement of the Whig Hooker whose "theory [of the origin of government] absolutely coincides with that of Locke" (1:214–23). (WSH)

HANSON, DONALD W. *From Kingdom to Commonwealth: The Development of Civic Consciousness in English Political Thought.* Cambridge: Harvard Univ. Press, and London: Oxford Univ. Press, 1970. A brief and thoughtful account of Hooker's political theory, taking into account the research of Munz, Shirley, and E. T. Davies. (EG)

HARDING, JOHN, ed. *The Sixth Book.* See above, section IV.

HARGRAVE, O. T. *The Doctrine of Predestination in the English Reformation.* Ph.D. dissertation, Vanderbilt University. Ann Arbor: University Microfilms, 1966. An investigation that shows that alongside the Calvinist understanding of predestination there existed other currents as well, placing Hooker (pp. 228–34) among the latter. (EG)

HARTH, PHILLIP. *Swift and Anglican Rationalism: The Religious Background of "A Tale of a Tub."* Chicago: Univ. of Chicago Press, and Toronto: Univ. of Toronto Press, 1961. Hooker is a major figure in this study of seventeenth-century English religious thought. (WSH)

HENDERSON, T. F. "Hooker, Richard." In *The Encyclopaedia Britannica,* 11th ed., 13:672–74. Cambridge: Cambridge Univ. Press, 1910. An old but impressive summary with attention to biography, philosophy, and politics. (EG)

HERR, ALAN FAGEN. *The Elizabethan Sermon: A Survey and a Bibliography.* Philadelphia: Univ. of Pennsylvania, 1940; reprinted New York: Octagon, 1969. Sees Hooker as a notable exemplar of the "florid" style (pp. 97–99). (WSH)

HIGHAM, FLORENCE. *Catholic and Reformed: A Study of the Anglican Church, 1559–1662.* London: S.P.C.K., 1962. A study of the seventeenth century with an introductory assessment of the Tudor period containing a few thoughtful but general references to Hooker. (EG)

HILL, WILLIAM SPEED. "The Doctrinal Background of Richard Hooker's *Laws of Ecclesiastical Polity.*" Ph.D. dissertation, Harvard University, 1964. Argues that the doctrinal views expressed in the *Tractates* and the MS answers to *A Christian Letter* underlie the political thought of the *Laws*; in revision for Twayne's English Authors Series. (WSH)

———— "Hooker's 'Preface,' chapters VIII and IX." *Notes and Queries,* n.s. 16 (1969): 457–59. Describes an inadvertent printing of an early draft of chapters viii and ix of the Preface as *The Dangers of New Discipline* (Oxford, 1642). (WSH)

———— "The Authority of Hooker's Style." *Studies in Philology* 67 (1970): 328–38. Concentrates on the sermons, finding there a tone of authority which derives from Hooker's skill in dialectic, his integrity in citing Scripture, and a pervasive humanity expressed through metaphor and tone. (GE)

———— "Doctrine and Polity in Hooker's *Laws.*" *English Literary Renaissance* 2 (1972) 173–93. See comment above, on "Doctrinal Background." (WSH)

———— "Hooker's *Polity*: The Problem of the 'Three Last Books'." *Huntington Library Quarterly* 34 (1971): 317–36. Summarizes and supports the arguments for the authenticity of the posthumous books, substantially accepting Gauden's claims for his edition (1662); supports Keble against Sisson and Houk in rejecting Book VI from the *Laws.* (WSH)

HILLERDAL, GUNNAR. *Reason and Revelation in Richard Hooker.* Lunds Universitets Årsskrift, n.s. 1, Vol. 54, no. 7. Lund: C. W. K. Gleerup, 1962. A diligent but superficial study from a Lutheran perspective which fails to note Hooker's consistent appropriation of the Thomistic correlation of reason and grace. (EG)

HOADLY, BENJAMIN. *The Original and Institution of Civil Government, Disscuss'd. Viz. I. An Examination of the Patriarchal Scheme of Government. II. A Defense of Mr. Hooker's Judgment, &c. against the Objections of several late Writers.* London: James Knapton, 1710. An early instance of the Whig appropriation of Hooker in the tradition of Locke's *Two Treatises of Government* by a prominent Latitudinarian and controversialist. (WSH)

HOOK, WALTER F. "Hooker, Richard." In *An Ecclesiastical Biography Containing the Lives of Ancient Fathers and Modern Divines, Interpreted with Notices of Heretics and Schismatics, Forming a Brief History of the Church in Every Age,* 6: 109–27. London: F. & J. Rivington, 1850. An outline with many quotations from Hooker. (EG)

HOOPES, ROBERT. *Right Reason in the English Renaissance*. Cambridge: Harvard Univ. Press, 1962. Places Hooker in an intellectual and ethical tradition that has both Christian and Platonic roots (pp. 123–32) and is notably characteristic of Christian humanist thought of the English Renaissance. (WSH)

HOUK, RAYMOND A., ed. *Book VIII*. See above, section IV.

HUDSON, WILLIAM T. "A Comparative Analysis of the Concepts of Natural Law and Political Obligation in St. Thomas Aquinas and Richard Hooker." M.A. dissertation, University of Chicago, 1954. A somewhat elementary account that sees Hooker as moving "away from the scholastic tradition and toward such modern political conceptions as the Grotian theory of government, and the conservative principle of reverence for the historic past and the continuity of tradition" (p. 3). (EG)

HUGHES, PHILIP. *The Reformation in England*. Vol. 3, *True Religion now Established*. London: Hollis & Carter, and New York: Macmillan, 1954; 3 vols. in 1, 5th rev. ed., London: Burnes & Oates, 1963. A learned Catholic appraisal that notes Hooker's dependence on scholasticism but maintains that he consistently sided with Protestantism. (EG)

HUNT, JOHN. *Religious Thought in England from the Reformation to the End of the Last Century: A Contribution to the History of Theology*, 1:56–70. London: Strahan, 1870. A lucid and reliable outline of major issues in Hooker's theology which analyzes in what sense Hooker is a "rationalist." (EG)

HUNT, THEODORE W. "Richard Hooker, The Elizabethan Ecclesiastic." *Homiletic Review* 28 (1894): 489–93. An old thumbnail sketch. (EG)

JACKSON, S. R. "Richard Hooker: An Approach to the Renaissance." *The Manitoba Arts Review* 2 (Spring, 1940): 22–33. [New York Public Library.] A semipopular account of Hooker's Thomism in its Renaissance context. (WSH)

JENSSEN, ERNST. "Das Licht der Vernunft (reason) in der Theologie Richard Hookers." In *Solange es "heute" heisst: Festgabe für Rudolf Hermann zum 70. Geburtstag*, pp. 147–52. Berlin: Evangelische

Verlagsanstalt, 1957. A philosophical definition of "reason and intellect" on the basis of the model of "adherence and evidence." (EG)

JORDAN, W. K. *The Development of Religious Toleration in England.* Vol. 1, *From the Beginnings of the English Reformation to the Death of Queen Elizabeth.* London: George Allen & Unwin, and Cambridge: Harvard Univ. Press, 1932. A classic study which observes (pp. 222–32) that Hooker had less of an historical role to play in the emergence of religious toleration than his reputation as an irenicist would suggest. (WSH)

KAVANAGH, ROBERT V. "Reason and Nature in Hooker's *Polity.*" Ph.D. dissertation, University of Wisconsin, 1944 (abstracted in *Summaries of Doctoral Dissertations*, University of Wisconsin, 1949, 9: 490–91). A brilliant exposition of Hooker's intellectual heritage; the first study to note explicitly that the reason to which Hooker appeals is reason aided by grace. (EG)

KEARNEY, H. F. "Richard Hooker: A Reconstruction." *Cambridge Journal* 5 (1952): 300–11. Following the work of W. Oakeshott (intro. to Hobbes' *Leviathan*), Kearney argues that Books 1 and VIII of the *Laws* contradict one another and that there is a fundamental incoherence in Hooker's political thought. (WSH)

KLEIN, ARTHUR J. *Intolerance in the Reign of Elizabeth Queen of England.* Boston and New York: Houghton Mifflin, 1917; reprinted Port Washington, N.Y.: Kennikat Press, 1968. A comparison of Jewel and Hooker on authority (pp. 118–24). (EG)

KNOX, S. J. *Walter Travers.* See above, section II.

KOENEN, JOSEF. *Die Busslehre Richard Hookers: Der Versuch einer anglikanischen Bussdisziplin.* Freiburger Theologische Studien, No. 53. Freiburg im Breisgau: Herder, 1940. A thorough Catholic interpretation of Hooker's Anglican view of penance. (EG)

KRAPP, GEORGE P. *The Rise of English Literary Prose.* New York: Oxford University Press, 1915. A general discussion, emphasizing dignity, order, and restraint in Hooker's style. (GE)

KÜHLWETTER, K. VON. "Hooker, Richard." In *Evangelisches Kirchenlexikon*, edited by Heinz Brunotte and Otto Weber, 2:200–01.

Göttingen: Vandenhoeck & Ruprecht, 1958. A summary with bibliographical references, including several German works. (EG)

LECKY, W. E. H. *History of the Rise and Influence of the Spirit of Rationalism in Europe.* Rev. ed. New York: D. Appleton, 1878. A well-known older work that views Hooker as a rationalistically inclined liberal who qualified his final conclusions in order to conform with his times. (EG)

LECLER, JOSEPH. *Toleration and the Reformation.* Translated by T. L. Westow. 2 vols. London: Longmans, and New York: Association Press, 1960. Originally published as *Histoire de la tolérance au siècle de la reforme.* 2 vols. Aubier: Editions Montaigne, 1955. A scholarly French Catholic work observing that Hooker viewed outward religious conformity as binding yet followed the ideal of comprehension in doctrinal matters (2:398–403). (EG)

LEWIS, C. S. *English Literature in the Sixteenth Century Excluding Drama.* Vol. 3, The Oxford History of English Literature. Oxford: Clarendon Press, 1954; reprinted 1959. A fresh and sympathetic appreciation of Hooker's reasoned opposition to Cartwright's "Barthianism," which Lewis defines as "a flattening out of all things into common insignificance before the inscrutable Creator." (EG)

LITTLE, DAVID. *Religion, Order, and Law: A Study in Pre-Revolutionary England.* New York: Harper & Row, Harper Torchbooks, 1969, and Oxford: Basil Blackwell, 1970. In this application of the thought of Max Weber to sixteenth-century England, there is an important discussion of Hooker (pp. 147–66). (JB)

LOOTEN, C. "Un avocat de l'Eglise anglicane: Richard Hooker (1554–1600): Of the Laws of Ecclesiastical Polity (1592–3 et 1597)." *Revue d'Histoire Ecclésiastique* 33 (1937): 485–534. An extensive summary intended for an audience not familiar with Hooker's work. (WSH)

MCADOO, HENRY R. *The Spirit of Anglicanism: A Survey of Anglican Theological Method in the Seventeenth Century.* London: Adam & Charles Black, and New York: Charles Scribner's Sons, 1965. Hooker is a major figure throughout this study. Of particular interest is ch. 1, "Hooker and Liberal Method: The Tew Circle." (JB)

McGRADE, ARTHUR S. "Public Religion: A Study of Hooker's *Polity* in View of Current Problems." Ph.D. dissertation, Yale University, 1961. McGrade challenges the thesis of Munz and of Kearney that there is a fundamental contradiction between the political thought of Book 1 of the *Laws* and its application to the English monarchy in Book VIII. (WSH)

—— "The Coherence of Hooker's Polity: The Books on Power." *Journal of the History of Ideas* 24 (1963): 163–82. See comment on preceding item.

—— "The Public and the Religious in Hooker's *Polity*." *Church History* 37 (1968): 404–22. A provocative essay which argues that Book v "has both a definite structure of its own and an important function in the argument" of the *Laws* as a whole, whose aim McGrade sees as "a defense of Christianity as a 'public' religion ...on three levels...the political [Books VI–VIII], the everyday [Book v], and the intellectual [Books I–IV]." (WSH)

McLACHLAN, H. J. *Socinianism in Seventeenth Century England*. London: Oxford Univ. Press, 1951. Interesting discussions of Anglican theologians, especially Hooker, Laud, and Chillingworth. (JB)

McNEILL, JOHN T. "Richard Hooker: The Laws of Ecclesiastical Polity." In *Books of Faith and Power*, pp. 61–88. New York: Harper & Bros., 1947. An outline and evaluation by a famous church historian who attributes Hooker's appeal to thoughtful reflection and to his style. (EG)

MALONE, MICHAEL T. "The Doctrine of Predestination in the Thought of William Perkins and Richard Hooker." *Anglican Theological Review* 52 (1970): 103–17. An incisive and thorough analysis. (EG)

MAROT, D. H. "Aux Origines de la Théologie Anglicane: Ecriture et Tradition chez Richard Hooker (†1600)." *Irénikon* 30 (1960): 321–43. A scholarly discussion that relates Hooker to major issues raised in the ecumenical movement. (EG)

MARSHALL, JOHN S. "Richard Hooker and the Anglo-Saxon Ideal."

Sewanee Review 52 (1944): 381–92. A convinced but unconvincing claim that Hooker's main virtues are uniquely Anglo-Saxon. (EG)

————— "Hooker's Theory of Church and State." *Anglican Theological Review* 27 (1945): 151–60. Argues that Hooker christianized Aristotle's theory of the state by reference to the experience of Israel, the writings of Paul, and the example of England. (WSH)

————— "Hooker's Doctrine of God." *Anglican Theological Review* 29 (1947): 81–88. A statement of great enthusiasm for Hooker which asserts that both explicit and implicit views reveal a biblical understanding. (EG)

————— *Hooker's Polity in Modern English.* Sewanee, Tenn.: The Univ. Press at the Univ. of the South, 1948. The latest of a long tradition of paraphrase. (WSH)

————— "Richard Hooker and the Origins of American Constitutionalism." In *Origins of the Natural Law Tradition*, edited by A. L. Harding, pp. 48–68. Dallas: Southern Methodist Univ. Press, 1954. Argues that through Locke and the authors of the American Constitution, Hooker's view of natural law lies behind American constitutional thought. (WSH)

————— *Hooker's Theology of Common Prayer: The Fifth Book of the Polity Paraphrased and Expanded into a Commentary on the Prayer Book.* Sewanee, Tenn.: The Univ. Press at the Univ. of the South, 1956. Attempts "to discover a general pattern of positive argument" in Book v and by paraphrase to "lay bare Hooker's fundamental conception of public worship" (p. iii). (WSH)

————— "Freedom and Authority in Classical Anglicanism." *Anglican Theological Review* 65 (1963): 54–73. A brief exposition of the philosophical ethos which Hooker shared with the Caroline divines. (EG)

————— *Hooker and the Anglican Tradition: An Historical and Theological Study of Hooker's Ecclesiastical Polity.* Sewanee, Tenn.: The Univ. Press at the Univ. of the South, and London: Adam & Charles Black, 1963. A provocative study of Hooker's theology with particular attention to its Anglican context and Thomistic method. (EG)

MASIH, INAYAT. "A Study of Richard Hooker's Doctrine of Church Polity." Th.M. thesis, Protestant Episcopal Theological Seminary in Virginia, Alexandria, Va., 1954. Not available for consultation except at the Seminary. Mr J. H. Goodwin, Librarian, describes it as "substandard." (EG)

MASON, A. J. "Richard Hooker." In *Typical English Churchmen from Parker to Maurice: A Series of Lectures*, edited by William E. Collins, 1:25–34. The Church Historical Society, Vol. 65. London: S.P.C.K., 1902. A popular summary of Hooker's life. (EG)

MAURICE, FREDERICK DENISON. *Modern Philosophy: Or, A Treatise of Moral and Metaphysical Philosophy from the Fourteenth Century to the French Revolution, with a Glimpse into the Nineteenth Century.* London: Griffin, Bolur, 1862; reprinted as *Moral and Metaphysical Philosophy*, Vol. 2. London: Macmillan, 1890. A plea (pp. 189–98) that Hooker be read as no mere controversialist, that he transcends the polemics of his age even as he shares their deepest presuppositions. (WSH)

MESSENGER, ERNEST C. *The Reformation, the Mass and the Priesthood: A Documented History with Special Reference to the Question of Anglican Orders.* Vol. 2, *Rome and the Revolted Church*, pp. 316–19. London: Longmans, Green, 1937. A pre-ecumenical Catholic work that evaluates Hooker as "little more than a Zwinglian." (EG)

MICHAELIS, GOTTFRIED. *Richard Hooker als politischer Denker: Ein Beitrag zur Geschichte der naturrechtlichen Staatstheorien in England im 16. und 17. Jahrhundert.* Historische Studien, 225. Berlin: Emil Ebering, 1933; reprinted Vaduz: Kraus, 1965. Argues that the real interest and importance of Hooker lies in his role in the development of the theory of social contract. (WDJCT)

MORE, PAUL ELMER, and CROSS, FRANK LESLIE, eds. *Anglicanism: The Thought and Practice of the Church of England, Illustrated from the Religious Literature of the Seventeenth Century.* Milwaukee: Morehouse, 1935. Hooker is one whose works are quoted in this anthology. Introductory essays by More and by Felix Arnott help to locate Hooker's place among the Caroline divines. (JB)

MORREL, GEORGE W. "Richard Hooker, Theologian of the English Reformation." *Christianity Today* 10 (September 16, 1966): 8–10. A claim that Hooker was in basic theological agreement with the Continental Reformation. (EG)

—— *The Systematic Theology of Richard Hooker.* Th.D. dissertation, Pacific School of Religion, 1969. Ann Arbor, Mich.: University Microfilms, 1970. A detailed investigation of the systematic character of Hooker's thought without attention to its sources. (EG)

MORRIS, CHRISTOPHER. "Richard Hooker." In *The Great Tudors*, edited by Katharine Garvin, pp. 537–50. London: Ivor Nicholson & Watson, 1935; reprinted London: Eyre & Spottiswoode, 1956. A lively, popular evocation of Hooker the man and his times. (WSH)

—— *Political Thought in England: Tyndale to Hooker.* The Home University Library of Modern Language, 225. London: Oxford Univ. Press, 1953; reprinted 1965. A shrewd and readable summary that concludes that "Hooker was a very great political philosopher judged by any standards" (pp. 172–98). (WSH)

MORRIS, JARVIS S. "Richard Hooker's Doctrine of the Eucharist as Found in the Fifth Book, 'Of the Laws of Ecclesiastical Polity'." Th.D. dissertation, Union Theological Seminary, New York, 1936. A scholarly study that interprets Hooker's Eucharistic *via media* in reference to the Continental Reformation. (EG)

MOZLEY, J. B. *A Treatise on the Augustinian Doctrine of Predestination.* London: John Murray, 1855; 3d rev. ed., 1883. An old but learned study that compares Hooker with St Augustine on predestination (pp. 386–89). (EG)

MUNZ, PETER. *The Place of Hooker in the History of Thought.* London: Routledge & Kegan Paul, 1952; reprinted New York: Greenwood Press, 1970. An important study of Hooker's indebtedness to the thought of Aquinas, Marsilius of Padua, Aristotle, and Plato; noteworthy for its conclusion that, as a systematic thinker, Hooker was ultimately inconsistent. (WSH) [See above, pp. 10, 50–53 —*ed.*]

—— "Hooker, Richard." In *The Encyclopedia of Philosophy*, edited by Paul Edwards, 4:63–66. New York: Macmillan & The Free Press, 1967. An abstract of Munz's longer study, emphasizing Hooker's "stubborn Aristotelianism" and his consequent neglect of a nascent Renaissance Platonism. (WSH)

MURRAY, ROBERT H. *Richard Hooker and His Teaching.* Church of England Handbooks, 6. Liverpool: J. A. Thompson; London: Simpkin, Marshall, Hamilton, Kent [1924]. A somewhat popular exposition of Hooker's main theological concerns, by a well-known scholar. (EG)

——— *The Political Consequences of the Reformation: Studies in Sixteenth-Century Political Thought.* London: Ernest Benn, 1926; reprinted New York: Russell & Russell, 1960. Hooker, "a Bayard of ecclesiastical controversy," provides a serene coda to Murray's survey of the turbulent world of Machiavelli, Luther, Calvin, and Bodin; abridges *Richard Hooker and His Teaching* (above). (WSH)

NASH, HENRY S. "A Statesman of the English Church." *American Journal of Theology* 7 (1903): 563–69. A review of *The Fifth Book,* ed. Ronald Bayne. (EG)

NELSON, GEORGE. *Analysis of the Fifth Book of Hooker's Ecclesiastical Polity in the Form of Question and Answer.* London: Christian Knowledge Society, 1890. [Not seen.] [Univ. of Pennsylvania.]

NEW, JOHN F. H. *Anglican and Puritan: The Basis of Their Opposition, 1558–1640.* London: Adam & Charles Black, and Stanford: Stanford Univ. Press, 1964; reprinted 1965. A concise, if somewhat hasty, contrast. (EG)

NORTHROP, F. S. C. "Richard Hooker and Aristotle." In *The Meeting of East and West: An Inquiry Concerning World Understanding,* pp. 171–81. New York: Macmillan, 1946; reprinted New York: Collier, 1966. A spirited, popular account of the differences between British and American democracy, among which is the "organic, hierarchical conception of the good state" (p. 172) articulated by Hooker. (WSH)

NOVARR, DAVID. *The Making of Walton's "Lives."* See above, section II.

ORR, ROBERT R. "Chillingworth versus Hooker: A Criticism of

Natural Law Theory." *Journal of Religious History* 2 (December 1962): 120–32. Treats Chillingworth on Hooker. Challenges Cassirer's remark (*Platonic Renaissance*, trans. James P. Pettegrove, pp. 35–36) on "close similarity between ideas" of the two men. Chillingworth is willing to entertain a far more critical view of reason as it tackled the problems of faith; the two have antithetical "images of the human mind." (WSH)

—— *Reason and Authority: The Thought of William Chillingworth.* Oxford: Clarendon Press, 1967. There are important discussions of Hooker, especially on Scripture and authority (pp. 108–13, 147–53). (JB)

OSBORN, JAMES M. "Johnson on the Sanctity of an Author's Text." *PMLA* 50 (1935): 928–29. Notes Samuel Johnson's intention of editing Hooker and the need to paragraph text; from MS report (Bodleian MS Malone 30, fols. 64^v, 65^r) of conversation with Edmond Malone. (WSH)

PAGET, FRANCIS. *An Introduction to the Fifth Book of Hooker's Treatise of the Laws of Ecclesiastical Polity.* Oxford: Clarendon Press, 1899; 2d ed., 1907. The Bishop of Oxford, a prominent nineteenth-century student of Hooker, has much to say which is still of great value. (JB)

PAMP, FREDERICK E., Jr. "Walton's Redaction of Hooker." See above, section II.

PARRIS, J. R. "Hooker's Doctrine of the Eucharist." *Scottish Journal of Theology* 16 (1963): 151–65. A scholarly evaluation with critical references to several older studies. (EG)

PATRIDES, C. A. "The 'Universall and Public Manuscript' of Commonplaces." *Neophilogus* 47 (1963): 217–20. John Dove as plagiarist of Hooker. (WSH) [See above, pp. 101–2 —*ed.*]

PAUCK, WILHELM. *Das Reich Gottes auf Erden: Utopie und Wirklichkeit. Eine Untersuchung zu Butzers "De Regno Christi" und zur englischen Staatskirche des 16. Jahrhunderts.* Arbeiten zur Kierchengeschichte, 10. Berlin and Leipzig: Walter de Gruyter, 1928. A brief but brilliant assessment (pp. 159–70) of Hooker's main contribution by a famous historian of the Reformation. (EG)

PERCY, H. C. "Richard Hooker and Izaak Walton." *Hibbert Journal* 41 (1942): 81–82. A verse commemoration. (WSH)

PLATT, DONALD OLIVER. "The Doctrine of the Church in the Church of England, from the accession of Elizabeth I to the outbreak of the Civil War, 1558–1642." Ph.D. dissertation, Cambridge University, Corpus Christi College, 1955. The dichotomy between the physical and the spiritual, adopted from his contemporaries, is seen as an essential principle; ch. 7 offers interpretations of natural law, reason, tradition, society, royal supremacy, church, ministry, and the sacraments, Appendices V–VII are also devoted to Hooker. (EG)

POLLARD, ARTHUR. *Richard Hooker*. Writers and Their Work, 195. London: Longmans, Green, 1966. A brief but sympathetic introduction. (WSH)

PORTER, H. C. *Reformation and Reaction in Tudor Cambridge*. Cambridge: Cambridge Univ. Press, 1958. Part III, "The Universe of Grace," is a notably full exposition of the doctrinal issues that underlie Hooker's sermons of the 1580s. (WSH)

PREVITE-ORTON, C. W. "Marsilius of Padua." Annual Italian Lecture of the British Academy, 1935. In *Proceedings of the British Academy*, 21. London: Humphrey Milford, 1935. Previté-Orton shows (pp. 31–32) how much Book VIII of the *Laws* owes to Marsilio's *Defensor Pacis*. (WSH) [See above, pp. 64–65 —ed.]

RANKE, LEOPOLD VON. "Zur Geschichte der Doctrin von den drei Staatsgewalten." *Sämmtliche Werke*, 24. Leipzig: Duncker & Humbolt, 1872. An outline of Hooker's political theory by an old master. (EG)

REARDON, B. M. G. "Richard Hooker's Apology for Anglicanism." *Hibbert Journal* 52 (1954): 278–85. An anniversary eulogy. (EG)

REMUSAT, CHARLES DE. *Histoire de la Philosophie en Angleterre depuis Bacon jusqu'à Locke*, 1 : 125–36. Paris: Didier, 1878. A brief outline of Hooker's interpretation of law. (EG)

ROSS, MALCOLM M. "Ruskin, Hooker, and 'the Christian Theoria'." In *Essays in English Literature from the Renaissance to the Victorian*

Age: Presented to A. S. P. Woodhouse 1964, edited by Millar Mac-Lure and F. W. Watt, pp. 283–303. Toronto: Univ. of Toronto Press, 1964. Argues that in Vol. 2 of *Modern Painters* Ruskin was indebted to Hooker for the substance of his religious theory of art. (WSH)

Rowse, A. L. *The England of Elizabeth: The Structure of Society.* New York: Macmillan, 1950; reprinted 1961. A scholarly study that attempts to record "the essence of Hooker's mind" (pp. 483–88). (EG)

Sabine, George H. *A History of Political Theory.* New York: Henry Holt, 1937; 3d rev. ed., 1961. A summary statement of Hooker's importance as a political thinker in a standard textbook; Sabine sees Hooker's *Laws* as "the last great statement of... the medieval tradition" (pp. 439–42). (WSH)

Sack, Karl Heinrich. *Richard Hooker von den Gesetzen des Kirchenregiments im Gegensatze zu den Forderungen der Puritaner: Ein Beitrag zur Geschichte der anglikanischen Kirche und Theologie im sechzehnten Jahrhundert.* Heidelberg: Carl Winter, 1868. The first German book-length study; it contains numerous quotations from the *Laws* translated into German. (EG)

Saintsbury, George. *A History of English Prose Rhythm.* London: Macmillan, 1912. Argues that Hooker's prose lends itself to poetic scansion, but Saintsbury's conclusions remain impressionistic ("undulating sweeps... wing-like motion"). (EG)

Sambayya, Emani. "The Eucharistic Doctrine of Richard Hooker and Herbert Thorndike." S.T.M. thesis, Union Theological Seminary, New York, 1950. A somewhat superficial study that restates the central eucharistic insights of Hooker. (EG)

Schmidt, M[artin]. "Hooker." In *Die Religion in Geschichte und Gegenwart,* 3:448–49. 3d rev. ed., Tübingen: J. C. B. Mohr (Paul Siebeck), 1959. A concise summary in a standard reference work with a bibliography. (EG)

—— "Die Rechtfertigungslehre bei Richard Hooker." In *Geist und Geschichte der Reformation: Festgabe Hanns Rückert zum 65. Geburtstag dargebracht von Freunden, Kollegen und Schülern,* pp. 377–96.

Arbeiten zur Kirchengeschichte, 38. Berlin: Walter de Gruytei, 1966. A scholarly study of justification by a Wesley expert. (EG)

SCHNACK, E. *Richard Hooker und seine Stellung in der Entwicklung der englishen Geistesgeschichte im 16. Jahrhundert.* Thesis, University of Halle, 1923. [Not seen.]

SCHÜTZ, PAUL. *Religion und Politik in der Kirche von England: Auf Grundneuer Quellen untersucht an der Epoche ihres Ursprungs.* Gotha and Stuttgart: Friedrich Andreas Perthes, 1925. [Princeton Theological Seminary.] A sketchy and self-assured introduction to the essence of English Christianity which is not always justified by the facts. (EG)

—— *Richard Hooker: Der grundlegende Theologe des Anglikanismus. Eine Monographie zur Reformationsgeschichte Englands und zu den Anfängen der Aufklärung.* Göttingen: Mittelstelle für Mikrokopie, Vandenhoeck & Ruprecht, 1952. A revision of his 1922 thesis which regards Hooker's theology as an expression of the spirit of the Thirty-Nine Articles with a patristic and Catholic accent as well as a clear anticipation of rationalism. (EG)

SEABURY, WILLIAM J. "Paget on Hooker's Fifth Book." *The Church Eclectic* 27 (1899): 784–94. A review of Paget's *Introduction* (1899). (WSH)

SECOR, PHILIP B. *Richard Hooker and the Christian Commonwealth.* Ph.D. dissertation, Duke University, 1959. Ann Arbor, Mich.: University Microfilms, 1960. A wide-ranging and well-informed account, emphasizing Hooker's recourse to "historic public reason"; there are sympathetic discussions of the Royal Supremacy (pp. 2–47), the origins of government (201–47), the Real Presence (253–60), the church (260–97), the "Christian commonwealth" (297–317), and religious toleration (325–35). (WSH)

SHIRLEY, F. J. "Hooker and the Jesuits." *Church Quarterly Review* 113 (1931): 12–37. A scholarly comparison of Hooker with contemporary Jesuit political thought. (EG)

—— *Richard Hooker and Contemporary Political Ideas.* Church Historical Society. London: S.P.C.K., 1949. A useful but largely derivative survey of Hooker's political ideas and those of his leading Protestant and Catholic contemporaries. Shirley attacks the authenticity of Book VII in its present form and argues that the passages supporting a "prelatical" conception of episcopacy are a seventeenth-century interpolation by Bishop Gauden. (WDJCT)

SIMPSON, PERCY. "Proof-Reading by English Authors of the Sixteenth and Seventeenth Centuries." *Proceedings of the Oxford Bibliographical Society* 2 (1928): 20–25. Reprinted in *Proof-Reading in the Sixteenth, Seventeenth and Eighteenth Centuries*, pp. 76–79. London: Oxford Univ. Press, 1935. Pages cited describe the printer's copy for Book V (Bodleian MS Add. C. 165). (WSH)

SISSON, C.J. *The Judicious Marriage of Mr. Hooker*. See above, section II.

SMYTH, CHARLES. "A Religious Realist." *Listener* 52 (1954): 326–27. A very brief popular sketch. (EG)

SOUTHGATE, W. M. *John Jewel and the Problem of Doctrinal Authority*. Harvard Historical Monographs, 49. Cambridge: Harvard Univ. Press, 1962. An important study of Hooker's patron, Bishop Jewel, comparing (pp. 135–45) the sense in which each could be called a "rationalist." (WSH)

STALEY, VERNON. *Richard Hooker*. See above, Section II.

STANLEY, A. P. "Richard Hooker." *Good Words* 14 (1873): 26–32. A sermon preached on the occasion of the restoration of Hooker's church at Bishopsbourne, November 14, 1872. (WSH)

STONE, DARWELL. *A History of the Doctrine of the Holy Eucharist*, 2:239–49. London: Longmans, Green, 1909. An older study expressing the view that Hooker did not define the exact manner of Christ's eucharistic presence. (EG)

STUEBER, SISTER M. STEPHANIE. "Richard Hooker's Place in the History of Renaissance Christian Humanism." Ph.D. dissertation, St Louis University, 1954. An exhaustive study, particularly useful for its evidence that the *Laws* was "designed...as a forensic oration and executed in a Ciceronian style" (pp. 400ff.). (WSH)

—— "The Balanced Diction of Hooker's *Polity*." *PMLA* 71 (1956): 808–26. A largely theoretical paper, arguing that Hooker attempts to reestablish the "reason-faith balance of Christian humanism" by emphasizing reason to repudiate Puritan fideism; Hooker's diction is functional to this end because he uses words "to express the nature of things," as distinguished from the Euphuists' "purely ornamental" diction. (GE)

SURLIS, PAUL. "Natural Law in Richard Hooker (c. 1554–1600)." *Irish Theological Quarterly* 35 (1968): 173–85. A summary of Hooker's teaching on natural law, emphasizing its affirmation of the validity of reason, its Thomistic roots, and its ecumenical implications for a renascent moral theology in the Church of England. (WSH)

SWAN, CAROLINE D. "The Quaintness of 'The Judicious Hooker'." *Atlantic Monthly* 37 (1876): 727–34. An effusive rescension of Walton, together with appreciative observations on Hooker's "quaint" Elizabethan diction. (WSH)

SYKES, NORMAN. "Richard Hooker." In *The Social & Political Ideas of Some Great Thinkers of the Sixteenth & Seventeenth Centuries,* edited by F. J. C. Hearnshaw, pp. 63–89. London: George C. Harrap, 1926; reprinted New York: Barnes & Noble, 1949. This is a helpful essay by one of the ablest and most learned of modern church historians. (JB)

―――― "Hooker, Richard." In *Encyclopaedia of the Social Sciences,* 7:459. New York: Macmillan, 1932. A brief but trenchant summary. (WSH)

―――― "Richard Hooker and Today." *Spectator* 193 (November 12, 1954): 571–72. A brief tribute on the occasion of the quatercentenary of Hooker's birth. (WSH)

―――― *Old Priest and New Presbyter: The Anglican Attitude to Episcopacy, Presbyterianism and Papacy since the Reformation.* Cambridge: Cambridge Univ. Press, 1956; reprinted 1957. An authoritative exposition of the Anglican position in which the *Laws* figures as a central text, especially in ch. 1, "The Godly Prince and the Godly Bishop." (WSH)

TALBERT, ERNEST W. *The Problem of Order: Elizabethan Political Commonplaces and an Example of Shakespeare's Art.* Chapel Hill:

Univ. of North Carolina Press, 1962. A full analysis of the conventional elements in Hooker's political thought, emphasizing its similarities to that of Sir Thomas Smith in the *De Republica Anglorum*. (WSH)

TAYLOR, HENRY O. "The Anglican *Via Media*: Richard Hooker." In *Thought and Expression in the Sixteenth Century*, 2:159–82. New York: Macmillan, 1920; reprinted New York: Frederick Ungar, 1959. A survey of Hooker's thought in an early work of intellectual history. (WSH)

THOMPSON, ELBERT N. S. "Richard Hooker among the Controversialists." In *Renaissance Studies in Honor of Hardin Craig*, pp. 262–72. Stanford: Stanford Univ. Press, 1941. Also issued in *Philological Quarterly* 20 (1941): 454–64. A sensitive and wide-ranging appreciation, which views Hooker in the light of later writers' responses to the same issues, notably those of Milton. (WSH)

THORNTON, LIONEL S. *Richard Hooker: A Study of His Theology*. English Theologians. London: S.P.C.K. and New York: Macmillan, 1924. A semipopular, older study of Hooker's theological system which sees Hooker as "the father of Anglo-Catholic theology." (EG)

TILLYARD, E. M. W. *The Elizabethan World Picture*. London: Chatto & Windus, and New York: Macmillan, 1943; reprinted New York: Random House, Modern Library Paperbacks [1959]. A famous and very readable sketch of Elizabethan social, political, and cosmological assumptions, in which Hooker figures prominently as evidence of orthodox views. (WSH)

TUTTLE, D. S. "Hooker and the Post-Reformation Period." In *Leading Persons and Periods in English Church History: Delivered in Christ Church, St. Paul, and in Gethsemane Church*, Minneapolis, pp. 107–38. Milwaukee: The Young Churchman Co., 1899. [The Library of Congress.] A perfervid rehearsal of Walton. (WSH)

URBAN, LINWOOD. "A Revolution in English Moral Theology." *Anglican Theological Review* 53 (1971): 5–20. A thesis that Hooker modifies St Thomas' definition of the relationship between the law of nature and moral law, which leads to the position of Bishop Butler that regards the moral law as autonomous. (EG)

VOEGELIN, ERIC. *The New Science of Politics: An Introduction*. Charles R. Walgreen Foundation Lectures. Chicago and London: Univ. of Chicago Press, 1952; 7th impression, 1969. A critique of Puritanism as a type of Gnostic revolutionary movement in line with such "Western Gnostic sectarians" as Scotus Erigena, Dionysius Areopagita, Joachim of Flora, John Calvin, Diderot, D'Alembert, Karl Marx, and "the patristic literature of Leninism-Stalinism." Hooker is identified as a faithful representative of "the classic and Christian tradition." (EG)

WASHBURN, E. A. "Richard Hooker." In *Epochs in Church History and Other Essays*, edited by C. C. Tiffany, pp. 199–238. New York: E. P. Dutton, 1883. A popular statement emphasizing Hooker's *via media* position. (EG)

WHIPPLE, E. P. "Hooker." *Atlantic Monthly* 22 (1868): 674–82. A popular sketch. (EG)

WILLEY, BASIL. "Humanism and Hooker." In *The English Moralists*, pp. 100–23. London: Chatto & Windus, and New York: W. W. Norton, 1964; reprinted Garden City, N.Y.: Doubleday, Anchor Books, 1967. A sympathetic exposition of Hooker's attempt "to separate and delimit the spheres of Nature and Grace, Reason and Revelation" (p. 103). (WSH)

WILLIAMS, R. R. "Richard Hooker and the Church and State Report." *The Churchman* 85(1971): 97–104. [Not seen.]

WILMER, RICHARD H. "Hooker on Authority." *Anglican Theological Review* 33 (1951): 102–08. A concise formulation. (EG)

WOLIN, SHELDON S. "Richard Hooker and English Conservatism." *Western Political Quarterly* 6 (1953): 28–47. A perceptive analysis of Hooker as the authentic fountainhead of the British conservative tradition later exemplified by Edmund Burke. (WSH)

WOODHOUSE, A. S. P. "Religion and Some Foundations of English Democracy." *Philosophical Review* 61 (1952): 503–31. A persuasive brief that the Anglicanism of Hooker is as much a part of the political traditions of British democracy as the presbyterianism of the Puritans. (WSH)

WOODHOUSE, H. F. "The Authenticity of Hooker's Book VII.'

Church History 22 (1953): 3–7. Does not accept Shirley's argument (*Hooker*, pp. 41–57) against the authenticity of Book VII, or Houk's and Sisson's arguments for it. Concludes that "we should be extremely chary about advancing any great claim on a theological or historical point based only on book VII" (p. 7). (WSH)

———— *The Doctrine of the Church in Anglican Theology 1547–1603.* London: S.P.C.K., and New York: Macmillan, 1954. A scholarly study with detailed attention to Hooker's ecclesiology. (EG)

———— "Permanent Features of Hooker's Polity." *Anglican Theological Review* 42 (1960): 164–68. A spirited claim that Hooker is still worth reading. (EG)

YODER, SAMUEL A. "The Prose Style of Richard Hooker's *Of the Laws of Ecclesiastical Polity*: A Study in Cultural History." Ph.D. dissertation, Indiana University, 1937. Emphasizes the influence of classical rhetoric, particularly on the structure of the *Laws*, and the Latinate aspects of Hooker's style. (GE)

———— "*Dispositio* in Richard Hooker's 'Laws of Ecclesiastical Polity'." *Quarterly Journal of Speech* 27 (1941): 90–97. A brief discussion of the Aristotelian rhetoric of the *Laws*, both in overall organization about a single thesis and in its predominantly syllogistic reasoning. (WSH)

YOUENS, F. A. C. *Analysis of Hooker's Ecclesiastical Polity, Book V: With Introduction, Notes, and Examination Questions.* London: Robert Scott, 1912. [University of Cincinnati Library.] A lengthy point-by-point summary intended as a tool for training Episcopal clergymen in another generation. (EG)

[Anon.] *A Christian Letter of certaine English Protestants...vnto that Reverend and learned man,* Mr. R. Hoo....[Middleburgh, Holland], 1599; facsimile, New York: Da Capo Press, 1969 (No. 202, The English Experience); reprinted in Bayne, ed., *The Fifth Book*, pp. 589–635. The only Puritan reply to Hooker in his lifetime; charges him with doctrinal error; Hooker's annotated copy survives (Corpus Christi College, Oxford, MS 215b), as do drafts of answers to its charges (*Works*, 1888, 2: 537–50, 556–97). (WSH)

[Anon.] "The Dean of Christ Church on Hooker and the Puritans."

Church Quarterly Review 49 (October 1899): 116–29. A review of Paget, *Introduction* (1899). (EG)

[Anon.] "Hooker in the Modern World." *Times Literary Supplement* (May 11, 1946), pp. 217–18. A review of Davies, *The Political Ideas of Richard Hooker*, which urges the relevance of Hooker's political thought "to the problem of rebuilding a Christian Society in a world largely divorced from the Christian tradition" (p. 217). (WSH)

[Anon.] "Richard Hooker." *Times Literary Supplement* (April 30, 1954), p. 281. A commemorative piece, on the occasion of the 400th anniversary of Hooker's birth. (WSH)

[Anon.] *The Teaching of St. Augustine and Hooker Respecting the Divine Will.* Points of Theology, 1. Oxford and London: J. Parker, 1879. [Not seen.]

ADDENDUM

COHEN, EILEEN Z. "The Visible Solemnity: Ceremony and Order in Shakespeare and Hooker." *Texas Studies in Literature and Language* 12 (1970): 181–95. Argues that Shakespeare's reading of the *Laws* in the 1590s, influenced specific themes in the "second tetralogy" of history plays (*Richard II–Henry V*). (WSH).

NOTE ON THE CONTRIBUTORS

W. D. J. CARGILL THOMPSON is Lecturer in Ecclesiastical History, University of London King's College. He was educated at King's College, Cambridge, where he held the Lightfoot University Scholarship in Ecclesiastical History and was Fellow and Lay Dean of the College. He has also taught at the University of Sussex. In 1957–58 he held a Commonwealth Fund Fellowship for study at Harvard University and the Henry E. Huntington Library, and in 1964–65 an Alexander von Humboldt Fellowship for study at Göttingen. He has published extensively on Luther and on various aspects of the English Reformation.

H. C. PORTER is Lecturer in History at the University of Cambridge. He has taught at the University of Toronto and the University of California at Berkeley, and in 1956–57 he held a Proctor Visiting Fellowship at Princeton University. His books include *Reformation and Reaction in Tudor Cambridge* (1958; based on the Cranmer Prize Essay for 1952), *Erasmus and Cambridge*, with D. F. S. Thomson (1963), and *Puritanism in Tudor England* (1970), a collection of contemporary documents. He is at work on a study of England and the North American Indian, 1500–1700, and he has contributed numerous articles on the theological controversies of Tudor England in the past decade. For the Folger Edition of Hooker's *Works* he is preparing annotation and commentary on the Preface and Books I–IV of the *Laws*.

W. SPEED HILL is General Editor of the forthcoming Edition of Hooker's *Works*, sponsored by the Folger Shakespeare Library. A recipient of degrees from Princeton University and Harvard University, he held a Woodrow Wilson Fellowship, 1957–58 and fellowships at the Folger and Newberry libraries in the summer of 1969. He currently teaches English at New York University. He has recently published a critical bibliography of the early editions of Hooker (1970) and has contributed articles on Hooker, Jonson, and Spenser to various journals. He is preparing the text of Book v of the *Laws* for the Edition.

EGIL GRISLIS is Professor of Historical Theology at the Hartford Seminary Foundation, Hartford, Connecticut. Born in Latvia, he studied at the University of Heidelberg before coming to the United States in 1949. He holds degrees from Gettysburg College, Lutheran Theological Seminary at Gettysburg, and Yale University, and he taught at Duke University before assuming his present position. In 1964–65 he held an American Association of Theological Schools Fellowship for study at Heidelberg. He has published widely on topics in Reformation theology, including articles on Luther, Calvin, and Hooker. He has in preparation a book-length study of Hooker's theology, from which the present essay is taken, and has responsibility for the commentary on Hooker's doctrinal works, *The Divine Tractates*, for the Folger Edition.

JOHN E. BOOTY is Professor of Church History at the Episcopal Theological School at Cambridge, Massachusetts. Before assuming his present post, he taught at the Virginia Theological Seminary, Alexandria, Virginia. He is the author of *John Jewel as Apologist of the Church of England* (1963), and he has edited Jewel's *Apology* for the Folger Shakespeare Library (1963). He has studied at Princeton University and the University of London, the latter on a Fulbright Fellowship, 1957–58; he was a Fellow of the Folger Library in 1964. He has contributed many articles on Elizabethan church history to various journals and is editing the Book of Common Prayer for the Folger Library. For the Folger Edition he is editing a collection of contemporary reaction to Hooker's *Laws*, as well as preparing the commentary for Book v.

GEORGES EDELEN is Professor of English at Indiana University, Bloomington. He was educated at Georgetown University and Harvard University, where he also taught for three years. A recipient of a Folger Library Fellowship, he has recently published an edition of William Harrison's *Description of England* (1968) for the Library. He has also written on Renaissance prose, and he has in preparation a monograph on Hooker's style, from which his present essay is excerpted. He is preparing the text of the Preface and Books I–IV of the *Laws* for the Folger Edition.

THE FOLGER EDITION:
AN HISTORICAL NOTE

THE FOLGER LIBRARY EDITION
OF THE WORKS OF RICHARD HOOKER

General Editor, W. Speed Hill

327

Powel Mills Dawley
  The General Theological Seminary (ret.)
Passerin d'Entrèves
  University of Turin
C. W. Dugmore
  University of London King's College
O. B. Hardison, Jr.
  The Folger Shakespeare Library
Robert M. Kingdon
  The University of Wisconsin
Mortimer Levine
  West Virginia University
Christopher Morris
  King's College, Cambridge
Peter Munz
  Victoria University of Wellington
John M. Steadman
  The Henry E. Huntington Library and Art Gallery
H. R. Trevor-Roper
  Oriel College, Oxford
Howard Webber
  The M.I.T. Press
James M. Wells
  The Newberry Library

THE FOLGER EDITION
An Historical Note

W. Speed Hill

The *Works* of the judicious Hooker have enjoyed a distinctly cyclical popularity. The editions printed in his lifetime, as the late Professor Sisson informed us, were slow to sell out. But once the enterprising William Stansby had inherited the business of John Windet in 1611, he was quick to reprint the *Laws of Ecclesiastical Polity* in a handsome new format, and the volume became a steady seller for a generation. Between 1611 and 1639, a new edition (or part edition) was called for every seven years, on the average, from which we can infer an annual sale of between 180 and 200 copies, a demand that would gladden the heart of many publishers, then and now. After the interregnum, Hooker was scarcely less valuable as a commercial property, for between 1662 and 1723, no fewer than six folio editions of the *Works* appeared in London and one in Dublin. Thereafter, no new editions appeared for sixty years, until the Clarendon Press edition of 1793. The first in the now familiar octavo format, it was reprinted twice before John Keble re-edited the *Works* in 1836, an edition that appeared four times with Keble's apparatus and three without, not counting the American editions that were derived from it, nor the less reputable editions that continued to sell in the nineteenth century —Dobson's in 1825, Hanbury's in 1830, as well as others of less distinguished parentage. The Church and Paget rescension of Keble in 1888, however, seemed to exhaust nineteenth-century interest in Hooker, and the *Works* have not been edited as a whole since.

The present Edition, then, comes at the end of a long and remarkably homogeneous publishing tradition. Though it has been in prospect since November 1967, it has a prehistory. Properly speaking, it began at the University of North Carolina when O. B. Hardison, Jr., and Ernest W. Talbert proposed such an edition to the University Press at Chapel Hill as a joint venture with the Clarendon Press. But the omens were unfavorable, the project never secured the proper institutional backing, and its sponsors turned to other matters. In the meantime, Howard Webber, formerly an editor at the North Carolina Press, had become Director of the Press at Western Reserve University, now Case Western Reserve. He urged me to submit a prospectus to the Press. It was favorably received by the Press's Editorial Committee, and, so encouraged, I set about organizing the project. Taking as a model the St Thomas More Project at Yale University—and with the aid and support of two of its stalwarts, Richard S. Sylvester and R. S. Schoeck—I assembled an Editorial Committee of scholars with a lively interest in Hooker. In addition to myself, Sylvester, and Schoeck, we secured Georges Edelen, an acute student of Hooker's style; David Novarr, whose work on Walton had taken him deeply into Hooker and the seventeenth century; and John Booty, whose work on Jewel had admirably prepared him for editing and commenting on Hooker's work in the same tradition. We also drew together a formal Board of Advisers, to whom we could appeal as the occasion arose for particular assistance in matters of personnel, editorial queries, and the like. Correspondence and travel for consultation took up most of the first two years, though the Editorial Committee did meet twice in the early stages of the project—once in a bedroom at the Taft in New York City and once at the Press's offices in Cleveland. By the end of the summer of 1969 the preliminary planning was complete and fully half of the volumes formally assigned. Simultaneously, I had set about compiling a formal descriptive bibliography of the early editions as a foundation for establishing the text anew, based on the incomparable collection of early folios at the Folger Library, which has been published in trial format prior to its reissue, revised and corrected as necessary, in the final volume of the *Complete Works*.

O. B. Hardison, who was at that time succeeding to the directorship of the Folger, suggested that we resubmit our prospectus, duly amended to take into account the progress of the past two years, to the Library for consideration by its newly formed Committee on Library Publications. In November the Library agreed in principle to sponsor the project as "The Folger Library Edition of the Works of Richard Hooker." By this time, its General Editor had moved to New York University and its original sponsor, Howard Webber, had accepted the directorship of the Press of Massachusetts Institute of Technology. William R. Crawford, his successor at the Press in Cleveland, was as hospitable to the Edition as his predecessor had been, however, and once a contract had been entered into between the Press and the General Editor for the Editorial Committee in June 1970, a formal agreement was signed with the Folger.

Since then the Editorial Committee has convened twice at the Folger. Volumes have been assigned as follows:

Of the Laws of Ecclesiastical Polity. Preface, Books I–IV
    text: Georges Edelen
    commentary: H. C. Porter
Of the Laws of Ecclesiastical Polity. Book v
    text: W. Speed Hill
    commentary: John Booty
Of the Laws of Ecclesiastical Polity. The Posthumous Books
    Book vi: T. S. Healy, S.J. (text and commentary)
    Books vii and viii:
        text: P. G. Stanwood
        commentary: Arthur S. McGrade
Tractates and Sermons
    text: Laetitia Yeandle
    commentary: Egil Grislis

Contemporary Commentary
    John Booty (text and commentary)
Bibliography, Documents, Index
    W. Speed Hill

The first fruits of the Edition are the preliminary *Bibliography* (The Press of Case Western Reserve University, 1970) and the present volume of essays, conceived as a survey of the issues to which the commentary must address itself, commissioned by the Press. As an example of the value of publicity, the Folger has recently been offered and has purchased a manuscript copy of John Earle's Latin translation of Books I–V of the *Laws*, since the seventeenth century thought to have been lost or destroyed. (The remaining loss now, of course, is the missing manuscript of Book VI, known to have been prepared by Hooker's amanuensis, Benjamin Pullen, for the press and read in the 1590s by his friends and former students, Edwin Sandys and George Cranmer.) As all volume assignments are expected to come to hand between September 1972 and September 1974, a completion date of 1980—or even sooner—is not impossible, even taking into account the inevitable delays that attend upon such a complex and far-flung effort.

If there is a *moralitas* to this brief *fabula*, it is a dual one. First, there is an agreed-upon need for a modern edition of Hooker, good as Keble's was. With rare exceptions, the institutions to which I have gone for support have recognized this need and acted favorably upon it—notably the American Philosophical Society and the American Council of Learned Societies, with grants-in-aid to forward the project, in addition to the Folger and my own University. Second, a measure of simple good fortune (Hooker would have called it Divine Providence) has been no less necessary for its success. That the Edition has fallen to hand with such apparent ease continues to amaze and delight me.

INDEXES

GENERAL INDEX

Note: *citations from annotations in Bibliography are in italics.*

335

Hooker (*cont.*)

viii, ix, early printing of, *301*; cited, 133, 150; compared with Bancroft, 131; echoes of Bancroft, 16; sets tone of *Laws*, 14, 148

— Book I; argument, 19, 20, 22; character of, distinct from II–IV, 18–19; echoes Aristotle's *Politics*, 36–37; emphasizes government by consent, 41–42; law of reason discussed, 27–28; method of argument described, 18; no contemporary parallels, 19; précis, *295*

— Book II: on natural law, 135–36; on Scripture, 90, 105

— Book III: chapter viii controversial, 215; cited by Hall, 235 n. 14; on Scripture and church polity, 35, 104

— Book IV, cited, 136, 235 n. 14

— Book V: aim, 136; announced topic, 146; argument, *307*; Bayne's edition of, *310*; cited, 65, 138, 235 n. 14; dedicated to Whitgift, 146; fragment published in 1642, 145; influenced by Cranmer, 140; influenced by Jewel, 16; length, 136; place in *Laws*, *306*; printer's copy of, *284, 286, 315*; publication, 134, 138, 146; revision, 134, 146

— Book VI: early draft, 70 n. 29; MS notes on, 135, *285*; part of *Laws*, 289, *302*; revision, 146; topic, 137

— Book VII: authenticity, 69 n. 26, *314, 318*; cited, 235 n. 14; defense of episcopacy in, 16, 56–57; early draft of, 70 n. 29;

first edition of, *288*; Marsilius quoted in, 52

— Book VIII: aim 20, 50; cited, 235 n. 14; completion, 66, 70 n. 29; consent, theme of, 38–39, 82–83; consistency with earlier Books, 53, 66–67; debt to Marsilius, *312*; defense of Royal Supremacy, x, 10; Dublin MS, 74 n. 71; echoes of Aristotle's *Politics*, 36–37; legal knowledge in, 46; *pactum societatis/subjectionis*, 42–43; parallels, 64–65; subject, H's description of, 78; text, order of, 72 n. 50; theme, 22–23

— Books I, III, as basis for defense of Royal Supremacy, 53, 66–67

— Books I–III: arguments of, x; arguments of, anticipated in Sermons, 128

— Books I–IV, 257; dating, *297*; publication, 134, 145–46

— Books I–V: known in seventeenth century, 230; Latin translation of, *285*; publication and sale of, 235 n. 11, 329–30

— Books I, VIII, contradictions between, *304, 305–6*

— Books II–IV: controversial character of, 19, 148; debt to Whitgift in, 16, 19; length of, 146

— Books V–VIII, 19, 135–40, 257

— Books VI–VIII (Posthumous Books): authenticity, x, 4, *288, 290, 302*; publication 134–35, 146, 147, 156 n. 43, *287*; revision, 140, *294*; unfinished, 51

Natural knowledge, limits to, 106–7

Natural law. *See* Law: natural

Nature: and grace, 105, *318*; harmony of, and cosmos, 102–3; potentialities of, 98; references to, in Fawkner, 236 n. 19. *See also* Law: Natural; Reason

Neill, Stephen, 234 n. 2

Nicodemus for Christ. . . . See Fawkner, Anthony

Nobility, threatened by Puritans, 84, 95, 143

Nonconformity, Puritan, 149, 150–51. *See also* Dissent, Protestant

Nonresidence, H on, 14

Norris, Sylvester, *An Antidote or Soveraigne Remedie . . .*, 224; cites H, 212, 224

Novarr, David, x, 4

Nowell, Alexander, Dean of Westminster, 96

Obedience, 98, 149–50, 181. *See also* Church of England, conformity to

Objectivity, problem of, *300*

Ockham, William of, 30

Of the Laws of Ecclesiastical Polity. See Hooker, Richard: works, individual

Order: Anglican ideal, 97, 127, 215; Elizabethan commonplace, *316*; H's concern for, 102–3, 112, 150, 229, 259, 262, *300*; public, 96; Puritan concern for, 236 n. 27; as reason, for H, 164; Whitehead on, in nature, 260

Order, power of, topic of Book V, 146

Original sin. *See* Sin, original

Overall, John, Bishop of Norwich, 81

Oxford Movement, interest in H, 159–60

Oxford University: Aristotelianism in,

in sixteenth century, 21–22; Corpus Christi College, xiii–xiv, 21–22, 119

Pactum societatis/subjectionis, in Book VIII, 42–43

Paget, Francis, Bishop of Oxford, 23, 160, 230; *Introduction* reviewed, *314, 319*

Papacy: Marsilius of Padua's attacks on, 52, 74 n. 74; authority of, rejected by H, 211

Papists, benefit from agitation for reform, 139

Parker, Matthew, Archbishop of Canterbury: character, 96; on church music, 94; compared to H, 94, 111; on Puritan discipline, 96; on disobedience to laws of church, 95–96; under Edward VI, 94; on established religion, 95–96; on insularity of English church, 94; on limits of conscience, 94; motto, 97; policy of *moderatio*, xi, 93–97; on popular control of church, 95–96; on Puritans, 95–96; on "reasonableness" of ecclesiastical law, 95; on zeal, 95–96, 96–97

Parliament, ecclesiastical authority, 50, 62–63, 66, 76 n. 84, 79, 80–81, 89, 92, 97; legislative powers, 48; representative character, 34. *See also* Commons, House of

Parliament of 1593, 134, 140–42

Pauck, Wilhelm, 6

Paul, Saint: cited by H on predestination, 127–28; cited by Travers at Temple, 125, 127; on natural law, 30, 107; used by H, *306–7*

Paul's Cross, H summoned to preach at, 119

Paul's Cross Sermon (1588/89). *See* Bancroft, Richard

INDEX OF PASSAGES
CITED OR DISCUSSED

Note: references are to *Works* (1888), by Book, chapter, and section

Index of Passages Cited